THE KOREAN WAR

WARS OF THE UNITED STATES
(Editor: Richard L. Blanco)
Vol. 8

GARLAND REFERENCE LIBRARY
OF SOCIAL SCIENCE
Vol. 189

WARS OF THE UNITED STATES
(Richard L. Blanco, General Editor)

THE KOREAN WAR
An Annotated Bibliography

Keith D. McFarland

GARLAND PUBLISHING, INC. • NEW YORK
1986

Library of Congress Cataloging-in-Publication Data

McFarland, Keith D., 1940–
 The Korean War, an annotated bibliography.

 (Wars of the United States ; vol. 8) (Garland
Reference library of social science ; v. 189)
 Includes indexes.
  1. Korean War, 1950–1953—Bibliography. 2. Korean
War, 1950–1953—United States—Bibliography. I. Title.
II. Series: Wars of the United States ; v. 8.
III. Garland reference library of social science ;
v. 189.
Z3319.K6M38 1986   016.9519'042   83-48204
ISBN 0-8240-9068-3

Printed on acid-free, 250-year-life paper
Manufactured in the United States of America

To Mark

CONTENTS

GENERAL EDITOR'S PREFACE

In his THE KOREAN WAR: AN ANNOTATED BIBLIOGRAPHY, Keith McFarland has compiled a timely study of a major event in American history. This "limited war" was actually a bitter and protracted struggle in which the Unites States and its allies in the United Nations committed armed forces to the mainland of eastern Asia. There, near the borders of the Union of Soviet Socialist Republics and the Peoples Republic of China, the U.S. and the U.N. assisted in the defense of the Republic of South Korea against an invasion by (Communist) North Korea.

To provide the reader with the best and most readily obtainable material in the English language about the participation of the United States in this conflict, Professor McFarland provides terse, colorful summaries of the rich literature on this subject. Whatever the reader's interests—the decision to intervene, the skirmishes and battles, the roles of the United States Army, Navy, Marines and Air Force, the participation of U.N. units, the debate at home about risking a confrontation with Communist powers, or the famous controversy between President Harry Truman and General Douglas MacArthur—the researcher will find in this volume ample items on a particular topic. There are over 2,300 entries here conveniently and professionally annotated. Organizing his material into twenty-two broad categories, with numerous subdivisions, Dr. McFarland, Dean of Graduate Studies and Research at East Texas State University College, covers a wide span of information concerning the origins of the war, the various campaigns, the diplomatic aspects, and the social-economic-political ramifications of America's determination to defend the territorial integrity of a fledgling Asian republic.

The scope of this work is comprehensive for the author cites books, memoirs, monographs, essays from popular magazines, articles from military and scholarly journals, theses and Ph.D. dissertations, collections of speeches and documents as well as hundreds of "first-hand" accounts by Americans who fought on the front line. Furthermore, Dr. McFarland has enhanced the value of this unique research tool by listing detailed entries from a wide variety of source material about subjects which have intrigued the public since the 1950°s, such as personalities of key U.S. generals, the performance of black troops, the effectiveness of military

medicine, the influence of psychological warfare, the treatment of
U.S.-U.N. prisoners of war, and the evacuation of the wounded by helicopters. Not only has the writer provided us with ample references about
the war itself, but he has included invaluable sections about the impact
of the struggle on society, the effects of the war on South Korea, the
tempo of American politics in the era, the interpretations of the struggle
by journalists, and the views of writers who dramatized the experience in
novels. With such a variety of subjects from which to select a specific
topic--along with a convenient chronology of events and detailed author
and subject indices--a reader can quickly locate the most pertinent
material about a particular theme. McFarland's study is unquestionably
the most comprehensive bibliography about the Korean War in print. High
school and college students, those in graduate school, researchers in
the social sciences, and particularly, that vast audience known as
"general readers" who demonstrate an intense curiosity about their
nation's military heritage, will all benefit from this valuable
reference-work.

The Korean War erupted unexpectedly, barely five years after the
conclusion of World War Two. The United States and its United Nations
allies defended a small state against aggression thereby matching with
military might the glowing rhetoric of the era about protecting democracy
world-wide. The war--in which over 200,000 U.S. servicemen were casual-
ties--was a catalyst in consolidating American opinion to support overseas
intervention in areas considered vital to the national security. In a
manner that few observers comprehended, the Korean War demonstrated how
difficult it would be for the United States to wage similar limited warfare in Asia, especially in Vietnam.

Richard L. Blanco
Department of History
SUNY, Brockport

PREFACE

When I set out on this project, I did so with the naive assumption
that it could be completed in twelve to eighteen months. The
reasons for my optimistic assessment were primarily twofold. First,
I reasoned that since the Korean War had been a relatively small
conflict and had ended only thirty years before, there was not that
much that would have been or could have been written about it,
especially since I was limiting the scope of my study to works
written in English. Second, a computer search of nearly every data
base then available produced a listing of approximately 300 books
and articles on the war. Realizing the limitations of electronic
searches, I estimated that perhaps one-third of the pertinent works
had been identified. I therefore concluded that my study would
likely include in the neighborhood of a thousand sources. As the
project approached the 800 entry level, I realized that my estimate
had been low and so I raised it to 1,200. As the months passed so
did my upward revisions, and when I reached 1,800 citations, I
realized that the undertaking could become virtually endless. At
that point an arbitrary ceiling of 2,000 citations was set, but
after including other works that I felt had to be included, the
figure stood at more than 2,300.

This bibliography is a select one, and in all likelihood,
serious students of the conflict will search this book and be
disappointed that a certain article, book or dissertation that they
consider of utmost importance is not included. For such omissions,
I apologize. However, while some works have been left out, many,
including most key ones, are contained herein and hopefully their
citation and annotation will be of value to the serious researcher
and of interest to the history buff. Since this study includes only
works in English, the books of most major United States and British
publishers are included. Because of breakthroughs in the printing
industry in the 1950's, many Korean veterans published personal
accounts of the war (many of which are outstanding) at small private
presses, frequently in the author's hometown. Unfortunately, a
number of those excellent works probably escaped my attention.

Scholarly articles written from the time of the war to present
are cited as are articles from specialized journals which were
printed during the war. Citations of articles from contemporary
news magazines are not included, except in those cases where such a
work is of major importance. For the student of the conflict who
desires a running account of events, such weekly publications as
TIME, NEWSWEEK, US NEWS AND WORLD REPORT and FACTS ON FILE should be
consulted. THE READER'S GUIDE for the war years contains citations
of literally thousands of magazine articles dealing with all facets

of the conflict. Most of those articles are not cited in this work. The best day-to-day accounts of the war can be found in the NEW YORK TIMES and WASHINGTON POST.

While most pertinent doctoral dissertations written in United States universities are cited, only a limited number of master's theses are included. There is a real need for a comprehensive listing of what is bound to be a multitude of fine master's theses that have been written on various aspects of the war.

While this bibliographic study gives some indication of the extent of written works on the Korean War, I am convinced that the surface is just being scratched on the subject. Hopefully, the years ahead will see an outpouring of studies that will promote an understanding of the war and shed light on the lessons it has taught.

ACKNOWLEDGMENTS

Any person who has ever pursued a serious scholarly endeavor realizes that a surprisingly large number of supportive people contribute to the completion and success of the project. This study is no different, and thus I wish to express my appreciation to a number of people who assisted me.

Major thanks go to the general editor of this series, WARS OF THE UNITED STATES, Dr. Richard Blanco, of the State University of New York at Brockport. Although we had never met, he was trusting enough to select me to do the Korean War volume, then to stick with me through several delays brought on by a position change. For his confidence and support, I will be ever grateful.

If bibliographical studies do not accomplish anything else, they do make the lives of inter-library loan and reference librarians both interesting and frustrating. I certainly tested the mettle of the East Texas State University library staff, and while they probably mumbled to themselves on many occasions, "here he comes again," they always accomodated me in a most professional manner. To those librarians, especially Jan Kemp, Marsha Blair and Frank Newhouse of inter-library loan and Diane Saucier, Carolyn Trezevant and Scott Downing of reference services, I extend a most heartfelt, "Thank you."

If anyone went above and beyond the call of duty in this project, it was my secretary and typist, Marcia Lair, who typed this manuscript from 2,300 note cards that were as legible as a medical doctor's prescriptions. To say that I truly appreciate her efforts is an understatement of major proportions.

As any married scholar knows, few works of substance would be completed were it not for the support and encouragement of one's immediate family. Therefore, my final thanks go to four people who paid the heaviest price and contributed most to this undertaking--my wife, Nancy, and children, Mark, Carolyn and Dianna.

K.D.M.
Commerce, Texas
May 10, 1985

INTRODUCTION

Between mid-1950 and mid-1953 nearly one million men, women and
children died as a result of military hostilities that took place in
the small East-Asia nation of Korea. In addition to those who died,
there were another two million injured and untold thousands who were
missing and never accounted for. Among the American casualties were
33,629 servicemen who died in combat, 20,617 who died from injuries
and disease, and well over 150,000 who were wounded. While American
involvement was termed a police action, the conflict was, as the
casualties will attest to, in every sense of the word a war.

Even while United States servicemen were fighting and dying in
Korea, it was apparent they were engaged in a very different kind of
conflict, yet it was not evident that the war's impact on the
American way of conducting hostilities would be so far-reaching.
For the United States, the Korean War marked a major turning point
in the way the nation would pursue the age-old institution of war.

From the Revolutionary War through World War II, the American
military establishment had been given the task of defeating the
enemy on the field of battle so that the nation's political leaders
could impose their will upon the vanquished. In all of America's
conflicts, the military leaders had been given an essentially free
hand to defeat the enemy. By the mid-20th century, Americans, like
citizens around the world, had come to accept the concept of total
war as a legitimate and proper means by which to achieve political
ends. However, in Korea the rules and expectations were changed.

For the first time, the American military machine was held in
check by its civilian leaders. Military commanders had restrictions
placed on where they could fight, how they could fight, the targets
they could hit and the weapons they could utilize. The newly
imposed limitations were frustrating to players who had learned to
fight under the old, and very different, rules of meeting the enemy.

Not surprisingly, the warriors became increasingly frustrated
as they wrestled with a multitude of unique problems which were
encountered in the United States' first limited war. The change
from total to limited war, like most change, was difficult for many
Americans, military and civilian, to accept. Some, including the
supreme US-UN Commander, General Douglas MacArthur never did accept
it. Many others accepted it, but only amidst considerable
confusion, many misgivings and much frustration. Others accepted
the changes outwardly but with an inner uneasiness. Because of the
newness of conducting a limited war and the range of emotions that
such an event elicited, it was not surprising that the Korean War
aroused, among Americans at large, feelings of hostility, resentment
and confusion the likes of which had not been experienced in the
nation since the days of the Mexican-American War more than one
hundred years before.

One of the major difficulties in studying any war is the fact that those individuals most directly involved in the conflict and thus in many ways most knowledgeable about its political and military details are frequently unable to examine the experience in an objective and analytical manner. Thus, while the participants can provide considerable information, it generally requires a more detached look to determine the lessons of a particular conflict. In practical terms this means that it ordinarily takes a minimum of twenty years for any nation to begin to place a war in its proper historical perspective. Unfortunately, from the time the war in Korea ended until the United States was again deciding on a major military commitment in Vietnam only twelve years elapsed. Because of that short time span, the lessons of Korea were not yet understood and the nation made more blunders in Southeast Asia in the 1960's and early 1970's than it should have.

While the attention of military historians in the 1980's is increasingly on the war in Vietnam, it is important that they not ignore the war in Korea. The United States has fought just two limited wars and the possibility of engaging in another such conflict seems more likely than does that of fighting a nuclear war. Consequently, it is essential that we study both limited conflicts and learn from both. In fact it is my firm conviction that the study of the war in Korea will teach us no less than the war in Vietnam. It is my hope that this work will be of some assistance to the scholars of the future as they search for the meaning and lessons of the war in Korea.

ABBREVIATION FOR CITED PERIODICALS
(Periodicals spelled out in text are not listed.)

ADMIN SCI Q	Administrative Science Quarterly
ADV HERT	Adventist Heritage
AERO HIST	Aerospace Historian
AERO AL	Aero Album
AERON ENG R	Aeronautical Engineering Review
AEROP	Aeroplane
AIR FORCE	Air Force Magazine
AIR TR	Air Trails
AIR UNIV Q R	Air University Quarterly Review
AIRP HIST	Airpower Historian
AM ACAD POL SOC SCI ANS	American Academy of Political and Social Science Annals
AM AVI	American Aviation
AM AVI HIST SOC J	American Aviation Historical Society Journal
AM HERT	American Heritage
AM HIST ILL	American History Illustrated
AM J EPID	American Journal of Epidemiology
AM J INTER LAW	American Journal of International Law
AM J PSY	American Journal of Psychiatry
AM LEG MAG	American Legion Magazine
AM MERCURY	American Mercury
AM PERS	American Perspective
AM POL SCI R	American Political Science Review
AM Q	American Quarterly (Belgium)
AM SCH	American Scholar
AM SOC R	American Sociological Review
AN AM AC POL SOC SCI	Annals of the American Academy of Political and Social Science
ARM FOR SOC	Armed Forces and Society
ARMY	Army – The Magazine of Landpower
ARMY DIG	Army Digest
ARMY INFO DIG	Army Information Digest

ARMY LOG	Army Logistician
ARMY Q	Army Quarterly
ARMY Q DEF J	Army Quarterly and Defense Journal (Great Britain)
ARZ WEST	Arizona and the West
ASIA Q	Asia Quarterly
ASIAN AFF	Asian Affairs
ASIAN FOR	Asian Forum
ASIAN PRO	Asian Profile (Hong Kong)
ASIAN SUR	Asian Survey
ATLANTIC	Atlantic Monthly
AVI AGE	Aviation Age
AVI HIST SOC J	Aviation History Society Journal
AVI WK	Aviation Week
BEE-HIVE	The Bee-Hive
BERK J SOC	Berkeley Journal of Sociology
BRAS AN	Brassey's Annual: The Armed Forces Year-Book
BT SUR	British Survey
BUL BT PSY SOC	Bulletin of the British Psychological Society
BUL CON ASIAN SCHS	Bulletin of Concerned Asian Scholars
BUL INST STUDY USSR	Bulletin of the Institute for the Study of the USSR (West Germany)
BUL NY ACA MED	Bulletin of the New York Academy of Medicine
BUS WK	Business Week
CAN ARMY J	Canadian Army Journal
CAT WORLD	Catholic World
CHAP	The Chaplain
CHINA Q	China Quarterly
COM FOR J	Combat Forces Journal
COMP POL STUDIES	Comparative Political Studies
COMM	Commentary
CONT R	Contemporary Review
CUR HIST	Current History
DEPT STATE BUL	US Department of State Bulletin
DIP HIST	Diplomatic History
EAS WORLD	Eastern World
ED PUB	Editor and Publisher
ED REC	The Educational Record
ENC	Encounter
FAR EASTERN Q	Far Eastern Quarterly
FAR EASTERN SUR	Far Eastern Survey
FLY	Flying
FOR AFF	Foreign Affairs
FOR POL REPS	Foreign Policy Reports

FOR SER J	Foreign Service Journal
GLB LAU	Globe and Laurel
HIST TEACHER	History Teacher
INF	Infantry
INF SCH Q	Infantry School Quarterly
INTV	Interavia
INTER AFF	International Affairs
INTER CON	International Conciliation
INTER HIST R	International History Review
INTER J	International Journal (Canada)
INTER PER	International Perspective
INTER R MIL HIST	International Review of Military History
INTER STUDIES N	International Studies Notes
INTER STUDIES Q	International Studies Quarterly
JAP J AM STUDIES	Japanese Journal of American Studies
J ABN SOC PSY	Journal of Abnormal and Social Psychology
J AM HIST	Journal of American History
J AMA	Journal of the American Medical Association
J ASIAN STUDIES	Journal of Asian Studies
J ASIATIC STUDIES	Journal of Asiatic Studies (South Korea)
J BLACK STUDIES	Journal of Black Studies
J COMM	Journal of Communication
J COM FAM STUDIES	Journal of Comparative Family Studies
J CON RESO	Journal of Conflict Resolution
J CONT ASIA	Journal of Contemporary Asia
J KOREAN AFF	Journal of Korean Affairs
J NEGRO HIST	Journal of Negro History
J POL	Journal of Politics
J POL MIL SOC	Journal of Political and Military Sociology
J SOC IS	Journal of Social Issues
J UNI SER INST IND	Journal of the United Service Institute of India
JOU Q	Journalism Quarterly
KOREA JA	Korea Journal
KOREA WORLD AFF	Korea and World Affairs (South Korea)
KOREAN AFF	Korean Affairs
KOREAN SUR	Korean Survey
KOREANA Q	Koreana Quarterly
LAB HIST	Labor History
LIB Q	Library Quarterly
MARINE CORPS GAZ	Marine Corps Gazette
MIL AFF	Military Affairs
MIL CHAP	The Military Chaplain
MIL ENG	Military Engineer
MIL HIST J	Military History Journal

MIL R	Military Review
MIL SURG	Military Surgeon
MILTA	Militaria
MOD CHINA	Modern China
MONT R	Monthly Review
MONT LAB R	Monthly Labor Review
NATION	The Nation
NAT GEO	National Geographic
NAT R	National Review
NAV AVI N	Naval Aviation News
NAV W C R	Naval War College Review
NEGRO HIST BUL	Negro History Bulletin
NEW AM MERCURY	New American Mercury
NEW STATS NAT	New Statesman and Nation
NY TIMES B R	New York Times Book Review
NY TIMES MAG	New York Times Magazine
NO DAK Q	North Dakota Quarterly
PAC AFF	Pacific Affairs
PAC HIST R	Pacific Historical Review
PAC SPEC	Pacific Spectator
PEG	Pegasus
POINTER	The Pointer
POL AFF	Political Affairs
POL Q	Political Quarterly
POL SCI Q	Political Science Quarterly
POP MECH	Popular Mechanics
PRES STUDIES Q	Presidential Studies Quarterly
PROB COM	Problems of Communism
PROL	Prologue
PSY	Psychiatry
PUB ADM R	Public Administration Review
PUB INT	Public Interest
PUB OP Q	Public Opinion Quarterly
QM R	Quartermaster Review
QUEEN'S Q	Queen's Quarterly
READ DIG	Reader's Digest
RED RIV VAL HIST R	Red River Valley Historical Review
R AM HIST	Reviews in American History
R POL	Review of Politics
ROCKY MT SOC SCI J	Rocky Mountain Social Science Journal
ROY ARM CORPS J	Royal Armoured Corps Journal (Great Britain)
ROY UNI SER INST J	Royal United Service Institution Journal (Great Britain)
SAT EVE POST	Saturday Evening Post
SCH EX	School Executive
SIG	Signal
SOC CAS	Social Casework

SOC ED	Social Education
SOC PROB	Social Problems
SOC SCI Q	Social Science Quarterly
STUDIES HIST SOC	Studies in History and Society
STUDIES SOV UNION	Studies on the Soviet Union
TWEN CENT	Twentieth Century
UKR Q	Ukranian Quarterly
UN BUL	United Nations Bulletin
UN WORLD	United Nations World
UNI SER EM R	United Services and Empire Review
US AIR SER	US Air Services
USA AVI DIG	US Army Aviation Digest
US ARM FOR MED J	United States Armed Forces Medical Journal
US NAVAL INST PROC	US Naval Institute Proceedings
US NEWS W R	US News and World Report
UTAH HIST Q	Utah Historical Quarterly
VEN	Ventures
VIR Q R	Virginia Quarterly Review
WEST PENN HIS MAG	Western Pennsylvania History Magazine
WILSON Q	Wilson Quarterly
WIS MAG HIST	Wisconsin Magazine of History
WORLD AFF	World Affairs
WORLD POL	World Politics
YALE R	Yale Review

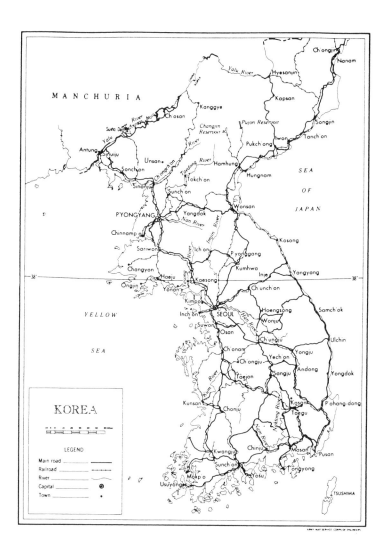

KOREAN WAR CHRONOLOGY

1950

June 25   North Korean Army invades the Republic of Korea
US requests meeting of the UN Security Council
UN Security Council, with Soviet Union not
    represented, adopts by a 9-0-1 vote a resolution
    calling for "immediate cessation of hostilities"
President Truman authorizes US Commander, Far East,
    General MacArthur, to furnish military supplies to
    ROK

June 26   ROK appeals to US and UN for aid and other steps
    to secure peace and security
UN Commission on Korea rejects North Korean
    allegations that ROK attacked first

June 27   Truman orders US air and sea forces to give ROK
    forces cover and support
UN Security Council votes 7-1-2 to adopt US
    resolution calling for members to furnish aid to
    South Korea to repel the attack and restore peace

June 28   North Koreans take control of Seoul, the South
    Korean capitol

June 29   MacArthur flies to Korea to evaluate situation

June 30   Truman authorizes air attacks on North Korea,
    naval blockade of entire Korean coast and use of
    US ground troops in South Korea.

July 1   First US troops arrive in South Korea

July 2   US rejects Nationalist China's offer of 33,000
    troops for Korea

July 5   US Army Task Force Smith encounters North Korean
    force near Osan in first combat action

July 7   UN authorizes US to establish unified UN Command in
    Korea

July 8   Truman names MacArthur UN Commander

July 12-13   US troops retreat across Kum River

July 13   General Walton Walker named commander of US troops
                    in Korea (Eighth US Army)

July 18   US 1st Cavalry and 25th Division arrive in Korea

July 20   UN forces abandon Taejon

July 31   Chinju falls to North Koreans; US First Marines and
                    Army 2nd Infantry reach Korea

August 1   UN Forces in Pusan Perimeter

August 6-8   MacArthur secretly confers with Averell Harriman
                    and Generals Norstad, Almond and Ridgway about
                    possible landing at Inchon

August 14-16   US counterattacks stall Reds near Taegu

August 25   Chinese Reds reported massing near Korean frontier

September 1-3   Reds launch major attacks on Pusan perimeter
                    but efforts nullified by UN forces

September 12   US Secretary of Defense Johnson forced to resign by
                    President Truman, General George Marshall named new
                    Secretary

September 15   Successful UN invasion of Inchon

September 18   Kimpo Airfield recaptured by UN Forces

September 22   US Eighth Army breaks out of Pusan Perimeter

September 28   UN Forces retake Seoul

September 30   ROK Forces cross 38th Parallel

October 4   UN approves crossing 38th Parallel

October 7   US 1st Cavalry crosses 38th Parallel near Kaesong

October 12-13   Truman and MacArthur confer at Wake Island
                    on the conduct of the war

October 19   US troops capture North Korean capital of
                    Pyongyang

October 25   US troops attack port of Wonsan

October 26   ROK Forces reach Yalu River
                    ROK Forces capture Chinese prisoners near Sudong

October 27-31   Chinese Communist troops attack ROK forces

October 30   US troops forty miles from Yalu River

November 2   Chinese attack US 8th Army near Unsan

November 6   MacArthur estimates 60,000 Chinese in the conflict

November 24   Troops of US 7th Division reach Yalu
                    UN launches major drive to the Yalu, MacArthur
                       says he hopes "to keep my promise to the GI's
                       to have them home by Christmas"

November 25-27   Chinese launch major counterattack and inflict
                       heavy casualties on US troops 1st Marine Division
                       hit on west side of Changjin Reservoir and US 7th
                       Division on east and begin fight to breakout

December 5   Reds take Pyongyang

December 7   US announces that as of November 26, 5,616 men had
                       been killed, 21,764 wounded and 5,062 missing; thus
                       making it the 4th costliest war in the nation's
                       history

December 9   1st Marines and 7th Infantry complete breakout begun
                       November 27

December 15   UN troops withdraw below 38th Parallel

December 23   General Walker killed in jeep accident; General
                       Ridgway named as replacement

December 24   UN troops complete evacuation of North Korea

1951
January 4   Reds recapture Seoul and drive UN forces thirty to
                       fifty miles south of 38th Parallel

January 25   US and ROK Forces launch counter offensive--advance
                       toward Han River

January 25-   Bitter fighting near Chipyong
February 25

February 11-17   Chinese launch major offensive--little progress

February 21   US IX and X Corps launch Operation Killer

February 28   Red resistance crushed South of the Han River

March 7   Operation Ripper by US IX and X Corps advances
                 across the Han in central and eastern
                 portions of country

March 15   US troops recapture Seoul

April 11   President Truman removes General MacArthur as
                 Supreme Commander and names General Ridgway as
                 his replacement
                 General James Van Fleet takes command of Eighth Army

April 22-28   Chinese launch major offensive

April 30   UN Forces halt enemy advances north of Seoul and
                 the Han River

May 16-19   Chinese launch all-out offensive against
                 UN forces

May 20   Chinese offensive halted; UN forces begin counter-
                 attack

May 24   US forces cross 38th Parallel at two places

June 1-30   Front stabilizes

June 30   General Ridgway broadcasts to Chinese the UN's
                 willingness to open cease-fire negotiations

July 10   UN and Communist negotiators begin peace talks at
                 Kaesong

August 23   Negotiations suspended by Communists when UN
                 refuses to acknowledge and apologize for alleged
                 plane attack on the neutral zone at Kaesong

August 25   US B-29's raid Rachin, North Korea, just 20 miles
                 from Siberia, in a controversial attack

September 26	Biggest air battle of the war as 155 Red and 101 UN planes clashed near Sinanju
October 25	Truce talks resume at a new site, Panmunjom, six miles from former site of Kaesong
November 12	US Army ordered to cease offensive operations and pursue an active defense
December 12	Negotiations establish subcommittee to begin work on exchange of prisoners

1952
January 19	USAF reported 457 aircraft lost thus far in the war
February 10	Top US jet ace, Major George A. Davis, killed in dogfight over Northeast Korea
February 17	US 24th Infantry Division, first force to fight in Korea, withdraws to Japan
March 13	Disorder in UN POW camp on Koje Island, twelve Reds die
March 26	US reports the 123 deaths experienced the week of March 15-21 made it the lightest casualty week of the war; so far 18,616 reported dead
May 7	Red prisoners at Koje Island POW camp take US General Francis T. Dodd, camp commander, captive
May 11	General Dodd released
May 12	General Mark Clark replaces General Ridgway as US and UN Commander
May 23	General Dodd demoted to Colonel by Secretary of Army Frank Pace, Jr.
June 23-26	US planes knock out five major hydroelectric power plants in the Yalu River district
July 10	First anniversary of peace negotiations with tentative agreements on all issues except exchange of prisoners
July 11-12	Biggest UN air raid of the war, a 24-hour attack on North Korean capital of Pyongyang

August 1-29   US steps up air attack on North Korea, ending
                  with August 29th 1,403 sorties against Pyongyang

Sept. 20-24   Reds step up land attacks along truce line
                  but all advances are rebuffed

October 1   Fifty-two Communist POW's killed in uprising at
                  camp at Cheju Island

October 1   USAF reports sixty-two Red MIG-15's shot down in
                  September, a one-month record in the war

October 6-24   Reds launch biggest land attack in a year and
                  are repulsed by UN troops

October 8   Truce talks suspended

December 2-5   US President-elect Dwight Eisenhower honors
                  election promise and visits the Korean battlefield

1953
February 11   General Maxwell Taylor replaces General Van Fleet
                  as Commander of US 8th Army

February 22   General Clark, UN, Supreme Commander, proposes that
                  sick and injured prisoners be exchanged before an
                  armistice agreement is reached

March 28   North Korean Premier Kim Il Sung and General Peng
                  Teh-huai, Commander of Red Chinese Volunteers in
                  Korea, accept proposal of exchange of sick and
                  injured POW's and urge resumption of negotiations
                  at Panmunjom

April 6   Negotiations on exchange of ill prisoners begins

April 11   Negotiators agree to exchange 605 UN prisoners
                  for 6,030 Communists

April 20   Exchange of sick prisoners begins--takes seven days

April 25   Full scale negotiations reopened

May 12   Withdrawal of 1st US Marines from the battle line
                  after thirty-three months of action

May 25   UN negotiators make "final" offer on POW's;
                  proposal approved by South Korea

June 1-30   USAF shoots down seventy-four MIG's, a one-
                month record for the war

June 8   Allied and Communists negotiators sign agreement
                on POW's thus removing the last obstacle to the
                signing of an armistice
                Vigorous ROK opposition to tentative agreement

June 16-30   Communists launch major land attack on central
                and eastern fronts; some of the allies' heaviest
                artillery and mortar attacks of the war

June 18   President Rhee endangers armistice agreement by
                releasing 25,000 POW's rather than turn them over
                to a custodial commission

June 20   Reds halt truce negotiations over Rhee's action

July 8   Communists agree to resume talks

July 11   Rhee agrees to truce agreement

July 13   Reds launch their biggest land drive in two years

July 16-18   UN troops repel advances and stabilize lines

July 20   Talks resume

July 27   Armistice signed, 10:10 a.m.; hostilities end,
                10:10 p.m.

August 5-   POW exchange carried out
September 6

THE KOREAN WAR

I. REFERENCE WORKS
A. SOURCE GUIDES AND BIBLIOGRAPHIES

1. Albion, Robert G. NAVAL AND MARITIME HISTORY: AN ANNOTATED
    BIBLIOGRAPHY. Fourth Edition. Mystic, CT: Marine
    Historical Association, 1972.

    More than 5,000 books and dissertations on all aspects of
    US maritime history including a limited number of works on
    the US Navy in the post WWII and Korean War eras.

2. Allard, Dean C., et al. comps. U.S. NAVAL HISTORY SOURCES IN
    THE UNITED STATES. Washington: Naval History Division,
    Department of the Navy, 1979.

    Identifies manuscript, archival and other special
    collections on naval affairs and personnel. Lists the
    collections held in each state. Holdings cited include those
    for many individuals whose careers spanned the Korean War.
    Of importance only to the serious researcher.

3. American Historical Association. GUIDE TO HISTORICAL
    LITERATURE. New York: Macmillan, 1961.

    A listing and short annotation of nearly 20,000 historical
    works on all aspects of world history. This work has more than
    two dozen books and government reports on the Korean War and
    its background.

4. Armstrong, William J. "United States Naval Aviation History--
    A Guide to the Sources." AERO HIST, 1980 27 (2):109-112.

    Brief guide to the leading repositories of information on
    US naval aviation. Very little is said about collections that
    have Korean War materials, but there is a helpful listing of
    the locations, addresses and contact person at the libraries
    and collection sites.

5. Association of Asian Studies. CUMULATIVE BIBLIOGRAPHY OF
    ASIAN STUDIES 1941-1965: SUBJECT BIBLIOGRAPHY. 4 vols.
    Boston: Hall, 1970.

    Volumes 3 and 4 contain several hundred books, articles
    and government reports, all written in English, on all facets
    of the Korean conflict. One section is devoted entirely to the
    War, but other sections also contain many citations on the
    subject. Unfortunately, no index. Another volume, 1966-1970,
    published by Hall in 1972.

6. Backus, Robert L., comp. RUSSIAN SUPPLEMENT TO THE KOREAN
    STUDIES GUIDE. Berkeley: Institute of International
    Studies, University of California, 1958.

    Extensive bibliography which includes nearly 200 Russian
    language books and articles on the Korean conflict.

7. Beers, Henry P. BIBLIOGRAPHIES IN AMERICAN HISTORY,
    1942-1978. 2 vols. Woodbridge, CT: Research
    Publications, 1982.

    The most extensive list available of bibliographies, in
    English, on American History topics--nearly 12,000 entries.
    Various sections contain bibliographies dealing with topics
    related to the Korean War. Extremely valuable are sections
    on publications of the Defense, Air Force, Army and Navy
    Departments and Chapter 7 on Military and Naval topics.

8. Berton, Peter, and Eugene Wu. CONTEMPORARY CHINA: A
    RESEARCH GUIDE. Edited by Howard Koch, Jr. Stanford, CA:
    Hoover Institution, 1967.

    More than 2,000 entries on China since 1945 including nearly
    two dozen works on the Korean War. Cites key sources from Red
    China and Nationalist China, and master's theses and doctoral
    dissertations.

9. Besterman, Theodore. WORLD BIBLIOGRAPHY OF ORIENTAL
    BIBLIOGRAPHIES. Totowa, NJ: Rowman, 1975.

    Includes a listing of more than fifty bibliographies
    dealing with various aspects of Korea and its history. Cites
    five works on the Korean War.

10. Blanchard, Carroll H., Jr., comp. KOREAN WAR BIBLIOGRAPHY
    AND MAPS OF KOREA. Albany, NY: Korean Conflict Research
    Foundation, 1964.

    The most extensive bibliography yet published on the Korean
    War. Ten thousand citations, especially strong in articles
    and foreign language publications. Well organized. Maps.
    An indispensable source for serious students of the war but
    only covers works published through 1963.

11. Bolander, Louis H. "Books on Korea." US NAVAL INST PROC,
    1950 76 (9):1031-1032.

    Brief survey of more than a dozen books which provide
    background on the Korean War by looking at the nation's
    history, people and culture. Most books cited were published
    between 1944 and 1950.

12. Burns, Richard D., ed. HARRY S. TRUMAN: A BIBLIOGRAPHY OF
    HIS TIMES AND PRESIDENCY. Wilmington, DE: Scholarly
    Research, 1984.

Annotated bibliography of more than 3,000 books, articles and reports on all aspects of Truman's career, including many entries on his foreign policy and an entire chapter on the Korean War.

13. Chan, F. Gilbert. NATIONALISM IN EAST ASIA: AN ANNOTATED BIBLIOGRAPHY OF SELECTED WORKS. New York: Garland, 1981.

This work contains a chapter on Korean Nationalism. Discusses the Korean experience before examining more than thirty books, in English, on the topic and twenty-five works in Korean and Japanese.

14. Chung, Yong Sun, comp. KOREA: A SELECTED BIBLIOGRAPHY 1959-1963. Kalamazoo, MI: Korea Research and Publications, 1965.

Includes more than fifty books on the Korean War, including a number of North Korean publications.

15. Cline, Marjorie W., et al, eds. SCHOLAR'S GUIDE TO INTELLIGENCE LITERATURE: BIBLIOGRAPHY OF THE RUSSELL J. BOWEN COLLECTION. Frederick, MD: University Publications, 1983.

An excellent bibliography of more than 5,000 works on intelligence. Although there is no heading specifically on the Korean War there are numerous citations on Korean-related intelligence matters listed throughout the work.

16. Coletta, Paolo E., comp. A BIBLIOGRAPHY OF AMERICAN NAVAL HISTORY. Annapolis, MD: Naval Institute, 1981.

A listing of nearly 5,000 books, articles, documents, theses and dissertations on naval history, including 120 works on the Korean War. The author interprets naval history in a very broad sense, thus it includes general military studies as well as works on policy and strategy.

17. Craig, Harding. A BIBLIOGRAPHY OF ENCYCLOPEDIAS AND DICTIONARIES DEALING WITH MILITARY, NAVAL AND MARITIME AFFAIRS, 1577-1971. 4th ed. Houston: Rice University, Department of History, 1971.

Lists, by year, works dealing with the military. Key works in English and a number of foreign languages. Many of the encyclopedias and dictionaries contain references pertinent to the war in Korea.

18. Cresswell, Mary Ann, and Carl Berger. UNITED STATES AIR FORCE HISTORY: AN ANNOTATED BIBLIOGRAPHY. Washington: Office of Air Force History, 1971.

Nearly 1,500 entries on aviation developments. Books,

journals and government documents are covered. Includes more
than fifty citations on the Korean War. Brief annotations.

19. Dollen, Charles. BIBLIOGRAPHY OF THE UNITED STATES MARINES.
    New York: Scarecrow Press, 1963.

    This book lists more than 1,000 books and articles on the
    Marines and includes many works on the Korean War.

20. Dornbusch, Charles E. HISTORIES OF AMERICAN ARMY UNITS, WORLD
    WAR I AND II AND KOREAN CONFLICT, WITH SOME EARLIER
    HISTORIES. Washington: Department of the Army, Office of
    the Adjutant General, 1956.

    In spite of the title there are only a handful of citations
    on US Army units fighting in Korea, and they are difficult to
    locate in this volume listing more than 2,000 works.
    Researcher can benefit if searching for a specific unit.

21. Dornbusch, Charles E. HISTORIES, PERSONAL NARRATIVES, UNITED
    STATES ARMY. A CHECKLIST. Cornwallville, NY: Hope Farm,
    1967.

    Includes more than 2,500 entries, most of which are
    privately printed histories of specific units. Very few,
    less than 5%, deal with units in the Korean War.

22. Dornbusch, Charles E. POST-WAR SOUVENIR BOOKS AND UNIT
    HISTORIES OF THE NAVY, MARINE CORPS AND CONSTRUCTION
    BATTALIONS. Washington: Office of Naval History, 1953.

    Lists more than 125 publications, many privately printed,
    detailing the activities of specific units or ships involved
    in the Korean theater.

23. Estep, Raymond. "Notes on Air Force Bibliography: With a
    List of Basic Reference Guides." AIR UNIV Q R, 1959
    11 (1):113-120.

    Excellent introduction for persons wanting to research any
    aspect of US air power, including operations in Korea. Cites
    twenty essential guides such as bibliographies, indices, guides
    and handbooks. Includes many official studies which have not
    been published.

24. Freidel, Frank, ed. HARVARD GUIDE TO AMERICAN HISTORY. Vol.
    II. Cambridge: Belknap, 1974.

    This work, which is one of the standard guides for
    researching virtually any aspect of American History, has a
    section on the Korean War which lists more than fifty works
    on the conflict. No annotations.

25. Ginsburgs, George. SOVIET WORKS ON KOREA, 1945-1970. Los
    Angeles: University of Southern California, 1973.

Begins with an essay on Soviet literature on Korea in the
years after WWII. Lists more than 1,100 works including 133,
mostly newspaper and journal articles, on the Korean War.
Major topics such as: American oppression; violations of
international law; bacteriological warfare and North Korea
during the war, are all covered from the Soviet perspective.

26. Greenwood, John, comp. AMERICAN DEFENSE POLICY SINCE 1945:
     A PRELIMINARY BIBLIOGRAPHY. Lawrence: University Press of
     Kansas, 1973.

     This listing of nearly 2,500 books, articles and government
     publications on US defense matters includes over eighty works
     on the Korean War. Includes key bibliographies. No
     annotations or index.

27. Halperin, Morton H. LIMITED WAR: AN ESSAY ON THE DEVELOPMENT
     OF THE THEORY AND AN ANNOTATED BIBLIOGRAPHY. Cambridge, MA:
     Center for International Affairs, 1962.

     A brief look at the nature of limited war plus a review of
     key books and articles on limited wars. Includes an
     evaluation of many of the best works on the Korean War.

28. Henthorn, William E., comp. A GUIDE TO REFERENCE AND
     RESEARCH MATERIALS ON KOREAN HISTORY. Honolulu: East-West
     Center, 1968.

     Contains many Japanese and Korean language publications,
     limited citations on the Korean conflict.

29. Higham, Robin, et al. A GUIDE TO THE SOURCES OF UNITED
     STATES MILITARY HISTORY. Hamden, CT: Archon, 1975.

     A first rate scholarly guide to the field of American
     military history covering books and articles published
     through 1972. Although there is no chapter per se on the
     Korean War, a number of chapters dealing with the post WW II
     period cite works covering the conflict.

30. Higham, Robin, and Donald Mrozek, eds. A GUIDE TO THE
     SOURCES OF UNITED STATES MILITARY HISTORY: SUPPLEMENT I.
     Hamden, CT: Archon, 1981.

     A continuation of the first rate, scholarly guide to
     American military history which covers leading books and
     articles published between 1973 and 1978, along with several
     chapters on new topics. As in the original guide no specific
     section on Korea but top works on the conflict are cited in
     several chapters.

31. Higham, Robin, ed. OFFICIAL HISTORIES: ESSAYS AND
     BIBLIOGRAPHIES FROM AROUND THE WORLD. Manhattan: Kansas
     State University Library, 1970.

Examination of military history programs of more than thirty-five nations. Citations on works of various history units and commissions. Of limited value to students studying the Korean War because of lack of index. Digging will provide information on some of the nations involved in the Korean fighting. Brief mention of the work of the South Korean War History Compilation Committee.

32. Hufer, Klaus, ed. THE UNITED NATIONS SYSTEM--INTERNATIONAL BIBLIOGRAPHY. Vol. 1: LEARNED JOURNALS AND MONOGRAPHS 1945-1956. Bonn, West Germany: Verlag, 1976.

Contains forty-seven publications, most of which are in English, that focus on the diplomacy of the UN as it related to the Korean War and its background.

33. Imperial War Museum Library. THE WAR IN KOREA, 1950-1953, A LIST OF SELECTED REFERENCES. London: War Museum Library, 1961.

A mimeographed paper listing more than 350 books, pamphlets and journal articles, in English, on the Korean War. Good for materials on the armed forces activities of both Britain and the US.

34. Jessup, John E., and Robert W. Coakley. A GUIDE TO THE STUDY AND USE OF MILITARY HISTORY. Washington: Center of Military History, 1979.

Discusses the nature and uses of military history and explains the US Army's historical programs. Part two consists of seven bibliographical essays on various aspects of military history--including one on the US and the World since 1945, which covers more than thirty works on the Korean War.

35. Kim, Han-Kyo. STUDIES ON KOREA: A SCHOLAR'S GUIDE. Honolulu: University Press of Hawaii, 1980.

One of the best bibliographic studies available on Korea. More than 3,500 annotated entries divided into sixteen subject areas such as: government and politics, international relations, North Korea, economics, geography, education, culture and bibliographies. Includes thirty works specifically on the Korean War and more than that number on Korean politics from 1945-1953.

36. Koh, Hesung Chun. KOREA: AN ANALYTICAL GUIDE TO BIBLIOGRAPHIES. New Haven, CT: Human Relations Area Files, 1971.

Cites over 500 bibliographies on various aspects of Korean history and culture. Bibliographies included are in eight different languages and covers items published between 1896 and 1970.

37. Kreslins, Janis A. FOREIGN AFFAIRS BIBLIOGRAPHY, 1962-1972. New York: Bowker, 1976.

     One of the best bibliographic works available. This volume, which lists primarily books in English, contains more than seventy works on political, diplomatic and economic affairs in North and South Korea plus twenty-one books on the Korean War. Brief annotations.

38. Lambert, Norma K. CUMULATIVE INDICES TO MILITARY AFFAIRS 1937-1969. Manhattan: Kansas State University Library, 1969.

     Author, title, subject and review indices for works in MILITARY AFFAIRS, the journal of the American Military Institute. Poorly indexed. Items on Korea, of which there are only a handful, are difficult to find.

39. Lane, Jack C. AMERICA'S MILITARY PAST: A GUIDE TO INFORMATIONAL SOURCES. Detroit: Gale, 1980.

     More than 1800 annotated entries covering the range of American military history from the colonial period to Vietnam. Nearly fifty books and articles on the Korean War.

40. Lang, Kurt. MILITARY INSTITUTIONS AND THE SOCIOLOGY OF WAR: A REVIEW OF THE LITERATURE WITH ANNOTATED BIBLIOGRAPHY. Beverly Hills, CA: Sage, 1972.

     This study of more than 1,300 sociological works on war includes information on a score of studies directly related to the Korean War and several dozen topics that deal with it indirectly. Subjects covered on Korea include combat performance, stress, prisoners of war and impact of racial integration.

41. Lee, Chong-Sik. "Korea and the Korean War." SOVIET FOREIGN RELATIONS AND WORLD COMMUNISM. Edited by Thomas T. Hammond. Princeton, NJ: Princeton University, 1965, pp. 787-806.

     An excellent annotated bibliography of one hundred works, half of which are on the war.

42. Lee, Soon H. "Korea: A Selected Bibliography in Western Languages, 1950-1958." Master's Thesis. Catholic, 1959.

     Of the 500 books and published reports on various aspects of Korean history and culture, more than 175 deal with various aspects of the Korean War. No annotations.

43. Library of Congress. KOREA: AN ANNOTATED BIBLIOGRAPHY OF PUBLICATIONS IN FAR EASTERN LANGUAGES. Washington: Government Printing Office, 1950.

Thousands of works, primarily in Korean, Japanese and
Chinese, on a variety of topics dealing with Korea. Covers
the political turmoil that led to the war but there is
nothing on the war.

44. Library of Congress. KOREA: AN ANNOTATED BIBLIOGRAPHY OF
    PUBLICATIONS IN THE RUSSIAN LANGUAGE. Washington:
    Government Printing Office, 1950.

    Covers a wide range of topics on Korea as covered by
    Russian writers between 1917 and 1950. Author, title and
    subject index.

45. Library of Congress. KOREA: AN ANNOTATED BIBLIOGRAPHY OF
    PUBLICATIONS IN WESTERN LANGUAGES. Washington: Government
    Printing Office, 1950.

    Good coverage of books on Korean history, government
    and economics in the period from 1930 through 1950.

46. Marcus, Richard, ed. KOREAN STUDIES GUIDE. Westbrook,
    CT: Greenwood Press, 1974.

    Originally published in 1954 this is an annotated
    bibliography of some 500 works on modern Korea most of
    which were published between 1900 and 1951. Very little
    on World War II and after.

47. Millett, Allan R., and B. Franklin Cooling, III, comps.
    DOCTORAL DISSERTATIONS IN MILITARY AFFAIRS: A
    BIBLIOGRAPHY. Manhattan: Kansas State University Library,
    1972.

    A listing of more than 1,400 doctoral dissertations written
    in US universities on military topics. Organized along broad
    lines of world military affairs, including a breakdown by
    country, US topics and general studies on war and the
    military. Includes nearly two dozen entries on the Korean
    War. Annual updates are found in MILITARY AFFAIRS beginning
    with the February 1973 issue.

48. Nunn, G. Raymond. ASIA: REFERENCE WORKS: A SELECT
    ANNOTATED GUIDE. London: Mansell, 1980.

    Includes a section on South Korea which has annotated
    entries on 113 works, including reference books,
    encyclopedias and handbooks, yearbooks, dictionaries,
    biographical dictionaries, and bibliographies in Korean
    and western languages.

49. Okinshevoich, Leo, comp. UNITED STATES HISTORY AND
    HISTORIOGRAPHY IN POSTWAR SOVIET WRITINGS, 1945-1970.
    Santa Barbara, CA: Clio, 1976.

More than 3,600 entries, with brief annotations, of works in
Russian on post WWII topics. Includes two dozen general
entries on Korea plus twenty-three works on the Korean War.

50. O'Quinlivan, Michael, and James S. Santelli. AN ANNOTATED
     BIBLIOGRAPHY OF THE UNITED STATES MARINE CORPS IN THE
     KOREAN WAR. Washington: Historical Division, U.S. Marine
     Corps, 1962, revised 1970.

     Several hundred books and articles on various facets of
     Marine activities in Korea are included with a one sentence
     annotation on most.

51. Park, Hong-Kyu, comp. THE KOREAN WAR: AN ANNOTATED
     BIBLIOGRAPHY. Marshall, TX: Demmer, 1971.

     A brief annotated bibliography of some 125
     entries, including primary and secondary sources
     plus non-English publications.

52. Paszek, Lawrence J., comp. UNITED STATES AIR FORCE HISTORY:
     A GUIDE TO DOCUMENTARY SOURCES. Washington: Office of Air
     Force History, 1973.

     Tells of collections of documents that deal with the
     growth, development and activities of US air power.
     Describes collections at USAF center and depositories,
     national archives, federal records center, presidential
     libraries, library of congress and special collections.
     Cites thirteen collections that deal with the Korean War and
     includes reference to the personal papers of more than a
     dozen individuals involved in Korea.

53. Rhoads, Edward J.M., et al. THE CHINESE RED ARMY, 1927-1963:
     AN ANNOTATED BIBLIOGRAPHY. Cambridge, MA: Harvard University,
     1964.

     Looks at more than 600 publications on the Communist
     Chinese Army and the role it has played in the military and
     political history of the nation. Includes fifty-one items on
     the Korean War in English and Asian languages.

54. Roberts, Henry L. FOREIGN AFFAIRS BIBLIOGRAPHY, 1942-1952.
     New York: Harper, 1955.

     This work cites seventeen books on Korea and fifteen works
     on the Korean War. Most entries, with brief annotations, are
     for works in English but several are in other languages.

55. Roberts, Henry L. FOREIGN AFFAIRS BIBLIOGRAPHY 1952-1962.
     New York: Bowker, 1964.

     Continuation of a first rate bibliographic series has
     annotated entries on thirty-eight books dealing with the
     Korean War plus numerous entries on Korean politics and
     economics.

56. Roos, Charles, comp. BIBLIOGRAPHY OF MILITARY MEDICINE
    RELATING TO THE KOREAN CONFLICT, 1950-53. Washington:
    Government Printing Office, 1953.

    Lists nearly 200 works, primarily journal articles, that deal
    with all aspects of military medicine and services in Korea.

57. Roos, Charles, comp. BIBLIOGRAPHY OF MILITARY PSYCHIATRY,
    1947-1952. Washington: Government Printing Office, 1953.

    Cites several hundred works dealing with military
    psychiatry as related to US and British forces. Most entries
    deal with developments and activities during the Korean War.

58. Saunders, Jack. "Records in the National Archives Relating
    to Korea, 1945-1950." CHILD OF CONFLICT. Edited by Bruce
    Cumings. Seattle: University of Washington, 1983, pp.
    309-326.

    First rate bibliographical essay describing the extensive
    military and diplomatic records available on Korea at the
    National Archives. A must for the serious scholar who needs
    to go to the Archives to examine the primary sources.
    Describes the key Record Groups.

59. Scull, Roberta A. A BIBLIOGRAPHY OF UNITED STATES GOVERNMENT
    BIBLIOGRAPHIES, 1968-1973. Ann Arbor, MI: Pierin, 1975.

    Annotated listings of more than 1,200 bibliographies
    published by various agencies in the US Government. Includes
    several dozen works on the Far East, including Korean
    military affairs and history.

60. Shapero, Seymour. BRAINWASHING: A PARTIAL BIBLIOGRAPHY.
    Washington: American University, Special Operations
    Research Office, 1958.

    A listing of several hundred books and journal articles on
    brainwashing, including a number of entries on Communist
    techniques used on prisoners of war during the Korean
    conflict.

61. Shulman, Frank J. "American Doctoral Research on Korea,
    1970-74: A Brief Statistical Analysis and Bibliographical
    Listing." J KOREAN AFF, 1976 6 (1):61-80.

    A study based on more than 300 doctoral dissertations
    written in US universities notes that very few Americans are
    writing on Korea, most is done by those of Korean background
    teaching in the U.S. Concludes Korean Studies offer great
    opportunities for study but not enough is being done.

62. Shulman, Frank J. DOCTORAL DISSERTATIONS ON ASIA: AN
    ANNOTATED BIBLIOGRAPHICAL JOURNAL OF CURRENT INTERNATIONAL
    RESEARCH. Ann Arbor, MI: University Microfilms, 1975.

Semiannual compilation providing information on
dissertations completed and in progress on all aspects of
Asian culture and history. No subject index, but scanning of
issues reveals many dissertations on Korea, the war and its
antecedents. Very few entries are annotated.

63. Shulman, Frank J. DOCTORAL DISSERTATIONS ON JAPAN AND KOREA:
     A CLASSIFIED BIBLIOGRAPHICAL LISTING OF INTERNATIONAL
     RESEARCH. Ann Arbor, MI: University Microfilms, 1976.

     Cites more than 300 dissertations on all aspects of Korean
     history and culture including more than a dozen studies
     dealing with the Korean War and its background.

64. Shulman, Frank J. JAPAN AND KOREA: AN ANNOTATED BIBLIOGRAPHY
     OF DOCTORAL DISSERTATIONS IN WESTERN LANGUAGES, 1877-1969.
     Chicago: American Library Association, 1970.

     This compilation of more than 2,500 doctoral dissertations
     on all facets of Japanese and Korean life, culture and
     politics includes nearly 500 works on Korea of which ninety
     are on the post-WWII era and the Korean War.

65. Silberman, Bernard S. JAPAN AND KOREA: A CRITICAL
     BIBLIOGRAPHY. Tucson: University of Arizona, 1969.

     This annotated bibliography lists more than 300 works on
     Korea, including about twenty on the Korean war. Covers
     history, philosophy, religion, art, music, literature,
     economics and government. Well organized but index is weak.

66. Stapleton, Margaret L. THE TRUMAN AND EISENHOWER YEARS,
     1945-1960: A SELECTIVE BIBLIOGRAPHY. Metuchen, NJ:
     Scarecrow Press, 1973.

     A listing of more than 1,600 books and articles
     on US political, military, economic and social topics
     for the period under consideration. Cites more than
     seventy works on the Korean War.

67. Sunderman, James F. "Documentary Collections Related to the
     U.S. Air Force." AIR UNIV Q R, 1961 13 (1):110-126.

     Description of the principal collections of reference and
     documentary materials on US air power, including those
     depositories with holdings on the Korean War era. Tells
     where major collections are held and types of records located
     there. Places covered include: WAF Historical Division
     Archives; Air University Library; Air Force Museum; Research
     Studies Institute; Air Force Photo Files; National Archives;
     Library of Congress and many more.

68. TEN YEARS OF UNITED NATIONS PUBLICATIONS 1945 TO 1955:
     A COMPLETE CATALOG. New York: UN Department of Public
     Information, 1955.

Describes two dozen publications and reports on the Korean
issue. Includes reports of the UN Temporary Commission, UN
Military Command, UN Reconstruction Agency and the
Repatriation Commission.

69. U.S. Air Force Academy Library. AIR POWER AND WARFARE.
     Special Bibliography Series No. 59. US Air Force
     Academy, 1978.

     This work includes a listing of a dozen books and more
     than fifty journal articles dealing with US air power in
     the Korean conflict.

70. U.S. Air Force Academy Library. THE AMERICAN MILITARY AND
     THE FAR EAST. Special Bibliography Series No. 62. US Air
     Force Academy, 1980.

     A section in this publication devoted to the Cold War Years
     and Korean Conflict lists thirty-two books, eighteen journal
     articles and seven government publications on the Korean War.

71. U.S. Air Force Academy Library. MILITARY PLANNING IN THE
     TWENTIETH CENTURY. Special Bibliography Series No. 68, US
     Air Force Academy, 1984.

     Chapter 5 is devoted to planning during the Cold War and
     Korean War periods and contains a listing of more than twenty
     pertinent works.

72. U.S. Bureau of the Census. BIBLIOGRAPHY OF SOCIAL SCIENCE
     PERIODICALS AND MONOGRAPH SERIES: REPUBLIC OF KOREA,
     1945-61. Washington: Foreign Manpower Research
     Office, Bureau of the Census, 1962.

     Annotated entries of more than 260 periodicals and
     monograph series dealing with various aspects of life and
     culture in South Korea. Includes listings on such topics as
     history, politics, economics, education and bibliography.

73. U.S. Department of Army. COMMUNIST CHINA: RUTHLESS ENEMY OR
     PAPER TIGER? A BIBLIOGRAPHIC SURVEY. Washington:
     Government Printing Office, 1962.

     This bibliographical study includes more than 1,000
     annotated listings on Red China, including two dozen works on
     the Chinese Communist involvement in the Korean War. An
     appendix lists more than three hundred books and articles on
     the conflict in Korea. All works cited were published
     between 1950 and 1960.

74. U.S. Department of Army. COMMUNIST NORTH KOREA, A
     BIBLIOGRAPHIC SURVEY. Washington: Government Printing
     Office, 1971.

Annotated bibliography of books and articles on the political, historical, cultural and economic life of North Korea. Cites works in English and non-English publications.

75. U.S. Department of Army. "Korean War 1950-1953: A Bibliography." COMMUNIST CHINA: RUTHLESS ENEMY OR PAPER TIGER? A BIBLIOGRAPHIC SURVEY. Washington: Government Printing Office, 1962, pp. 125-135.

A listing of more than 100 books and 200 articles, written in English, on the Korean War. Very good reference for publications of various branches of the US Armed Forces.

76. U.S. Department of Navy. UNITED STATES NAVAL HISTORY: A BIBLIOGRAPHY, Sixth Edition. Washington: Government Printing Office, 1972.

More than 1,200 books and articles on US Naval history by period and topic. Brief annotation for works whose title does not make subject covered clear. About a dozen works directly on the Korean War and a similar number closely related to that subject.

77. U.S. Senate. THE UNITED STATES AND THE KOREAN PROBLEM: DOCUMENTS, 1943-1953. Washington: Government Printing Office, 1953.

A senate publication that contains numerous US documents relating to Korean policy from WWII through the end of the Korean War. Also includes key UN resolutions and reports.

78. Ward, Robert E., and Frank J. Shulman. THE ALLIED OCCUPATION OF JAPAN, 1945-1952: AN ANNOTATED BIBLIOGRAPHY OF WESTERN LANGUAGE MATERIALS. Chicago: American Library Association, 1974.

Extensive annotations are to be found on the more than 2,500 entries found in this work. Several dozen entries on General MacArthur and his career, including the Korean War and his dismissal.

79. Young, Walter E., comp. CAVALRY JOURNAL/ARMOR CUMULATIVE INDICES 1888-1968. Manhattan: Kansas State University Library, 1974.

Listing of articles, by author, subject and title of ARMOR: THE MAGAZINE OF MOBILE WARFARE which, as the title would indicate, focuses on US Army Armor activities. Includes several dozen articles on Korea but some are difficult to find because subject index is superficial.

B. HISTORIOGRAPHIES

80. Griffith, Robert. "Truman and the Historians: The
     Reconstruction of Postwar American History." WIS MAG HIST,
     1975 59 (1):20-50.

     Reviews the historical literature of the Truman
     Administrations, specifically domestic and foreign policy.
     Includes changing interpretations of the Cold War as well as
     the Korean War.

81. Leopold, Richard W. "The Korean War: The Historian's Task."
     WHISTLE STOP, 1977 5 (2):1-3.

     Sets forth subjects dealing with the Korean War which this
     well known historian believes should be studied further.
     Suggested areas, with justification, include: administrative
     history of the Truman presidency; armed forces in the Pacific
     before June 1950; the orders to the Seventh Fleet to prevent
     an attack on Formosa; UN establishment of a Commission for
     the Unification and Rehabilitation of Korea; 1951 MacArthur
     hearings and an examination of recruitment and training of
     armed forces. This paper, in somewhat different form, is
     found in Francis Heller, THE KOREAN WAR: A 25 YEAR
     PERSPECTIVE (Lawrence: University Press of Kansas, 1976).

82. Leopold, Richard W. "A Survey of Sources Relating to the
     Korean War." WHISTLE STOP, 1977 5 (2):insert, 4 pages.

     Excellent review of major sources of information on the
     war. Mention is made of key printed primary sources such as
     memoirs, legislative materials, State Department publications
     and important secondary works published before 1975. Also,
     looks at unpublished sources. This information also appears
     in the author's paper in Francis Heller, THE KOREAN WAR: A
     25 YEAR PERSPECTIVE (Lawrence: University Press of Kansas,
     1976).

83. Millett, Allan R. "The Study of American Military History
     in the United States." MIL AFF, 1977 41 (2):58-61.

     An assessment of the progress of military history from 1937
     through 1977. Tells of the reasons for its resurgence and
     lauds the contributions of both government and university
     historians. Cites some of the best attempts to synthesize
     the US experience and the contributions of the various
     military services. Excellent footnotes cite some of the most
     valuable military bibliographies and key articles on the
     subject.

84. Park, Hong-Kyu. "America and Korea, 1945-1953: A
     Bibliographical Essay." ASIAN FOR, 1971 3 (1):57-66.

     One of the top Korean War bibliographers surveys several
     dozen of the most important works on the coming of the
     conflict and the war itself, including military operations,
     Chinese intervention and the Truman-MacArthur controversy.

85.   Park, Hong-Kyu. "American Involvement in the Korean War."
      HIST TEACHER, 1958 16 (2):249-263.

      An excellent historiography which looks at thirty-five key
      books and scholarly articles on such facets of the war as
      origins, intervention, Truman-MacArthur controversy, peace
      negotiations, POW's and the impact of the war on the US.

86.   Park, Hong-Kyu. "The Korean War Revisited: A Survey of
      Historical Writings." WORLD AFF, 1975 137 (4):336-344.

      An assessment of fifty historical works on the Korean War,
      written in English through 1975. Cites a number of facets of
      the war which still need to be examined by scholars.

87.   Swartout, Robert, Jr. "American Historians and the Outbreak
      of the Korean War: An Historiographical Essay." ASIA Q,
      1979 (1):65-77.

      Discusses two schools of thought about the outbreak of the
      Korean War: (1) those who maintain the Soviet Union was
      behind it and (2) those who contend that South Korea, under
      Syngman Rhee and with the encouragement of General MacArthur,
      was responsible. Includes the authors who support those
      views. Finally, a third explanation, that North Korea under
      Kim Il-Sung planned and carried out the attack on its own, is
      suggested.

88.   Thompson, Mark E. "The Truman-MacArthur Controversy: A
      Bibliographical Essay." STUDIES HIST SOC, 1974 5 (2):66-73.

      Examines the key literature surrounding the 1951 dismissal
      of General MacArthur. Literature is divided between that
      which is favorable to the President, which generally contends
      he had no choice, and that supporting the General, which
      claims he was either a victim of poor communications or a
      scapegoat for a war that was not going well for the US.

89.   Warner, Geoffrey. "The Korean War." INT AFF, 1980 56
      (1):98-107.

      A bibliographical essay by a British historian which
      focuses on more than fifteen leading books that examine the
      matter of who was responsible for the start of the war and
      why the Red Chinese intervened. Looks at explanations of
      such historians as Robert Simmons, William Stueck, I.F. Stone
      and Allen Whiting and participants such as Mao, Khrushchev,
      Collins and Acheson.

90.   Wubben, H. H. "American Prisoners of War in Korea: A Second
      Look at the 'Something New in History' Theme." AM Q, 1970 22
      (1):3-19.

Excellent bibliographic essay reexamines the generally
accepted view that US prisoners of war in Korea were easily
duped by the enemy and readily collaborated with it and
concludes that such was not the case. Claims that the
American public readily accepted the enemies' claims without
searching for the real truth.

C. CHRONOLOGIES

91.   A CHRONICLE OF PRINCIPLE EVENTS RELATING TO THE KOREAN
      QUESTION, 1945-1954. Peking, China: World Culture, 1954.

      A detailed chronology of developments in North and
      South Korea from the Communist Chinese perspective.

92.   "A Chronology of Marine Corps Aviation in Korea." LEATHERNECK,
      1956 39 (11):47-50, 81.

      A brief listing of key activities of marine aviation from
      July 5, 1950, to July 27, 1953.

93.   Cooney, David M.   A CHRONOLOGY OF THE U.S. NAVY, 1775-1965.
      New York: Watts, 1965.

      This excellent chronology includes a month-by-month,
      virtually day-by-day account of naval activities in the
      Korean conflict.   Covers nearly all US naval vessels involved
      in the Korean theater.

94.   "Korea: A Chronology of Principal Events, 1945-1950." WORLD
      TODAY, 1950 6 (8):319-330.

      A listing of key diplomatic and political events taking
      place in Korea from the end of WWII through the outbreak of
      war.

95.   "Korean Chronology." LEATHERNECK, 1951 34 (11):28-29.

      Brief chronology of Marine operations in Korea from June
      25, 1950, through June 30, 1951.

96.   Loesch, Robert J.   "Korean Milestones 1950-53." ARMY INFO
      DIG, 1953 8 (9):52-59.

      Narrative account of the start of the Korean War followed
      by a chronological listing of significant military events
      throughout the conflict.

97.   Morley, James W. JAPAN AND KOREA: AMERICA'S ALLIES IN THE
      PACIFIC. New York: Walker, 1965.

      Essays on the relationships between Korea and Japan and
      their dealings with the U.S. Contains chronologies, brief
      bibliographies and tables on economic and defense matters
      from the 1940's to mid 1960's.

98. Toner, James H. "The Making of a Morass." MIL R, 1977 57
    (10):3-16.

    A chronicle of U.S. policy toward Korea from the end of
    WW II through the outbreak of war in 1950. Makes clear the
    U.S. military did not consider Korea vital to national
    security during that period.

99. U.S. Department of Navy. UNITED STATES NAVAL AVIATION,
    1910-1960. Washington: Government Printing Office, 1961.

    Contains a chronological listing of key events in US Naval
    and marine aviation activities including those during the
    Korean War.

100. U.S. Department of State. A HISTORICAL SUMMARY OF UNITED
     STATES-KOREAN RELATIONS, WITH A CHRONOLOGY OF IMPORTANT
     DEVELOPMENTS, 1834-1962. Washington: Government Printing
     Office, 1962.

     This chronology, which covers nearly 130 years of foreign
     relations, includes a brief account of the historical events
     leading to war in 1950, the war and its subsequent impact on
     official relations. Gives the US Government's explanation of
     what happened.

101. "The War in Korea--A Chronology of Events, 25 June
     1950-25 June 1951." WORLD TODAY, 1951 7 (8):317-328.

     A day-by-day listing of political and military events
     during the first year of the war.

                    D.   HANDBOOKS, GUIDES AND DICTIONARIES

102. American University. US ARMY AREA HANDBOOK FOR KOREA.
     Washington: Government Printing Office, 1958, and
     subsequent updates.

     A guide for US servicemen heading for Korea. This handy
     reference gives an overview of the social, cultural, economic
     and political history of both North and South Korea.

103. Dupuy, R. Ernest, and Trevor N. Dupuy. THE ENCYCLOPEDIA OF
     MILITARY HISTORY FROM 3500 BC TO THE PRESENT. Rev. ed.
     New York: Harper, 1977.

     Traces key wars and other military events from ancient
     times to the present following a chronological approach.
     Includes more than a dozen pages on the background, conduct
     and consequences of the Korean War.

104. Effenberger, David. A DICTIONARY OF BATTLES. New York:
      Crowell, 1967.

      Brief description of more than 1,500 military engagements
      from 1469 B.C. to 1966, including key battles of the Korean War.
      Tells situation, strategy and tactics, commanders involved and
      outcome.

105. FACTS ABOUT KOREA. Pyongyang: Foreign Languages Publishing
      House, 1961.

      An almanac which includes a comprehensive history of North
      Korea from the Communist viewpoint--a good counter to
      pro-western accounts.

106. Gaynor, Frank, ed. THE NEW MILITARY AND NAVAL DICTIONARY.
      New York: Philosophical Library, 1951.

      Defines and/or explains terminology, technical phrases and
      slang of all branches of the US armed forces. The fact that
      this work was prepared shortly after the Korean War began
      makes much of its information especially valuable to the
      student of the conflict. Includes organizational charts for
      the various services.

107. Hakwonsa Ltd. KOREA: ITS PEOPLE AND CULTURE. Seoul:
      Hakwonsa, 1970, 3rd ed.

      Handbook format looks at the geography, history, literature
      and art of Korea. This useful reference work has much
      statistical information. Survey of the nation's history
      includes a political and military overview of the Korean War.

108. Harkins, Paul D., and Philip Harkins. THE ARMY OFFICER'S
      GUIDE. New York: McGraw-Hill, 1951.

      Contains information designed for assisting the young US
      Army officer. Contains summaries of army manuals on such
      topics as tactics, drill, maintenance, map reading, hygiene,
      military justice, physical fitness, defense, guerrilla
      warfare and staff procedures. Concludes with a brief chapter
      on lessons to be learned from Korea.

109. KOREA ANNUAL 1964-1984. Seoul: Hapdong, 1964-1984.

      Emphasis is on current political, economic, social,
      educational and cultural developments in South Korea.
      General information on history, geography and people.
      Includes useful information such as ROK Army Chiefs of Staff,
      Chiefs of Naval Operations and Air Force Chiefs of Staff for
      Korean War period and after.

110. Korean Overseas Information Service. A HANDBOOK OF KOREA.
      Seoul: Ministry of Culture and Information, 1978.

Probably the best handbook available on South Korea, its people, history, culture, arts, literature, customs and contemporary developments such as industry, transportation, communication, education and sports. Excellent color photographs and many statistics. Overview of the Korean War and its consequences.

111. Oh, Chae Kyung. HANDBOOK OF KOREA. New York: Pageant, 1958.

The author, Director of Public Information, Republic of Korea, examines the country's agricultural, educational, industrial, economic and defense situation but does so by putting them in an historical setting. Emphasizes the Korean War and its impact. Good sections on geography, government and foreign affairs.

112. Quick, John. DICTIONARY OF WEAPONS AND MILITARY TERMS. New York: McGraw, 1973.

Excellent reference work which contains brief descriptions of most of the weapons and equipment used in Korea. Includes organizational and operational terms.

113. Schuon, Karl. U.S. MARINE CORPS BIOGRAPHICAL DICTIONARY. New York: Watts, 1963.

A biographical reference work which includes thumbnail sketches of many officers and enlisted men who served with distinction in Korea.

114. Shinn, Rinn-Sup, et al. AREA HANDBOOK FOR NORTH KOREA. Washington: Government Printing Office, 1969.

Department of Army guide looks at such topics as history, government and politics, economics, languages and culture. Includes a good bibliography on North Korea.

115. Spiller, Roger J., ed. DICTIONARY OF AMERICAN MILITARY BIOGRAPHY. 3 vols. Westport, CT: Greenwood, 1984.

Biographical essays on major US military figures, including many who played a role in the Korean War, such as MacArthur, Ridgway, Clark, Collins. Chronology of American military developments and entries by war. Each essay contains a treatment of the subject's life, a critical assessment and brief bibliography.

116. Thursfield, Henry G., ed. BRASSEY'S ANNUAL: THE ARMED FORCES YEAR BOOK, 1950-1954 editions. New York: Macmillan, 1950-1954.

Articles on various aspects of the British Armed Forces during the Korean War era. Includes survey of British activities in Korea as well as those of other Commonwealth nations. Also covers such topics as training, supply and weapons of British forces.

117. U.S. Department of Defense. SEMIANNUAL REPORT OF THE
      SECRETARY OF DEFENSE AND THE SEMIANNUAL REPORTS OF THE
      SECRETARY OF THE ARMY, SECRETARY OF THE NAVY, SECRETARY OF
      THE AIR FORCE, 1950 through 1953 reports. Washington:
      Government Printing Office, 1950-1953.

      These reports for the Korean War era contain a great deal
      of information, much of it statistical on manpower,
      equipment, expenditures, training and state of all US armed
      services. Very little per se about the war in Korea.

118. WEBSTER'S AMERICAN MILITARY BIOGRAPHIES. Springfield, MA:
      Merriam, 1978.

      Contains brief biographies of slightly more than one
      thousand individuals significant in US military history,
      including about thirty who were prominent in the Korean War.
      Includes sketches of and brief analysis of their military
      exploits.

119. WHO WAS WHO IN AMERICAN HISTORY - THE MILITARY. Chicago:
      Marquis Who's Who, 1975.

      Brief biographies of more than 10,000 US military leaders
      and heroes covering all American Wars. Since it includes
      only individuals who died prior to 1975, it includes
      relatively few individuals who served in Korea (approximately
      150).

                        E.   GEOGRAPHIES AND MAPS

120. Canada Department of Mines and Technical Surveys. KOREA: A
      GEOGRAPHICAL APPRECIATION. New York: Institute of Pacific
      Relations, 1952.

      A brief but useful study of Korean geography, including
      physical, human, economic and political characteristics.

121. Esposito, Vincent J., ed. THE WEST POINT ATLAS OF AMERICAN
      WARS, 1689-1953. 2 vols. New York: Praeger, 1959.

      Volume 2, section 3, contains seventeen maps and a brief
      summary of key operations in the Korean War.

122. MAPS OF KOREA. Washington: Korean Affairs Institute, 1945.

      Pamphlet containing eight pages of historical and
      contemporary maps of Korea.

123. McCune, Shannon. KOREA'S HERITAGE: A REGIONAL AND SOCIAL
      GEOGRAPHY. Rutland, VT: Tuttle, 1956.

      One of the very first works on Korean geography by an
      American. A general account of the geography of the nation
      followed by analysis of ten distinct regions. Weak on

climatic and physical factors but very strong on social and economic matters. A look at the post-Korean War division at the 38th parallel in a geographical context. Also discusses devastation from the war.

124. McCune, Shannon. "Maps of Korea." FAR EASTERN Q, 1946 5 (3):326-329

Brief account of the map coverage of the Korean peninsula. Notes that the area is very well mapped--a factor that was very important to the US when war came.

125. McCune, Shannon. "Recent Geographical Works on Korea." FAR EASTERN Q, 1952 12 (2):222-225.

Review essay of eight geographical studies on Korea that appeared between 1945 and 1952.

126. PHYSICAL GEOGRAPHY AND CLIMATOLOGY OF KOREA AND ADJACENT AREAS. Maxwell Air Force Base, AL: Air University, 1950.

Examines the topography, physical characteristics and climatic characteristics of Korea, Manchuria, North China, Southern Siberia and the Shantung Peninsula.

127. Zaichikov, V. T. GEOGRAPHY OF KOREA. New York: Institute of Public Relations, 1952.

This work, which was finished by its Russian author shortly after the Korean War started, was rushed into print in English because of a dearth of works on the topic. Looks at physical, political and economic factors.

128. Acheson, Dean. THE KOREAN WAR. New York: Norton, 1971.

The former US Secretary of State during the Korean war relies heavily on his previously published memoirs to write this defense of the administration's policies in Korea. Defends the decision to enter the war, not to seek congressional approval and to relieve General MacArthur.

129. Acheson, Dean. PRESENT AT THE CREATION: MY YEARS AT THE STATE DEPARTMENT. New York: Norton, 1969.

An excellent autobiography by the man who served as U.S. Secretary of State throughout the Second Truman Administration. Covers Acheson's years at State from 1941 to 1953 but is especially strong in dealing with Korea, both the decision to intervene and the conduct of the war. Puts U.S. policy in a global setting. Indispensable source when looking at the political and diplomatic conduct of the war.

130. Berger, Carl. THE KOREA KNOT: A MILITARY POLITICAL HISTORY. Philadelphia: University of Pennsylvania, 1957.

A brief general account of the background of the war and the war itself with emphasis on political events. Focus is almost solely upon the US and its role in the conflict. Examines such matters as the reasons for intervention and the dismissal of MacArthur in very objective fashion. Good overview but nothing new for the specialist.

131. Bernardo, C. Joseph, and Eugene H. Bacon. AMERICAN MILITARY POLICY: ITS DEVELOPMENT SINCE 1775. Harrisburg, PA: Stackpole, 1955.

Good but dated survey of US policy examines development of the armed services on the eve of the conflict in Korea plus a chapter on the war, America's conduct of it, armed forces policies, role of the reserves and the problems of fighting a peripheral war.

132. Brodie, Bernard. WAR AND POLITICS. New York: Macmillan, 1973.

Examines 20th Century US wars to determine what war is all about. Chapter 3 is devoted to Korea. Claims US entered the conflict because of feeling that the containment of communism was an American responsibility and that peace in the world was indivisible. The US backed into limited war because the doctrine was not yet known, and the Joint Chiefs of Staff

felt the Russians were using Korea as a front while they
prepared for a major attack in Europe.

133. Dupuy, R. Ernest. THE COMPACT HISTORY OF THE UNITED STATES
      ARMY. New York: Hawthorn, 1956.

      Brief history of the Army from colonial times through Korea
      gives scant attention to the latter. Mentions briefly the
      Truman-MacArthur controversy, the frustrations of limited war
      for the combatants, the "bugout" of American troops and the
      POW issue.

134. Dupuy, R. Ernest, and Trevor N. Dupuy. MILITARY HERITAGE OF
      AMERICA. New York: McGraw, 1956.

      This survey of America's wars from the Revolutionary times
      on includes a concise and well-written military/political
      account of the Korean War. The conclusion, which examines
      the results of the conflict and the lessons learned, includes
      statistics on casualties and the impact of air operations.

135. Cassino, Jay A., ed. PICTORIAL HISTORY OF THE KOREAN WAR.
      New York: Wise, 1951.

      Extensive photographic coverage of the first year of the
      fighting. Covers UN Command forces in every facet of the
      conflict. A Veteran of Foreign Wars memorial edition.

136. Cumings, Bruce, ed. CHILD OF CONFLICT: THE KOREAN-AMERICAN
      RELATIONSHIP, 1943-1953. Seattle: University of
      Washington, 1983.

      Collection of papers taken from two conferences held at the
      University of Washington to try and look at the
      Korean-American relationship in other than the Cold War
      framework. Scholarly works, including some by young authors,
      on such subjects as US policy between 1943-1950, the decision
      to advance to the Yalu, problems in achieving an armistice
      and records in the National Archives on Korea from
      1945-1950.

137. Donovon, Robert J. TUMULTUOUS YEARS: THE PRESIDENCY OF
      HARRY S. TRUMAN, 1949-1953. New York: Norton, 1982.

      An excellent account of Truman's second administration (an
      earlier volume covered the first). Gives a good overview of
      the background of the war, the decision to intervene, the
      conduct of the war and the search for peace. Very well
      researched and written. The author, as a White House
      correspondent during the period, relates many pieces of
      information not found elsewhere. Generally favorable to
      Truman.

138. Fehrenbach, T.R. THE FIGHT FOR KOREA: FROM THE WAR OF 1950
      TO THE PUEBLO INCIDENT. New York: Grosset, 1969.

Survey of the Korean issue for high school age readers.
Overview of the war, with background, military and political
activities, UN involvement and the uneasy truce of 1953.
That the armistice ushered in years of strain was evident in
the Pueblo affair.

139. Fehrenbach, T.R. THIS KIND OF WAR: A STUDY IN
     UNPREPAREDNESS. New York: Macmillan, 1963.

This account by a US Army Reserve Officer who fought in
Korea maintains that the US was not prepared politically,
militarily or psychologically for the limited war it found
itself in. The military ebb and flow of the war is handled
well as is the interaction between events on the front and
political and social events at home. Cites need to learn a
lesson from Korea and be prepared for future limited wars.

140. Fincher, Ernest B. THE WAR IN KOREA. New York: Watts, 1981.

A children's book which gives an overview of Korean history
but focuses on the Korean War, which it portrays as a
successful US effort to contain communism.

141. Forty, George. AT WAR IN KOREA. London: Allen, 1982.

An extremely well-illustrated general history of the war
from North Korean aggression to the signing of the armistice.
Traces the activities of various UN units but also focuses on
the UN soldier and what the conflict meant to him.

142. Fraser, Haynes R. "The Korean Conflict With Special Reference
     to the Theory and Dynamics of Collective Security."
     Doctoral Dissertation. Southern California, 1956.

The Korean War is used as a case study of the value of
using collective security as a means of halting and deterring
international aggression.

143. Gardner, Lloyd C., ed. THE KOREAN WAR. New York:
     Quadrangle, 1972.

The editor, a first-rate historian, leads off with an
inciteful and informative introduction which is followed by a
collection of twenty-two essays which appeared in the NEW
YORK TIMES MAGAZINE during the war. Essayists include
leading political figures, such as Dean Acheson and John
Foster Dulles, and leading news analyst like Arthur Krock and
James Reston.

144. Goulden, Joseph C. KOREA: THE UNTOLD STORY OF THE WAR. New
     York: Times, 1982.

While the title of this book is perhaps misleading since it
really offers no new explanations of the conflict, it is a

well-written, well-researched general history of the war.
Covers both diplomatic and military aspects of the conflict.
Objectivity is lacking when it comes to analyzing the roles
of Truman and Acheson, whom the author is extremely critical
of, and that of MacArthur, whose actions are nearly always
praised.

145.   Gurney, Gene. A PICTORIAL HISTORY OF THE UNITED STATES ARMY.
       New York: Crown, 1966.

       Contains a chapter on Korea with a brief narrative and
       nearly one hundred-fifty excellent photographs.

146.   Hassler, Warren W., Jr. WITH SHIELD AND SWORD: AMERICAN
       MILITARY AFFAIRS, COLONIAL TIMES TO THE PRESENT. Ames, IA:
       Iowa State, 1983.

       This integrated survey of US military affairs, which
       touches on policy, operations and leadership includes a
       superficial overview of the American involvement in the
       Korean War.

147.   Hatada, Takashi. A HISTORY OF KOREA. Santa Barbara, CA:
       ABC-Clio, 1969.

       Brief survey of Korea by a Korean-born Japanese.
       Intertwines political history with social and economic
       developments. Includes an overview of the war.

148.   Heller, Francis H., ed. THE KOREAN WAR: A 25-YEAR
       PERSPECTIVE. Lawrence, KS: Regents Press of Kansas, 1977.

       On the 25th anniversary of the US decision to enter the
       war, the Truman Institute hosted a meeting of living
       participants and scholars of the period. This is the
       published proceedings of that conference, including
       addresses, scholarly papers and open discussions. No new
       information from the administrative figures but several
       excellent papers.

149.   Hoxie, R. Gordon. COMMAND DECISION AND THE PRESIDENCY. New
       York: Reader's Digest, 1977.

       Surveys US national security policy and organization from
       Truman through Carter, with considerable emphasis on Truman.
       Narrative account of the background of the Korean War,
       decision to intervene, conduct of the war, MacArthur
       controversy and Eisenhower's ending of the conflict.

150.   James, D. Clayton. "The War That Faded Away." R AM HIST,
       1978 6 (4):544-547.

       Review article of Frances H. Heller's (ed) THE KOREAN WAR:
       A 25-YEAR PERSPECTIVE. Contains a brief survey of the major
       points made by participants in the 1975 conference on the war,

sponsored by the Truman Institute. Covers themes of
scholarly papers presented by Lawrence S. Kaplan, John E.
Wiltz, Robert R. Simmons and Richard W. Leopold.

151. Jervis, Robert. "The Impact of the Korean War on the Cold
     War." J CON RESO, 1980 24 (4):563-592.

     Argues that the Korean War had a dramatic impact on the
     nature of the Cold War because it led to major policy
     decisions that administrative leaders otherwise would not
     have been willing to make. The most important consequences
     were: high defense budgets; the militarization of NATO with
     resulting large armies in Europe; perceptions of a united
     Sino-Soviet block; awareness of the danger of limited wars
     and a global commitment to stop Communist expansion.

152. Johnson, Gerald. "The End of Incredulity." VIR Q R,
     1968 44 (4):531-542

     Claims that important events in the first half of the 20th
     Century can be explained logically, but key events starting
     with 1950 cannot be so explained because they have no
     comprehensible cause. Then examines six key events as
     examples and the Korean War is one of them.

153. KEY KOREAN WAR BATTLES FOUGHT IN THE REPUBLIC OF KOREA. APO
     San Francisco: Hq, Eighth United States Army, 1972.

     Narrative account of the more important military
     engagements in which US Army forces were involved during the
     Korean War.

154. Kim, Chum-kon. THE KOREAN WAR: THE FIRST COMPREHENSIVE
     ACCOUNT OF THE HISTORICAL BACKGROUND AND DEVELOPMENT OF THE
     KOREAN WAR (1950-1953). Seoul: Kwangmyong, 1973.

     This general history of the war and its background is
     written from a pro-ROK perspective and thus lacks the
     objectivity required of real history.

155. Kim, Se-Jin, and Chang-Hyun Cho, eds. KOREA: A DIVIDED
     NATION. Silver Springs, MD: Research Institute of Korean
     Affairs, 1977.

     A comparative survey of North and South Korea. While much
     attention is given to economic and political developments in
     both Koreas, part one of the book presents a sound study of
     the history of the nation through the Korean War.

156. King, O.H.P. TAIL OF THE PAPER TIGER. Caldwell, ID: Caxton,
     1961.

     Personal account of the war as seen through the eyes of an
     Associated Press correspondent who covered most of the
     conflict. Focus is on military operations and experiences of
     US and UN combat troops.

157. Koenig, William J. AMERICANS AT WAR: FROM THE COLONIAL WARS TO
      VIETNAM. New York: Putnam's, 1980.

      The chapter on "Korea - The First Limited War" is a
      pictoral history of the conflict from beginning to end.
      Excellent photographs including some very rare ones in color.
      Emphasis is on military activities.

158. KOREA--USA CENTENNIAL, 1882-1982. Seoul: Yonhap, 1982.

      This slick-cover look at one hundred years of relations
      between the two nations is primarily a work of mutual praise
      and adulation, but its survey of key events, including the
      Korean War, includes many good photographs. Includes a good
      twenty-seven page chronology of Korean-American relations.

159. "The Korean War, 1950-1953" in R. Ernest Dupuy and Trevor N.
      Dupuy, THE ENCYCLOPEDIA OF MILITARY HISTORY. New York:
      Harper, 1970.

      Brief background of the conflict, followed by a detailed
      chronology of military operations and concluding with the
      major developments of the war. Statistics on killed, wounded
      and POW's.

160. Kurland, Gerald. KOREAN WAR. Charlotteville, NY: Sam Har,
      1984.

      Extremely brief overview of the political and military
      aspects of the conflict.

161. Lawson, Don. THE UNITED STATES IN THE KOREAN WAR. New York:
      Abelard, 1964.

      A book for juveniles which covers in general terms the
      political and military aspects of the war. Includes many
      examples of individual heroism.

162. Leckie, Robert. CONFLICT: THE HISTORY OF THE KOREAN WAR,
      1950-1953. New York: Putnam's, 1962.

      A very good survey of the political and military
      developments of the war from its beginning to end. Generally
      sympathetic to MacArthur and his position and critical of
      Truman's policy and the handling of the dismissal. Strong on
      the North Korean Army and its leadership.

163. Leckie, Robert. THE WAR IN KOREA: 1950-1953. New York:
      Random, 1963.

      A book written for juveniles to tell the story of the
      Korean War. Political and military account which portrays
      the conflict as a contest between the forces of good versus
      those of evil.

164. Leckie, Robert. THE WARS OF AMERICA. New York: Harper,
      1968.

      Readable survey of the US military experience from the
      Revolutionary war through Vietnam. Overview of the Korean
      War covers background, the opposing forces, the major
      campaigns, Truman-MacArthur feud and a critique of the
      limited war. Surprisingly, because of the generally
      pro-military position of the author, the account is critical
      of MacArthur.

165. Marshall, S.L.A. THE MILITARY HISTORY OF THE KOREAN WAR.
      New York: Watts, 1963.

      Very brief, illustrated overview of the war covering
      primarily military developments. Written for a juvenile
      audience.

166. Matloff, Maurice, ed. AMERICAN MILITARY HISTORY.
      Washington: US Government Printing Office, 1969.

      A general survey of America's wars from the Revolution to
      Vietnam. Designed for use in Army ROTC courses. A chapter
      is devoted to the conduct of the Korean War.

167. Meredith, Ray. THE AMERICAN WARS: A PICTORIAL HISTORY FROM
      QUEBEC TO KOREA 1755-1953. Cleveland: World, 1955

      Includes a section on Korea which gives an overview of the
      military contributions of all the military services.

168. Middleton, Harry J. THE COMPACT HISTORY OF THE KOREAN WAR.
      New York: Hawthorn, 1965.

      An extremely good one-volume account of the military
      aspects of the war from the North Korean invasion to the
      stalemate of 1952-53. Of value and interest to the general
      reader but may not be of interest to the serious student of
      the conflict.

169. Miller, Francis T. WAR IN KOREA AND THE COMPLETE HISTORY OF
      WORLD WAR II. N.p., 1955.

      General narrative of political and military events of the
      first few months of the war.

170. Miller, John Jr. et al. KOREA, 1951-1953. US Government
      Printing Office, 1956.

      A photographic history of the US Army in action in Korea
      during the last two years of the war. Uses official Army
      photos.

171. Millett, Allan R., and Peter Maslowski. FOR THE COMMON
          DEFENSE: THE MILITARY HISTORY OF THE UNITED STATES. New
          York: Free Press, 1984.

          This excellent survey of the American military experience
          from Colonial Times to the present contains a twenty-page
          overview of the Korean War. Looks at several of the key
          political-military decisions of the conflict.

172. Millis, Walter. ARMS AND MEN: A STUDY IN AMERICAN MILITARY
          HISTORY. New York: Putnam's, 1956.

          In this classic study of the evolution of American policy
          from 1775 to 1955, the author claims that war and preparation
          for war have had a major and continuing impact on all of
          American society. Briefly examines the Korean War which he
          concludes was a good move politically but militarily came
          close to being a disaster. Conduct of the war frustrated
          politicians, military leaders and the public because of the
          uniqueness of a limited war.

173. Nath, Pran. A CONDENSED STUDY OF THE WAR IN KOREA.
          Dehradun, India: E.D.B., 1968.

          The military campaigns of the conflict are set forth by
          using a question and answer format.

174. "1945-1953: The Korean War." ARMY INFO DIG, 1963
          18 (9):31-34.

          Very brief and superficial account of the background of the
          war and the major military aspects of the conflict. Straight
          narrative with no analysis.

175. O'Ballance, Edgar. KOREA 1950-1953. London: Faber, 1969.

          Political and military history of the war. Places the
          conflict in the context of international politics and the
          domestic affairs of the nations involved.

176. Park, Pong-Shik. "The Korean War 1950-1953." KOREA J, 1967 7
          (July 1): 15-20.

          A Korean scholar looks at some of the problems related to
          the Korean War. Specifically he examines: the relations
          between the US and USSR as one of the major causes of the
          war; the characteristics of UN forces; and the meaning of the
          Armistice agreement which was opposed by the ROK.

177. Poats, Rutherford M. DECISION IN KOREA. New York: McBride,
          1954.

          Narrative account of the war from beginning to end by an
          American correspondent who spent the entire period in Korea
          and Japan. Sees the war as an excellent example of

collective security in action and maintains war was necessary
to show the Communists that aggression would be resisted,
however, sees it primarily in a negative light--a war that is
frustrating, disheartening, uninspiring and unpopular.
Praises MacArthur's early performances but is supportive of
Truman when dismissal comes.

178. Portway, Donald. KOREA: LAND OF THE MORNING CALM. London:
      Horrap, 1953.

      A general history and analysis of the war and its
      consequences for the Korean people by a former British army
      engineer and educator. Mildly critical of the US and its
      policy toward Korea, the author urges giving Koreans greater
      control of their destiny.

179. Rees, David. KOREA: THE LIMITED WAR. New York: St. Martin's,
      1964.

      One of the top two or three comprehensive accounts of the
      war. The British author presents a well-written, objective
      narrative of the events leading up to the war as well as the
      military and political aspects of the conflict. Puts the US
      decision to intervene in the context of the containment
      policy.

180. Rees, David, ed. THE KOREAN WAR: ITS HISTORY AND TACTICS.
      New York: Crescent, 1984.

      One of the best single volume works on the conflict focuses
      on the military aspects. Excellent photographic coverage.
      Primarily narrative with some analysis. For a popular
      audience.

181. Republic of Korea, Ministry of National Defense. THE HISTORY
      OF THE UNITED NATIONS IN THE KOREAN WAR. 5 vols. Seoul:
      Ministry of National Defense, 1972-1974.

      While lacking objectivity about the UN contributions in
      Korea, this multi-volume work does cover rather thoroughly the
      military and service activities of the twenty-one nations,
      including the US, who were involved.

182. Stebbins, Richard P. THE UNITED STATES IN WORLD AFFAIRS,
      1950. Also 1951, 1952, 1953 vols. New York: Harper, for
      the Council on Foreign Relations, 1950-1953.

      An excellent overview and good analysis of the place of the
      US in World Affairs. Does a fine job of relating foreign
      relations to the domestic scene as it integrates
      congressional, State Department and administration attitudes
      and actions. Good overview of the political and military
      aspects of the Korean crisis.

183. Stratton, Samuel S. "Balance Sheet on Korea." US NAVAL INST
      PROC, 1954 80 (4):367-373.

      Recaps the reasons for the Korean War, the UN intervention
      and conduct of the conflict before concluding that it was US
      sea power that made containment of the Communist forces
      possible. Examines the containment policy which it
      criticizes on some points but concludes it is currently the
      most suitable policy.

184. Thomas, Robert C. THE WAR IN KOREA. Aldershot, England: Gale,
      1954.

      Brief military account of the war by a British Army officer.
      Praises the UN response as he praises nations for going to war
      for no personal gain. Very favorable to General MacArthur.

185. Toner, James H. "Candide as Constable: The American Way of
      War and Peace in Korea, 1950-1953." Doctoral Dissertation.
      Notre Dame, 1976.

      Analyzes the events of the Korean War in the light of the
      American national experience. Uses the perspective of widely
      held beliefs, customs and values as factors that influenced
      US political and military policy in Korea.

186. US Military Academy Department of Military Art and
      Engineering. OPERATIONS IN KOREA. West Point, NY: US
      Military Academy, 1956.

      Brief overview of the military activities of all US armed
      forces in the Korean War.

187. Veterans of Foreign Wars. PICTORIAL HISTORY OF THE KOREA WAR,
      1950-1953. N.p.: Veterans Historical Book Service, 1954.

      Excerpts of UN Command reports are used to tie together
      this extensive photographic work of all aspects of the
      conflict.

188. Voorhees, Melvin B. KOREAN TALES. New York:
      Simon, 1952.

      Essentially a collection of essays on the war from a
      Lieutenant Colonel who was the chief censor of the Eighth
      Army in Korea. Includes subjects like the plight of the
      Koreans, key military personalities like Walker and Ridgway,
      problems of a multi-national fighting force, minor engagements
      and grim stories of combat.

189. Weigley, Russell. HISTORY OF THE UNITED STATES ARMY.
      New York: Macmillan, 1967.

A general history from Colonial militias to the army of the mid-1960's. Probably the best single volume history of the US Army. A scholarly work that is well written. Includes a chapter on the war in Korea. Good footnotes but no bibliography.

III. BACKGROUND TO THE WAR
A. KOREA TO 1945

190. Bridgham, Philip L., and William L. Neumann. "Korea and the
      United States." AM PERS, 1950 4 (3):225-245.

      A brief history of American-Korean relations between 1866
      and the outbreak of the Korean War. Claims that the US has
      bungled its relations throughout the period and that its
      failures in the post-WWII period were responsible for the
      nation being plunged into war.

191. Chien, Frederick F. THE OPENING OF KOREA. Hamden, CT: Shoe
      String, 1967.

      This look at Chinese diplomacy toward Korea from 1876-1885
      includes an in-depth look at the US-Korean Treaty of 1882.

192. Chung, Kyung Cho. KOREA TOMORROW. New York: Macmillan, 1956.

      A well-researched and -written reference work on Korea and
      its people. In addition to history it covers society,
      customs, religion, literature, language, politics and
      economics. Includes a chronology and maps.

193. Conroy, Francis H. THE JAPANESE PENETRATION OF KOREA:
      1868-1919. Philadelphia: University of Pennsylvania, 1960.

      Well-written, scholarly account of Japanese policy toward
      Korea contends it was not a well-conceived and agreed upon
      policy of imperialism but a divisive issue that was heavily
      influenced by domestic considerations.

194. Dallin, Davis J. SOVIET RUSSIA AND THE FAR EAST. New Haven,
      CT: Yale University, 1948.

      Outstanding survey of policy toward China, Japan and Korea
      from 1931 through 1947. Sees the policy as one of pursuing
      continual expansionism as evidenced in post-war Korea.
      Maintains that the US lack of clarity and consistency in
      Korea helped the Soviet cause there.

195. Deuchler, Martina. CONFUCIAN GENTLEMEN AND BARBARIAN ENVOYS:
      THE OPENING OF KOREA, 1875-1885. Seattle: University of
      Washington, 1977.

      The decade examined marked a major turning point in Korean
      history, and the nation turned from unilateral dependence on

China to identify with Japan and the West. That change and
the impact of foreign goods and new ideas that came to the
country are examined in this scholarly study.

196. THE FAR EASTERN QUARTERLY: SPECIAL NUMBER ON KOREA. New
      York: Columbia University, 1946.

      Contains six articles on Korea by American authorities on
      Korea. Generally covers developments in the 1930's and early
      1940's. The opening article by J. Ernest Fisher is extremely
      pro-American in regard to post-war policies. Other articles
      on economics, geography and history.

197. Fowler, Wilton. AMERICAN DIPLOMATIC HISTORY SINCE 1890.
      Northbrook, IL: AHM, 1975.

      Bibliographic work listing more than 2,800 works on US
      foreign policy includes more than 25 books and articles on
      the diplomatic background of the Korean War.

198. Grajdanzev, A.J. MODERN KOREA. New York: Day, 1944.

      A comprehensive history of Korea from the time of Japanese
      annexation until just prior to the end of WWII. Focus is on
      political, economic and social developments.

199. Harrington, F. H. GOD, MAMMON, AND THE JAPANESE: DR. HORACE
      N. ALLEN AND KOREAN-AMERICAN RELATIONS, 1884-1905.
      Madison: University of Wisconsin, 1944.

      Biography of an American missionary in Korea. Allen, who
      was ultimately appointed American Minister to Korea, did a
      great deal to protect American interest in that nation.

200. Kim, C.I. Eugene. KOREA AND THE POLITICS OF IMPERIALISM,
      1876-1910. Berkeley: University of California, 1967.

      Scholarly study describes and analyzes the circumstances
      which led to the Japanese annexation of Korea and the
      establishment of a military dictatorship in 1910. Success
      was not so much due to Japanese skill as it was the Korean
      lack of unity.

201. Kim, C.I. Eugene, and Doretha E. Mortimore, eds. KOREA'S
      RESPONSE TO JAPAN: THE COLONIAL PERIOD, 1910-1945.
      Kalamazoo, MI: Western Michigan University, 1975.

      A collection of 15 scholarly articles on various aspects of
      Korea's reaction to Japanese rule.

202. "Korea." LIFE, 1950 29 (2):73-79.

      Capsule history of the nation from 1122 B.C. to the outbreak
      of the Korean War. Brief geographical description and look
      at the Korean people.

203. Lee, Chong-Sik. THE POLITICS OF KOREAN NATIONALISM.
      Berkeley: University of California, 1964.

      A condensed version of the author's dissertation. An
      in-depth study of the development of Nationalism in Korea
      from 1905 through the end of WWII. Includes a look at key
      political figures in the movement.

204. McCune, George M., and John A. Harrison. KOREAN-AMERICAN
      RELATIONS. DOCUMENTS PERTAINING TO THE FAR EASTERN
      DIPLOMACY OF THE UNITED STATES. Vol 1. THE INITIAL PERIOD,
      1883-1886. Berkeley: University of California, 1951.

      Documents surrounding Korean-American relations between 1883
      and 1886. During that period Korea was the central point and
      the US the neutral in a contest between Japan, China, Russia
      and England.

205. Matray, James I. "An End to Indifference: America's Korean
      Policy During WWII." DIP HIST, 1978 2 (2):181-196.

      Shows how WWII brought an end to America's long tradition
      of indifference to Korea. Traces Roosevelt's WWII thinking,
      discussions and decisions on the future of Korea following the
      defeat of Japan. Tells how the President moved to acceptance
      of a Korean trusteeship.

206. Nalty, Bernard C., and Truman Stonebridge. "Our First Korean
      War." AM HIST ILL, 1967 2 (5):10-19.

      In June 1871 the US Marines launched an unauthorized attack
      on several fronts on the Salee River in Korea. The action was
      motivated by the refusal of Korean leaders to open their
      country to trade and the mistreatment of American missionaries.
      The attacks accomplished nothing and the US forces withdrew.

207. Nelson, M.F. KOREA AND THE OLD ORDERS IN EASTERN ASIA.
      Baton Rouge: Louisiana State University, 1945.

      A brief examination of Korea's international status from the
      nation's earliest history through the end of WWII.

208. Oliver, Robert T. KOREA: FORGOTTEN NATION. Washington:
      Public Affairs Press, 1944.

      Condemns the Japanese control of Korea and sets forth the
      desire of the Koreans to be independent. Discusses the
      independence movement and urges the US support for it. Tells
      of the activities of the Korean Provisional Government, which
      was in exile, and Syngman Rhee.

209. Osgood, Cornelius. THE KOREANS AND THEIR CULTURE. New York:
      Ronald, 1951.

      A first-rate book on the political and cultural history of

Korea from ancient times to the Chinese intervention in the
Korean War. The author, an anthropologist, gives excellent
insight into the influence of environment on the Korean
people.

210. Palmer, Spencer J. KOREAN-AMERICAN RELATIONS: DOCUMENTS
     PERTAINING TO THE FAR EASTERN DIPLOMACY OF THE UNITED
     STATES. VOL II, 1887-1895. Berkeley: University of
     California, 1963.

     Second of projected three volumes on Korean-American
     relations between 1883 and 1905. Documents exchanged between
     the two countries during a period when Japanese influence was
     already beginning to grow. See item 204 for Vol. I.

211. Rhee, Syngman. JAPAN INSIDE OUT: THE CHALLENGE OF TODAY.
     New York: Revell, 1941.

     Warns the United States that Japan has aggressive designs
     in the Pacific and utilizes the danger of that threat to set
     forth the need for Korea to shed Japanese control and receive
     its independence.

212. Scalapino, Robert A., and Chong-Sik Lee. "The Origins of the
     Korean Communist Movement." J ASIAN STUDIES, 1960 20
     (2):149-167.

     Examines the development of communism in the Far East in
     the aftermath of WWI. Focuses on the movement in Japanese
     controlled Korea through 1925.

213. Sohn, Pow-key, et al. THE HISTORY OF KOREA. Seoul: Korean
     National Committee For UNESCO, 1970.

     A good political survey of Korea from ancient times through
     the 1963 restoration of civilian government under Park Chung
     Hee, however very little on the Korean conflict.

214. Suh, Dae-Sook, comp. DOCUMENTS OF KOREAN COMMUNISM, 1918-
     1948. Princeton, NJ: Princeton University, 1970.

     A useful compilation of reports, speeches and
     correspondence that supplements the author's work on Korean
     Communism prior to 1949.

215. Suh, Dae-Sook. THE KOREAN COMMUNIST MOVEMENT, 1918-1948.
     Princeton, NJ: Princeton University, 1967.

     Scholarly study of the Communist revolutionary movement in
     Korea shows the feuding and internal struggles that
     characterized the movement through the end of WWII.
     Following the war, Kim Il-Sung fashions a political defeat of
     the old line. Rejects the idea that Russia dominated
     politics in North Korea. Excellent bibliography.

216. Weems, Clarence N., ed. HULBERT'S HISTORY OF KOREA. 2 Vols.
        London: Routledge, 1962.

        Updated and editorially worked reprint of Homer B.
        Hulbert's 1905 classic history of Korea from ancient times
        through 1904. The editor does a good job of telling where
        later research calls into question or refutes the author's
        original positions.

217. Weems, Clarence N. KOREA: DILEMMA OF AN UNDERDEVELOPED
        COUNTRY. New York: Foreign Policy Association, 1960.

        This pamphlet #144 in the Headline Series traces Korea's
        history from ancient times to 1960 including both political
        and economic developments before, during and after the Korea
        War.

218. Woo-keun, Han. THE HISTORY OF KOREA. Honolulu: East-West
        Center, 1971.

        This general history, written by a professor at the Seoul
        National University, covers from primitive times to the fall
        of President Rhee in 1960. Very brief coverage of the post-
        WWII period and the Korean conflict.

                        B. KOREA, 1945-1950

219. "Background on Korea." ARMY INFO DIG, 1950 5 (8):10-17.

        Surveys the political developments in Korea from 1945
        through June 1950. Includes the division of the country,
        failure of Russia and US to reach an accord on the form of
        government, UN activities and establishment of the North and
        South Korean Governments. Straight narrative with little
        analysis.

220. Baldwin, Frank, ed. WITHOUT PARALLEL: THE AMERICAN-KOREAN
        RELATIONSHIP SINCE 1945. New York: Pantheon, 1974.

        Essays by eight scholars are unified by the theme that
        American intervention in Korea in the three decades following
        WWII was disastrous for the country and its people.
        Provocative essays by: Halliday, who claims that UN
        intervention was really US action to further its own policy;
        Simmons, who maintains US intervention in the Korean civil
        war led to untold harm; and other revisionist authors whose
        works are deserving of consideration.

221. Bell, Coral. "Korea and the Balance of Power." POL Q,
        1954 25 (1):17-29.

        Examines Korea in the post-WWII era and the Korean War
        period and shows how it became involved in the Soviet-US
        political-military tug-of-war. In getting caught up in the

Cold War conflict, Korea came to achieve a place of great
symbolic importance. Claims that major consequence of the
war was to move Europe closer to the US and Asia toward the
Soviet Union.

222.   Beloff, Max. SOVIET POLICY IN THE FAR EAST, 1944-1951.
       London: Oxford University, 1953.

       A sober, scholarly work by a recognized expert in Soviet
       foreign policy. Maintains that Russian Far Eastern Policy in
       the period examined was not a well-planned process, but a
       makeshift policy that Stalin developed in response to
       developments in that part of the world.

223.   Berry, Sidney B. "Land Reform in South Korea Since 1945."
       Master's Thesis. Columbia, 1953.

       Although land reform was one of the major goals of the
       American Military Government and the Republic of Korea
       between 1945 and 1950, no progress was made, and when the war
       came in 1950, all plans were shelved.

224.   Borg, Dorothy, and Waldo Heinrichs, eds. UNCERTAIN YEARS:
       CHINESE-AMERICAN RELATIONS, 1947-1950. New York: Columbia
       University, 1980.

       Collection of scholarly essays from a 1978 conference on US
       Far Eastern policy on the eve of the Korean conflict.
       Includes an excellent essay by John L. Gaddis on The Rise and
       Fall of the "Defensive Perimeter" Concept. Includes
       chronology of events.

225.   Borton, Hugh. "Korea Under American and Soviet Occupation,
       1945-1947" in Arnold Toynbee, ed. SURVEY OF INTERNATIONAL
       AFFAIRS, 1939-1946. Vol VII: THE FAR EAST, 1942-1946.
       London, 1955, pp. 428-473.

       Surveys developments in Korea in the two years following
       WWII as the US and Soviets became involved in a cold war
       conflict in the nation. Tells how the Russians attempted
       to dominate the North as the US searched for a solution to
       unifying the country.

226.   Borton, Hugh. "Occupational Policies in Japan and Korea."
       AM ACAD POL SOC SCI ANS, 1948 225 (1):146-155.

       Explains the political, economic and social goals of the US
       Military Government in post-WWII Korea.

227.   Brun, Ellen, and Jacques Hersh. "The Korean War: 20
       Years Later." MONT R, 1973 25 (2):44-53.

       Retrospective examination of US policy in Korea from 1945-
       1950. Places major blame for the war on the US by contending
       that its imperialist-motivated interference in Korean affairs
       was responsible.

228. Buhite, Russell D. SOVIET-AMERICAN RELATIONS IN ASIA,
      1945-1954. Norman, OK: University of Oklahoma, 1981.

      Maintains that the US was forced to expand its presence
      and influence in the Far East in the post-war period because
      of Soviet moves to restore its position there. Claims that
      American policy was merely a response to the Soviet challenge
      and thus did not understand such important considerations as
      nationalism. Although it looks at the entire Far East
      considerable attention is given to Korea.

229. Caldwell, John C., and Lesley Frost. THE KOREAN STORY.
      Chicago: Regnery, 1952.

      Criticizes the US Department of State's Korean policy
      prior to the June 1950 attack.

230. Chang, Paul T. "Political Effect of World War II on Korea:
      With Special Reference to the Policies of the United States."
      Doctoral Dissertation. Notre Dame, 1953.

      Looks at the development of US policy toward Korea in the
      final months of WWII plus the occupation of the country and
      establishment of the American Military Government. Covers the
      friction between US and Soviet Union in the period of
      occupation.

231. Cho, Soon-Sung. "The Failure of American Military Government
      in Korea." KOREAN AFF, 1963 (2) 331-347.

      Maintains the US Military Government established in Korea
      at the end of WWII was unclear as to its mission and
      consequently carried out a confused and disorganized policy
      which left the country in chaos and helped lay the basis for
      the Korean War. Sees Korean difficulties stemming from both
      Russian designs and US incompetence.

232. Cho, Soon-Sung. "Hodge's Dilemma: Failure of Korean
      Trusteeship." KOREAN AFF, 1965 4 (May):58-74.

      Places blame for the failure of the Korean Trusteeship not
      on the head of the American Military Government, General John
      Hodge but upon the decisions made by US Secretary of State
      James Byrnes in the December 1945 Foreign Ministers Conference
      in Moscow. The agreements reached doomed any possibility of
      a unified Korea.

233. Cho, Soon-Sung. KOREA IN WORLD POLITICS, 1940-1945.
      Berkeley: University of California, 1967.

      A political and military history of Korea with special
      emphasis on the post-WWII period. In this well-researched
      study of US policy in Korea, the author concludes that in

spite of the good intentions of Washington policy makers, there were numerous blunders which were detrimental to Korea and made the outbreak of war in 1950 virtually inevitable.

234. Cho, Soon-Sung. "United States Policy Toward the Unification of Korea, 1943-1950." Doctoral Dissertation. Michigan, 1960.

Excellent study on the background of the Korean War from the view that Russia and the US must share blame for inability to work out a political settlement for a united Korea. Goes into WWII diplomacy dealing with the future of Korea.

235. Chung, Henry. THE RUSSIANS CAME TO KOREA. Washington: Korean Pacific, 1947.

A look at Soviet policies in Korea in the eighteen months following WWII. The author, a Korean nationalist, calls for the US to halt Soviet expansionist tendencies in Korea.

236. Chung, Kyung Cho. KOREA TOMORROW: LAND OF THE MORNING CALM. New York: Macmillan, 1956.

Historical survey with the last half of the book examining the post-WWII era, including the Korean War. Well-organized and well-written--good for the broad picture.

237. Chung, Yong Hwan. "John Wook Moon: Statesman and Educator." Master's Thesis. East Texas State, 1977.

Looks at the life of an American educated Korean scholar who, between 1945 and 1949, filled important posts under the US Army Military Government and the Republic of Korea. His service as Director of Foreign Affairs under the Military Government was concerned primarily with problems of repatriation. Provides a good understanding of what was happening within South Korea in the aftermath of WWII.

238. Chung, Yong Hwan. "Repatriation Under the United States Army Military Government in Korea, 1945-1948." ASIAN FOR, 1976 8 (2):25-44.

Between 1945 and 1948 there was considerable repatriation of Koreans from Manchuria, China, Japan and North Korea to South Korea and repatriation of Japanese from South Korea, the void left by the latter and the impact of those returning led to considerable friction that helped bring on war several years later.

239. Cumings, Bruce. "Korea: The Politics of Liberation, 1945-1947." Doctoral Dissertation. Columbia, 1975.

Examination of group interaction between various factions of Koreans and the occupying forces of the US and Russia.

240. Cumings, Bruce. THE ORIGINS OF THE KOREAN WAR: LIBERATION
     AND THE EMERGENCE OF SEPARATE REGIMES 1945-1947.
     Princeton, NJ: Princeton University, 1981.

     Excellent scholarly study of the background of the war.
     Claims that the conflict was inevitable following the
     decisions of 1945 that ultimately led to the establishment
     of separate regimes in North and South.

241. Dobbs, Charles M. "American Foreign Policy, the Cold War, and
     Korea: 1945-1950." Doctoral Dissertation. Indiana, 1978.

     Looks at US policy toward Korea in the post-war era and
     concludes that there was no policy, since officials in Washington
     initially ignored the problems of Korea and later were unsure
     as to how they should handle them. When war came the US was
     forced to defend an area which was indefensible and
     strategically unimportant.

242. Dobbs, Charles M. THE UNWANTED SYMBOL: AMERICAN FOREIGN
     POLICY, THE COLD WAR AND KOREA, 1945-1950. Kent, OH: Kent
     State University, 1981.

     Traces United States policy toward Korea from the end of
     WWII through the commitment of troops in 1950. A well-
     researched account that maintains the United States had
     no policy but drifted into a growing but reluctant commitment
     to South Korea, which became a symbol of its defense of the
     free world.

243. Dulles, John Foster. "The Korean Experiment in
     Representative Government." DEPT STATE BUL, 1950 23
     (574):12-13.

     Dulles' speech before the ROK National Assembly on June 19,
     1950, a week before the North Korean attack. Pledges the
     support of the US to South Korea and notes the close ties
     between the Rhee Government and the UN.

244. Elzy, Marten I. "The Origins of American Military Policy,
     1945-1950." Doctoral Dissertation. Miami, 1975.

     Shows how and why US military policy relied so heavily on
     airpower and atomic weapons, at the expense of conventional
     forces, in the period under study. Demand for manpower
     demobilization, fear of depression and belief in total,
     atomic warfare are all examined as factors. Helps explain
     why US troops originally sent to Korea did so poorly.

245. Faulkner, Maurice. "Korean Music and American Military
     Government, 1945-1946." KOREAN SUR, 1955 5 (1):10-12.

     The Director of Music for the Bureau of Education in the
     Military Government of Korea tells how a complete program

of music education was organized and implemented in the
first year of US occupation. School music was developed
at all levels from elementary through the university level.

246. Foltos, Lester J. "The Bulwark of Freedom: American
     Security Policy For East Asia, 1945-1950." Doctoral
     Dissertation. Illinois, 1980.

     While looking at US Far Eastern policy in general,
     considerable attention is devoted to Korean policy. Shows
     how Truman attempted to implement the Yalta agreement on
     Korea and later bowed to pressure to give limited economic
     and military aid to the ROK but avoided any firm commitments
     to defend it. When the North Korea attack came, however,
     Truman reversed his course and came to the South's defense,
     thus, reversing his earlier position.

247. Gaddis, John L. "Korea in American Politics, Strategy and
     Diplomacy, 1945-1950" in Yonosuke Nagai and Akira Iriye,
     eds. THE ORIGINS OF THE COLD WAR IN ASIA. New York:
     Columbia University, 1977, pp. 277-298.

     Criticizes US policy makers for their decisions in regard
     to Korea in the post-WWII period because of their inability
     to anticipate the consequences of their actions. The latter
     was true even when making the decision to intervene. Sees
     the decision as made primarily in response to, or
     anticipation of, developments in the larger international
     arena.

248. Gaddis, John L. "The Strategic Perspective: The Rise and
     Fall of the 'Defensive Perimeter' Concept, 1947-1951" in
     Borg, Dorothy, and Waldo Heinrichs, eds. UNCERTAIN YEARS:
     CHINESE-AMERICAN RELATIONS, 1947-1950. New York: Columbia
     University, 1980, pp. 61-118.

     Following WWII the US strategic frontier shifted from the
     West Coast to the Asian offshore islands but not the Asian
     mainland. Consequently, by 1949-1950, the State and Defense
     Departments were in agreement that South Korea was not of
     strategic importance, and plans were made accordingly.
     However, when the North attacked the South, the agreed upon
     policy was ignored and the decision was made to intervene.

249. Gane, William J. "Foreign Affairs of South Korea, August 1945
     to August 1950." Doctoral Dissertation. Northwestern, 1951.

     Examines the activities of the foreign office of the US
     Army Military Government as well as UN efforts to form a
     unified and independent Korea plus SCAP's supervision of
     Korean affairs between 1945 and 1948.

250. Garthoff, Raymond L. "Sino-Soviet Military Relations."
     AM ACAD POL SOC SCI ANS, 1963 349 January:81-93.

Looks at Russian-Chinese relations in the fifteen years
after WWII and concludes it was never a good relationship.
Points out that in immediate post-war years Soviet support
was quite limited. In the Korean War years, weapons and
supplies were made available, but the Chinese had to
purchase them. Soviet policy was always cautious and aid
was limited.

251. Gayle, John S. "Korea, Honor Without War." MIL R,
        1951 30 (10):55-62.

Details the actions of the US occupation forces of
the 7th Infantry Division in Korea from August 1945 until
withdrawal in 1949. Claims the occupying soldiers were
not properly prepared, either in the manner they were
informed or indoctrinated, for the task assigned them.

252. Gayn, Mark J. JAPAN DIARY. New York: Sloane, 1948.

Somewhat misleading title since nearly one-third of the
book is devoted to Korea. Extracts from the personal
diary of an American foreign correspondent who observed
US occupation of Japan and Korea in the immediate post-WWII
period. Most observations are on conditions in 1946.

253. Gitovich, A., and B. Bursov. NORTH OF THE 38TH PARALLEL.
        Shanghai: Epoch, 1948.

A Communist tract which examines developments in North
Korea from the end of WWII until early 1948. Discusses
goals and objectives of the North Korean regime and
maintains they are being thwarted by the imperialist
policies of the US.

254. Gordenker, Leon. "The United Nations Commissions in Korea,
        1947-1950." Doctoral Dissertation. Columbia, 1958.

Studies the establishment, activities, accomplishments and
failures of the various UN commissions sent to deal with
problems in Korea.

255. Gordenker, Leon. THE UNITED NATIONS AND THE PEACEFUL
        UNIFICATION OF KOREA. The Hague: Nijhoff, 1959.

An expanded version of the author's Ph.D. dissertation
which examines the role of the UN in Korea from 1947
until the outbreak of war three years later. Notes both
the failures and accomplishments of the UN in dealing with
the problem.

256. Gordenker, Leon. "United Nations, the United States
        Occupation and the 1948 Election in Korea." POL SCI Q,
        1958 73 (3):426-450.

Background to the election held under the auspices of the

UN to establish an independent South Korea. Looks at
earlier efforts of the US and UN to bring about a unified
Korea.

257. Green, Adwin W. EPIC OF KOREA. Washington: Public
     Affairs Press, 1950.

     A popular "all about Korea" book published shortly after
     the outbreak of war. Covers history, culture and society of
     Korea, with special emphasis on the period from 1945 to 1950.
     Very biased against US policies and the performance of the
     Military Government.

258. Grey, Arthur L., Jr. "The Thirty-Eighth Parallel."
     FOR AFF, 1951 29 (3):482-487.

     Examines the decision to divide Korea at the 38th
     Parallel at the end of WWII and refutes the widespread
     impression the issue was settled at Yalta. The decision
     was actually formulated in the US War Department in the
     late summer of 1945. Shows that unlike decisions on
     Germany, Korean decisions were made, by the military, on
     the eve of the Japanese surrender.

259. Hah, Chong-Do. "Bitter Diplomacy: Postwar Japan-Korea
     Relations" in Robert K. Sakai, ed. STUDIES ON ASIA 1964.
     Lincoln: University of Nebraska, 1964, pp. 63-93.

     The friction between Japan and Korea was intense in the
     period following WWII because of long-term hostility that
     developed during decades of Japanese occupation and questions
     of repatriation.

260. Hah, Chong-Do. "The Dynamics of Japanese-Korean Relations,
     1945-1963." Doctoral Dissertation. Indiana, 1967.

     Examines the foreign relations of Japan and Korea focusing
     upon international conflict between the two nations in the
     1950's. Tells how the hostility of the post-war period gave
     way to better relations when war came to Korea.

261. Halliday, Jon. THREE ARTICLES ON THE KOREAN REVOLUTION,
     1945-1953. London: AREAS, 1972.

     Collection of scholarly studies by a British socialist.
     Generally critical of Western explanation of what took
     place in Korea in the post-WWII era and the start of the
     war. Sees the West as thwarting the will of the Korean
     people.

262. Harlowe, W.N. "Korea, Foreign Policies of the Two
     Republics, 1948-1950." Master's Thesis. California:
     Berkeley, 1953.

     The governments of both North and South Korea had very

little say over their nations' foreign policies because they
were caught up in the conflict between East and West.
Their policies were in reality those of Russia and the
United States, both of whom were concerned more about
their future than that of Korea.

263. Henderson, Gregory. KOREA: THE POLITICS OF THE VORTEX.
      Cambridge: Harvard University, 1968.

      Scholarly political history of Korea from the Yi dynasty to
      the mid-1960's gives special attention to post-WWII
      developments, including the war. Is critical of US policy;
      claims US had a muddled Korean policy. When US failed to
      rule strongly, Korean society disintegrated.

264. Iriye, Akira. THE COLD WAR IN ASIA: A HISTORICAL
      INTRODUCTION. Englewood Cliffs, NJ: Prentice, 1974.

      An interpretative history of the origins of the Cold War in
      Asia places events in the context of Asian-Pacific and
      US-East Asian relations. Covers the 20th Century but focuses
      on the 1940's and early 1950's, including an overview of the
      Korean War.

265. Jessup, Philip C. THE BIRTH OF NATIONS. New York: Columbia
      University, 1974.

      As special US representative to the UN and US
      Ambassador-at-large in the post-WWII era, Jessup observed and
      was involved in the breakup of empires and the birth of
      nations. He recounts his experiences and observations of the
      creation of nine nations in that period. One of the nations
      he examines is Korea. With the failure to find a unification
      formula for that country, there came the birth of two Koreas.

266. Joseph, Robert G. "Commitments and Capabilities: United
      States Foreign and Defense Policy Coordination, 1945 to the
      Korean War." Doctoral Dissertation. Columbia, 1978.

      In the years following WWII, the Truman Administration made
      increased political, economic and military commitments
      throughout the world at the same time it was decreasing the
      nation's military capabilities. Consequently, the US was not
      prepared militarily when war came in Korea.

267. Judd, Walter H. "The Mistakes That Led to Korea." READ DIG,
      1950 57 (343):51-57.

      A US congressman cites what he considers the errors of the
      Truman Administration that led to the war. The mistakes
      include: the decision to divide Korea at the 38th Parallel;
      the failure to build up the South Korean Army; the 1949
      withdrawal of US troops; Truman's January 1950 announcement
      the US would not provide military aid to Formosa; and
      Acheson's January 1950 speech in which he failed to include
      South Korea in the US's Far East defense perimeter.

268. Kang, Han Mu. "The United States Military Government in
       Korea, 1945-1948." Doctoral Dissertation. Cincinnati, 1970.

       This analysis and evaluation of US policy in Korea is
       critical of the policy makers in Washington. Shows the
       problems facing the commander of the American occupation
       forces, General John Hodge, and the Soviet mood which made
       his task even more difficult.

269. Kim, C.I. Eugene. "Civil-Military Relations in the Two
       Koreas." ARM FOR SOC, 1984 11 (1):9-31.

       Describes the influence of the Soviet Union on North
       Korea's civil-military relations and that of the US on South
       Korea. Shows how the military became a dominant political
       factor in both Koreas, but in the North, it was dominated by
       one man, Kim Il-sung, while in the South military power was
       fragmented. Traces that influence in the decades after the
       war.

270. Kim, Jinwung. "American Policy and Korean Independence:
       An Appraisal of Military Occupation Policy in South Korea,
       1945-1948." Doctoral Dissertation. Brigham Young, 1983.

       Claims that US occupation of Korea in the post-WWII era
       prevented a revolutionary movement from making headway and
       assured that the South Korean Government would be very
       conservative.

271. Kotch, John B. "United States Security Policy Toward
       Korea, 1945-1953." Doctoral Dissertation. Columbia, 1976.

       Studies the origins of US security policy toward South
       Korea. Looks at the problems in post-WWII Korea which led
       to the UN creation of the ROK and the origin and evolution
       of the UN Command after war came in 1950. Gives considerable
       attention to the problems existing between US diplomatic and
       military personnel in Korea and those back in Washington.

272. Kublin, Hyman. "Korea and Japan: Neighbor's Keepers?"
       US NAVAL INST PROC, 1955 81 (10):1085-1091.

       Examines the centuries old, bitter feud between the
       Japanese and Koreans but focuses on their hostilities and
       differences between 1945 and 1954. Claims that if they do
       not settle their differences they are apt to fall
       individually into the Communist camp. Urges establishment of
       diplomatic relations as a first step.

273. Kwak, Jae-Hwan. "United States-Korean Relations: A Core
       Interest Analysis Prior to US Intervention in the Korean
       War." Doctoral Dissertation. Claremont, 1969.

Analyzes core (generally a geographical area considered
essential to national security) interest of the US toward
Korea prior to the Korean War. Maintains that in the pre-war
period US policy makers did not consider Korea in her core
interest but did in her idealogical interest. Characterizes
US Korean policy as one of indecision.

274. Latourette, Kenneth S. THE AMERICAN RECORD IN THE FAR EAST,
1945-1951. New York: Macmillan, 1952.

An assessment of US policy and actions in the Far East
following WWII. Does a good job of showing the complexity of
problems facing policy makers in regard to Korea, China, Japan,
India and Southeast Asia. Maintains that while some mistakes
were made they were not due to treasonous acts.

275. Lee, Soon-won. "Korean-Japanese Discord, 1945-1965: A Case
Study of International Conflict." Doctoral Dissertation.
Rutgers, 1967.

Includes a review of Japanese-Korean relations prior to 1945
and a study of friction in the post-WWII period. Looks at such
factors as: property claims, territorial disputes, repatriation,
relations under SCAP and the role of the US in the almost
continual conflict between the two Far Eastern nations.

276. Lee, U-Gene. "American Policy Toward Korea, 1942-1947,
Formulation and Execution." Doctoral Dissertation.
Georgetown, 1973.

Maintains that the US decision to divide Korea at the end
of WWII was based primarily on the basis of what would best
weaken Japan and hasten its surrender.

277. Lee, Won Sul. THE IMPACT OF THE UNITED STATES OCCUPATION
POLICY ON THE SOCIO-POLITICAL STRUCTURE OF SOUTH KOREA,
1945-1948. Doctoral Dissertation. Western Reserve, 1962.

The Social and Political impact on Korean society of: the
American Military Government; the Trusteeship Controversy;
the Korean Interim Government; and the establishment of the
Republic of Korea. Looks at some of the social reforms under
the US military government.

278. Lee, Young-Woo. "Birth of the Korean Army, 1945-1950:
Evaluation of the Role of US Occupation Forces." KOREA
WORLD AFF, 1980 4:639-656.

Shows how the character of the ROK armed forces was
drastically influenced by US advisors and their post-WWII
policies. Also examines Soviet influence on the North Korean
Army.

279. McCune, George M. "Korea: The First Year of Liberation."
PAC AFF, 1947 20 (1):3-17.

An examination of the political and economic situation in
Korea in late 1946. Contends that the occupation policies of
Russia and the US led to chaos for the Korean people as the
super-powers fought for ideological superiority. Appeals
for unification of North and South.

280. McCune, George M. "The Korean Situation." FAR EASTERN Q,
1948 17 (3):197-202.

Brief description of political developments in Korea from
the end of WWII through mid-1948. Sets forth the US and
Soviet positions and the role of the UN.

281. McCune, George M. "The Occupation of Korea." FOR POL REP,
1947 23 (15):186-195.

Examines the collapse of Japanese control in Korea at the
end of WWII as well as developments, political and economic,
in both the American and Soviet occupation zones between 1945
and 1947. Critical of the super powers for agreeing in
December 1945 to a plan establishing a free and independent
Korea but then failing to implement it.

282. McCune, George M. "Occupation Policies in Korea." FAR
EASTERN SUR, 1946 15 (1):33-37.

Covers the occupation policies and procedures of the Soviet
Union and the US in Korea in the months immediately following
the defeat of Japan.

283. McCune, George M. "Post-War Government and Politics of Korea."
J POL, 1947 9 (4):605-623.

Surveys Soviet and US occupation policies in Korea in the
two years following the expulsion of the Japanese. Covers
the establishment of the American Military Government in the
South under Lieutenant General John R. Hodge and explains its
administrative organization. Explains the utilization of
People's Committee's to govern the North. By 1947, it
claims, the extreme rightist were entrenched in the South and
the extreme leftist in the North.

284. McCune, George M., and Arthur L. Grey, Jr. KOREA TODAY.
Cambridge: Harvard University, 1950.

Written before the outbreak of the war, this work includes a
brief account of the history of old Korea, Korea as a Japanese
colony and the social, political and economic problems that
developed in the post-WWII era.

285. Masao, Okonogi. "The Domestic Roots of the Korea War" in
Yonosuke Nagai and Akira Iriye, eds. THE ORIGINS OF THE
COLD WAR IN ASIA. New York: Columbia University, 1977,
pp. 299-320.

Rejects the view that domestic factors were largely
irrelevant in explaining the origins of the Korean War.
Argues that domestic politics were internationalized while
international politics became internalized thus leading to
war.

286. Materi, Irma T. IRMA AND THE HERMIT: MY LIFE IN KOREA.
      New York: Norton, 1949.

      Humorous account of life in Korea by the wife of a US
      Army Major. The author spent 19 months in the country
      during the period of post-WWII Army occupation. Includes a
      good deal about the history and culture of Korea.

287. Mathews, Naiven F. "The Public View of Military Policy,
      1945-1950." Doctoral Dissertation. Missouri-Columbia, 1964.

      Claims that public opinion played a definite role in
      influencing US military policy between WWII and the outbreak
      of war in Korea. Sees confidence in the atomic bomb and the
      Air Force's ability to deliver it as key in the demise of the
      Army and Navy that was so apparent in the summer of 1950.

288. Matray, James I. "Captive of the Cold War: The Decision to
      Divide Korea at the 38th Parallel." PAC HIST R, 1981
      50 (2):145-158.

      Claims that the division of Korea at the 38th Parallel was
      due to: deterioration of US-Soviet relations; Truman's
      belief that it was necessary to prevent complete Soviet
      control of the country; and Stalin's feeling it was the best
      deal which Russia could get at that time.

289. Matray, James I. "Korea: Test Case of Containment in Asia"
      in Bruce Cumings, ed. CHILD OF CONFLICT. Seattle:
      University of Washington, 1983, 169-193.

      Rejects the view that Truman's decision to withdraw US
      troops from Korea in 1949 indicated a reluctance to practice
      containment outside of Europe. From 1946 on Truman resisted
      pressure from military advisors to withdraw from South Korea
      while supporting the State Department position of not
      abandoning the South and championing a vast economic aid
      program.

290. Mauck, Kenneth R. "The Formation of American Foreign Policy in
      Korea, 1945-1953." Doctoral Dissertation. Oklahoma, 1978.

      Explores the forces which led to the development of US
      policy toward Korea and eventually resulted in a bilateral
      security agreement following the Korean War.

291. Meade, Edward G. "A Military Government Experiment in Korea."
      Doctoral Dissertation. Pennsylvania, 1949.

An examination of the establishment and operation of the
American Military Government in Korea in 1945-1946. A
revision of this dissertation was published in 1951 under the
title, AMERICAN MILITARY GOVERNMENT IN KOREA.

292. Meade, Edward G. AMERICAN MILITARY GOVERNMENT IN KOREA.
      New York: King's Crown, 1951.

      An account of the establishment and operations of the
      American military government from October 1945 to October
      1946, along with an analysis of its successes and its
      shortcomings. An insider's view since the author was an
      administrator in that government.

293. Millis, Walter, ed. THE FORRESTAL DIARIES. New York:
      Viking, 1951.

      The US Secretary of Navy, 1944-1947, and the first
      Secretary of Defense, 1947-1949, kept very insightful diaries
      of what was happening in Washington. Although the diary ends
      in 1949, it contains frequent references to the problem of
      Korea in the post-WWII years.

294. Min, Byong-tae. "Political Development in Korea: 1945-1965."
      KOREA J, 1965 5 (9):28-33

      Survey of South Korean political developments from the end
      of WWII through the two decades that followed. Sympathetic
      toward US efforts to achieve unification and formation of the
      Republic of Korea. Sees US-UN defense of the nation as a
      noble and worthy cause.

295. Mitchell, C. Clyde. KOREA: SECOND FAILURE IN ASIA.
      Washington: Public Affairs Institute, 1951.

      Sees the fall of China to Communism as the first failure in
      Asia and the inability to establish a free country in Korea
      as the second. Reviews developments in North and South Korea
      from the end of WWII through Chinese intervention in the Korean
      War.

296. Mitchell, Richard H. THE KOREAN MINORITY IN JAPAN.
      Berkeley: University of California, 1967.

      Traces the hostilities and controversies surrounding
      Koreans living in Japan. The friction that has developed
      over that issue served as a sore spot that prevented
      settlement of basic disputes and prevented normal diplomatic
      relations from the end of WWII on.

297. Morris, William G. "The Korean Trusteeship, 1941-1947."
      Doctoral Dissertation. Texas, 1975.

      During WWII US leaders became convinced that Korea needed
      tutelage or chaos would prevail; thus, they came, primarily

for humanitarian views, to accept the idea of a trusteeship
in the post-war period. Unfortunately, plans could not be
completed before Japan collapsed, and the US commander of
occupation forces, General John R. Hodge, did not handle the
situation well, thus forcing the US to turn the future of
Korea over to the UN.

298. Nagai, Yonosuke, and Akira Iriye, eds. THE ORIGINS OF THE
     COLD WAR IN ASIA. New York: Columbia University, 1977.

     Collection of seventeen essays, many of which deal with
     Korean policies of nations such as the US, Soviet Union,
     Communist China and Britain in the early phases of the cold
     war. Good material on the background of the conflict from
     an international perspective.

299. Nam, Byung Hun. "Educational Reorganization in South Korea
     Under the United States Army Military Government, 1945-1948."
     Doctoral Dissertation. Pittsburgh, 1962.

     Describes the US Army's reorganization of the educational
     system, the schools and higher education in the occupation
     period following WWII. Reveals that considerable time and
     attention were devoted not only to political issues but
     education as well.

300. Oliver, Robert T. WHY WAR CAME IN KOREA. New York: Fordham
     University, 1950.

     Critical account of US policy toward Korea, especially in
     the post-WWII era, by a former Counselor to the Korean
     delegation to the UN. Claims that US's "blundering good
     will" led to a militarily weak South Korea because of a
     desire to prove to Russia and the world that it had no
     designs in that country. Also argues that Russia made no
     headway in winning South Koreans to communism and therefore
     had to destroy it.

301. Pak, Hyung Koo. "Social Changes in the Educational and
     Religious Institutions of Korean Society Under Japanese and
     American Occupation." Doctoral Dissertation. Utah State,
     1965.

     Analyzes the role that the Japanese occupation of 1910-1945
     and US occupation of 1945-1948 had on Korean educational and
     religious institutions. While Japan made decisions on the
     models to be followed, American policy was to let the Koreans
     have considerable freedom of choice, and thus they retained
     much of their original culture.

302. Park, Hong Kyu. "American-Korean Relations, 1945-1953: A
     Study in United States Diplomacy." Doctoral Dissertation.
     North Texas,
     1981.

Traces the US move from limited interest in Korea at the
end of WWII to substantial involvement when war came to that
country in 1950. The original US objective was to restore
South Korea's border, but after the Inchon success, the
decision was made to unify the country; however, after
Chinese intervention, the original objective was embraced.
The armistice, he claims, almost degenerated into a US
sponsored coup against President Rhee.

303. Park, Hong Kyu. "US-Korean Relations, 1945-1947." ASIAN
     PRO, 1980 8 (1):45-52.

     Examines the failure of US-Soviet negotiators
     to reach an agreement on Korean unification in the
     immediate post-WWII period.

304. Park, No-Yong. "Cross Currents in Korea." CUR HIST,
     1946 11 (63):389-396.

     Examines the futile 1946 negotiations between the US and
     Russia as they attempted to reach agreements on the political
     future of Korea. Discusses Soviet and American policy and
     the factionalism present in Korea. Sees the Korean people
     caught in a conflict between the super powers and concludes
     it is uncertain which power will get its way.

305. Parr, E. Joan. "Korea - Its Place in Korea." POL Q,
     1952 23 (4):352-367.

     Evaluates US Secretary of State Dean Acheson's September
     1950 statement that UN intervention in Korea marked a turning
     point in history. Says that while not a turning point,
     because major powers have not altered their goals or
     attitudes, the UN action is significant because it showed a
     willingness to meet aggression. Considerable discussion of
     UN handling of the June-July 1950 crisis.

306. Paul, Mark. "Diplomacy Delayed: The Atomic Bomb and the
     Division of Korea, 1945" in Bruce Cumings, ed. CHILD OF
     CONFLICT. Seattle: University of Washington, 1983, pp.
     67-91.

     Sees the atomic bomb as being the key to understanding US
     policy toward Korea in 1945. Maintains Truman delayed
     discussion of Far Eastern issues, including Korea, until he
     knew if the atomic bomb would be available. Thus, when the
     bombs were used and the war quickly ended, the future of
     Korea had not been decided and hasty decisions were made on
     division and occupation--hasty decisions that contained the
     seeds of the Korean War.

307. Pelz, Stephen. "US Decisions on Korean Policy, 1943-1950:
     Some Hypotheses" in Bruce Cumings, ed. CHILD OF CONFLICT.
     Seattle: University of Washington, 1983, pp. 93-132.

     Sets forth the view that the major cause of the Korean War

was the mismanagement of Korean issues by Presidents
Roosevelt and Truman. Looks at the decision-making process
and concludes Roosevelt saw Korea as a minor problem which
would go away under a trusteeship, and Truman inherited that
concept and never rethought that decision. Furthermore,
Truman did not make the US position clear, thereby inviting
the 1950 attack on the South.

308. Potts, William E. "Korea: 1945 to 1950." ARMOR, 1950 59
      (5):27-29.

      Brief narrative of political events impacting Korea from
      the 1943 Cairo Conference to the outbreak of the Korean War.
      Tells of the political, economic and military problems which
      the US faced in that country. Lauds the US contribution of
      providing South Korea self-government.

309. Republic of Korea, National Unification Board. A WHITE PAPER
      ON THE SOUTH-NORTH DIALOGUE IN KOREA. Seoul: Unification
      Board, 1982.

      While dealing with attempts in the early 1980's to open
      communications toward possible unification, this study gives
      a brief, but very good, account of the political factors that
      led to the war. Surveys the war. Statistics on both armies
      at the beginning of the war.

310. Rhee, Insoo. "Competing Korean Elite Politics in South Korea
      After World War II, 1945-1948." Doctoral Dissertation. New
      York, 1981.

      The inter-relationship of the political activities of the
      South Korean political elites with the policies and practices
      of the US and Soviet occupying powers.

311. Rhee, Syngman. THE GOAL WE SEEK. Washington: Korean
      Pacific, 1947.

      The influential Korean nationalist makes a plea to the
      American public and policy makers to pursue vigorously a
      policy which will provide for a unified and independent
      Korea.

312. Rose, Lisle A. ROOTS OF TRAGEDY: THE UNITED STATES AND THE
      STRUGGLE FOR ASIA, 1945-1953. Westport, CT: Greenwood,
      1976.

      A survey of US foreign policy in Asia in the aftermath of
      WWII by a US Foreign Service Officer, claims US officials
      were unable to identify with Asian aspirations for
      independence. At no place is that truer than in Korea is a
      thesis he develops by examining the situation from the US's
      1945 occupation through the Korean War.

313. Sandusky, Michael C. AMERICA'S PARALLEL. Alexandria, VA:
      Old Dominion, 1984.

In-depth look at the decision to divide Korea at the 38th
Parallel at the end of WWII. Looks at the Soviet and
American positions at war's end and discusses motives which
led both sides to agree to the division.

314. Skroch, Ernest J. "Quartermaster Advisors in Korea." QM R,
     1951 31 (2):8-9, 118-123.

     The activities of the Quartermaster Advisory Section of the
     US Military Advisory Group to the Republic of Korea (KMAG) in
     the year prior to the Korean War and the first year of the
     conflict. KMAG established the ROK Army Quartermaster which
     assumed the responsibility of supplying food, clothing and
     many consumable items. Explains the functioning of the South
     Korean Group.

315. Stueck, William. THE ROAD TO CONFRONTATION: AMERICAN POLICY
     TOWARD CHINA AND KOREA, 1947-1950. Chapel Hill:
     University of North Carolina, 1980.

     Shows how US policy toward China and Korea was intertwined
     from the end of WWII through November 1950. Sees the Truman
     Administration's concern and search for credibility as a major
     factor in the US commitment to halt aggression--a willingness
     to show Russia it could and would act militarily, with other
     than A-bombs, to halt communist aggression.

316. Sunoo, Harold Hakwon. AMERICA'S DILEMMA IN ASIA: THE CASE
     OF SOUTH KOREA. Chicago: Nelson, 1979.

     Well-written study of Korea in the 20th Century contains
     excellent chapters on the post-WWII liberation, Soviet-US
     controversy, the Korean War and the personal and political
     life of Syngman Rhee. Sees US intervention as a means to
     halt communism not save South Korea. Maintains a primary
     reason for Chinese troops and Russian material support to
     North Korea was if the latter fell the communist cause would
     have suffered a severe setback in Asia. Generally critical
     of US policy toward Korea in the 20th Century.

317. Tavrov, G. "The Korean Question." INTER AFF (Moscow),
     1956 2 (Feb):82-96.

     Historical survey of the situation in Korea, from the end of
     WWII through the Geneva Conference, as seen from the Soviet
     perspective. Indicates the Russians wanted to pursue policies
     favored by the majority of Koreans but they were thwarted at
     every turn by US obstructionism.

318. Tewksbury, Donald G. SOURCE MATERIALS ON KOREAN POLITICS AND
     IDEOLOGIES. New York: International Secretariat:
     Institute of Pacific Relations, 1950.

Collections of treaties, speeches, proclamations and
constitutions. Divided into three sections, one of which
deals from the end of WWII through the 1950 attack. In
spite of the title the book has very little information on
politics and ideologies.

319. US Army. SOUTH KOREAN INTERIM GOVERNMENT ACTIVITIES.
     Seoul: US Army, South Korean Interim Government, 1947-1948.

     Official record of the activities of the US Command and the
     South Korean Interim Government during the period August 1947
     through August 1948 when the transition was being made from
     the US Military Government to creation of the Republic of
     Korea.

320. US Department of State. THE CONFLICT IN KOREA: EVENTS PRIOR
     TO THE ATTACK ON JUNE 25, 1950. Washington: Government
     Printing Office, 1951.

     Traces political developments in Korea from the end of WWII
     through the beginning of the Korean War.

321. US Department of State. FOREIGN RELATIONS OF THE UNITED
     STATES, 1945. Vol. VI: THE BRITISH COMMONWEALTH, THE FAR EAST.
     Washington: Government Printing Office, 1969.

     1945 diplomatic exchanges of US officials in Washington and
     the Far East on policies of the US toward Korea. Includes
     exchanges between Truman and Rhee, matters of division,
     occupation, handling of Japanese, indecision about what
     political course to follow.

322. US Department of State. FOREIGN RELATIONS OF THE UNITED
     STATES, 1946. Vol. VIII: THE FAR EAST. Washington:
     Government Printing Office, 1971. Also 1947, Vol. VI: THE
     FAR EAST, 1972.

     The exchanges between US and Soviet officials on Korea and
     the failures to reach agreement on the form of government and
     taking the issue to the UN General Assembly are covered in
     these two volumes. Many exchanges between the military
     commanders in the Far East and Washington and inside the
     State Department are included.

323. US Department of State. FOREIGN RELATIONS OF THE UNITED
     STATES, 1948. Vol. VI: THE FAR EAST AND AUSTRALASIA.
     Washington: Government Printing Office, 1974. Also 1949,
     VOL. VII: THE FAR EAST AND AUSTRALASIA. PT 2., 1976.

     Inside information on the US and the UN Temporary
     Commission on Korea, preparation for elections, establishment
     of the ROK, assessment of strategic value to US, decision to
     withdraw and evacuation of US military forces are covered in
     these volumes of US diplomatic and military documents.

324. US Department of State. KOREA: 1945-1948. Washington:
     Government Printing Office, 1948.

     The official US explanation of its Korea policy from the
     end of WWII until early 1948. Includes numerous documents
     on the initial negotiations and agreements with the Soviet
     Union plus items relating to the establishment and operation
     of the American Military Government and documents from
     the UN's dealings with the issue.

325. US Department of State. KOREA'S INDEPENDENCE. Washington:
     Government Printing Office, 1947.

     The US Government's official version of negotiations with
     the Soviet Union between 1945 and 1947 on matters related to
     Korea.

326. US Department of State. MUTUAL DEFENSE ASSISTANCE AGREEMENT
     BETWEEN THE UNITED STATES AND KOREA (JANUARY 26, 1950).
     Washington: Government Printing Office, 1950.

     Sets forth the provisions of the January 26, 1950,
     agreement to help strengthen the ROK Army by supplying $10
     million in US military equipment.

327. US Department of State. THE RECORD ON KOREAN UNIFICATION,
     1943-1960. Washington: Government Printing Office, 1960.

     A brief narrative of US foreign policy toward Korea as seen
     by the Department of State.

328. US House of Representatives Committee on Foreign Affairs.
     BACKGROUND INFORMATION ON KOREA. House Report 2495, 81st
     Cong. 2d Sess. Washington: Government Printing Office,
     1950.

     Excerpts from official US Government documents are used in
     the study of US policy toward Korea from 1945 to mid-1950.
     Examines wartime agreements, impasse between US and USSR, the
     UN and the Korean problem, withdrawal of American and Soviet
     troops, US assistance and the military and political events
     of June and July 1950.

329. Vinacke, Harold M. FAR EASTERN POLITICS IN THE POST-WAR
     PERIOD. New York: Appleton, 1956.

     General, but solid, narrative of the Far East in the decade
     following WWII. Two chapters are devoted to Korea, one on
     the period up to the war and the other on the conflict and the
     truce.

330. Vinacke, Harold M. THE UNITED STATES AND THE FAR EAST,
     1945-1951. Stanford, CA: Stanford University, 1952.

     An excellent survey of the US role in the Far East in the

post-war period. Good overview of America's policy toward
China, Japan and Korea. Good background for the general
reader.

331. Wedemeyer, Albert C. "1947 Wedemeyer Report on Korea."
       CUR HIST, 1951 20 (118):863-865.

       In the summer of 1947 President Truman sent Lt. General
Wedemeyer on a fact finding trip to the Far East. The
portion of the report on China was released in 1949, but the
portion dealing with Korea was suppressed until May 1, 1951.
This report cites the Soviet threat to South Korea and says
the US should strengthen its economic and military commitment
if it is to thwart a communist takeover. For the complete
report see: Wedemeyer, Lt. Gen. A.C. REPORT TO THE
PRESIDENT: APPRAISAL OF ECONOMIC AID PROGRAM IN KOREA,
SEPTEMBER 1947. Washington: Government Printing Office,
1951.

332. Weems, Benjamin B. REFORM, REBELLION AND THE HEAVENLY WAY.
       Tucson: University of Arizona, 1964.

       Claims that the Korean nationalist movement was influenced
by Ch'ondogyo, the religion of the heavenly. Examines the
movement in three time periods, including the years from 1945
to 1950.

333. "Why We Are Fighting in Korea." US NAVAL INST PROC, 1950
       76 (9): 1016-1017.

       A US Navy public relations piece which traces,
chronologically, events in Korea from the 1947 establishment
of the UN Joint Commission through President Truman's June
30, 1950, decision to commit ground troops. Places blame on
Russia for the failure to have a united Korea.

334. Widener, Alice. "The Korean Failure." AM MERCURY, 1952
       74 (341):12-24.

       Critical account of the failed US foreign policies as
related to Korea from 1945 through late 1952. Places blame
on Truman and the State Department for failing to make clear
it would resist aggression in Korea. Then when war came they
missed opportunities to win a quick victory or an acceptable
truce. Claims that the Korean war has been a defeat for the
US rather than the success that is claimed.

335. Woodall, Emery. "A Study of the Judicial System of Korea
       (1945-1948)." KOREAN SUR, 1953 2 (4):6-8, 10.

       The development of a legal system in Korea under the US
Military Government is described. Tells of the problems of
doing away with the Japanese system and instituting a
Democratic system.

336.   Woodman, Dorothy. "Korea, Formosa and World Peace." POL Q,
       1950 21 (4):364-373.

       Contains good background on the coming of the War. Critical
       of US policy in Korea after WWII and sees Korea getting
       caught up in the US-USSR feud. Tells of political situation
       in Korea on eve of attack. Claims that if a settlement is to
       be reached North Korea and Red China need to be brought into
       the negotiations which should be conducted by the UN.

                    C. DEMOCRATIC PEOPLE'S REPUBLIC OF KOREA

337.   Baik, Bong. KIM IL SUNG: BIOGRAPHY. 3 volumes. Tokyo:
       Miraisha, 1969-1970.

       Translation of the most detailed biography of Il Sung,
       published in Pyongyang in 1968. Standard North Korean
       explanation of the patriot's role.

338.   Brun, Ellen, and Jacques Hersh. "Aspects of Korean Socialism."
       J CONT ASIA, (Sweden) 1975 5 (2):138-152.

       From the end of WWII on, North Korea followed a rather
       independent style of socialism. Prior to the Korean War
       there was only limited socialism but the war speeded up the
       process considerably as the government attempted to bring
       about greater industrialization.

339.   Cumings, Bruce G. "Kim's Korean Communism." PROB COM, 1974 23
       (2):27-41.

       Describes the unique aspects of communism as developed in
       North Korea by Kim Il-Sung in the post-WWII years. It was
       extremely nationalistic and self-reliant and relied a great
       deal on politicalization of the nation's social organization.

340.   Democratic People's Republic of Korea. BRIEF HISTORY OF THE
       REVOLUTIONARY ACTIVITIES OF COMRADE KIM IL-SUNG. Pyongyang:
       Foreign Languages Publishing House, 1969.

       The North Korean Government's official account of the
       political activities, style and accomplishments of the
       revolutionary leader.

341.   Dutt, Vidya P., ed. EAST ASIA: CHINA, KOREA, JAPAN, 1947-1950.
       London: Oxford University, 1958.

       Selected documents including more than one hundred pages of
       items related to North and South Korea. Introduction is a
       brief history of Korea from 1947 through 1949. Includes
       documents of the US and Russia concerning the Korean
       political disagreement, UN documents dealing with the
       problem, reports and speeches from North and South Korean
       leaders, items dealing with US-South Korean relations and
       those of Russia and North Korea.

342. Felton, Monica P. THAT'S WHY I WENT. London: Lawrence, 1953.

        Recounts a 1951 British delegation of women who traveled to
        North Korea at the invitation of that government. Extensive
        coverage of trip but several chapters are devoted to life in
        the North during the war. The visitors were shown documents
        which allegedly proved that South Korea and the US planned
        and carried out the attack--an explanation the author
        accepts.

343. Harlowe, W.N. "Korea, Foreign Policies of the Two Republics,
        1948-1950." Master's Thesis. California, Berkeley, 1953.

        How the newly formed North and South Korean Governments
        foreign policies were dominated by their close ties with the
        Soviet Union and the US respectively.

344. Hun, Ryu. STUDY OF NORTH KOREA. Seoul: Research Institute of
        Internal and External Affairs, 1966.

        An anti-communist history of North Korea from the end of
        WWII through 1965. Counters the communist line on the
        origins and conduct of the Korean War.

345. Kim, Chang-sun. FIFTEEN-YEAR HISTORY OF NORTH KOREA.
        Washington: Joint Publications Research, 1963.

        Survey of the history of the North Korean People's Republic
        from its establishment in 1948 until early 1963. The
        functioning of the government during the war years and the
        politics under Kim Il-Sung are treated relatively
        objectively.

346. "Kim Il-song." ARMY DIG, 1969 24 (10):32.

        Brief survey of the North Korean leader from his birth in
        1912 through 1965. Notes that as Premier, General Secretary
        of the Central Committee and the Korean Labor Party and
        Supreme Commander of the Armed Forces Kim was all-powerful.

347. Kim, Joungwon A. DIVIDED KOREA: THE POLITICS OF DEVELOPMENT,
        1945-1972. Cambridge, MA: East Asian Research, 1975.

        The emergence, birth and political development of North and
        South Korea pays particular attention to the role of
        political leaders and their utilization of political forces
        for their ends and those of their countries.

348. Kim, Youn-Soo. "North Korea's Relationship to the USSR: A
        Political and Economic Problem." BUL INST STUDY USSR, (West
        Germany) 1971 18 (6):34-48.

        Surveys North Korean-USSR foreign relations from 1945 to

1970. In the post-WWII period the relationship between the
two nations was very close, however, during the Korean War,
North Korea became very upset at Russia's refusal to
intervene on her behalf. Consequently, the war drove North
Korea and China closer together, but when the war ended, the
North, for economic reasons, turned to a position of
independent neutralization.

349. Kiyosaki, Wayne S. NORTH KOREA'S FOREIGN RELATIONS: THE
        POLITICS OF ACCOMMODATION, 1945-1975. New York: Praeger,
        1976.

        Shows North Korea's interaction with Moscow and Peking in
        the post-war era. Focuses primarily on political relations
        with minimal coverage of economics and military interaction.
        Shows how lukewarm Russian support in Korea turned the North
        increasingly to China.

350. Koh, Byung Chul. THE FOREIGN POLICY OF NORTH KOREA. New
        York: Praeger, 1969.

        Analysis of North Korean foreign policy from the late
        1940's to the mid-1960's includes a good background on the
        emergence and early years of the Kim Il-Sung's North Korean
        Government. Tells how the North built its political base
        between 1945-1950 then attempted to achieve unification by
        force in 1950. Unification is the constant goal through the
        period examined.

351. Lee, Chong-Sik. "Kim Il-Song of North Korea." ASIAN SUR,
        1967 7 (6):374-382.

        Surveys the North Korean leader's life and political style.
        Looks at his childhood and youth, his life as an anti-Japanese
        guerrilla, his selection as the "Soviet man" and his style of
        leadership.

352. Nam, Koon Woo. THE NORTH KOREAN COMMUNIST LEADERSHIP, 1945-
        1965. University, AL: University of Alabama, 1974.

        Analyzes the process by which Kim Il-Sung consolidated his
        power in the two decades following WWII. Initial political
        cunning was increasingly replaced by liquidation of rival
        factions and their leaders.

353. Paige, Glenn D. THE KOREAN PEOPLE'S DEMOCRATIC REPUBLIC.
        Stanford, CA: Hoover Institution, 1966.

        Briefly examines North Korean development from Japanese
        control to its entry into the communist party-state system in
        1948 to the integrative and nationalist implications of the
        Korean War and the intensive socialist development in the
        eleven years following hostilities.

354. Peterson, William S. "Creation of the Korean Democratic
        People's Republic." Master's Thesis. Columbia, 1951.

Narrative account of the role of the Soviet Union in
setting up the North Korean government in September 1948.
Maintains the puppet government of Kim Il-Sung was clearly
established to further Soviet interests in the Far East.

355. POLITICAL SURVEY OF THE D.P.R.K., 1945-1960.
      Pyongyang: Foreign Languages Publishing House, 1960.

      Maintains that the Soviet Union successfully liberated the
      Northern position of Korea but could not assist the South
      because the US followed a policy of "National Division." This
      tract discusses the Korean War in terms of a war being fought
      by Koreans for freedom and independence.

356. Scalapino, Robert A. NORTH KOREA TODAY. New York: Praeger,
      1963.

      Collection of nine scholarly articles from a special issue
      of CHINA QUARTERLY which examines social, political and
      economic developments in North Korea from 1945 to the early
      1960's. Also looks at foreign policy, control of the army
      and the consequences of the Soviet-Red China split.

357. Scalapino, Robert A., and Chong-Sik Lee. COMMUNISM IN KOREA.
      2 volumes. Volume I, THE MOVEMENT and Volume II, THE
      SOCIETY. Berkeley: University of California, 1972.

      VOL. I. is an in-depth historical account of the development
      of the Communist movement, especially under Kim Il-Sung in the
      post-WWII period. Relates both domestic and foreign policies
      of North Korea. Vol. II examines the social, political and
      economic systems of North Korea.

358. Shapiro, Jane P. "Soviet Policy Towards North Korea and
      Korean Unification." PAC AFF, 1975 48 (3):335-352.

      Examines the Soviet policy toward Korea from the end of
      WWII to 1973. From the time of occupation until the 1953
      armistice Russia attempted to sovietize the North and
      encourage unification of both Koreas. After 1953 Russia
      attempted to be more accommodating to the North so it would
      be neutral in any conflict between Russia and China.

359. Suh, Dae-Sook. "A Preconceived Formula for Sovietization:
      The Communist Takeover of North Korea." STUDIES SOV UNION,
      1971 11 (4):428-442.

      Studies Kim Il-Sung's methods of seizing power in North
      Korea in the post-WWII period. Soviet officials first formed
      a genuine coalition, then established a communist-dominated
      coalition before permitting Il-Sung to assume control.

360. US Department of State. NORTH KOREA: A CASE STUDY IN THE

TECHNIQUES OF TAKEOVER. Washington: Government Printing Office, 1961.

Examines the Soviet occupation and domination of North Korea and the methods utilized to become dominant. Based on late 1950 interrogation of North Korean government officials and official documents of the North Koreans and Russians.

361. Washburn, John N. "Soviet Russia and the Korean Communist Party." PAC AFF, 1950 23 (1):59-65.

An overview of the relationship between the Soviet Union and Communist Party in North Korea from 1919 to 1950, with emphasis on the period after WWII. Includes discussion of top party officials in North Korea on the eve of the war.

362. Yang, Key P. "The North Korean Regime, 1945-1955." Master's Thesis. American, 1958.

This study of the political development and government institutions of the communist-backed North Korean Government relies heavily on North Korean documentary sources. Includes an extensive bibliography.

363. YESTERDAY, TODAY: US IMPERIALISM, MASTERMIND OF AGGRESSION IN KOREA. Pyongyang: Korean People's Army Publishing House, 1977.

This account of the Korean War claims that the war was started by South Korean aggression which was stimulated by US pressure. Contains a preface by Kim Il-Sung.

364. Yoo, Se Hee. "The Communist Movement and the Peasants: The Case of Korea" in John W. Lewis, ed., PEASANT REBELLION AND COMMUNIST REVOLUTION IN ASIA. Stanford, CA: Stanford University, 1974, pp. 61-76.

Korean communist targeted the peasants of Korea as likely targets for converts. The efforts, which had their origins in the post-WWI period, intensified during WWII and in the post-WWII eras.

D. REPUBLIC OF KOREA

365. Allen, Richard C. (pseudonym). KOREA'S SYNGMAN RHEE: AN UNAUTHORIZED PORTRAIT. Rutland, VT: Tuttle, 1960.

A rather thorough and relatively objective study of the political life of Korea's war-time President up until his 1960 overthrow. The author, who supposedly had first-hand knowledge of the events and people about which he wrote, acknowledges that Rhee had faults such as being inflexible and egotistical but also comes to his defense on certain policies and practices.

366.   Bernstein, Barton J.   "Syngman Rhee: The Pawn as Rook: The
       Struggle to End the Korean War." BUL CON ASIAN SCHS, 1978
       10 (1):38-47.

       Examines the negotiations to end the war, focusing on South
       Korean President Rhee. Shows the difficulties the Truman and
       Eisenhower administrations had with Rhee as he thwarted their
       efforts to reach a settlement by threatening to take action
       that would wreck the chances of reaching an agreement.
       Rhee's motive was to gain increased economic and military aid
       and a mutual defense treaty, and he achieved his goal.

367.   Brill, James H. "KMAG Rings the Bell for Freedom." ARMY
       INFO DIG, 1965 20 (6):59-60.

       Brief statement on the function of the United States
       Military Group to the Republic of Korea (KMAG), which was
       established in 1949 and twenty-five years later was providing
       military advice and humanitarian service to the people of the
       Republic of Korea.

368.   Bullitt, William C. "The Story of Syngman Rhee." READ DIG,
       1953 63 (377):37-43.

       The author, a distinguished US diplomat and friend of Rhee
       for thirty-five years, sketches the life of the South Korean
       President and tells the pressures the US put on him in the
       summer of 1953 to accept the armistice terms. Very laudatory
       of Rhee and his commitment to his nation.

369.   Fisher, Earnest. "Korea's First National Election." KOREAN
       SUR, 1958 7 (8):5-7, 13.

       First-hand account of the way the American Military
       Government in Korea planned for and carried out the UN
       Temporary Commission on Korea's call for an election in May
       1948 to establish a government.

370.   Gibney, Frank. "Syngman Rhee: The Free Man's Burden."
       HARPER'S, 1954 208 (1245):27-34.

       Character study of Rhee is relatively balanced. Points out
       that on one hand the South Korean war time leader was an
       invaluable rallying point for his people because of his
       courage and uncompromising stand during the dark days of the
       war. On the other hand he turned his National Assembly into
       a rubber stamp and utilized mob violence in support of his
       program. Sketches his career before and during the Korean
       conflict.

371.   Hon, Pyo Wook. "The Problem of Korean Unification: A Study
       of the Unification Policy of the Republic of Korea,
       1948-1960." Doctoral Dissertation. Michigan, 1963.

Examines the background of the unification policy as it
developed in South Korea after WWII before proceeding to a
look at the policy as it emerged under Syngman Rhee. The
coming of war in 1950 put the plans on hold and in spite of
ROK desires to deal with the issue in the armistice
negotiations no progress was made. Hostilities developed
during the war then precluded any progress from 1953 to 1960.

372. Kim, Se-Jin. THE POLITICS OF MILITARY REVOLUTION IN KOREA.
Chapel Hill: University of North Carolina, 1971.

While focusing on the use of the military in the 1960's,
this scholarly study provides good background on the rise of
right-wing political parties in the post-WWII era and the
party feuds that ultimately saw Syngman Rhee rise to power.
Examines Rhee as a political organizer.

373. KMAG Public Information Office. THE UNITED STATES ADVISORY
GROUP TO THE REPUBLIC OF KOREA, 1945-1955. Tokyo: Diate,
n.d.

Administrative history of KMAG follows its organization and
activities from the pre-Korean War period through the
fighting and into the post-war years. Stresses the
benevolent policies of the group.

374. KOREAN REPORT, 1948-1952. Washington: Korean Pacific, 1952.

A review of Republic of Korean governmental procedures from
its creation in 1948 through the summer of 1952. Shows the
administrative difficulties of establishing a new government
and then functioning under two years of wartime conditions.

375. Kuznets, Paul W. ECONOMIC GROWTH AND STRUCTURE IN THE
REPUBLIC OF KOREA. New Haven, CT: Yale University, 1977.

Economic developments under the US Military Government, the
early period of independence and the Korean War are covered
in this study.

376. Kwon, Chan. "The Leadership of Syngman Rhee: The Charisma
Factor as an Analytical Framework." KOREANA Q, 1971 13
(Spring):31-48.

Lauds the leadership of the South Korean President and
shows the impact that it had on the nation's political and
cultural history. Maintains that his fostering of personal
charisma was a major ingredient in his success.

377. Merrill, John. "Internal Warfare in Korea, 1948-1950: The
Local Setting of the Korean War" in Bruce Cumings, ed.,
CHILD OF CONFLICT. Seattle: University of Washington,
1983, pp. 133-162.

A persuasive case is made that the origins of the war rested in internal rather than external factors. Tells of the guerrilla conflict in the South, including violent opposition to US policy. With the defeat of Southern partisans in 1950, the war turned to conventional warfare. Covers a topic virtually ignored by those looking at the cause of the war.

378. Moon, Chang-Joo. "Development of Politics and Political Science in Korea after WWII." KOREANA Q, 1968 10 Autumn:282-302.

Survey of the political developments in South Korea and the role played by political scientists in the creation, emergence, development and demise of the Rhee government.

379. Oh, John Kie-Chiang. KOREA: DEMOCRACY ON TRIAL. Ithaca: Cornell University, 1968.

Analyzes the emergence of and political problems encountered in establishing the Republic of Korea and the fifteen years that followed. In spite of the difficulties, the transition to Western Democracy was successful and beneficial to South Koreans.

380. Oliver, Robert T. "The Republic of Korea Looks Ahead." CUR HIST, 1948 15 (85):156-161; 15 (86):218-221.

Examines the establishment of the Republic of Korea and assesses its future. Positive factors include the homogenity of its people, freedom of international debts, industriousness of its citizens and the fact that the new government represents a strong break with the past. Negative factors also loom large, especially the divisions brought about by the tug-of-war between Russia and the US and the Soviet desire to gain control of the region; thus, the nation's future is very questionable.

381. Oliver, Robert T. "A Study in Devotion." READ DIG, 1956 69 (411):113-118.

This study of the Austrian born wife of Syngman Rhee, Francesca Donner, who he married in 1934 traces Rhee's struggle through WWII, the post-war period and the Korean War through her eyes. Tells of her activities in those tumultuous times.

382. Oliver, Robert T. SYNGMAN RHEE: THE MAN BEHIND THE MYTH. New York: Dodd, 1954.

The first full length biography of the controversial South Korean President is an extremely laudatory account by an American educator who is a long-time friend of Rhee. In spite of its lack of objectivity it does give some good insights into Rhee's thinking on the war and the activities of some of the men who surrounded him.

383. Oliver, Robert T. "Syngman Rhee and the United Nations."
      PAC SPEC, 1953 7 (4):426-434.

      The author, a good friend of Rhee, traces the history of
      relations between the Republic of Korea and the UN. Ends
      with Rhee's denunciation of the Panmunjom armistice, which he
      claims is another Munich. Includes sources of friction
      between US and South Korea and discussion of Korean domestic
      politics during the war.

384. Reeve, W.D. THE REPUBLIC OF KOREA: A POLITICAL AND ECONOMIC
      STUDY. London: Oxford University, 1963.

      Scholarly study of South Korea's First Republic under
      Syngman Rhee. Focuses on political, economic and
      administrative activities, accomplishments and shortcomings.

385. Robb, H.L. "Korea--Scene of Action." MIL ENG, 1950 42
      (289):356-360.

      Background of Korea for US Army Engineers tells of engineer
      activities in that country from the end of WWII through the
      withdrawal in 1949. Tells of the improvements at harbors
      such as those at Inchon and Pusan and the huge airfield at
      Kimpo. Tells of major roads and bridges, water supply and
      sewage disposal plants, electric plants and the problems
      encountered in working with Korean laborers.

386. Sawyer, Robert K. MILITARY ADVISORS IN KOREA: KMAG IN PEACE
      AND WAR. Army Historical Series. Washington: Government
      Printing Office, 1963.

      When the US withdrew from South Korea in 1949, it left a
      Korean Military Advisory Group of 500 military personnel to
      create and train an effective army of the Republic of Korea
      (ROK). This details the problem facing that group and the
      solutions they attempted to apply.

387. Shin, Roy W. "The Politics of Foreign Aid: A Study of the
      Impact of United States Aid in Korea From 1945 to 1966."
      Doctoral Dissertation. Minnesota, 1969.

      Claims the extension of US aid to South Korea before,
      during and after the Korean War significantly promoted
      economic development and democratic political practices.

388. US Senate, Committee on Foreign Relations, Historical Series.
      ECONOMIC ASSISTANCE TO CHINA AND KOREA: 1949-1950:
      HEARINGS HELD IN EXECUTIVE SESSION, EIGHTY-FIRST CONGRESS.
      Washington: Government Printing Office, 1974.

      The section of these June and July 1949 hearings dealing
      with Korea give a good understanding of the administration's

attitudes and feelings toward Korea just one year prior to
the outbreak of war. Contains testimony of US State and
Defense Department officials.

389. Vinocour, Seymour M. "Syngman Rhee: Spokesman for Korea: A
     Case Study in International Speaking." Doctoral
     Dissertation. Pennsylvania State, 1953.

     Rhee was an effective public speaker who rallied the South
     Korean people throughout the Korea War. This study examines
     his speeches from June 1951 through October 1952 and studies
     his techniques and his position on many issues, especially
     those related to the war.

390. Yim, Louise. MY FORTY YEAR FIGHT FOR KOREA. New York: Wyn,
     1951.

     An autobiography by a Korean woman who lived through the
     Japanese occupation, played a role in presenting Korea's case
     to the UN, and became Minister of Commerce and Industry under
     Syngman Rhee, only to be dismissed for alleged corruption.
     As accurate history it leaves much to be desired but does
     give some good insights into happenings in South Korea between
     1945 and 1950.

IV. THE ATTACK AND US DECISION TO INTERVENE
A. THE ATTACK AND WHO INITIATED IT

391. Acheson, Dean G. "Crisis in Asia--An Examination of US Policy."
DEPT STATE BUL, 1950 22 (551):111-118.

Complete text of Secretary of State Acheson's controversial
January 12, 1950, speech to the National Press Club in
Washington. It was this speech which the Secretary's critics
claim was a major factor in the coming of the Korean War
because it did not make clear that the US would defend Korea
in case of aggression. Although he did not include South
Korea in the defensive perimeter, he did imply assistance, if
needed, would be provided.

392. Chaffee, Wilbur. "Two Hypotheses of Sino-Soviet Relations as
Concerns the Instigation of the Korean War." J KOREAN AFF,
1976-77 6 (3-4):1-13.

Two explanations of Chinese-Soviet relations as they
impacted the coming of the Korean War. One hypothesis is
that the war was part of Soviet expansionism while another
idea is that Russia was caught in the dilemma of wanting to
control buffer zones in the Far East and wanting Mao's
friendship. This dilemma caused friction between Russia and
China and the former's refusal to give more support to North
Korea and China during the war.

393. Chu, Yong Bok. "Memoire." J KOREAN AFF, 1975 4 (4):68-75.

Recounts North Korea's preparations for war between 1946
and 1950. Tells of the importance of Soviet equipment and
the role of Soviet military advisors.

394. Cooper, A.C. "Lest We Forget." KOREAN SUR, 1956 5 (9):3-5.

The Anglican Bishop of Korea, who was taken prisoner by the
Communists in 1950 and released in April 1953, tells of the
June 1950 invasion and subsequent destruction that followed.
Says South Korea with its sense of fierce independence will
survive.

395. Crofts, Alfred. "The Start of the Korean War Reconsidered."
ROCKY MT SOC SCI J, 1970 7 (1):109-117.

Looks at the causes of the Korean War by focusing on the
issues of who started the war, the conspiracy doctrine and

Russia's failure to use the veto. The author concludes that
there is no evidence of an international conspiracy to start
the war; rather, the causes were indigenous.

396. Democratic People's Republic of Korea, Ministry of Foreign
Affairs. DOCUMENTS AND MATERIALS EXPOSING THE INSTIGATORS
OF THE CIVIL WAR IN KOREA. Pyongyang, Korea: 1950.

Collection of documents, allegedly captured from the
archives of the Syngman Rhee Government, which "show" that
South Korea was responsible for the initiation of
hostilities.

397. FACTS TELL. Pyongyang: Foreign Languages Publishing House,
1960.

A collection of "captured confidential documents" that
supposedly reveal that the Korean War was started by the
South Koreans with the support of US imperialists. Also
includes a report of a "Commission of the International
Association of Democratic Lawyers" which uncovered extensive
US Crimes in Korea. A good example of Communist propaganda.

398. Fleming, D. Frank. THE COLD WAR AND ITS ORIGINS, 1917-1960,
Vol. II, 592-601. Garden City, NY: Doubleday, 1961.

A scholarly work that contends that South Korea was
responsible for the start of the war.

399. Floyd, Samuel J. "Radio Free Korea." KOREAN SUR, 1955 4
(1):3-7.

A radio officer with the American Embassy in Seoul at the
time of the invasion tells of the evacuation of Seoul and the
subsequent establishment of radio operations in Taejon during
the weeks that followed. The radio was used to convince
South Korea to carry on the fight.

400. Garrett, Stephen A. "Afghanistan and Korea: Examining the
Parallels." USA TODAY, 1981 109 (2432):15-18.

Sees a parallel between the US reaction to the 1979 Soviet
invasion of Afghanistan and its 1950 response to the
communist invasion of South Korea. Claims both were seen as
reflecting broader Soviet strategy of aggression and
expansion. Looks at the war in Korea in some detail and
maintains it was not part of a new, grand Soviet strategy.

401. Gupta, Karunakar. "How did the Korean War Begin?" CHINA Q,
1972 (52):699-716.

Challenges the view that the war began with a North Korean
attack on the South. Maintains that there is a "strong
possiblity" that a ROK attack on the town of Haeju (North
Korea) actually triggered the war. Also cites accusations by
both sides that the other was responsible for the war.

402. Halliday, Jon. "The Korean War: Some Notes on Evidence and
        Solidarity." BUL CON ASIAN SCHS, 1979 11 (3):2-18.

        A British scholar looks at the Western versus Communist
        explanation of who started the Korean War and concludes that
        the pro-Western explanation is lacking. Examines Harold
        Noble's EMBASSY AT WAR and is very critical of its
        reliability. Same assessment of Riley and Schramm's THE REDS
        TAKE A CITY. Makes appeal for reunification of Korea.

403. Hitchcock, Wilbur W. "North Korea Jumps the Gun." CUR
        HIST, 1951 20 (115):136-144.

        After examining several theories of why the Soviet Union
        may have been behind the start of the Korean War, the author
        suggests that the Soviets not only did not initiate the war
        but may have been as surprised as the US that Kim Il-Sung
        launched the invasion.

404. Jung, Yong Suk. "A Critical Analysis on the Cause of the
        Korean War." J ASIATIC STUDIES, 1972 15 (1):85-94.

        Many critics of the Truman administration claimed that
        Secretary of State Dean Acheson's January 12, 1950, speech in
        which he failed to include Korea as one of the Far Eastern
        areas to be defended if attacked was a major reason why North
        Korea attacked South Korea. Claims the speech was not a
        cause of the war but failure of US to clarify its Far Eastern
        policy was a contributing factor.

405. Khrushchev, Nikita. KHRUSHCHEV REMEMBERS. Boston: Little,
        1970.

        In his memoirs (there is some debate on their authenticity)
        the Soviet Premier denies that Russia was behind the North
        Korean attack. He maintains that Premier Kim Il-Sung was the
        initiator of the war. In this book Khrushchev is the first
        top Soviet official to give a detailed account of the
        beginning of the war.

406. Kolko, Joyce and Gabriel. THE LIMITS OF POWER: THE WORLD
        AND UNITED STATES FOREIGN POLICY, 1945-1954. New York:
        Harper, 1972.

        One of the leading New Left historical works on American
        Diplomacy focuses on the Truman and Eisenhower
        Administrations and claims the US was really on the offensive
        in the post-war period, and Russia merely reacted to protect
        its interest. In regard to Korea they place the blame for
        the coming of war on the South with President Syngman Rhee
        and General Douglas MacArthur as major instigators.

407. Noble, Harold J. EMBASSY AT WAR. Seattle: University of
        Washington, 1975.

An insider's account of the first three months of the Korean War. The author, a journalist, was serving as first secretary to the American Ambassador to Korea, John Muccio, when the war broke out. Traces developments as Syngman Rhee and Muccio moved to keep things from collapsing in the summer of 1950. Good sketches of leading political and military figures in Korea at that time.

408. Noble, Harold J. "The Reds Made Suckers of Us All." SAT EVE POST, 1952 225 (6):30,76.

The first secretary of the American Embassy in Seoul at the time of the Korean War tells how the North was able to catch the South off-guard in June 1950. The North diverted attention from troop movements by making overtures on reunification talks. With attention focused on that issue, they were able to prepare for the attack. Maintains that US and South Korean officials had no solid evidence that an invasion was near.

409. Oliver, Robert T. "Why War Came in Korea." CUR HIST, 1950 19 (109):139-143.

An American scholar familiar with South Korea claims that war came because: (1) of the strategic importance of the nation; (2) Russia has wanted control of it for 75 years; (3) Russia built a strong North Korea; (4) South Korea was militarily weak; and (5) the US, unofficially and officially, did not make clear it would defend South Korea.

410. Pemberton, R.F. "Why Korea." MIL REV, 1953 32 (11):73-75.

Puts forth the view that while the war in Korea is in part a clash of East and West ideologies it is even more a clash of have-not nations and have nations and a desire on the part of Stalin and the members of the Politburo to gain and exercise more power. Only one thing can stop the Communists and that is superior military force. Digested from the April 1952 issue of THE ROYAL AIR FORCE QUARTERLY.

411. Pritt, Denis N. NEW LIGHT ON KOREA. London: Labour Monthly, 1951.

A pamphlet setting forth the position that the US and South Korea instigated the hostilities in Korea in June, 1950.

412. Raymond, Ellsworth. "Korea: Stalin's Costly Miscalculation." UN WORLD, 1952 (3):28-31.

A Soviet expert maintains that Russian support for communist aggression was a major political and economic blunder on the USSR's part. Politically it has led to

increased friction with Red China while economically the
costs of rearmament has ruined Soviet plans, especially those
for heavy industry.

413. Simmons, Robert R. "The Communist Side: An Exploratory
        Sketch" in Francis H. Heller, ed. THE KOREAN WAR: A 25-YEAR
        PERSPECTIVE. Lawrence: Regents Press of Kansas, 1977, pp.
        197-208.

        Contends that rivalry in the Korean Worker's Party in the
        North and appeals from South Korean based guerrillas
        influenced the outbreak of hostilities. Also claims that the
        war intensified friction between the Chinese Communist and
        North Koreans on one hand and the Soviet Union on the other
        because the latter did not provide adequate logistical
        support.

414. Simmons, Robert R. "The Korean Civil War" in Frank Baldwin,
        ed. WITHOUT PARALLEL: THE AMERICAN-KOREAN RELATIONSHIP
        SINCE 1945. New York: Pantheon, 1974, pp. 143-178.

        Maintains that the North Korean attack of June 1950 was
        not a Soviet directed offensive nor a case of unprovoked
        aggression but was an aspect of the Korean Civil War.

415. Simmons, Robert R. THE STRAINED ALLIANCE: PEKING,
        P'YONGYONG, MOSCOW AND THE POLITICS OF THE KOREAN CIVIL
        WAR. New York: Free Press, 1975.

        One of the best works on the origins of the war and the
        diplomacy throughout it. Examines the divisive forces in the
        Communist camp as the Soviet Union, China and North Korea
        were at odds. Maintains Kim Il-Sung attacked in 1950 because
        of an internal struggle with Pak Hon-yong, and consequently,
        the Soviet Union was not ready to get involved. It was the
        "strained alliance" between the three communist powers that
        best explains the nature of the Korean War.

416. Soh, Jin Chull. "The Role of the Soviet Union in
        Preparation For the Korean War." J KOREAN AFF, 1974 3
        (4):3-14.

        Russia provided North Korea with military equipment and
        training which enabled its army to perform very effectively
        in the early months of the Korean War. The Soviet assistance
        made a major contribution.

417. Soh, Jin Chull. "Some Causes of the Korean War of
        1950: A Case Study of Soviet Foreign Policy in Korea
        (1945-1950), With Emphasis on Sino-Soviet Collaboration."
        Doctoral Dissertation. Oklahoma, 1963.

        Examines the role of Russian foreign policy as a factor in
        the coming of the Korean War. Emphasis on diplomatic and
        military relations between Russia, Communist China and North
        Korea. The role of the Russians and Chinese Communists at
        the time of intervention is examined.

418. Stone, Isidor Feinstein. THE HIDDEN HISTORY OF THE
        KOREAN WAR. New York: Monthly Review, 1952 and 1969.

        In this controversial work the author, a journalist,
        maintains that the Korean War was actually brought about by a
        US-South Korean conspiracy--a charge later to be embraced to
        varying degrees by revisionist historians. Based on official
        US and UN documents and American and British newspapers.

419. Stueck, William. "Cold War Revisionism and the
        Origins of the Korean War: The Kolko Thesis." PAC HIST R,
        1973 42 (4):537-575.

        Critical analysis of the thesis of New Left historians
        Joyce and Gabriel Kolko that South Korea and the United
        States were to blame for the war in Korea. Stueck examines
        their various arguments and finds them wanting. Especially
        critical of their use of sources. This article is followed
        by an exchange of letters between the author and the Kolkos.

420. Stueck, William. "The Soviet Union and the Origins
        of the Korean War." WORLD POL, 1976 28 (4):622-635.

        A review article in which the author rejects the thesis of
        revisionist Robert Simmons who claims that the Soviet Union
        was as surprised as anyone when North Korea attacked the
        South in June 1950. Stueck concludes that the traditional
        view which holds that the Kremlin was behind the attack and
        approved it is still the most plausible.

421. Sweet, Joseph B. THE PRICE OF SURVIVAL. Harrisburg,
        PA: Military Service, 1950.

        Comprehensive estimate of the military situation of the US
        with respect to the rest of the world as of early 1950.
        Warns of the US drift to unpreparedness--a situation which
        became apparent in the early months of US fighting in Korea.

422. Temple, Harry. "Deaf Captains: Intelligence, Policy,
        and the Origins of the Korean War." INTER STUDIES N,
        1981-82 8 (3-4):19-23.

        Focuses on the emphasis US policy makers were putting on
        NSC-68 (National Security Council Policy Paper No. 68) as
        their guide to future action in 1950. Contends they were
        focusing so much attention on Western Europe and the Middle
        East that they ignored the increasingly explosive situation
        in Korea.

423. "Too Little, 45 Days Too Late." COLLIER'S, 1950 126
        (10):24-25.

        Maintains that top US government officials should have been
        aware that a North Korean attack was imminent because the

South Korean Defense Minister had sounded such a warning
forty-five days before the attack actually came. Claims
Truman and his advisors are responsible for the deaths of
many US servicemen. Ignores the fact that such warnings were
common in that period.

424. "U.P.'s Jack James was Going to Picnic June 25." ED
     PUB, 1950 83 (30):10.

     Account of the events of June 25, 1950, in Seoul, Korea for
     United Press correspondent Jack James, the man who broke the
     story of the North Korean attack. Tells of the unusual
     events that led to his scoop of the invasion.

425. US Department of State. "White Paper on Korea." CUR HIST,
     1950 19 (109):170-174.

     The official US government response to Soviet Deputy Foreign
     Minister Gromyko's July 4, 1950, statement blaming the US for
     the outbreak of hostilities in Korea. Covers background from
     WWII to the June 1950 crisis before examining the start of
     hostilities, which it claims were the result of North Korean
     aggression. Stresses the US was responding to appeals of the
     UN.

426. Vieman, Dorothy H. KOREAN ADVENTURE. San Antonio, TX:
     Naylor, 1951.

     Letters and diary accounts by an Army wife of her life in
     Korea from April 1949 to evacuation in June 1950 following the
     outbreak of hostilities.

427. Whang, Ho Youn. "Life Behind the Iron Curtain." KOREAN SUR,
     1955 4 (7):3-6, 12.

     Recollection of a young man who was with his family in Seoul
     when it was overrun by the North Koreans during the early days
     of the fighting. Tells how the "People's Committee" achieved
     order and how they put forth their propaganda.

428. WHO STARTED THE WAR? THE TRUTH ABOUT THE KOREAN CONFLICT.
     Seoul: Public Relations Association of Korea, 1973.

     South Korean explanation of who started the war claims that
     evidence is clear that the North Koreans, with Soviet
     encouragement unleashed an unwarranted attack on the South.

                    B. U.S. DECISION TO INTERVENE

429. Acheson, Dean. "The Responsibility for Decision in Foreign
     Policy." YALE R, 1954 44 (1):1-12.

     The former Secretary of State takes a theoretical look at
     foreign policy decision making and refers frequently to the

decision to intervene in Korea. Makes clear that the
decision is the President's with policy alternatives provided
by his advisors, primarily those from the State Department.
Notes the difficulty of making a "right" choice on a major
policy question.

430. "Act of Aggression." DEPT STATE BUL, 1950 23 (575):43-50.

Secretary of State Acheson reviews US and UN efforts to
restore peace in the days following the North Korean
invasion. Includes background from 1945 to 1950 as seen by
the US State Department. Official news releases on
Nationalist China's offer of troops and US refusal. Request
to the Soviet Union to assist in mediating the dispute. John
Foster Dulles speculates on the reasons for the aggression.

431. "Authority of the President to Repel the Attack in Korea."
DEPT STATE BUL, 1950 23 (578):173-178.

Department of State memorandum setting forth the authority
for President Truman's order to US armed forces to repel the
attack on South Korea. Cites Supreme Court cases dealing
with the authority as well as precedents set by US Presidents
who made similar commitments on eighty-five separate
occasions. Those interventions including where, date and why
are cited.

432. Bernstein, Barton J. "The Week We Went to War: American
Intervention in the Korean War." FOR SER J, 1977 54 (1):
6-9, 33-35; (2):8-11, 33-34.

A two-part article on the US decision to intervene in Korea
with the focus being on President Truman and Secretary of
State Acheson. Part one focuses on the two leaders' views of
Russian intentions in Korea while part two examines the
fateful meetings between June 26 and 30 when the
administration moved from a position of trying to evacuate
Americans to a commitment of US ground forces.

433. Campbell, Joel T. "Public Opinion and the Outbreak of War."
J CON RESO, 1965 9 (3):318-333.

Explores the theories of Lewis F. Richardson, based on
opinions prior to WWII and Korea, that maintain that war
among nations can be predicted by looking at public war
moods. The author rejects the hypothesis because, he
maintains, attitudes are affected by events. Also claims
that the methods used to gather public opinion prior to the
wars studied were inadequate.

434. Detzer, David. THUNDER OF THE CAPTAINS: THE SHORT SUMMER IN
1950. New York: Crowell, 1977.

Popular account of the US decision to intervene in Korea
and the immediate consequences of that action. Primarily
narrative, little analysis. Interweaves events in Washington
and Korea with the American social scene. Good sketches of
leading political figures.

435. Finletter, Thomas K. "The Meaning of Korea." ARMY INFO DIG,
     1951 6 (9):3-8.

     The US Secretary of the Air Force maintains that the nation
     became involved in Korea because of the need to support the
     ideals of the UN.

436. George, Alexander L. "American Policy-Making and the North
     Korean Aggression." WORLD POL, 1955 7 (2):209-232.

     Examines US foreign policy toward the Soviet Union and
     Korea on the eve of the Korean War and shows how officials of
     the Truman Administration reversed its policies when faced
     with North Korean aggression. Shows that various
     interpretations were given by US officials to the attack and
     what it meant for Korea and to overall Soviet intentions.

437. Goldman, Eric. "The President, The People, and The Power
     To Make War." AM HERT, 1970 21 (3):28-35.

     Looks at the Constitution and the power to make war and
     claims that it is a congressional prerogative but one that
     President Truman ignored in waging war in Korea. Maintains
     that Truman's abuse of the Constitution had unfortunate
     consequences for the entire nation.

438. Gromyko, Andrei A. "World Documents--Gromyko Statement."
     CUR HIST, 1950 19 (109):167-170.

     A July 4, 1950, statement by Soviet Deputy Foreign Minister
     Gromyko charging the US with aggression in Korea. This
     statement, released by TASS, the Soviet news agency, put
     forth the official Russian line on the reasons for the war.

439. High, Stanley. "We'll Remember Your Lies, Mr. Malik."
     READ DIG, 1950 57 (344):52-57.

     Critical account of the activities of Jacob A. Malik, the
     Soviet delegate to the UN at the time of the Korean War.
     Includes Malik's statements contending that the war was
     started by the South Koreans. Also contains his explanation
     of US-UN misrule in Korea between 1945 and 1950. Sees Malik
     as a mouthpiece for Russian lies.

440. Lilienthal, David E. THE JOURNALS OF DAVID E. LILIENTHAL.:
     Vol. III: VENTURESOME YEARS, 1950-1955. New York: Harper,
     1966.

     This third of five volumes of memoirs of the TVA leader and
     first chairman of the Atomic Energy Commission focuses on his
     return to private life in the early 1950's but gives good
     insight into a former government official who sees a number
     of pitfalls in pursuing the war in Korea.

441. Lofgren, Charles A. "Mr. Truman's War: A Debate and Its
      Aftermath." R POL, 31 (2):223-241.

      A constitutional law view of President Truman's June 27,
      1950, decision to commit US forces in Korea. The President's
      advocates claim that the UN Security Council Resolutions gave
      him the authority. Critics, led by Senator Robert Taft,
      argued that under the Constitution, Congress still had to
      approve US participation, even if after the fact.

442. Matray, James I. "America's Reluctant Crusade: Truman's
      Commitment of Combat Troops in the Korean War." HISTORIAN,
      1980 42 (3):437-455.

      Rejects the claim that Truman's decision to intervene
      marked a major reversal of US foreign policy. Maintains the
      action was consistent with past policy. Until the attack
      Truman believed Russia would not resort to open aggression
      and thus he made the decision to resort to military
      intervention to halt Soviet expansion.

443. Maurer, Maurer. "The Korean Conflict Was a War." MIL AFF,
      1960 24 (3):137-145.

      Throughout the Korean War US officials referred to the
      conflict as a "police action" rather than a war since war was
      never formally declared by Congress. The author maintains
      that in spite of the lack of legislative action, the conflict
      was in every true sense of the word a "war."

444. May, Ernest R. "Korea, 1950: History Overpowering
      Calculation" in Ernest R. May, LESSONS OF THE PAST: THE
      USE AND MISUSE OF HISTORY IN AMERICAN FOREIGN POLICY. New
      York: Oxford University, 1973, pp. 52-86.

      Excellent essay that examines why the Truman Administration
      ignored its own well-developed policy of avoiding any
      military engagement in Korea and made the decision in June
      1950 to intervene. Claims that Truman's temperament,
      commitment to containment and belief that the North Korean
      attack was similar to those of Germany, Italy and Japan in
      the 1930's and had to be stopped or it would lead to more
      aggression.

445. Muccio, John J. "Military Aid to Korean Security Forces."
      DEPT STATE BUL, 1950 22 (573):1048-1049.

      This statement issued by the US Ambassador to Korea on June
      9, 1950, just two weeks before the attack, notes that the US
      has adopted a policy providing political support, economic
      assistance and military aid to the South Korean government.
      Indicates that the Security Forces are almost entirely
      dependent upon the US.

446. Nagai, Yonosuke. "The Korean War: An Interpretation Essay."
      JAP J AM STUDIES, 1981 1:151-174.

Maintains that the Korean War gave the US a clear
opportunity to draw a line of containment in the Far East
thereby ending the ambiguity that had existed. Also supports
the view that Korea was for the Cold War what Pearl Harbor
was to WWII in so far as it was initiated with a surprise
attack and had a tremendous impact on American opinion.

447. "North Korean Forces Invade South Korea." DEPT STATE BUL,
      1950 23 (574):3-8.

      Covers UN Security Council request for action and the
      commitment of US air and naval forces to the defense of South
      Korea. Includes Ernest A. Gross' statement to the Security
      Council on June 25 and President Truman's June 27 order
      commiting US forces.

448. Organski, A.F.K. "Davids and Goliaths: Predicting the
      Outcomes of International Wars." COMP POL STUDIES, 1978 11
      (2):141-180.

      Four conflicts, including the Korean War, are examined to
      test three hypotheses: (1) the winner of a war will have
      capabilities equal or superior to those of the loser; (2)
      equality in capability will produce a draw; and (3) war
      results will not be related to capabilities. An application
      of the measure of national power to the four conflicts
      supported the first two hypotheses.

449. Paige, Glenn D. "Comparative Case Analysis of Crisis
      Decisions: Korea and Cuba" in C.F. Hermann, ed.
      INTERNATIONAL CRISES: INSIGHTS FROM BEHAVIORAL RESEARCH.
      New York: Free Press, 1972, pp. 41-55.

      Examination of the decisions to intervene in Korea and to
      take a strong stand in the Cuban missile crisis in terms of
      the decision making process.

450. Paige, Glenn D. THE KOREAN DECISION: JUNE 24-30, 1950.
      New York: Free Press, 1968.

      The definitive work on the Truman Administration's decision
      to intervene in Korea. This study of the decision-making
      process includes the most detailed events of what took place
      at the White House, State Department and Pentagon. Makes use
      of in depth personal interviews with the participants as well
      as official documents. Essential to an understanding of the
      US entrance into the war.

451. Paige, Glenn D. 1950: TRUMAN'S DECISION: THE UNITED STATES
      ENTERS THE KOREAN WAR. New York: Chelsea, 1970.

      Collection of statements, speeches, press interviews, radio
      addresses, UN documents and press accounts trace the Truman

administration's decision to commit forces in Korea. All
items were public releases made between January 5 and July 1,
1950. Use of reactions of military men, diplomats and
politicians gives a good understanding of the decision making
process.

452. Pelz, Stephen E. "When the Kitchen Gets Hot, Pass the Buck:
Truman and Korea." R AM HIST, 1978 6 (4):548-555.

A review article focusing on the US Department of State's.
FOREIGN RELATIONS OF THE UNITED STATES series 1950 volume 7
KOREA. The official papers from the State Department and
other agencies, such as the National Security Council and
Defense Department, are utilized to give an excellent inside
account of the US decision to enter the war and to pursue it
as it did in the remainder of 1950.

453. Price, Thomas J. "Constraints on Foreign Policy Decision
Making: Stability and Flexibility in Three Crises." INTER
STUDIES Q, 1978 22 (3):357-376.

Sees the US decision to enter the war in Korea as one of
three examples of foreign policy decision-making. Focuses on
stability and flexibility as the two major constraints on
political choices.

454. Purifoy, Lewis M. HARRY TRUMAN'S CHINA POLICY. New York:
New Viewpoints, 1976.

Examines Truman's China policy from 1947-1951 and sees it
influenced by McCarthyism and the hysteria it engendered.
Gives considerable attention to the US commitment in Korea
which the author sees not as the result of a reasoned policy
but response to a reaction against charges that the
administration had been soft on communism.

455. Rovere, Richard, and Arthur Schlesinger, Jr. "Correspondence:
Hidden History of Korean War." NEW STATS NAT, 1950 44 July
12, 1950:41-42.

Two well-known historians reject author I.F. Stone's
arguments in his book THE HIDDEN HISTORY OF THE KOREAN WAR.
They offer information which counters Stone's claims that:
South Korea started the war, that Truman deliberately
refrained from concluding peace and that the US cannot afford
peace. Stone offers a counter-rebuttal.

456. Shepherd, Lemuel C. "As the President May Direct." US NAVAL
INST PROC, 1951 77 (11):1149-1155.

The title comes from congressional legislation which
provides for a small military force responsive directly to
the President of the US--that force is the Marines. That
authority has been used frequently by Chief Executives and
such was the case in the summer and fall of 1950 when the
Marines were commited to Korea. Tells of the 1950 expansion,
commitment to battle and accomplishments of Marine Units.

457. Smith, Beverly. "Why We Went To War in Korea." SAT EVE POST, 1951 224 (18):22-23, 76-88.

     An excellent account of the decision making process as it unfolded in Washington the last week in June. Follows the President, Secretaries of State and Defense, key White House aides and the Joint Chiefs of Staff. The author interviewed many of the participants and had the opportunity to peruse numerous White House documents. Amazingly accurate considering it was written so soon after the events reported.

458. Snyder, Richard C., and Glenn D. Paige. "The United States Decision to Resist Aggression in Korea: The Application of an Analytical Scheme." ADMIN SCI Q, 1958 3 (3):341-378.

     The Truman Administration's decision to intervene in Korea is studied as a decision-making process. Concludes the decision was made because: (1) direct intervention was commensurate with the basic values threatened; (2) the objective could probably be achieved by limited military commitment; (3) the risks and costs were acceptable; (4) and the military means were immediately available.

459. Stevenson, Adlai E. "Korea in Perspective." FOR AFF, 1952 30 (3):349-350.

     US Senator and 1952 Democratic Presidential candidate puts the decision to intervene in historical perspective and concludes that it marked a major step in establishing a viable system of collective security by supporting the UN.

460. Tillema, Herbert K. APPEAL TO FORCE: AMERICAN MILITARY INTERVENTION IN THE ERA OF CONTAINMENT. New York: Crowell, 1973.

     Studies the concept of military intervention and focuses on four instances of armed US intervention since WWII. Of the four case studies, Korea is one. Looks at such matters as restraints on intervention and justifications for doing so. Bibliography cites twenty works on the Korean conflict.

461. US Department of State. FOREIGN RELATIONS OF THE UNITED STATES, 1950. Vol. VII: KOREA. Washington: Government Printing Office, 1976.

     US diplomatic and military documents dealing with the outbreak of the war, the decision to intervene, North Korean offensive, UN offensive and Chinese intervention. Contains information on the behind the scenes thinking and decisions of the President, Security Council, State and Defense Departments. Absolutely essential to the serious student of the war.

462. US Department of State. UNITED STATES POLICY IN THE KOREAN
        CRISIS. Washington: Department of State, 1950.

        Reviews the diplomatic position of the US during the first
        six days of the Korean War (June 25-July 1, 1950).

463. Warner, Albert L. "How the Korean Decision Was Made."
        HARPER'S, 1951 202 (1213):99-106.

        Traces events in Washington from June 24 when news of the
        North Korean attack was first received until June 30 when the
        orders to commit ground troops went out. Looks at the key
        decision makers, the important meetings and the evolution of
        the decision to intervene. Some major factual errors,
        which are to be expected in an article written so close to the
        events.

V. US-UN WARTIME POLICY AND DECISION-MAKING
    A. US MILITARY AND CIVILIAN LEADERS

464. Alberts, Robert C. "Profile of a Soldier: Matthew B.
      Ridgway." AM HERT, 1976 27 (2):4-7, 73-82.

      Traces the military career of the US General who was
      selected by President Truman to replace General MacArthur
      as UN Commander in Korea in April 1951. In 1952 he assumed
      command of NATO forces, and the following year became Army
      Chief of Staff. Includes information based on interviews.

465. Alexander, Jack. "Stormy New Boss of the Pentagon." SAT
      EVE POST, 1949 222 (5):26-27, 67-70.

      Feature story on Secretary of Defense Louis A. Johnson who
      Truman brought into office to make military unification a
      reality. The new Secretary, who had served as Assistant
      Secretary of War prior to WWII, was an aggressive politico
      who had created controversy wherever he went. Johnson, who
      was still in office when war came to Korea, made many enemies
      in the Pentagon, especially the Navy, during his first few
      months in office.

466. Bell, James A. "Defense Secretary Louis Johnson."
      AM MERCURY, 1950 70 (318):643-653.

      A journalistic account of the man who was Truman's
      controversial Secretary of Defense at the beginning of the
      Korean War. Traces briefly his career before becoming
      Secretary in 1949 and looks at the numerous controversies,
      especially those surrounding military unification, that he
      was involved in during the fifteen months before war came in
      Korea. Several months after this article was written, Truman
      fired Johnson.

467. Bess, Demaree. "Are Generals in Politics a Menace?"
      SAT EVE POST, 1952 224 (43):28-29, 135-137.

      Lauds the leadership abilities of the four surviving
      US Generals of the Army during the Korean War. Looks at
      MacArthur's service as Far East and UN Commander, Bradley's
      performance as Chairman of the Joint Chief's of Staff,
      Marshall's service as Secretary of Defense and Eisenhower's
      contributions to NATO.

468. Blumenson, Martin. MARK CLARK: THE LAST OF THE GREAT
      WORLD WAR II COMMANDERS. New York: Congdon, 1984.

      Scholarly study which looks at General Clark's long
      military career, including his service as UN Commander in
      Korea from 1952 to the end of the war, but focusing on his
      WWII service. Very laudatory of Clark as a military leader.

469. Bradley, Omar N. "The Path Ahead." ARMY INFO DIG,
      1950 5 (10):24-26.

      The Chairman of the Joint Chiefs of Staff tells why the
      US intervened in Korea and indicates the nation faces three
      immediate requirements: get more men and equipment to Korea;
      replace units sent there to restore the nation's defense
      capabilities; and the need for greater flexibility of
      military power.

470. Bradley, Omar N. "US Military Policy: 1950." COM FOR J,
      1950 1 (2):5-11.

      Puts forth the Chairman of the Joint Chiefs of Staff's
      analysis of the nation's military policy in the aftermath of
      the US entry into the Korean conflict. Notes the policy has
      shifted from containment to contesting communism, and the
      nation will resist the enemy at any cost. Stresses the
      importance of protecting Western Europe. Discusses the roles
      of the various services and examines the importance of
      certain weapons. Same article appeared in October 1950
      READER'S DIGEST.

471. Bradley, Omar N., and Clay Blair. A GENERAL'S LIFE: AN
      AUTOBIOGRAPHY BY GENERAL OF THE ARMY OMAR N. BRADLEY. New
      York: Simon, 1983.

      A candid memoir by one of America's most famous soldiers who
      served as Chairman of the Joint Chiefs of Staff during the
      Korean War. Good inside account of key military-political
      decisions. Excellent sketches of leading American and
      political figures; very critical of General MacArthur and
      Secretary of Defense Louis Johnson.

472. Bundy, McGeorge, ed. THE PATTERN OF RESPONSIBILITY.
      Boston: Houghton, 1952.

      A look at the public record of Secretary of State Dean
      Acheson from January 1949 to August 1951. Relies on
      quotations from public statements. The statements are linked
      in meaningful fashion by the editor. One chapter is devoted
      to Korea before the war and another looks at the period
      from aggression through the MacArthur dismissal and debate.

473. Clark, Mark W. FROM THE DANUBE TO THE YALU. New York:
      Harper, 1954.

The commander of the UN forces in Korea in the fifteen
months prior to the truce gives his assessment of the war,
the way it was conducted and the armistice agreement.
Maintains the US could have won the war militarily but lacked
the determination to do so. Recommendations of what the US
should do militarily to meet the Communist challenge.

474. Clark, Mark W. "The Truth About Korea." COLLIER'S, 1954
     133 (3):34-39; 133 (4):88-93; 133 (5):44-49.

     The US General who became Supreme Commander of UN Forces in
     Korea in May 1952 and held the post to the armistice gives
     his inside account of his activities. Tells of the
     frustrations of conducting a limited war. Addresses such
     things as the Koje uprisings, problems of negotiating with
     the enemy, problems created by President Rhee and limitations
     placed on air power. Overall is critical of US failure to
     pursue the war vigorously.

475. Clark, Mark W. "What Kind of Air Support Does the Army
     Want? An Interview with General Mark W. Clark." AIR FORCE,
     1950 33 (12):24-25, 52.

     The chief of the Army Field Forces in Korea discusses the
     need for, importance of and value of close air support for
     Army combat units. Reflections on the importance of such
     activity during the first five months of the war.

476. Coffin, Tris. "Stuart Symington: Our No. 2 President."
     CORONET, 1950 29 (2):130-135.

     Brief account of Symington's role as Chief of Defense
     Mobilization and Chairman of the National Security Resources
     Board in the early months of the Korean War. Reviews his
     current activities and modes of operation and recounts his
     career prior to that time, including Secretary of Air Force
     until shortly before the conflict in Korea began.

477. Coffin, Tris. "Vandenberg Runs Our Air Force Team."
     CORONET, 1951 30 (3):96-101.

     Sketch of the US Air Force Chief of Staff during the Korean
     War, General Hoyt S. Vandenberg. Assesses the General's mode
     of operation in the Pentagon. Describes his workday and
     examines his standing among his staff people. Covers his
     career from West Point through his combat missions over
     Europe in WWII and his appointment as Chief of Staff.

478. Collins, J. Lawton. LIGHTNING JOE: AN AUTOBIOGRAPHY.
     Baton Rouge: Louisiana State University, 1979.

     Focuses on the US Army General's WWII experiences but
     has a chapter on his service as Chief of Staff, 1949-1953.
     Section on Korea is a greatly condensed version of his
     1969 book, WAR IN PEACETIME.

479. Collins, Joseph Lawton. WAR IN PEACETIME: THE HISTORY
          AND LESSONS OF KOREA. Boston: Houghton, 1969.

      General Collins, who was the US Army Chief of Staff and then
      a member of the Joint Chiefs of Staff throughout the Korean
      War, gives an excellent inside account of the conflict from
      a military viewpoint. Good insights into decision-making
      processes and good analysis of US actions.

480. Davis, Burke. MARINE! THE LIFE OF LT. GEN. LEWIS B.
          (CHESTY) PULLER, USMC (RET.). Boston: Little, 1962.

      A biography of a career marine officer whose career
      culminated with his command of the US 1st Marines from
      September 1950 through May 1951. A good look at command
      problems as experienced at the Division level. Considerable
      attention is given to the Korean War.

481. Denson, John. "Ridgway, Will He Succeed Ike?" COLLIER'S,
          1952 129 (10):11, 66-69.

      Somewhat misleading title since the article looks at the
      question of whether General Ridgway is qualified to replace
      Eisenhower as Commander, SHAPE. Article really examines the
      General's performance as MacArthur's successor as Supreme
      Commander, Allied Powers and Commander in Chief, UN Command
      in Korea. Concludes he did a masterful job in Korea and tells
      why. Very favorable assessment.

482. Finletter, Thomas K. POWER AND POLICY. New York: Harcourt,
          1954.

      Although this authoritative analysis of US foreign and
      military policy was written by the wartime US Secretary of
      the Air Force after he left office in 1952, his thinking on
      the problems facing decision makers in the age of atomic
      weapons gives insight into his attitudes during the Korean
      War.

483. Graebner, Norman A. "Dean G. Acheson" in Norman A. Graebner,
          ed. AN UNCERTAIN TRADITION: AMERICAN SECRETARIES OF STATE
          IN THE TWENTIETH CENTURY. New York: McGraw, 1961, pp. 267-
          288.

      Good overview of Acheson's service as US Secretary of State
      from 1949-1953. Limited coverage of Korea but does put it
      into the broad context of US foreign policy during that period.
      No footnotes but brief bibliographical essay.

484. Hetzel, Frederick A., and Harold L. Hitchens. "An Interview
          With General Matthew B. Ridgway." WEST PENN HIS MAG, 1982
          65 (4):279-307.

      Recollections of a long and distinguished military career.
      Ridgway concentrates on the problems and frustrations of
      commanding the US Eighth Army in Korea in 1950-1951.

485. Hines, William. "Admiral Sherman: Chief of Naval Operations."
        AM MERCURY, 1950 71 (323):515-523.

        Brief look at the career, personality and mode of operation
        of the US Navy's Chief of Operations during the first year of
        the Korean War.

486. Hines, William. "General Collins: Army Chief of Staff."
        AM MERCURY, 1950 71 (321):266-273.

        Sketch of the US Army Chief of Staff during the Korean War.
        Traces his career and looks at his personal and professional
        characteristics.

487. Jurika, Stephen, Jr., ed. FROM PEARL HARBOR TO VIETNAM:
        THE MEMOIRS OF ADMIRAL ARTHUR W. RADFORD. Stanford, CA:
        Hoover Institution, 1980.

        Memoirs of the crucial years of the US Navy Admiral who is
        best known for his service as Chairman of the JCS but was
        Commander-in-Chief Pacific Fleet during the Korean War.
        Devotes several chapters to the war, including the outbreak,
        original commitments, Wake Island meeting, MacArthur
        dismissal and period of stalemate. Critical of the
        administration's conduct of the war.

488. Kennan, George F. MEMOIRS, 1925-1950. Boston: Little, 1967.

        The top US expert on Soviet affairs in the 20th century and
        author of the Containment Policy recounts his years in the US
        Foreign Service. Good account of the key decisions made on
        Korea, including intervention and crossing the 38th Parallel
        in the summer of 1950, just before he left the State
        Department. Shows how one of the top foreign policy minds
        viewed the North Korean attack.

489. McLellan, David S. "Dean Acheson and the Korean War."
        POL SCI Q, 1968 83 (1):16-39.

        A critical account of Acheson's role in the Korean War by
        one of the top Acheson scholars. The author criticizes the
        Secretary of State for miscalculating Chinese intentions,
        failing to provide the President with a realistic assessment
        of the situation and failing to push for the ouster of
        MacArthur early on.

490. McLellan, David S. DEAN ACHESON: THE STATE DEPARTMENT YEARS.
        New York: Dodd, 1976.

        Well-researched and -written study of Acheson's service as
        Secretary of State from 1949-1953. Excellent on Far Eastern
        policy prior to Korea, the decision to intervene, conducting
        the war and relief of MacArthur. Good on background and
        analysis and is quite objective.

491. Martin, Harold H. "Lightning Joe, The GI's General."
      SAT EVE POST, 1951 223 (31):20-21, 121, 123-127.

      An inside look at US Army Chief of Staff during the Korean
      War, General Joe Collins. Describes his life at the Pentagon
      during the period and shows his mode of operation. Includes
      a brief sketch of his life, including his noted WWII career
      as a tank commander.

492. Mosley, Leonard. MARSHALL: HERO FOR OUR TIMES. New York:
      Hearst, 1982.

      Laudatory biography of George C. Marshall's long and
      distinguished career includes four chapters on his service as
      Secretary of Defense from the fall of 1950 until the fall of
      1951. Written for a popular audience; no footnotes. Will be
      useful until the third volume of Forrest Pogue's work on
      Marshall appears.

493. "The New Chief of Staff." COM FOR J, 1953 4 (21):8-9.

      Brief account of the career of General Matthew B. Ridgway
      with emphasis on his command of the US Eighth Army in Korea.

494. Ridgway, Matthew B. THE KOREAN WAR. New York: Doubleday,
      1967.

      Memoirs of the war by the US General who assumed command of
      the US Eighth Army in Korea in late 1950. Taking a dis-
      pirited, ill-equipped Army that was merely holding on, he
      instilled a confidence and developed an esprit that few
      Americans on the scene and at home thought possible.
      Excellent analysis of key US military figures; he gives
      credit where it is due and criticizes where he feels it is
      justified.

495. Ridgway, Matthew B. "My Battles in War and Peace: The
      Korean War." SAT EVE POST, 1956 228 (35):36, 127-130.

      Ridgway's account of his command of the US Eighth Army in
      Korea. Tells of the Communist onslaught when he assumed
      command in December 1950 and how the situation was stabilized.
      Tells of working with President Rhee.

496. Ridgway, Matthew B. SOLDIER: THE MEMOIRS OF MATTHEW B.
      RIDGWAY, as told to Harold H. Martin. New York: Harper,
      1956.

      The General who succeeded General Walker in 1950 and
      General MacArthur in April 1951 and remained Commander of the
      Eighth Army and UN Command until April 1952 recalls primarily
      his WWII experiences but does devote one chapter to his years
      in Korea. Ridgway's in depth account of Korea can be found
      in his later book, THE KOREAN WAR.

497.   Roosevelt, Kermit. "The Army's Bright Young Boss." SAT
         EVE POST, 1950 223 (18):27, 154.

         Looks at the career and thinking of the Secretary of the
         Army when war broke out in Korea, Frank Pace, Jr. The man
         from Arkansas was just 38 years old when he assumed his
         position less than four months before war came. Pictures
         Pace as an able administrator, loyal to the President.
         Covers Pace's activities in the days following the North
         Korean attack.

498.   Schnabel, James F. "Ridgway in Korea." MIL R, 1964 44
         (3):3-13.

         An examination of General Matthew Ridgway's command of the
         8th Army in Korea in 1950-51 and as UN and Far East Commander
         in 1951-52. Very favorable to Ridgway, especially of his
         ability to maintain morale of US troops in the trying period
         after Chinese intervention.

499.   Schoenebaum, Eleanora, ed. POLITICAL PROFILES: THE TRUMAN
         YEARS. New York: Facts on File, 1978.

         Contains brief biographies of 435 key figures in the Truman
         Administration and in key federal agencies during his years
         in office. Includes some analysis and assessment of their
         contributions along with suggestions for further reading.
         Most of the key administrative officials including those in
         the State and Defense Departments are included.

500.   Shisler, Michael F. "General Oliver P. Smith's Life Was a
         Commitment to Excellence." MARINE CORPS GAZ, 1978 62
         (11):42-48.

         A recap of the thirty-four year military career of Smith
         whose service culminated with his command of the 1st Marine
         Division in the Inchon Invasion and the Chosin Reservoir
         operation.

501.   Smith, Gaddis. DEAN ACHESON. New York: Cooper, 1972.

         A scholarly examination of US Foreign policy from 1945-1953
         but especially adroit examination of Acheson's years as
         Secretary of State (1949-1953). Favorable assessment of the
         Secretary and his handling of the Korean crisis from the time
         of attack through the armistice negotiations that were still
         going on when he left office.

502.   "A Soldier's Soldier." ARMY INFO DIG, 1953 8 (9):2-4.

         Brief sketch of the US Army Chief of Staff during the
         Korean War, General J. Lawton ("Lightning Joe") Collins.

503. Taylor, Maxwell D. SWORDS AND PLOWSHARES. New York: Norton,
      1972.

      Memoirs of a US General who is best known for his service
      as Army Chief of Staff (Eisenhower) and Chairman, Joint
      Chiefs of Staff (Kennedy), but who was also commander of the
      Eighth Army in Korea during the latter stages of the war.
      Tells of his Korea experience and reveals that atomic weapons
      were not used because of the limited number available.

504. Taylor, Maxwell D. THE UNCERTAIN TRUMPET. New York: Harper,
      1959.

      The former US Army Chief of Staff and Commander of the
      Eighth Army is critical of the US's conduct of the Korean War
      in this appeal for a move away from massive retaliation and
      toward a flexible response.

505. US Senate, Committee on Foreign Relations, Historical Series.
      REVIEWS OF THE WORLD SITUATION: 1949-1950: HEARINGS HELD
      IN EXECUTIVE SESSION, EIGHTY-FIRST CONGRESS. Washington:
      Government Printing Office, 1974.

      These secret sessions between Secretary of State Acheson
      and other top State Department officials immediately before
      the Korean War and in the six months after intervention give
      good inside information as to how the administration
      perceived the war in Korea.

506. Van Fleet, James. "Catastrophe in Asia." US NEWS W R, 1954
      37 (Sept. 17):24-28.

      The former commander of the US Eighth Army in Korea wrote
      this article shortly after his retirement in 1953 but did not
      release it until a year later. It is critical of the
      restraints put upon the military by the political decisions
      of US-UN leaders. Feels the war could have been won if
      shackles had been taken off the military. Urges that such
      restrictions not be put on US troops in future wars.

507. "Who's Who in Defense." ARMY INFO DIG, 1951 6 (5):23-33.

      Organization charts along with photographs and names of the
      leaders in the US defense structure in mid-1951. Includes the
      Office of the Secretary of Defense, Joint Chiefs of Staff and
      Departments of Army, Navy and Air Force.

                              B.   INTELLIGENCE

508. Arnold, Joseph C. "Omens and Oracles." US NAVAL INST PROC,
      1980 106 (8):47-53.

      Examines the collection, use and misuse of intelligence
      information by US authorities on three occasions, including

the Chinese entry into the Korean War in the fall of 1950.
Critical of US intelligence failure.

509. Ashman, Harold L. "Intelligence and Foreign Policy: A
      Functional Analysis." Doctoral Dissertation. Utah, 1973.

      Studies the nature and functions of intelligence and makes
      a case study of three instances where the system broke down.
      The US intelligence failure at the start of the Korean War is
      examined. Shows importance of intelligence in
      decision making and the unfortunate consequences when it is
      inaccurate.

510. Ben-Zvi, Abraham. "Hindsight and Foresight: A Conceptual
      Framework for the Analysis of Surprise Attacks." WORLD
      POL, 1976 28 (3):381-395.

      Puts forth the thesis that when policy makers face
      conflicting intelligence they tend to make certain
      assumptions rather than make a reassessment of the situation.
      Examines the breakdown of intelligence that led to the
      surprise Chinese intervention in the Korean War.

511. Brecher, Michael. "State Behavior in International Crisis:
      A Model." J CON RESO, 1979 23 (3):446-480.

      Studies of the start of WWII, the Korean War and Cuban
      missile crisis are used to develop twenty-three hypotheses
      to develop common attributes of information processing,
      consultation, decisional forums and the consideration
      of alternatives in meeting international crises.

512. Danford, Robert W. "Cameras on the Battlefield." ARMY INFO
      DIG, 1954 9 (7):49-55.

      Focuses on use of Army photography for tactical use (most
      attention has been given to Air Force work in this area).
      Observation aircraft were frequently used, but the
      development of panoramic strips by ground cameras was a new
      and useful development that came out of the Korean War.

513. DeWeerd, Harvey A. "Strategic Surprise in the Korean War."
      ORBIS, 1962 6 (3):435-452.

      Critical account of US handling of intelligence from Korea
      just prior to the outbreak of war in 1950. Contends that
      while the intelligence gathering and evaluation appeared to
      be sound, it failed to foresee an attack which it should have
      detected. Cites the information which he feels should not
      have been overlooked.

514. Fleming, Kenneth. "Hell Run Over Korea." LEATHERNECK, 1950
      33 (10):18-20.

      US Marine carrier-based photographers provided photos of

the Pusan perimeter and thereby aided in its defense.
Details the hazards of securing such pictures.

515. FOURTH AERIAL PHOTO INTERPRETATION COMPANY: ITS HISTORY AND
      MEN, KOREA, 1951-53. N.p., 1953.

      Short narrative along with numerous photographs of the
      unit's activities in Korea. Privately printed, yearbook
      format.

516. Haight, Frederick. "Mister Pak Takes Over." READ DIG,
      1953 62 (371):63-66.

      Examines the contributions of a Korean interpreter who knew
      a number of Chinese dialects and thus aided the 31st US
      Infantry Regiment by gathering valuable intelligence
      information from Chinese POW's. Condensed from KIWANIS
      MAGAZINE, March 1953.

517. Huie, William B. "Untold Facts in the Korean Disaster." NEW
      AM MERCURY, 1951 72 (326):131-140.

      Indictment of US intelligence as displayed in its
      ineptitude in Asia in 1950. Says that administration
      officials were unaware of the moves of Chinese troops or when
      they did have information did nothing about it. Lists a
      dozen actions by the Russians and or Chinese communist where
      American intelligence faltered.

518. Infield, Glenn B. UNARMED AND UNAFRAID. New York: Macmillan,
      1970.

      Looks at the use of air reconnaissance for intelligence
      gathering by the US military from Civil War times through
      Vietnam. One chapter is devoted entirely to the Korean
      experience. Title comes from the fact that the missions are
      flown from unarmed aircraft, with no air cover provided.

519. "Jet F95 Photo Unit Maps North Korea." NAV AVI N, 1951
      September:31.

      Describes how Detachmen Easy utilized three F95-2P aircraft
      for missions over North Korea to produce intelligence photos.
      The unit flew 160 sorties from the aircraft carrier PRINCETON
      during a six-month period in 1951 and took 14,000
      photographs.

520. Karig, Walter, et al. "The Man Who Made Inchon Possible"
      in Donald Robinson, ed. THE DIRTY WARS. New York:
      Delacorte, 1968.

      Account of US Navy Lieutenant Eugene F. Clark, an American
      guerrilla, who worked his way into Inchon two weeks prior to
      the invasion and provided valuable intelligence information
      to the UN Command.

521. Kolbenschlag, Richard P. "The United States Air Force Tactical Reconnaissance in the Korean Conflict." Master's Thesis. Pennsylvania State, 1963.

    Describes the use of US air reconnaissance of US armed forces to gather intelligence.

522. Norman, Lloyd. "Washington's War." ARMY, 1960 10 June:38-49.

    The US was ill-prepared for war in Korea in 1950 because of various factors including: defense economy moves, over-confidence in the role of A-bombs and conclusion of the JCS that strategically Korea was not important. Communist attack was a surprise because of failure of US intelligence. Covers the invasion and US decision to intervene. Claims the lessons of unpreparedness must be learned.

523. Park, Sun B. "Operation Dragonfly." USA AVI DIG, 1981 27 (6):7-9.

    The first use of air reconnaissance for ground troops in Korea was performed in July 1950 by the US 24th Infantry Division Aviation Section. The missions flown in that month were called Operation Dragonfly. Tells of the aircraft used and the missions performed until the US Air Force organized the Mosquito unit on August 1, 1950.

524. "Photographic Reconnaissance in Korea." AIR UNIV Q R, 1952 5 (2):54-64.

    An overview of the process of air reconnaissance by the US Air Force in Korea. Shows how the photos are taken and processed and then how the photo interpreters generate information used by the planners of bombing missions. Just as important was assessment of damage done by raids. Uses photos to demonstrate how the information is gained and utilized.

525. Politella, Dario. OPERATION GRASSHOPPER. Wichita, KS: Longo, 1958.

    Army aviation activities are covered in this volume which focuses on reconnaissance operations. Foreword is written by General Mark Clark.

526. Poteat, George H. "Strategic Intelligence and National Security: A Case Study of the Korean Crisis (June 25-November 24, 1950)." Doctoral Dissertation. Washington, 1973.

    Strategic surpise is the focus of this study on the Chinese entrance into the Korean War. The author reconstructs the intelligence available to Washington policy makers and

concludes they should have expected intervention, but their
decisions were based on pre-conceived notions which colored
their vision.

527. Pratt, James M. "Regimental S2, Korea." INF SCH Q,
      1952 40 (2):67-72.

      Explains the responsibilities of the intelligence officer
      serving in Korea. Tells how to interrogate POW's and how to
      utilize patrols.

528. Strobridge, William F. "Squad Reconnaissance Patrol, Korea."
      INF SCH Q, 1952 40 (2):88-94.

      Account of a night reconnaissance patrol by a squad from the
      7th Regiment, 3rd Division in the vicinity of Chon'Gong'Ni.

529. Vale, Charles F. "Combat Through the Camera's Eye."
      ARMY INFO DIG, 1953 8 (3):54-59.

      Shows how the US Army successfully utilized tactical
      photography in Korea. Signal Corps cameramen would make
      panoramic views of entire fronts facing infantry units and
      intelligence officers would secure valuable information
      concerning enemy positions. That data was then utilized in
      planning operations. Tells of problems of taking and
      processing the photos.

                    C. MILITARY DECISIONS

530. Bernstein, Barton J. "New Light on the Korean War." INTER
      HIST R, 1981 3 April:256-277.

      The well-known revisionist historian reveals new
      information, from recently declassified documents, about the
      Korean War. Among his revelations are: that serious talks
      took place early in the war about bombing Manchuria and using
      the atomic bomb; some advisers felt it would be a good time
      for war with Russia; MacArthur reported use of Chinese
      communist troops as early as July 1950; Truman's dislike of
      MacArthur preceded the war; villages suspected of harboring
      the enemy were destroyed; Eisenhower considered the use of
      tactical atomic weapons; and Eisenhower considered abandoning
      or overthrowing South Korean President Rhee.

531. Bernstein, Barton J. "The Policy of Risk: Crossing the
      38th Parallel and Marching to the Yalu." FOR SER J, 1977
      54 (3):16-22, 29.

      A narrative on the US decision to cross into North Korea to
      pursue the enemy. Contends it was clearly a political
      decision and examines the interplay between President Truman,
      Secretary Acheson and General MacArthur in the decision.

532. Betts, Richard K. SOLDIERS, STATESMEN, AND COLD WAR CRISES.
     Cambridge: Harvard University, 1977.

     This examination and analysis of military advice and
     influence on civilian policy makers and the use of military
     force looks at the impact of the Joint Chiefs of Staff on
     Truman's decision to intervene in Korea. Also looks at their
     position on the use of nuclear weapons and the MacArthur
     controversy.

533. Brodie, Bernard. STRATEGY IN THE MISSILE AGE. Princeton,
     NJ: Princeton University, 1959.

     This classic study gives considerable attention to the
     impact of the Korean War on American strategic concepts.
     Deals with the frustrations of pursuing a limited war and
     examines the US's non-use of nuclear weapons.

534. Carpenter, William M. THE KOREAN WAR: A STRATEGIC
     PERSPECTIVE THIRTY YEARS LATER. New York: Crane, 1980.

     A comparative study of the military strategies employed by
     the US-UN and communist camps in the conflict.

535. CIA RESEARCH REPORTS: JAPAN, KOREA, AND THE SECURITY OF
     ASIA. Frederick, MD: University Publications, n.d.

     This microfilm collection of hundreds of reports, which
     cover the years from 1946 through the early 1970's, includes
     many studies on situations in Korea before, during and after
     the war. Topics covered include strategic importance of
     Korea to US, likelihood of Chinese intervention into the
     Korean War, possible Soviet intervention and Chinese military
     capabilities.

536. Doty, Mercer M. "The Decision to Cross the 38th Parallel
     in Korea During the United Nations Counteroffensive
     in the Fall of 1950." Master's Thesis. Pittsburgh, 1963.

     Examines the political and military considerations of the
     President, State and Defense Departments in making the
     decision to carry the war into the North.

537. Hammond, Paul Y. ORGANIZING FOR DEFENSE: THE AMERICAN
     MILITARY ESTABLISHMENT. Princeton, NJ: Princeton
     University, 1961.

     This study of the impact of public attitudes and political
     realities on the policies and operations of the US armed
     services includes a look at the post-WWII period as well as
     the Korean War era. Contends the war went a long way to
     providing true unification of the Armed Forces.

538. Hartmann, Frederick H. "The Issues in Korea." YALE R,
     1952 42 (1):54-66.

Supports the US decision to intervene then explores three
policy alternatives: (1) withdraw from the conflict; (2)
engage in an all-out war with Red China; (3) and negotiate a
compromise settlement. Rejects the first two and says
pursuing the third alternative will be very difficult because
the conflict is at a stalemate.

539. Heichal, Gabriella T. "Decision Making During Crisis: The
      Korean War and the Yom Kippur War." Doctoral Dissertation.
      George Washington, 1984.

Maintains that there is not generally a surpise development
in wartime action that calls for a major decision but rather
there is a problem with the flow of information. In
examining the Chinese Communist entry into the Korean War,
the author concludes the failure of the US to foresee entry
was due to a mishandling of intelligence information.

540. Hoyt, Edwin C. "The United States Reaction to the Korean
      Attack: A Study in the Principles of The United Nations
      Charter as a Factor in American Policy Making." AM J
      INTER LAW, 1961 55 (1):45-76.

A legalistic study of the Truman Administration's decision
to enter the conflict in Korea through the UN. Examines the
UN charter and shows how the US was able to use it to advance
the foreign policy of containment.

541. Huntington, Samuel P. THE COMMON DEFENSE: STRATEGIC
      PROGRAMS IN NATIONAL POLITICS. New York: Columbia
      University, 1961.

An examination of American military policy, specifically
strategic programs, from 1945 to 1960. Looks at the patterns
of politics and decision making as they affected the change
from a strategy of mobilization to one of deterrence. Tells
how the Korean War forced the nation to follow a policy of
military mobilization, especially after Red China entered the
war, and still provide the build up of forces to keep Russia
from expanding elsewhere.

542. Kissinger, Henry A. NUCLEAR WEAPONS AND FOREIGN POLICY.
      New York: Harper, 1957.

This classic study on the impact of nuclear weapons gives
considerable attention to the Korean War because it sets
forth so vividly the problems of nuclear war. According to
the author the war did not fit into American strategic
thought; thus, there was much confusion and conflict between
the commanders in the field and political officials in
Washington.

543. Krasner, Michael A. "Foreign Policy Stereotypes: The
      Decision to Cross the 38th Parallel." Mil R, 1972 52 (10):
      17-26.

Claims that Truman's decision to cross the 38th Parallel was mistakenly made on the assumption that the Chinese people shared a faith in democratic idealogy and were historically tied with the US and therefore would never enter the war against the UN forces.

544. LaFeber, Walter. "Crossing the 38th: The Cold War in Microcosm" in Lynn H. Miller and Ronald W. Pruessen REFLECTIONS ON THE COLD WAR. Philadelphia: Temple University, 1974, pp. 71-90.

In-depth study of the Truman decision of September 1950 to cross the 38th Parallel. The author, a first-rate diplomatic historian, sees the decision as a militarily costly one which marked a major turning point in the Cold War since the US decided not merely to contain but hurl back communist aggression.

545. Lapp, Ralph E. "Would the Atomic Bomb End the War in Korea?" REPORTER, 1953 8 (1):31-33.

Rejects the idea that the use of A-bombs would bring an end to the war in Korea. Discusses the problems of their use and notes that the circumstances under which they were used in WWII were quite different. Warns that their use could lead to all-out world war.

546. Lichterman, Martin. "To the Yalu and Back" in Harold Stein, ed. AMERICAN CIVIL-MILITARY DECISIONS: A BOOK OF CASE STUDIES. Birmingham, AL: University of Alabama Press, 1963, pp. 569-639.

In-depth study of the decision-making policy of US civil and military authorities in arriving at limits placed on the advance of land forces in the fall and early winter of 1950-51. Limited consideration of restrictions on air and naval operations. Shows how political, economic and military considerations impacted decisions.

547. Lo, Clarence Y.H. "Civilian Policy Makers and Military Objectives: A Case Study of the US Offensive to Win the Korean War." J POL MIL SOC, 1979 7 (2):229-242.

Rejects the standard explanation that places responsibility for the UN-US advance to the Yalu River in 1950 on General MacArthur and claims that the policy was supported and approved by top civilian policy makers in the Truman Administration. Thus, the civilian policy makers while claiming to be advocates of limited war actually supported "absolutist" policies such as those favored by MacArthur.

548. Lyons, Gene M. MILITARY POLICY AND ECONOMIC AID: THE KOREAN CASE, 1950-1953. Columbus: Ohio State University, 1961.

During the Korean War there was continual conflict between the UN's reconstruction policy and US military policy. This study probes that controversy and then criticizes the policy makers in Washington for pursuing only a military victory and failing to have a reconstruction policy.

549. Marshall, Thomas L. "The Strategy of Conflict in the Korean War." Doctoral Dissertation. Virginia, 1969.

Case study in limited warfare focuses on the conduct of the war and its outcome. Looks at preparedness of the US and Red China to fight a limited war, the self-imposed limitations and reasons for them. Attention is also given to bargaining over the outcome of the war which saw inspection procedures and a post-war conference disposed of before the final issue--repatriation of POW's.

550. Matray, James I. "Truman's Plan for Victory: National Self-Determination and the Thirty-Eighth Parallel Decision in Korea." J AM HIST, 1979 66 (2):314-333.

President Truman's decision to send UN troops across the 38th Parallel was motivated by his conviction the conflict was part of the world-wide Soviet-US conflict and thus offered a great opportunity to halt Soviet expansion. Also maintains the President was desirous of assuring that all Koreans would have an opportunity for self-determination and they would choose Democracy thereby inflicting a major setback on the Russians.

551. Miller, George H. "Shall We Blow Them Up?" US NAVAL INST PROC, 1953 79(2):151-155.

Asks whether the US should try and administer a "knock out" blow in the Korean War and if so should it be aimed at North Korea, Communist China or Russia. Says we cannot do it because we do not know when to hit or if we did, it would widen the war more than desired. Claims the people in US are too impatient and the nation must develop patience and be willing to negotiate while fighting.

552. Ohm, Chang-Il. "The Joint Chiefs of Staff and US Policy and Strategy Regarding Korea, 1945-1953." Doctoral Dissertation. Kansas, 1983.

In the post-WWII era the JCS did not see Korea as being of strategic importance to the US; however, the political decision to intervene put them in a position of supporting the war. That fact made them willing to accept limited war and stalemate as legitimate war objectives.

553. Ragle, George L. "Dragonflies Over Korea." COM FOR J, 1950 1 (4):32-33.

Describes the contributions of L-5's, L-4's and L-17's,
light liaison aircraft in Korea. Cavalry and Infantry
divisions used the light aircraft for reconnaissance,
directing artillery fire and air drops to isolated units.

554.   RECORDS OF THE JOINT CHIEFS OF STAFF, PART 2: 1946-53:
       THE FAR EAST. Frederick, MD: University Publications, 1980.

Microfilm--14 reels. Thousands of pages of unpublished
documents used by the JCS in policy decision-making.
Considerable attention given to Korea in such reports as
Military Importance of Korea (1947), Implications of a Full
Scale Invasion From North Korea 1950, Chinese Communist
Intervention (1950), Possible Employment of Atomic Bombs in
Korea (1950) and dozens more. Extremely valuable in studying
US military policy.

555.   RECORDS OF THE JOINT CHIEFS OF STAFF, PART 2: 1946-53:
       MEETINGS OF THE JCS. Frederick, MD: University
       Publications, 1980.

Microfilm--8 reels. Minutes of the meetings contain the
discussions, decisions and supporting documents of the JCS
prior to and during the Korean War. Essential for those
doing in-depth research on military aspects of the conflict.
Contains many items not declassified until the late 1970's.

556.   Stratton, Samuel S. "Korea: Acid Test of Containment."
       US NAVAL INST PROC, 1952 78 (3):237-249.

Argues that while the American people shot first then asked
questions as to why the nation was involved in Korea, there
is no question that the reason was to implement the policy of
containment. Traces the development of containment from the
appearance of George Kennan's 1947 article through Truman's
decision to commit troops. Says negotiating peace will be
difficult, and it is too early to tell if containment will
work.

557.   Stueck, William. "The March to the Yalu: The Perspective
       From Washington" in Bruce Cumings, ed. CHILD OF CONFLICT.
       Seattle: University of Washington, 1983, pp. 195-237.

Uses many previously classified US State and Defense
Department documents to study the decision-making
process as applied to: (1) the September 1950 US advance
north of the 38th Parallel to unify Korea; and (2) the
refusal of the US to halt the army's advance toward the Yalu
following the intervention of the Chinese Communist.

558.   Twining, Nathan F. NEITHER LIBERTY NOR SAFETY: A HARD LOOK
       AT US MILITARY POLICY AND STRATEGY. New York: Holt, 1966.

The US Air Force General who served as Chairman of the
Joint Chiefs of Staff in the late 1950's is extremely

critical of US civilian and military policy makers' conduct of
the Korean War. Criticizes the failure to build up
patriotic fervor, the announcement that the atomic bomb would
not be used and restrictions on enemy targets and concludes the
US effort there showed that the nation was really a "Paper
Tiger."

559. US Department of State. UNITED STATES POLICY IN THE KOREAN
      CONFLICT. Washington: Department of State, 1951.

      Official US diplomatic documents that cover the period
      between July 1, 1950, and February 1, 1951.

560. Weigley, Russell F. THE AMERICAN WAY OF WAR: A HISTORY OF
      UNITED STATES MILITARY STRATEGY AND POLICY. New York:
      Macmillan, 1973.

      Traces the evolution of American military strategy. The
      chapter on Korea focuses on General MacArthur and the
      frustrations he encountered in fighting a limited war.
      Also, examines how Secretary of Defense George Marshall used
      the conflict to prepare the nation's defenses for a policy of
      deterrence.

561. Williams, Ralph E., Jr. "The Great Debate: 1954." US
      NAVAL PROC, 1954 80 (3):247-255.

      Says the US must decide in 1954 if it should put all of its
      eggs in the basket of airpower and A-bombs or provide a
      balanced force. Says the nation was basically facing the
      same questions it had in 1951 when it considered carrying the
      war to Red China and using atomic bombs. Concludes that
      strategic airpower is important but so are conventional
      forces.

562. Worden, William. "We Won Back Korea--and We're Stuck
      With It." SAT EVE POST, 1950 223 (21):31, 153.

      Claims that as of early November 1950 the war in Korea is
      all but over and all the US has accomplished is to gain
      control over many filthy villages and responsibility for
      "twenty million miserable human beings." Sees a very dim
      future for South Korea, even with massive US aid.

563. Yahraes, Herbert. "The Mysterious Mission of ORO." SAT
      EVE POST, 1952 224 (34):36-37, 75, 77, 80-82.

      Sets forth the workings of the US Army's Operations
      Research Office (ORO), a think tank established under
      contract with Johns Hopkins University in 1948 and which
      became extremely active during the Korean War. Its studies
      led to such ideas that B-29's were excellent planes for close
      support of ground troops, napalm was the best tank killer and
      psychological warfare should be made a highly personal
      matter.

D. PROBLEMS OF LIMITED WARS

564. Clapp, Archie J. "Their Mission is Mobility." MIL R, 1953
      33 (5):35-40.

      Criticizes the current US policy in Korea which accepts
      stalemate. Maintains that by adding four or five full
      strength divisions the Eighth Army could get mobile and go on
      the offensive. Says the current US policy is man-poor and
      machine-rich and when mobility fails for lack of men, which
      it has, the contest is in favor of the side which values
      human life the least--which is the communist.

565. Deagle, Edwin A., Jr. "The Agony of Restraint: Korea, 1951-
      1953." Doctoral Dissertation. Harvard, 1970.

      This study examines the problems of making key
      civil-military decisions in Korea because of the restraints
      imposed by a limited war. Conducting a limited war was as
      difficult for policy makers as it was frustrating for the
      American public.

566. Guttmann, Allen, ed. KOREA AND THE THEORY OF LIMITED WAR.
      Lexington, MA: Heath, 1967, 1972.

      Examination of the question of whether or not limitations
      should have been put on the military in the Korean War. Uses
      Truman and MacArthur as embodying the divergent views. Uses
      contemporary statements of those two plus other military and
      civilian leaders. Six scholars present essays of their
      views.

567. Halperin, Morton H. "The Limiting Process in the Korean War"
      in Allen Guttmann, KOREA AND THE THEORY OF LIMITED WAR.
      Lexington, MA: Heath, 1967, pp. 92-106.

      Why did both sides impose limitations on themselves in
      Korea? This study examines such issues as why nuclear
      weapons were not used by the US and why did both sides limit
      the targets their warplanes could hit. Legalistic
      limitations are also cited.

568. Hudson, G.W. "The Privileged Sanctuary." TWEN CENT, 1951
      149 (887):4-10.

      Critical of the US and British policy of limited war which
      enables the Chinese Communists to wage war against UN forces
      while retaining complete immunity for its own territory. Sees
      such action as a political defeat for US, Britain and
      majority of UN members.

569. Johnstone, William C. "The United States as a Pacific
      Power." CUR HIST, 1970 58 (344):193-195, 243.

In the first half of the 20th century the US felt it
wielded tremendous power, religious, economic and political
in the Pacific, but the war in Korea marked the beginning of
a realization of the limits of that power.

570. Lai, Nathan, Yu-jen. "United States Policy and the Diplomacy
      of Limited War in Korea: 1950-1951." Doctoral Dissertation.
      Massachusetts, 1974.

      Studies the nature and problems of fighting a limited war,
      using the Korean War as a case study. Looks at how and why
      the decision to enter the war and cross the 38th Parallel
      was made by the US and why China entered the war. Concludes
      that limited war succeeded in preventing a global conflict
      and kept the North from taking over the South.

571. Lichterman, Martin. "Korea: Problems in Limited War" in
      Gordon B. Turner, ed. NATIONAL SECURITY IN THE NUCLEAR AGE.
      New York: Praeger, 1960, pp. 31-56.

      An analysis of the difficulties the US encountered in
      fighting a limited war in Korea. Uses the conflict as a
      case study in limited war.

572. Lofgren, Charles A. "How New is Limited War." MIL R,
      1967 47 (7):16-23.

      Looks at the definitions and concepts of limited war and
      after examining the Korea war concludes that it "does not fit
      the modern definition of a limited war." Claims that Vietnam
      was first limited war in the nuclear age.

573. Martin, Wayne R. "An Analysis of United States International
      Relations Before and During Limited War." Doctoral
      Dissertation. Southern California, 1970.

      Examines US international relations before and after the
      wars in Korea and Vietnam and concludes there was not a major
      change in relations as a result of those military conflicts.

574. O'Brien, William V. THE CONDUCT OF JUST AND LIMITED WAR.
      New York: Praeger, 1981.

      In-depth look at the Catholic Church's doctrine of a "just
      war" especially as applied to limited war. Uses the conflict
      in Korea as one of his three case studies.

575. Osborne, John. "Report From the Orient: Guns Are Not
      Enough." LIFE, 1950 29 (8):77-85.

      A US observer of the bitter fighting in the early weeks of
      the war tells of the savagery on both sides, especially by
      South Korean police and marines. Warns that the US must find
      political settlements for this and similar wars because of
      the difficulty of fighting a guerrilla war in Asia.

576. Osgood, Robert E. LIMITED WAR: THE CHALLENGE TO AMERICAN
     STRATEGY. Chicago: University of Chicago, 1957.

     Examines the question of how the US can promote its
     interest without running the risk of all-out nuclear war.
     Claims it can be accomplished by a capacity for total war and
     a willingness to pursue limited war. Examines US
     containment in Korea before, during and after the Korean War
     and concludes that experience can tell us much about the role
     of limited war.

577. Richards, Guy. "Re-Estimate of the Situation: The Tortoise
     Boat of 1950." US NAVAL INST PROC, 1950 76 (10):1057-1067.

     Maintains that the Korean War shocked the American people
     and its leaders and destroyed many myths about the way future
     wars would be fought. Notes that obsolescence of the Army and
     Navy was far from true, and the Air Force was not the answer
     to all military confrontations. Blames America's lack of
     preparedness on poor leadership at all levels and on
     unwillingness for citizens to accept the austerity and
     self-denial necessary to provide for its defense.

578. Thomas, James A. "Limited War: The Theory and the Practice."
     MIL R, 1973 53 (2):75-82.

     The Korean and Vietnam wars had demoralizing effects on the
     US Army because the expectation of achieving victory
     conflicted with the restrictions imposed by limited war.
     Maintains Army training should include psychological training
     to prepare soldiers to handle the concept of limited war.

579. Traverso, Edmund. KOREA AND THE LIMITS OF WAR. Menlo Park,
     CA: Addison, 1970.

     Brief assessment of the political and military benefits,
     problems and frustrations resulting from the Truman
     Administration's decision to fight a limited war.

580. "Year of No Decision." COLLIER'S, 1951 127 (26):22-23.

     Assesses the Korean War from a US perspective, a year after
     entry. Concludes it is a new type of war, one in which its
     goals are confusing and less noble than originally thought.
     Notes that the nation's leaders cannot describe the pattern
     of victory nor of a conflict being fought under new rules,
     specifically one in which UN military power is being held
     back for political reasons. Critical of the fact that US
     policy seems to be a passive one.

VI.   RAISING AND TRAINING US ARMED FORCES
A.   THE DRAFT

581.   Anderson, Martin, ed.   CONSCRIPTION: A SELECT AND ANNOTATED
       BIBLIOGRAPHY.   Stanford, CA: Hoover Institution, 1976.

       Excellent annotations on nearly 1,800 works.   The title is
       misleading in that the focus is on general military policy
       not just conscription.   Cites books, articles and government
       documents.   Most works deal with the US but there is a
       chapter dealing with foreign countries.   Approximately
       twenty-five entries cover the Korean War period, but since
       the index covers only authors and titles, they are very
       difficult to find.

582.   "Building Our Military Power."   ARMY INFO DIG, 1950
       5 (9):3-10.

       Describes the various actions taken by the US Congress,
       President and Armed Services to meet the manpower needs which
       the war in Korea thrust upon the nation.   Includes selective
       service changes, extensions of enlistments and tours of duty,
       modification of enlistment requirements, recall of reservists
       and national guard units, raising of service strengths and
       expansion of training facilities.

583.   Drake, William.   "After the Army What?"   AMERICAN, 1953
       155 (4):40-41, 88-91.

       Many draftees who served in the US Army in Korea were
       surprised to discover that when they were mustered out of
       the service their responsibilities were not over since most
       had reserve obligations.   This article tries to make some
       sense out of the complex reserve system, with its categories
       of Ready Reserve, Standby Reserve and Retired Reserve.

584.   Drake, William.   "What Veterans Can Expect From Uncle Sam."
       AMERICAN, 1953 155 (6):106-108.

       Brief explanation of the benefits which Korean War veterans
       were entitled to after being released from active duty.
       Answers questions about such things as separation pay,
       education benefits, insurance, loans, medical care,
       unemployment and job assistance.

585.   Drake, William.   "Your Chances in the Draft."   AMERICAN,
       1952 154 (5):24-25, 83-88.

Claims the US Selective Service System is running with reasonable efficiency in meeting the manpower needs for the Korean War. Its activities are traced during the first two years of the fighting. Explains the draft laws and how local boards tend to carry them out. Answers questions about who is likely to be called and those apt to be deferred.

586. Gerhardt, James M. THE DRAFT AND PUBLIC POLICY: ISSUES IN MILITARY MANPOWER PROCUREMENT 1945-1970. Columbus: Ohio State University, 1971.

Traces the evolution of US military manpower procurement in the twenty-five years following WWII. Major emphasis is placed on the period immediately prior to and during the conflict in Korea. One of the major sections is "Korean Rearmament and Cold War Policy (1950-1952)."

587. Goodman, Robert C. "The Soldier Who Went AWOL to Korea." COLLIER'S, 1953 131 (25):30, 32-39.

The story of Private Robert Von Kuznick who when he was not permitted to go to Korea, went AWOL, slipped undetected on to a troop ship and went to Korea where he joined up with and served in the 73rd Medium Tank Battalion, 7th Division.

588. Larson, Zelle A. AN UNBROKEN WITNESS: CONSCIENTIOUS OBJECTION TO WAR, 1948-1953. Doctoral Dissertation. Hawaii, 1979.

Traces attitudes of conscientious objectors from the time of the Berlin crisis through the Korean War.

589. Lehman, Milton. "What Happens When You're Drafted Now?" SAT EVE POST, 1951 224 (10):36-37, 163, 165.

Compares the induction and assignment process of US soldiers during the Korean War with procedures ten years earlier and concludes the Army is doing a much better job of finding the best man for the job. Also notes the treatment of the inductees is much more civilized.

590. Martin, Harold H. "Why Ike Had to Draft Fathers." SAT EVE POST, 1953 226 (9):27, 72, 74, 76.

Tells how the Eisenhower Administration moved to plug a draft loophole which was enabling 13,000 US students a month to turn temporary deferments into permanent exemptions by becoming fathers. While the move was denounced by drafted "fathers," it was hailed by local draft boards.

591. Simmons, Curt. "How to Get Along in the Army." AMERICAN, 1952 153 (6):20-21, 119.

The author, a baseball star for the Philadelphia Phillies, was called to active duty in September 1950 when his National Guard unit was activated. Tells of his eighteen months of service which took him to Germany. Gives advice to men facing the draft and tells them to enjoy and take advantage of the experience. Shows how even the famous had their lives affected by the Korean War.

592. Stavisky, Sam. "Who Will be Drafted This Time?" SAT EVE POST, 1951 223 (30):28-29, 96.

Examines the problems encountered by the US Selective Service System and its Director, General Lewis B. Hershey, to provide the manpower needed for the armed services. Notes those who are exempted, such as WWII veterans and college students, and the large number physically and mentally unfit. Looks at various ways to meet military manpower needs.

593. Suchman, Edward, et al. "Student Reaction to Impending Military Service." AM SOC R, 1953 18 (3):293-304.

Report on a survey of how college students facing the draft during the Korean War felt about those prospects. Shows the subjects had generally negative attitudes about being called, were not concerned or worried about such service, did not view it as a serious disruption of their lives, approved the current deferment policy and showed little guilt over their privileged status.

594. Whitman, Howard. "Why the Draft Makes Our Young Men Angry." COLLIER'S, 1952 130 (11):15-18.

The problem of raising Army troops for the war in Korea is the topic of this critical assessment. Contends that the draft of men eighteen-and-a-half to twenty-six, with the oldest taken first, is a mistake since it disrupts marriages and careers more than if they took eighteen year olds first.

B. MOBILIZING THE RESERVES

595. Benson, Larry. "The USAF's Korean War Recruiting Rush ... and the Great Tent City at Lackland Air Force Base." AERO HIST, 1978 25 (2):61-73.

With the outbreak of war the US Air Force lifted quota restrictions and thus accepted nearly all qualified volunteers. Before long the service's only basic training center, Lackland Air Force Base at San Antonio, Texas, was swamped by 70,000 airmen. Details the problems and solutions of handling and training such a large number of troops.

596. Brayton, Abbott A. "American Reserve Policies Since World War II." MIL AFF, 1972 36 (4):139-142.

Traces the evolution of the US Government's military
reserve policies from 1945 through 1968. Looks at the
problems caused by the creation of a separate Air Force in
1947 and the status of the reserves when war broke out in
Korea. Problems of mobilization in 1950 and 1951 are
examined as is the 1952 Armed Forces Reserve Act which was
designed to prevent the recurrence of problems that come in
the Korean mobilization.

597. Carmichael, Leonard, and Leonard C. Mead, eds.   THE
     SELECTION OF MILITARY MANPOWER: A SYMPOSIUM.   Washington:
     National Academy of Sciences, 1951.

     Report on a symposium held during the Korean War to study
     the selection and classification of military manpower.
     Covers such things as human resources, medical factors and
     utilization.

598. Coggins, Thomas M. "Replacements Are Coming." MARINE
     CORPS GAZ, 1953 37 (6):50-54.

     Looks at the processing and training of Marine recruits
     at Camp Pendleton, California, for service in Korea.

599. Giusti, Ernest. MOBILIZATION OF THE MARINE CORPS
     RESERVE IN THE KOREAN CONFLICT, 1950-51. Washington:
     Government Printing Office, 1951, 1967.

     Examines the administrative aspects of mobilizing Marine
     Corps Reserve Units and individuals from the summer of 1950
     through June 1951. Stresses the need for a well-trained,
     well-equipped reserve force.

600. Harvey, Holman. "Weekend Warriors." READ DIG, 1951
     58 (346):47-49.

     Relates the fine performance of civilian fliers of the
     Naval Air Reserve, many of whom were called to active duty
     upon the outbreak of war in Korea. These carrier-based
     pilots provided close air support for ground troops in the
     crucial early months of the conflict.

601. Hershey, Lewis B. "Mobilization of Manpower." QM R,
     1950 30 (3):4-5, 144-147.

     The Director of the US Selective Service System tells the
     problems in providing the military personnel needed to
     fight the war in Korea and meet the other defense needs.
     Explains how the factors of age, acceptability, dependency,
     occupational needs and status as veterans will impact the
     raising of a three million-man military force.

602. Hill, Jim D. THE MINUTE MAN IN PEACE AND WAR: A HISTORY
     OF THE NATIONAL GUARD. Harrisburg, PA: Stackpole, 1964.

Traces the evolution of the National Guard from the
colonial period to the early 1960's. Examines the
organization of the Guard prior to Korea, its call to
active duty and contributions to the US-UN effort.

603. Jacobs, Eugene C. "Medical Screening of Military Manpower."
MIL SURG, 1953 112 (2):112-118.

Maintains that the US's greatest weakness is lack of manpower,
but careful medical screening, including utilization of the
Army's physical profile serial system in conjunction with
classification based on occupational skill, can result in a
high degree of military efficiency by putting the right man
in the right job. Explains the screening system used by the
military.

604. Jones, James C. "Recall." LEATHERNECK, 1951 34 (11):14-21.

The role of the Reserve is emphasized in this look at the
US Marines during the first year of the war. Emphasizes that
the accomplishments could not have been made without the
availability of qualified reservists.

605. Koner, Marvin. "Ted Williams--Still a Big Leaguer."
COLLIER'S, 1953 132 (3):62-65.

In May 1952 one of baseball's greatest sluggers, Ted
Williams of the Boston Red Sox and a man who had served
three years in WWII, was recalled to active duty as a reserve
captain in the US Marines. He was sent to Korea where he
flew combat missions in a Panther jet fighter. For a time
his flight Operations Officer was John Glenn. This
illustrated account tells of Williams' activities.

606. McManes, K.M. "The Armed Forces Reserve Act." MIL SURG,
1953 112 (3):162-166.

Describes the provisions of the 1952 Reserve Act, called a
Magna Carta for US reservists because it spelled out their
rights, duties and obligations in a single piece of
legislation. Special emphasis is given to the impact of the
act on Navy Reserve Forces.

607. Mahon, John K. HISTORY OF THE MILITIA AND THE NATIONAL
GUARD. New York: Macmillan, 1983.

Extremely brief overview of the National Guard during the
Korean War. Tells of the Army units ordered into service and
notes they constituted less than 1% of ground soldiers who
served. Three-fourths of the Air Guard units were called to
duty during the first year of the war. Includes basic
provisions of the 1952 Armed Forces Reserve Act.

608. "National Guard Units Federalized." ARMY INFO DIG, 1950
5 (10):39-47.

Photographic essay on President Truman's July 31, 1950,
order calling four National Guard Divisions into Federal
service. Looks at the activation of the 28th, 40th, 43rd
and 45th Divisions as well as other smaller units.

609. Pertl, M.C. "Filling a Newly Activated Armored Division."
      ARMOR, 1951 60 (5):47-49.

      Tells what happened at Ft. Hood, Texas, in April 1951
      when the reactivation of the US First Armored Division
      brought 13,000 fillers from nine reception centers to the
      base at a rate of 400 a day. Tells of the processing
      problems and procedures.

610. REPORT OF THE MOBILIZATION OF THE NORTH DAKOTA NATIONAL
      GUARD, KOREAN EMERGENCY. Bismarck, ND: 1952.

      Official administrative account of the legal, logistical
      and practical problems that had to be overcome by one
      state's National Guard when mobilized during the War.

611. Reserve Officers of Public Affairs Unit 4-1. THE MARINE
      CORPS RESERVE: A HISTORY. Washington: Division of
      Reserves, Headquarters, US Marine Corps, 1966.

      Contains excellent chapters on the Korean War era focusing
      on the mobilization of the reserves and their military
      performance in Korea, political developments at home which
      culminated with the Marine Corps Bill and the story of what
      was going on in the Marine Reserves in the states.

612. "Rugged Reserves." ALL HANDS, 1952 (421):14-17.

      The call up of Marine reserves in the first year of the war
      and the major contributions they made to overall operations.

613. Ruppersberg, Anthony Jr., and Collins Wright. "Medical
      Processing of a National Guard Infantry Division."
      US ARM FOR MED J, 1953 4 (2):267-280

      Sets forth the processes and problems associated with the
      medical processing of the 37th Infantry Division, Ohio
      National Guard, which was called to active duty in late
      1951. The entire process, which included the examination
      of more than 7,000 guardsmen, was accomplished in eighteen
      weeks.

614. Stickney, W.W. "The Marine Corps Reserve." MARINE
      CORPS GAZ, 1957 41 (11):36-41; 42 (1):40-47.

      Historical survey of the role of the Marine Reserve from
      1914 onward puts emphasis on the Korean War period.

615. Stickney, W.W. "Marine Reserves in Action." MIL AFF,
      1953 17 (1):16-22.

Includes the recall, mobilization and service rendered
by US Marine Reserves in the Korean War.

616. Tallent, Robert W. "Replacement." LEATHERNECK, 1951
      34 (10):14-19.

Traces the processing and training of Marine Corps
personnel at Camp Pendleton and carries the account through
the placing of the men in units of the 1st Marine Division in
Korea.

617. Winegarden, Calman R., and Joseph S. Teizel. "National
      Manpower Needs and Supply 1952-53." MONT LAB R, 1952
      74 (3):263-266.

Examines the manpower needs of the US if it was to meet
the civilian and military needs of a nation in time of
limited war. Claims that an additional 3-1/2 million
workers will be needed by the end of 1953 and that goal
could be achieved if the government would make an
intensive effort to expand the workforce.

C. TRAINING

618. Arrington, Leonard J., et al. "Sentinels on the Desert:
      The Dugway Proving Ground (1942-1963) and Deseret Chemical
      Depot (1942-1955)." UTAH HIST R, 1964 32 (1):32-43.

A history of Dugway, which was a center for chemical
warfare research, and Deseret, a chemical storage facility,
shows how the outbreak of war in Korea led to reactivation
and expansion of the facilities.

619. Bender, Averam B. "From Tanks to Missiles: Camp Cooke/
      Cooke Air Force Base (California)." ARZ WEST, 1967
      9 (3):219-242.

Traces the development of an armored and infantry training
center from its establishment in 1941 until it was redesig-
nated Vandenberg Air Force Base. Inactivated from 1946 to
1950 it boomed from 1950 to 1953 as it became a primary
training facility for troops headed to Korea.

620. Carter, Warren R. "USAF Pilot Training." AIR UNIV Q R,
      1952-53 5 (4):3-17.

At the outbreak of the war in Korea, US pilots were given
general training in the Air Training Command and sent to
another command for advanced training in a specific aircraft.
In late 1950, primarily as a manpower move, the decision was
made to provide both basic and advanced training in the
command. This article explains the new program including
curriculum, training aircraft and objective.

621. Collier, John T. "Military Training--World War II and
      Korea." ARMY INFO DIG, 1953 8 (5):25-31.

      Contends that training of US combat troops in Korea was
      essentially the same as that utilized during WWII. Some
      training, such as tactical operations at night, was dis-
      continued in the post-war period, but the extensive use
      of such tactics by the enemy in Korea forced the reinstitu-
      tion of such training for American soldiers.

622. Finan, James. "The Making of a Leatherneck." AM
      MERCURY, 1951 72 (328):453-460.

      Tells of the importance of the training and discipline
      instilled in US Marines and how it was evident in the
      Chosin Reservoir operation. Then examines the training of
      Marine recruits at the Parris Island, South Carolina, "Boot
      Camp" and shows how the fighting man is moulded.

623. "Marine Corps Boot Camp." US NAVAL INST PROC, 1953
      79 (8):887-895.

      Photographic essay on the US Marines boot training taking
      place at Parris Island, South Carolina, and the Recruit
      Depot at San Diego, California, during the Korean War.

624. Newbold, William G., and J.L. Fernandez. "Korean Experience
      Applied in Training." ARMY INFO DIG, 1953 8 (10):47-54.

      Tells of the extensive use of combat-experienced veterans
      of the Korean conflict to train US infantrymen at Fort
      Benning, Georgia. Sharing their experiences with the
      trainees drove home the importance of what they were
      teaching.

625. "Training For Combat." ARMY INFO DIG, 1951 6 (1):34-39.

      Photographic essay looks at what takes place in basic
      training as new recruits are turned into trained soldiers.
      Training photos.

626. US Air Force Arctic-Desert-Tropic Information Center.
      "Survival Training in the USAF." AIR UNIV Q R, 1952-53
      5 (4):71-84.

      In WWII survival of aircraft crews downed in enemy
      territory was dependent primarily on skills the men had
      picked up on their own, but with the war in Korea, one in
      which many aircraft were downed behind enemy lines,
      survival training was given a high priority. Explains
      the training program as it applied to such things as
      surviving the crash, providing food and water, coping with
      the environment and ways to improve the chances of being
      rescued.

627. Witt, William H. "Realism in Training." ARMY INFO DIG,
     1951 6 (9):24-34.

     War in Korea led to a number of changes in the way US
     soldiers were trained. Some WWII methods, such as the
     infiltration course, using live ammunition, were reinstituted
     and some new innovations such as the concurrent and
     integrated methods were added. Does an excellent job of
     describing Army basic training. Good illustrations.

                    D. BLACKS AND WOMEN IN THE MILITARY

628. Banks, Samuel L. "The Korean Conflict." NEGRO HIST BUL,
     1973 36 (6):131-132.

     Claims that black US soldiers experienced considerable
     racism and bigotry in Korea. The author, who was stationed
     in Korea in the last months of the war, maintains that blacks
     were primarily in combat assignments but received relatively
     few promotions. While there may have been integration in the
     Army during the war there was no equality.

629. Bogart, Leo. "The Army and Its Negro Soldiers." REPORTER,
     1954 11 (2):8-11.

     Tells of an April-July 1951 study, by a private research
     firm, for the US Army to determine how integration was
     working. The author, who headed the research team, tells how
     the information was gathered from 13,000 soldiers and what it
     showed. It concluded that it worked reasonably well after an
     initial reaction against it by members of both races.

630. Bogart, Leo, ed. SOCIAL RESEARCH AND THE DESEGREGATION OF
     THE US ARMY. Chicago: Markham, 1969.

     Interviews of white and black US Army troops in integrated
     units in Korea shows that most troops had a positive reaction
     to the experience. Based on two 1951 Army field reports.

631. Clark, Mark W. "Negro Battalions 'Weakened Battle Line."
     US NEWS W R, May 11, 1956:54-56.

     The Chief of the Army Field Forces in Korea in 1952-53
     maintained, several years after the war ended, that
     integration did not work well in Korea, and he still did not
     believe in it. He believed that in Korea the injection of
     blacks into squads began the weakening process and that while
     many blacks performed well as individuals, collectively blacks
     tended to perform poorly.

632. Curtin, Ann. "Army Women on Active Duty." ARMY INFO DIG,
     1953 8 (6):22-30.

During the Korean War strength of the Women's Army Corps
(WAC) increased from 7,200 to 11,500, and they were utilized
in all Army career fields but six, primarily in the combat
and maintenance fields. Brief guide to current regulations
and requirements applicable to women during the Korean War
period.

633. Dalfiume, Richard M. DESEGREGATION OF THE US ARMED FORCES:
      FIGHTING ON TWO FRONTS 1939-1953. Columbia: University of
      Missouri, 1969.

      This excellent scholarly study of military integration
      maintains that while some progress was made in the period
      between 1948 and 1950, it was the Korean War experience
      which led, by 1954, to the virtual end of segregation and
      discrimination in the US military.

634. Davis, Benjamin J. "On the Use of Negro Troops in Wall
      Street's Aggression Against the Korean People." POL
      AFF, 1950 29 (9):47-57.

      Communist indictment of the US's imperialistic war of
      aggression against the people of North Korea. Claims that
      the Truman Administration is exploiting American Negro
      troops by using them to fight a war that is designed to
      help Wall Street make more money.

635. Gropman, Alan L. THE AIR FORCE INTEGRATES, 1945-1964.
      Washington: Office of Air Force History, 1978.

      Coverage of US Air Force use of blacks during the Korean
      War is extremely superficial but does deal with the way the
      press covered integration. Shows that instances of racism
      were still present. Maintains that the Air Force record of
      integration during the Korean War was superior to that of the
      other services.

636. Herman, Ruby E. "Women's Army Corps Trains at Fort Lee."
      ARMY INFO DIG, 1951 6 (6):26-32.

      Describes the organization and operation of the Women's
      Army Corps Training Center during the Korean War. The Center
      was organized and operated entirely by women. Traces the
      trainees' basic training duty assignments and additional
      training in the Leader Course.

637. Holm, Jeanne. WOMEN IN THE MILITARY: AN UNFINISHED
      REVOLUTION. Novato, CA: Presidio, 1982.

      Examines the role of women in the US armed forces in the
      20th century with a chapter devoted to their activities and
      contributions in the Korean War. Deals primarily with the
      need for women during Korea and the Pentagon's failure to
      come up with a program to attract women into the military.
      Maintains that mobilization of large numbers of women was not
      possible by the volunteer means employed.

638. Leiser, Ernest. "For Negroes, It's a New Army Now."
       SAT EVE POST, 1952 225 (24):26-27, 108, 110, 112.

       As a result of the success of racial integration of US
       combat units in Korea, the Army speeded up the process
       world-wide. Tells of the success in the process and
       focuses upon the 272nd Field Artillery Battalion in
       Germany as an example of the changes being made.

639. "Lessons From Korea: Army View of Segregation." US NEWS
       W R, May 11, 1956:56, 58.

       Reports on a 1951 study, still classified secret, by the US
       Army to determine "How did Negro soldiers perform in Korea
       when mixed into white companies." Based on more than 12,000
       questionnaires and 1,200 interviews, the conclusion is that
       it did work--that blacks in integrated units "tended to
       approach" the average performance level. Tells how the
       information was gathered as well as the findings.

640. MacGregor, Morris J. INTEGRATION OF THE ARMED FORCES
       1940-1965. Washington: Government Printing Office, 1981.

       In-depth examination of integration of US forces. Chapters
       on the Air Force and Navy and another on the Army give good
       explanations of how the war in Korea speeded up the process.
       Very good in showing how the initial showing of segregated
       units was so poor that it led to integration, and when
       efficiency improved it stimulated further action. An
       official account which relies heavily on unpublished
       documents.

641. Mandelbaum, David G. SOLDIER GROUPS AND NEGRO SOLDIERS.
       Berkeley: University of California, 1952.

       After examining the importance of the group as a factor in
       determining why men fight, the author turns to the
       integration of Negro troops into white units. Based
       primarily on the US experience in Korea, the author concludes
       that when Negroes are distributed in white units they are
       quickly accepted by the group and become good soldiers. When
       placed in black units, they accept the second class status
       that it implies, and they lose confidence in themselves.
       Concludes, therefore, that segregation is unnecessary and
       inefficient.

642. Marshall, Thurgood. "Summary Justice--The Negro GI in
       Korea." CRISIS, 1951 58 (5):297-304, 350-355.

       Charges that the thirty-nine black soldiers of the US 24th
       Infantry Regiment who were court-martialed and convicted were
       victims of Army racism. The author, who later became the
       first black US Supreme Court Justice, went to Korea in 1951
       to investigate the courts-martial. He concluded justice was
       not served, and General MacArthur was responsible. Most of
       the convictions were subsequently reversed.

643. Martin, Harold H. "How Do Our Negro Troops Measure Up."
      SAT EVE DIG, 1951 223 (51):30-31, 139, 141.

      Claims that racial segregation of US Army troops deprives
      the nation of many first class fighting men. Maintains that
      while the record of the all black 24th Infantry was bad, the
      performance of black soldiers in integrated units was good.

644. Murray, Paul T. "Blacks and the Draft: A History of
      Institutional Racism." J BLACK STUDIES, 1971 2 (1):57-76.

      A look at the process by which blacks were selected for
      military service in four US wars in the 20th century.
      Concludes that in WWI blacks were over-represented in the
      services and in WWII were under-represented, and in Korea,
      the first war in which integrated units were used, blacks
      were again over-represented.

645. Nelson, Dennis D. THE INTEGRATION OF THE NEGRO IN THE
      US NAVY. New York: Farrar, 1951.

      Traces the place of the Negro in the American Navy from
      WWI to the early stages of the Korean War. Shows that
      considerable progress was made just prior to the Korean War
      and that conflict led to further advances.

646. Nichols, Lee. BREAKTHROUGH ON THE COLOR FRONT.
      New York: Random, 1954.

      Claims that integration of combat units in Korea worked
      quite well. Based on Army study called project Clear, still
      unreleased, that gathered data from more than 13,000 officers
      and enlisted men, black and white, who served in Korea.

647. Reddick, Laurence D. "The Negro Policy of the American
      Army Since World War II." J NEGRO HIST, 1953 38
      (2):196-215.

      Examines the period from 1945-1952. Maintains the Korean
      War drastically changed the racial struggle issue by:
      heightening the interest of blacks in the military; the
      enemy making the war a color question; black troops
      receiving many military honors; and the fact that black
      troops received more favorable publicity in the press than
      they ever had.

648. Sondern, Frederic. "US Negroes Make Reds See Red."
      READ DIG, 1954 64 (381):37-42.

      In spite of communist convictions that the most likely
      POW's to convert to their cause would be Negroes such was
      not the case. In fact black prisoners were quite
      successful in resisting enemy propaganda and frequently
      hamstrung their would be indoctrinators. Ultimately, only
      three blacks elected to stay in China.

649.   Stapleton, Bill. "Fourth Squad, Third Platoon."
           COLLIER'S, 1951 127 (2):9-11.

           Describes the exploits which won Sergeant First Class
       Arthur C. Dudley, a black, the Distinguished Service Cross.
       In fighting at the Naktong River in early August 1950, he
       personally killed fifty enemy soldiers in one engagement.
       Dudley's squad, which was part of the 19th Infantry
       Regiment was composed of whites, blacks and South Koreans.

650.   Stillman, Richard J., II. INTEGRATION OF THE NEGRO IN
           THE US ARMED FORCES. New York: Praeger, 1968.

           Covers the integration of the military from 1940 to 1953
       with special emphasis on how the Korean War greatly
       facilitated the process.

651.   Walker, Wilbert L. WE ARE MEN: MEMORIES OF WORLD WAR II
           AND THE KOREAN WAR. Chicago: Adams, 1972.

           Personal narratives from American blacks who served in
       combat during the two wars.

VII. US ARMY IN KOREA
A. OVERVIEW OF ARMY OPERATIONS

652. Appleman, Roy E. SOUTH TO THE NAKTONG, NORTH TO THE YALU,
      JUNE-NOVEMBER 1950. Vol. I in the series, THE UNITED STATES
      ARMY IN THE KOREAN WAR. Washington: Government Printing
      Office, 1960.

      Focuses on the military aspects of the first six months of
      the conflict. An excellent, in depth study of US, UN and
      North Korean activities. Extensive use of official documents
      and interviews. The first of five volumes in the series is a
      definitive work on the early fighting.

653. Baya, G. Emery. "Army Organization Act of 1950." ARMY INFO
      DIG, 1950 5 (8):28-37.

      Three days after war broke out in Korea, President Truman
      signed into law an act providing authority for the
      reorganization of the US Army--it actually consolidated and
      revised many laws enacted in the past. The Army organization
      provided was that which was used throughout the Korean War
      and thus needs to be studied and understood by the serious
      student of the war.

654. Bradley, Omar N. "A Soldier's Farewell." SAT EVE POST,
      1953 226 (8):20-21, 56-64.

      Upon his departure as Chairman of the Joint Chiefs of
      Staff, General Bradley reflects on the status of the nation's
      defenses and the developments from 1949 through mid-1953.
      Tells how the Korean conflict led to the expansion and
      strengthening of the armed services.

655. Busch, George B. DUTY, THE STORY OF THE 21ST INFANTRY
      REGIMENT. Sendai, Japan: Hyappan, 1953.

      A unit history of the 21st from the time it entered the war
      in early July 1950 through the armistice three years later.
      Few units saw more combat action than this one.

656. Controvich, James T. UNITED STATES ARMY UNIT HISTORIES:
      A REFERENCE AND BIBLIOGRAPHY. Manhattan, KS: Military
      Affairs/Aerospace Historian, 1983.

      Some very valuable information on the Korean War is
      included, such as: Order of Battles; Organic Units to
      Divisions; Ground Participation Credits and Unit
      Participation; Commanding Generals of various units and
      excellent bibliography which cites many histories for
      units which fought in Korea.

657. David, Alan A., ed. BATTLEGROUND KOREA: THE STORY OF THE
      25th INFANTRY DIVISION. Tokyo: Kyoya, 1952.

      Administrative history of the division traces the military
      activities from initial involvement in the conflict in July
      1950 and the two years that followed. Includes a listing of
      unit citations and awards and a listing of those killed in
      action.

658. David, Alan A., ed. BAYONET. Tokyo: Toppan, 1952.

      A history of the US 7th Infantry Division during the first
      two years of the Korean conflict.

659. Dolcater, Max W., ed.   3RD INFANTRY DIVISION IN KOREA.
      Tokyo: Toppan, 1953.

      In-depth account of the Division and its units throughout
      the Korean War. Includes photographs, maps, listing of
      awards and men killed in action.

660. Eighth US Army, Military History Section. THE FIRST TEN
      YEARS: A SHORT HISTORY OF THE EIGHTH UNITED STATES ARMY,
      1944-1954. Tokyo: Army AG Administration Center, 1954.

      This survey of the Eighth Army focuses its attention on the
      war in Korea.

661. Farner, F., ed. THE FIRST TEAM. Atlanta: Love, 1952.

      Unit history of the US First Cavalry Division in Korea from
      July 18, 1950, to January 18, 1952. Yearbook type format.

662. Gugeler, Russell A. COMBAT ACTIONS IN KOREA. Washington:
      Combat Forces, 1954.

      Vivid accounts of numerous small unit actions throughout the
      war. Covers infantry attacks by both sides, artillery fights,
      armored drives, ambushes, heroic actions and analyzes each
      action. Intended for instructional purposes of men leading
      other men into combat.

663. Hermes, Walter G. "The United States Army in the Korean War:
      The Last Two Years, July 1951-July 1953." Doctoral
      Dissertation. Georgetown, 1966.

      Political-military history of the conflict. Looks not only
      at the problems of negotiating a settlement but the numerous
      problems of conducting a war in those circumstances. Examines
      the fact that the US carried on a butter and guns policy which
      led to many problems on the homefront.

664. Hewes, James E., Jr. FROM ROOT TO MCNAMARA: ARMY
      ORGANIZATION AND ADMINISTRATION, 1900-1963. Washington:
      Government Printing Office, 1975.

A survey of the organization and administration of the War
Department and Department of Army in the 20th century.
Includes coverage of the executive structure in place at the
outbreak of the Korean War and the changes brought about as a
consequence of the conflict.

665. Jacobs, Bruce. SOLDIERS: THE FIGHTING DIVISIONS OF THE
      REGULAR ARMY. New York: Norton, 1958.

Surveys the twenty-one divisions of the Regular US Army, by
examining their combat in the 20th century, including those
which fought in Korea. The US Army Divisions which fought in
Korea and are covered are: 2nd, 43rd, 7th, 24th and 25th
Infantry and 1st Cavalry. Brief bibliography for each
division.

666. Liell, William. "United States Airborne." J UNI SER
      INST IND, 1962 92 (387):139-148.

Describes the use of US airborne troops in WWII and Korea.

667. Mahon, John K., and Romana Danysh. INFANTRY, PART I:
      REGULAR ARMY. Washington: Government Printing Office, 1972.

A volume in the Army Lineage series covers the lineage,
honors and campaigns of infantry units of the active Army in
the various US wars, including Korea. Includes a brief
history of the Infantry Branch from the Revolutionary War on,
including the Korean War.

668. Marshall, S.L.A. "Our Army in Korea--the Best Yet."
      HARPER'S, 1951 203 (1215):21-27.

A look at the US Eighth Army in Korea during the first
year of the war. Examines the conditions it experienced and
its ability to adapt to this different kind of war. Concludes
that the men of the Eighth Army are "the hardest hitting, most
workmanlike soldiers" he has seen in uniform.

669. Meloy, G.S., Jr. "The Eighth Army Story." ARMY INFO DIG,
      1963 18 (6):2-13.

A brief history of the US Eighth Army which focuses on the
years 1949-1962. The war period is covered as well as the
post-war military and humanitarian objectives. Tells of the
establishment of The Military Armistice Commission and the
problems of its continuing activities. Tells of the role of
other UN forces in maintaining the peace.

670. Miller, John, Jr. et al. KOREA, 1950. Washington:
      Government Printing Office, 1951.

Official photographic account of the US Army in Korea from
the outbreak of war through the Chosin Reservoir compaign.
Photographs portray the American fighting man engaged
in a noble cause.

671. Miller, John, Jr., et al. KOREA 1951-1953. Washington:
      US Government Printing Office, 1956.

      Pictorial history of the last two and a half years of the
      war. Excellent photographs taken by official photographers
      set the US-UN policy in a most favorable light. Brief
      narrative.

672. Munroe, Clark C. THE SECOND UNITED STATES INFANTRY DIVISION
      IN KOREA, 1950-1951. Tokyo: Toppan, 1952; SECOND TO NONE:
      THE SECOND UNITED STATES INFANTRY DIVISION IN KOREA, 1951-
      1952. Tokyo: Toppan, 1953; SECOND TO NONE: THE SECOND
      UNITED STATES INFANTRY DIVISIONS, 1 JANUARY 1953-31 DECEMBER
      1953. Tokyo: Toppan, 1954.

      Privately printed, yearbook format with narrative and human
      interest photographs of the Division's experiences, military
      and social, in the Korean War.

673. IX Corps, Historical Section. THE IX CORPS IN KOREA: A BRIEF
      INFORMAL HISTORY OF IX CORPS IN KOREA, 23 SEPTEMBER 1950 TO
      1 SEPTEMBER 1954. Tokyo: Army AG Administration Center,
      1954.

      Brief overview of military operations of units in the IX
      Corps.

674. O'Connell, William R. THE THUNDERBIRDS, A 45TH DIVISION
      HISTORY: THE STORY OF THE 45TH DIVISION'S ACTIONS IN THE
      KOREAN CONFLICT. Tokyo: Toppan, 1953.

      This Oklahoma unit of the National Guard was ordered into
      Federal service on September 1, 1950, at Muskogee, Oklahoma,
      and was sent to Korea where it remained until war's end.
      This traces the unit's activities throughout its Korean
      service.

675. OUTLINE HISTORY OF THE 187TH AIRBORNE REGIMENTAL COMBAT
      TEAM. Korea: Headquarters, 187th, 1953.

      Brief account of operations in Korea.

676. Schnabel, James F. POLICY AND DIRECTION: THE FIRST YEAR.
      Vol. III in the series, THE UNITED STATES ARMY IN THE
      KOREAN WAR. Washington: Government Printing Office, 1972.

      An official history based primarily on US Army records.
      After surveying developments from 1945 to 1950 it focuses on
      the key military and political decisions made by US policy
      makers from the outbreak of hostilities through June 1951.
      Also strong on US combat operations during the first year of
      fighting.

677. Seventh Infantry Division, Public Information Office.
      BAYONET: A HISTORY OF THE 7TH INFANTRY DIVISION IN KOREA.

Tokyo: Dai Nippon, 1953.

Semi-official account of the activities of the division
from initial involvement in Korea in the summer of 1950
through the end of 1952. Methodical administrative history
written by unit historians.

678. Stadtmauer, Saul A., ed. A PICTORIAL HISTORY OF THE
     VICTORY DIVISION IN KOREA. Tokyo: Koyosha, 1953.

     This account of the Twenty-fourth Infantry Division's
     activities throughout the war in Korea contains excellent
     photographs taken by combat photographers.

679. Stubbs, Mary L., and Stanley R. Connor. ARMOR-CAVALRY, PART
     I: REGULAR ARMY AND ARMY RESERVE. Washington: Government
     Printing Office, 1969. PART II: ARMY NATIONAL GUARD.
     Washington: Government Printing Office, 1972.

     Volumes in the Army Lineage Series cover official lineage,
     honors and campaigns, including those in the Korean War, of
     all major Army, Army Reserve and National Guard Units.
     Includes a brief history of Armor (Armor and Cavalry) units
     in US wars including Korea.

680. US Army, 1st Cavalry Division. THE FIRST CAVALRY DIVISION
     IN KOREA, 18 JULY 1950-18 JANUARY 1952. Atlanta: Love, 1957.

     A social-military history of the division from its initial
     commitment to the conflict in the early weeks of the war until
     it was withdrawn and sent to Hokkaido, Japan eighteen months
     later.

681. "A Year in Korea." ARMY INFO DIG, 1951 6 (7):31-38.

     A pictorial account showing some of the many facets of US
     Army operations in Korea during the first twelve months of
     combat.

     B. INITIAL ACTIONS AND PUSAN PERIMETER (JUNE-SEPT. 1950)

682. Barth, George B. "The First Days In Korea." COM FOR J,
     1952 2 (8):21-24.

     Firsthand account of the first two weeks of Army activity
     in Korea by the Brigadier General who commanded the artillery
     of the 24th Division. Good account of initial military
     decisions by Generals William F. Dean and John Church. Tells
     of the initial overconfidence that quickly faded.

683. Bell, James. "The Brave Men of No Name Ridge." LIFE,
     1950 29 (9):34.

     Focus on US combat troops fighting in the first Battle of
     the Naktong, August 1950.

684. Duncan, David. "The First Five Days." LIFE, 1950 29
      (2):20-27.

      LIFE photographer Duncan, who was one of the first
      Americans on the scene, uses words and photos to set forth
      events from the evacuation of US citizens and first US air
      victories to General MacArthur's visit to the front.

685. Edwards, James W. "Action at Tongmyongwon." INF SCH Q,
      1951 38 (1):66-83.

      Describes the August 21-24, 1950, operations of the 2nd
      Battalion, 23rd Infantry as an example of an infantry
      battalion in defense in the early days of the war. The
      unit action halted a North Korean attempt to establish a
      bridgehead across the Naktong River.

686. Edwards, James W. "Naktong Defense." INF SCH Q, 1951
      38 (2):77-92.

      Account of the defensive actions of the 2nd Battalion,
      23rd Infantry, 2nd Infantry Division from August 31 to
      September 16, 1950. The battalion held a front 18,000
      yards wide and virtually destroyed two North Korean
      Divisions that tried to dislodge it for two weeks.

687. Glasgow, William M., Jr. "Korean Ku Klux Klan."
      COM FOR J, 1952 2 (7):18-24.

      On the night of August 31, 1950, more than 2,000 torch-
      carrying North Koreans attacked the 2nd Platoon, Company
      B, 23rd Infantry, 2nd Division, cutting it off. For two
      days the men worked to rejoin the battalion. This account
      of the attack and the move through enemy-held territory
      to get back comes from the platoon leader.

688. Gugeler, Russell A. "Attack Along a Ridgeline."
      COM FOR J, 1954 4 (10):22-27.

      The disastrous attack of the 2nd Platoon Company A,
      1st Battalion, 34th Infantry on North Korean positions
      along the Naktong River on August 15, 1950. Of the
      thirty-six men in the platoon, twenty died and six were
      wounded.

689. Harrity, Ralph D. "A Forward Observer Reports From
      Korea." COM FOR J, 1951 1 (9):28-29.

      Describes the problems and dangers facing US Army forward
      observers in the early phases of the war. Tells the
      organization of the observer section and the equipment
      utilized. Tells how they adjusted to the fluid situations.

690. Higgins, Marguerite. "The Terrible Days in Korea."
     SAT EVE POST, 1950 223 (8):26-27, 110-112.

     Firsthand account of the early days of combat in the war by
     the famous female war correspondent. Tells of the bloody
     Seoul to Taejon retreat. Relates the advantages of the
     communist forces and the collapse of ROK forces. Some
     sermonizing on the need to stop communist aggression.

691. Hoyt, Edwin P. THE PUSAN PERIMETER. Briarcliff Manor,
     NY: Stein, 1984.

     Well-written, popular history of the first few months of
     the war examines such phenomena as the invasion, dissolution
     of the Korean Army, the US-UN intervention, initial US
     setbacks and the establishment of the defensive perimeter
     around the port city of Pusan.

692. "Korea: Test of Strength." COM FOR J, 1950 1 (1):38-40.

     Describes the first two weeks of US military involvement
     in Korea. Presents political background and climatic
     factors and predicts that guerrilla fighting will be
     important in a prolonged war. Predicts that the North
     Koreans will not be driven north anytime soon.

693. Lantham, Henry J. "I Saw Us Almost Get Licked in Korea."
     SAT EVE POST, 1950 223 (18):28-29, 131-133.

     Views of a US congressman who visited the front in Korea
     early in the war notes that the US came close to suffering a
     severe defeat and was able to prevent it by the valor of its
     armed forces personnel. Concludes the war is extremely
     vicious and that in view of America's unpreparedness, it
     has done well.

694. Maddox, Robert. "War In Korea: The Desperate Times."
     AM HIST ILL, 1978 13 (4):26-38.

     Describes US military action from initial involvement in
     early July 1950 to consolidation of the Pusan Perimeter in
     August. Focuses on "Task Force Smith," which experienced
     50% casualties in the first action of US troops and the
     24th Infantry Division which suffered serious setbacks
     attempting to hold back the advancing North Koreans.
     Shortages of weapons and communications equipment
     contributed to costly American defeats.

695. Martin, Harold H. "The Colonel Saved the Day." SAT EVE
     POST, 1950 223 (11):32-33, 187, 189-190.

     Tells of Lt. Col John Michaelis, commander of the US 27th
     Regiment, who in the early weeks of the war, held his unit
     together in a vicious enemy attack near Chindong-ni. For

his performance, the West Point graduate received a battlefield promotion to full Colonel. (Shortly thereafter he
became a Brigadier General.)

696. Parks, Floyd L. "Defense Begins at Home." ARMY INFO DIG,
     1953 8 (1):7-12.

     Blames the poor showing of the US Army during the early
     weeks of the Korean War on the nation's unwillingness to
     provide adequate defense in time of peace. Notes that units
     were understrength, ill-equipped and poorly trained because
     the public was unwilling to accept the responsibility for a
     proper defense. Urges that the same mistake not be made
     again.

697. Price, Joseph E. "The Wages of Unpreparedness: The United
     States Army in the Korean War, July 1950." Master's Thesis.
     East Texas State, 1982.

     An excellent study of the reasons behind the extremely
     poor showing of the US Army during the first months of the
     Korean War. While the author, a former Marine Officer,
     places some blame on the Congress, the President and the
     American people, he is most critical of the Army's leader-
     ship, from Washington down to the unit level. Cites short-
     comings of conditioning, training and discipline that should
     have been addressed.

698. Quinn, Joseph M. "Catching the Enemy Off Guard." ARMOR,
     1951 60 (4):46-48.

     Covers the advance of Task Force Dolvin of the 89th Tank
     Battalion which helped lead the breakout of the Pusan
     perimeter in September 1950 and then proceeded to drive the
     enemy up the peninsula.

699. Russell, George H. "Defense On An Extended Front." INF
     SCH Q, 1953 43 (2):60-64.

     Relates the techniques used by the 23rd Infantry Regiment
     in successfully defending a 16,000 yard frontage on the
     Taegu-Pusan perimeter in August and September 1950.

700. Tate, James H. "The First Five Months." ARMY INFO DIG,
     1951 6 (3):40-54.

     Narrative account of US Army operations in Korea. Includes
     the various operations, the units involved, the commanders
     and the contributions of ROK units.

701. "Tie-in In ... Korea." ARMOR, 1950 59 (6):34-36.

     Account of the September 1950 actions of Task Force Lynch
     of the 3rd Battalion, 7th Cavalry Regiment, First Cavalry
     Division. The Force initially moved 25 miles north and

secured a crossing of the Naktong River at Sonsan then
fought its way 102 road miles to meet with the 7th Infantry
Division at Osan. Describes the various engagements.

C. INCHON, THE DRIVE NORTH AND RETREAT (SEPT.-DEC. 1950)

702. Canzona, Nicholas A. "Is Amphibious Warfare Dead?"
      US NAVAL INST PROC, 1955 81 (9):987-991.

      Maintains that amphibious warfare is not dead and will
      be extremely important in the future because of the
      likelihood of limited war. Uses the US experience in
      Korea to back up his argument.

703. Canzona, Nicholas A. "The Twelve Incredible Days of
      Colonel John Page." READ DIG, 1956 69 (408):84-89.

      For a twelve-day period from November 29 through December
      9, 1950, a US Army artillery officer undertook a number
      of difficult assignments that aided in the withdrawal
      of US Marines from the Chosin Reservoir. In his last
      heroic deed he killed sixteen enemy soldiers in the
      evacuation process before losing his life. The Marines
      awarded him the Navy Cross and in 1956, after the time
      limit had expired for receiving the Congressional Medal
      of Honor, legislation was passed enabling the awarding
      of the medal.

704. Deal, E. Lafayette. "Defense of the Low Ground."
      COM FOR J, 1952 2 (12):18-21.

      Describes a pitched battle between the 1st Platoon, Company
      B, 187th Airborne Regimental Combat Team and a Communist
      Chinese force which attacked its position at Samdung, North
      Korea, on November 24-25, 1950. The engagement saw the US
      force kill fifty-nine enemy and capture eighty-nine while its
      total casualties were three wounded men.

705. Dill, James. "Winter of the Yalu." AM HERT, 1982
      34 (1):33-48.

      A Lieutenant in the 31st Field Artillery Battalion,
      7th Division recounts his unit's march North to the
      Yalu and the rapid retreat from Kapsan to Hungnam in
      late 1950, following the Chinese Communist entry into
      the war. The suffering inflicted by the harsh winter
      and the enemy is vividly described.

706. Doyle, James H., and Arthur J. Mayer. "December 1950
      at Hungnam." US NAVAL INST PROC, 1979 105 (4):44-55.

      Account of the mass evacuation of the US Army's X Corps

and its support units from the North Korean port of
Hungnam in December 1950. The evacuation was performed
by a US naval force which also removed extensive supplies
and many Korean refugees.

707.   Flynn, John R. "Pursuit!" INF SCH Q, 1952 41 (1): 94-98.

Describes the exploits of Company K, 7th Cavalry on a
September 23-24, 1950, dash from Sangju to Poun, South Korea,
a distance of thirty-six miles. The operation led to the
capture of forty-four prisoners, the killing of eighteen
enemy soldiers, and the capture of the town of Poun. This
was an important part of the 3rd Battalion's movement from
Tabu-dong to Osan, for which the unit received the
Distinguished Unit Citation.

708.   Fralish, John C. "Roadblock." COM FOR J, 1953 3
       (6):32-37.

Account of a retrograde movement by the 503rd Field
Artillery Battalion, 2nd Division in North Korea when
the Chinese Communist entered the war in late November
1950. Describes the problems of extracting men and units
from positions when surrounded by enemy forces.

709.   Gavin, John A. "Bear Facts." MIL R, 1954 33 (11):18-31.

On December 5, 1950, the author assumed command of the 31st
Infantry Regiment, 7th Infantry Division, a unit which had
suffered considerably in the fighting against the Chinese
Communists at the Chosin Reservoir. He describes what was
involved in reorganizing and re-equipping the regiment and
tells the role of noncommissioned officers, company commanders
and battalion and regimental staffs.

710.   Glasgow, W.M. "Near Perfect Attack." INF SCH Q, 1954
       (2):49-55.

On September 15, 1950, Company B, 23rd Infantry was
involved in an attack that was the beginning of the breakout
of the Pusan perimeter. This account details a near-perfect
attack which saw effective use of air, artillery and armor
support of an infantry movement. Shows the importance of
coordinated attacks.

711.   Hamele, Louis F. "Inside the Infantry Division." MIL R,
       1953 33 (3):32-42.

Claims that the US 7th Infantry Division's withdrawal from
the Yalu River to the Changjin Reservoir, a distance of
eighty miles, without serious incident in late November and
early December 1950 was due to the superior organization of
the US infantry division with its flexibility, mobility,
superior communications and logistical support.

712. Henderson, Lindsey P., Jr. "Company L's Four Days."
         COM FOR J, 1951 2 (2):13-19.

         Recounts the fighting of Company L, 21st Infantry around
         Anju, North Korea, November 4-7, 1950. The engagement
         marked one of the first major encounters of Communist
         Chinese forces by US troops. Notes the optimism that the
         American soldiers had in early October that the war would
         soon be over. The account is taken from a journal kept
         by a Lieutenant in Company L.

713. Hoyt, Edwin P. ON TO THE YALU. Briarcliff Manor, NY:
         Stein 1984.

         The second volume in Hoyt's series of the US military in
         the Korean War starts with the coming of the Inchon
         invasion, continues with the decision to cross the 38th
         Parallel and traces the advance north until the Communist
         Chinese entered the conflict in full force in November 1950.

714. "The Invasion." LIFE, 1950 29 (14):23-31.

         Photo essay on the Inchon invasion complete with maps
         and sketches. MacArthur's observation of the attack and
         his visit ashore are also covered.

715. Lynch, James H. "Task Force Penetration." COM FOR J,
         1951 1 (6):10-16.

         Recounts the five-day 178 mile trek of a task force of the
         US 7th Cavalry Regiment from Tabu-dong to Osan in September
         1950. The force experienced a night fight at the Naktong-ni
         river crossing and an intense engagement at Habong-ni. The
         force killed or captured more than 700 of the enemy, captured
         or destroyed twenty tanks and fifty vehicles.

716. Marshall, S.L.A. THE RIVER AND THE GAUNTLET: DEFEAT OF
         THE EIGHTH ARMY BY THE CHINESE COMMUNIST FORCES, NOVEMBER
         1950 IN THE BATTLE OF THE CHONGCHON RIVER KOREA. New York:
         Morrow, 1953.

         One of the United States' foremost military analysts who
         was on the scene describes the longest retreat in American
         history as the US Eighth Army nearly disintegrated as it
         raced south toward the 38th Parallel to avoid being
         trapped by the Chinese Army. An excellent, sound account of
         one of the most embarrassing engagements in United States
         history.

717. Marshall, S.L.A. "They Fought To Save Their Guns."
         COM FOR J, 1953 3 (10):10-18.

         Tells the story of the virtual destruction of the US 2nd
         Infantry Division in North Korea on November 30-December 1,
         1950. The field and anti-aircraft artillery of the 2nd,

aided by elements of the 3rd Battalion, 38th Infantry, fought
valiantly to break out of the Kunuri Gauntlet. Shows the
chaos that prevailed in rapid retrograde movements.

718. Marshall, S.L.A. "This is the War in Korea." COM FOR
         J, 1951 1 (11):15-21.

         Observations by Colonel Marshall after spending from
         November 1950 to March 1951 on the front lines in Korea.
         While sent there to study Chinese tactics and suggest
         ways to combat them, his observations are primarily on
         the problems and performance of the US Eighth Army.
         Concludes that in spite of the difficulty of fighting in
         such adverse conditions the US soldiers were performing
         better than they had in WWI and WWII. Examines the
         enemy and concludes that they are not good soldiers.
         Also claims as myth the stories about frenzied charges.

719. Schnabel, James F. "The Inchon Landing: Perilous
         Gamble or Exemplary Boldness." ARMY, 1959 9 (10):50-58.

         Details the planning, by US military and civilian leaders,
         of the Inchon invasion. Details the geographical strategic
         and tactical considerations in the key decisions.

720. Tate, James H. "The Eighth Army's Winter Campaign."
         ARMY INFO DIG, 1951 6 (8):42-57.

         Narrative account of US Army action in Korea from
         the intervention of the Chinese Communist forces in
         November 1950 to the major attacks of April 1951.
         Includes the withdrawal from the Yalu as well as US
         operations such as Thunderbolt, Killer and Ripper.
         The second in a three-part series on the army during
         the first year of the war.

721. Wurtzler, Herbert W., and Edward C. Williamson.
         "Attempted Evacuation of Tanks." COM FOR J, 1952
         3 (3):33-34.

         Unsuccessful attempt of the 57th Ordnance Recovery
         Company to evacuate sixteen M46 tanks from Pyongyang in
         early December 1950. The tanks ultimately had to be
         destroyed by the US Air Force to keep them from falling
         into enemy hands.

              D. STALEMATE (JAN. 1951-JULY 1953)

722. Ahern, Neal J. "Killer Offensive." COM FOR J, 1952
         3 (4):34-36.

         In General Ridgway's "Killer" offensive in the late
         winter of 1951, Company L, Blue Battalion, 35th Infantry,
         with a new commanding officer, half of the men new replace-

ments and fifty men understrength successfully attacked and
captured five objectives and inflicted heavy casualties in
an operation near Osan.

723. "Battlefield Bunker Busting." ARMOR, 1952 61 (4):32-33.

      Photo story of a bunker busting operation by the Tank
      Company of the 31st Infantry Regiment, 7th Infantry
      Division in mid-1952.

724. Breault, Louis A., et al. "The Second Year in Korea."
      ARMY INFO DIG, 1952 7 (11):19-27.

      Surveys the activities of the US Army in Korea from
      January to June 1952 with special emphasis on the truce
      talks at Panmunjom, ground operations, air action, the
      war at sea and civil assistance to the Koreans.

725. Brown, Jack G. "Task Force Hazel to Ch'unch'on."
      ARMOR, 1952 61 (5):34-37.

      Recounts the May 24-25, 1951, operation of a force
      made up of units of the 32nd Infantry Regiment, 7th
      Division. The force moved from Hongch'on to Ch'unch'on
      rapidly thus surprising, routing and destroying many
      enemy forces, but it was not of sufficient size to
      adequately follow-up its initial successes.

726. Carmen, Jonathan (pseudonym). "Korea--Third Phase."
      COM FOR J, 1952 3 (5):24-26.

      The "new" war or "third phase" in Korea is a war of
      artillery and mortar fire with the armies digging
      deeper into the mountains. This phase of the war was
      characterized by battles such as: Heartbreak Ridge,
      Iron Horse Mountain and The Hook.

727. Carter, Stan. "The Men Who Put the Heart in
      Heartbreak Ridge." COLLIER'S, 1951 128 (24):
      22-23, 76-78.

      Descriptive account of one of the longest, bloodiest
      battles of the Korean War--thirty days. French and US
      soldiers of the 23rd Infantry Regiment attacked the
      enemy stronghold from September 12 to October 12, 1951,
      and suffered 1,650 dead and wounded while inflicting
      nearly 10,000 casualties on the enemy.

728. Chamberlain, William. COMBAT STORIES OF WORLD WAR II AND
      KOREA. New York: Day, 1962.

      Series of short stories on small unit actions in units of
      the US Eighth Army in the winter of 1950-51. Stereotypes
      of all the war heroes Americans have heard about.

729.   Chrietzberg, James, Jr. "Support for the Combat Patrol."
       INF SCH Q, 1954 44 (1):24-31.

       Details the planning and carrying out of a combat patrol
       by members of the 2nd Battalion, 27th Infantry near Kumwha,
       Korea, on November 11, 1951. Shows value of fire support
       for patrols. This action saw no US casualties and at
       least nine enemy soldiers killed.

730.   Colton, Willard A. "The Deadly Patrol of Lt. McGuire."
       SAT EVE POST, 1952 224 (47):38-39, 124, 127.

       Firsthand account by a 22 year old Army Lieutenant of what
       frontline soldiers encountered when fighting a war that had
       turned into a stalemate. Good descriptions of such things
       as close air support, attacks on enemy bunkers, fear and
       evacuation of wounded.

731.   Craven, Virgil E. "Operation Touchdown Won Heartbreak
       Ridge." COM FOR J, 1953 4 (5):24-49.

       Operation Touchdown, the last major UN offensive in the
       Korean War, took place October 5-15, 1951. In this action
       the 2nd Infantry Division drove five miles against Red forces
       who were well-entrenched in the rugged terrain. The two key
       objectives in the operation, Heartbreak Ridge and Kim Il Sung
       Ridge saw bitter fighting with US forces suffering more than
       3,000 casualties and the enemy 21,000. Details the planning
       and fighting.

732.   Deal, E. Lafayette. "The Fight for Hill 148." INF SCH Q,
       1954 44 (1):42-49.

       A squad leader of Company B, 187th Regimental Combat Team,
       tells of the problems, failures and successes of an attack on
       March 26, 1953, on a communist position in the Uijongbu
       Corridor. Why the enemy did not defend the position more
       vigorously was unclear to the attackers.

733.   "Enemy Field Defense in Korea." MIL R, 1953 33 (6):
       89-94.

       Describes and illustrates how, after the front line became
       static late in 1951, the communist constructed defensive
       fortifications. Details use of gun emplacements and use
       of mines and antitank obstacles. Digested from May 1952
       issue of BRITISH ARMY JOURNAL.

734.   Fehrenbach, T.R. CROSSROADS IN KOREA: THE HISTORIC
       SIEGE OF CHIPYONG-NI. New York: Macmillan, 1966.

       This book for junior high age readers examines the fierce
       two-day battle (Feb. 1951) between US and Chinese forces.
       Examines the strategies of both sides and describes the
       fierce fighting. Includes a chronology of the war.

735. Freedman, Sam. "Tankers at Heartbreak." ARMOR, 1952
          61 (5):24-27.

          Tells of the US tank operations which took place October
          10, 1951, when the 72nd Tank Battalion, along with a
          battalion of the 38th Infantry, made a successful major
          thrust which marked the end of enemy action at Heartbreak
          Ridge. Sixty-eight Sherman Tanks were used in the
          operation.

736. Groth, John. STUDIO: ASIA. Cleveland: World, 1952.

          A well-written, well-illustrated account of the war in
          Korea by an author and artist who gained notoriety in WWII.
          Good account of the life of US soldiers, in combat and in
          seeking recreation, in 1952. Includes many good accounts
          of life in UN units from France, Turkey and Greece.

737. Harris, William W. PUERTO RICO'S FIGHTING 65TH US
          INFANTRY: FROM SAN JUAN TO CHORWON. Novato, CA:
          Presidio, 1982.

          Traces the history of the Regiment from the Spanish-
          American War to Korea where it focuses on the unit's
          performance in the battle of Chorwon which took place in
          June 1951. In that key engagement the 65th stormed the
          heights overlooking the village and forced the Chinese to
          withdraw. The author, who commanded the unit in Korea,
          gives a good inside view of his troops and their
          accomplishments.

738. Heasley, Morgan B. "Mountain Operations in Winter."
          MIL R, 1952 32 (3):11-18.

          Maintains that the US Army experience in Korea proves that
          infantry divisions are capable of successfully conducting
          mountain operations in winter. Follows the actions of the
          1st Cavalry Division during the period January 20 through
          February 15, 1951, in a campaign southeast of Seoul.

739. Hoyt, Edwin P. THE BLOODY ROAD TO PANMUNJOM. Briarcliff
          Manor, NY: Stein, 1985.

          This concluding work in the author's trilogy on the
          military aspects of Korea covers from the US retreat from
          the Yalu in late 1950 and the stalemate that lasted from
          early 1951 until the summer of 1953.

740. Hughes, David R. "Hold That Hill." INF SCH Q, 1953
          42 (2):38-52.

          Detailed account and analysis of Company K, 3rd Battalion
          7th Cavalry, which successfully resisted numerous enemy
          attacks to drive them off Hill 339 near Yonchon in
          September 1951.

741. Long, William F., Jr., and Walter M. Turner. "Challenge
      Accepted." COM FOR J, 1952 2 (6):12-16.

      Recounts an April 1951 action in which the 1st Battalion,
      7th Infantry Regiment, 3rd Infantry Division was drawn from
      reserve to attack a Chinese Communist force that had a
      Belgian Battalion nearly surrounded. In the attack, which
      inflicted heavy casualties and enabled the Belgians to
      withdraw, Associated Press correspondent John Randolph won
      the Silver Star for rescuing four wounded soldiers.

742. Marshall, S.L.A. "Bayonet Charge." COM FOR J, 1951
      1 (11):22-32.

      Recounts the exploits of Company E, 27th Infantry Regiment,
      25th Division in January and February 1951, specifically
      Operation Punch, a coordinated armor-infantry attack. What
      is best known in this action was the most extensive bayonet
      charge by American troops since the Civil War. In that
      successful advance on Hill 180 nearly fifty of the enemy were
      killed including eighteen by bayonet.

743. Marshall, S.L.A. PORK CHOP HILL: THE AMERICAN FIGHTING
      MAN IN ACTION--KOREA, SPRING 1953. New York: Morrow,
      1956.

      One of America's top military analysts gives a vivid
      account of the 48-hour battle of Pork Chop Hill where the
      31st Infantry, 7th Infantry Division fought a series of
      bloody engagements at the platoon and company level and
      won the contest for the strategically unimportant spot
      simply by outlasting the enemy. Good account of the US
      fighting man in action.

744. Martin, Harold H. "How We Stopped the Biggest Chinese
      Offensive." SAT EVE POST, 1951 224 (5):28-29, 83-85.

      In April and May 1951 the Red Chinese launched a major
      offensive in a broad area north of Seoul. The attack
      broke a hole in the front being held by the 6th ROK, but
      the units on its flanks, the 1st Marines and 24th Army
      Division along with the 3rd Division, stopped the advance
      but only after suffering heavy losses.

745. Martin, Harold. "The Two Terrible Nights of the 23rd."
      SAT EVE POST, 1951 223 (47):22-23, 154-157, 159.

      For three days and two nights, February 13-15, 1951, the
      US 23rd Regiment, 2nd Division, supported by a French
      Battalion withstood fanatical attacks by Chinese Communist
      forces at Chipyong-ni. Traces the movement of the 23rd
      from its arrival at Pusan on August 5, 1950, till February
      1951.

746. Munroe, Clark C. "Armor Holds the Hills." ARMOR, 1953
       62 (1):11-14.

       Goes into great detail on a bitter September 21, 1952,
       engagement between the US 245th Tank Battalion and a large
       North Korean force. Describes the positioning of ten US
       tanks and the part they played in the intense fighting which
       saw the American unit successfully defend its position.

747. Murphy, Edward L. "Night Fighting." COM FOR J, 1953
       4 (4):18-20.

       During the first year of the war the UN troops generally
       attacked during the day while the communists attacked at
       night. Night defense offered many advantages and enemy
       casualties were generally heavy while for the defender
       they were low. Uses a number of skirmishes of Company F,
       17th Infantry in early 1951 to show advantages of night
       defense.

748. "Operation Ripper." INF SCH Q, 1951 39 (2):5-31.

       Background and conduct of the successful assault
       crossing of the Han River by the US 25th "Tropic
       Lightning" Division on March 7, 1951. Photographs.

749. Patterson, Bob. "Korean Klambake." KOREAN SUR,
       1953 2 (8):4-7.

       Firsthand account of how a US Infantry Company, supported
       by ROK soldiers, succeeded in repelling a major Chinese
       Communist offensive on "Old Baldy" in March 1953.

750. Perez, Gines. "On Top of the Ridgeline." INF SCH Q,
       1953 42 (1):56-63.

       The commander of the US 21st Infantry occupied a prominent
       ridge line near Kumsong--in accordance with Army doctrine.
       That commander wrote a letter questioning that doctrine
       and urging that in some cases the main line of resistance
       be located forward of the crest.

751. Pickett, George B., Jr. "Task Force Crombez at Chip'
       yong-ni." ARMOR, 1952 61 (4):34-38.

       Tells of an armored task force that successfully relieved
       a surrounded unit composed of the 23rd Infantry Regiment of
       the 2nd Division with a UN battalion attached. The action
       which took place in February 1951 saw units of the 6th Tank
       Battalion, 70th Tank Battalion and 5th Cavalry Division
       make-up task force Crombez.

752. Piercefield, Fremont, and John Donnelly. "Combat Outpost
       in Korea." COM FOR J, 1952 2 (10):12-16.

Tells of a reinforced platoon of Company B, 1st Battalion,
32nd Infantry, 7th Division which in April 1951 established
an outpost near the Hwachon Reservoir and held it for seven
days against the enemy which launched two unsuccessful night
attacks.

753.   Sawyer, Bickford E., Jr. "A Week With Easy Company."
       INF SCH Q, 1952 40 (1):84-96.

Describes seven days of typical rifle company combat in
Korea by following Company E, 2nd Battalion, 23rd Infantry
Regiment for one week in March of 1951. Action was near
Yangjimal and Norunbau.

754.   Sherrod, Robert. "Something's Got to Give in Korea."
       SAT EVE POST, 1953 225 (34):30, 115.

Looks at the frustrations experienced by US combat troops
in late 1952 as the stalemate continued. A war correspondent
visiting the front finds American commanders and soldiers
wanting to be given a strategic objective then given the
freedom to go after it. The political restraints of a
limited war were extremely hard for the American military to accept.

755.   Small, Ballard. "Night Raid on Hill 528." COM
       FOR J, 1953 4 (1):42-44.

Accounts of operations that achieve nothing are rare but
this is such a story. Tells of an April 21, 1952 raid by a
platoon of the 23rd Infantry, 2nd Infantry Division near
Kumhwa, North Korea. While the mission was to capture
prisoners, none were taken, and after setting off a few
grenades in the bunkers, the attackers retreated.
No known enemy were killed or wounded while friendly
forces suffered three wounded.

756.   Tate, James H. "Spring Campaign in Korea." ARMY
       INFO DIG, 1951 6 (11):13-23.

The third article in the author's series on US Army
operations during the first year of the war looks at
events from the April 1951 action in the Iron Triangle
sector to the Kaesong conferences that summer.

E.   WEAPONS, EQUIPMENT AND VEHICLES

757.   Batterton, R.J., Jr. "Random Notes on Korea." MARINE
       CORPS GAZ, 1955 39 (11):28-34.

A Marine Lt. Colonel comments on a number of items and
principles important to the combatant in Korea. Among the
things covered are: entrenching tools, sandbags, barbed
wire, mines, various weapons, foxholes and trench systems,

defensive positions and night patrols.

758.   "Battlefield Tank Recovery in Korea." ARMOR, 1952
         61 (1):28-29.

         Details a recovery operation by the maintenance platoon
         of the US 70th Tank Battalion. Because of the high cost of
         this weapon, such operations were given a high priority.
         A photo essay.

759.   Beech, Keyes. "These Soldiers Have Charmed Lives."
         SAT EVE POST, 1952 225 (11):35, 176.

         The use of new "bulletproof vest" by US combat troops
         in Korea saved numerous lives. Cites the experiences of
         a number of soldiers who benefited from the new body
         armor.

760.   Bullene, E.F. "Wonder Weapon." COM FOR J, 1952
         3 (4):25-28.

         Describes how the US Army's Chemical Corps utilized
         napalm (jellied gasoline) in mines, flame throwers and
         bombs. All US forces combined utilized, on an average,
         more than 65,000 gallons a day.

761.   Burns, Robert L. "Armor in the Hills." ARMOR, 1951
         60 (5):34-35.

         Assessment of the US M4A3EA tank by a tank platoon leader
         of the US 70th Heavy Tank Battalion. Contends that that tank
         has proved its ability to negotiate practically any type of
         dry terrain.

762.   Cocklin, Robert F. "Artillery in Korea." COM FOR J,
         1951 2 (1):22-27.

         Examines the role of artillery operations in support of
         the infantry. Praises new developments such as the target-
         grid method of observed fired and the six gun battery. Is
         critical of the US Army for not supplying adequate bull-
         dozers (to prepare gun positions), good maps, reliable
         communications equipment and reliable ammunition.

763.   Colton, Willard A. "Korea's Ridge Running Tankers."
         ARMOR, 1953 62 (3):11-13.

         In Korea US Army tankers learned a new lesson--how to
         fights in mountainous terrain. Describes the December 1951
         operation of the 31st Infantry Regiment in the Mundung-ni
         Valley where tanks climbed ridges to destroy enemy bunkers.
         In the months that followed, tank operations became
         commonplace.

764. Dolan, Michael J. "Napalm." MIL R, 1953 33 (6):9-18.

      Examines the use of napalm in Korea by US forces. Tells
      what napalm is, where it originated, how it is made, how it
      is exploded, and its use in flame throwers, bombs and
      artillery. Concludes it is an effective, versatile and
      fear-provoking weapon.

765. Downey, Fairfax. SOUNDS OF THE GUNS. New York: McKay, 1956

      This informal history of American artillery from colonial
      times through the Korean War makes brief mention of the
      use and effectiveness of artillery.

766. Dunn, Jerry T. "Self-Propelled Artillery in Positional
      Warfare." COM FOR J, 1953 4 (4):14-17.

      How the 937th Field Artillery armed with 155mm self-
      propelled guns adjusted to the military stalemate that
      made the final months of the conflict an artilleryman's
      war.

767. "Fire Bomb." AIR UNIV Q R, 1951 4 (3):73-78.

      During the war the US Air Force made extensive use of
      napalm fire bombs for both close support and inter-
      diction. This brief photo story shows the effectiveness
      of the weapon.

768. "Fire Bomb." NAV AVI N, 1951 May:8-11.

      Discusses the key role that napalm fire bomb was
      playing for US forces in Korea. Describes the
      preparation and use of the weapon, especially delivery
      by air.

769. Garn, Phil R. "75-mm Rifle Platoon in Korea." INF SCH
      Q, 1952 40 (1):51-60.

      Contends that the 75-mm recoilless rifle is one of the
      best supporting weapons both in the attack and defense.
      Based on the evaluation of a platoon leader in the 23rd
      Infantry who utilized the weapon extensively from August
      through December 1950.

770. Hazelrigg, Charles B. "The More We Get Together."
      INF SCH Q, 1952 41 (1):41-46.

      A tank commander in the 23rd Infantry, 2nd Division and
      later the 72nd Tank Battalion relates the importance of
      tankers and infantrymen understanding what is expected of
      the other and the need for cooperation. Uses experiences
      from the first few months of the war to proves his point.

771. Hindman, E.R. "Forgotten Killers." INF SCH Q,
      1953 43 (1):32-41.

      Use of land mines by the US Army in Korea. Stresses
      importance of proper recording of mine fields. Good
      examples of problems and solutions when using mines.

772. Holmes, Robert H. "The Need for Body Armor." COM FOR J,
      1952 3 (2):19-23.

      This article does much more than look at the importance
      of body armor in reducing wounds in Korea. It examines
      different kinds of wounds, mortality rates from such wounds,
      and tells under what kinds of conditions soldiers are hurt
      in Korea. Very valuable for understanding medical problems
      and developments.

773. Hughes, William R., and Larry W. Coker. "Vehicles for
      the Infantry." COM FOR J, 1953 3 (8):28-31.

      Describes the characteristics of vehicles most utilized
      by the US infantry in Korea. Includes discussion of the
      jeep (1/4-ton truck), 3/4-ton M37, and 2 1/2-ton cargo
      truck M35.

774. Kintner, William. "Don't Jump to Tanks." ARMOR,
      1951 60 (3):43-45.

      Warns that the US should not, in view of the recent
      success of the tank in Korea, undertake a major tank
      development program because it would conflict with the
      more essential tactical air program.

775. Larrabee, Eric. "Korea: The Military Lesson." HARPER'S,
      1950 201 (1206):51-57.

      Critical assessment of the military equipment forced upon
      US soldiers in Korea. The author contends US troops are
      saddled with a great deal of equipment that is not useful
      in the kind of war being fought. Says the American fighting
      man would be better off if he had the bare essentials, just
      like his communist enemy.

776. La Voie, Leon F. "Make Mine SP." COM FOR J, 1952
      2 (7):32-34.

      The value of self-propelled artillery in Korea was
      initially a question mark because of questions about how it
      would work in the mountainous, rice-paddied terrain.
      The self-propelled 155mm howitzer, M41 quickly proved to
      have the mobility and devastating punch that US ground
      troops were looking for. Claims self-propelled are
      superior to towed artillery pieces.

777. McFalls, Carroll. "Armor in Korea: Infantry-Tank Team."
      COM FOR J, 1952 2 (11):27-29.

Discusses the use of the infantry-tank team in the 1st
Cavalry Division. Covers organization, tactics,
communications, reconnaissance, patrols and logistics.

778. McFalls, Carroll. "Armor in Korea: The Maintenance
      Platoon." COM FOR J, 1952 3 (3):38-39.

      Focuses on the Maintenance Platoon of the 70th Tank
      Battalion to describe its organization, mission and
      operations in combat conditions. Suggests changes in
      terms of manpower and equipment that could improve
      efficiency.

779. McFalls, Carroll. "Bunker Destruction by Tank
      Cannon." ARMOR, 1952 61 (2):10-14.

      In the summer and fall of 1951 both sides dug in on the
      rugged terrain of Korea. The Chinese forces soon developed
      an elaborate bunker system, and in the spring of 1952 US
      forces began a sustained effort to destroy those strongholds.
      Tells how the bunkers were constructed and how American tank
      crews attacked them. Relates how difficult destruction is.

780. Marshall, S.L.A. COMMENTARY ON INFANTRY OPERATIONS
      AND WEAPONS USAGE IN KOREA, WINTER OF 1950-51. Chevy
      Chase, MD: Operations Research Office, The Johns
      Hopkins University, 1951.

      Analysis of US military tactics, operations and weapons
      performance in Korea. Favorable assessment of soldier's
      fighting capabilities, somewhat critical of defensive
      tactics and night operations and some artillery pieces.

781. Mesko, Jim. ARMOR IN KOREA. Carrolton, TX: Squadron,
      1983.

      Overview of the role of armor throughout the war. Covers
      key battles in which armor was involved. Strategy and tactics
      are discussed and data is included on tanks, self-propelled
      guns and tank retrievers. Includes many photographs, a
      number of which are in color.

782. Miller, Walter L. "The Uses of Flame in Korea."
      COM FOR J, 1954 4 (8):37-39.

      Flame was used extensively both offensively and defensively
      by UN troops in Korea. Describes the characteristics and use
      of emplaced, light mechanized and portable flame throwers as
      well as flares and bunker bombs.

783. Morgan, John J. "The New 81-mm Mortar." INF SCH Q,
      1953 42 (1):89-92.

Compares and contrasts the characteristics of the 81-mm
Mortar, M29 which began replacing the US Army's 81-mm
Mortar, M1 in 1952.

784. Multop, Charles. "A Heavy Weapon's Company in Korea."
      INF SCH Q, 1951 39 (2):80-87.

Personal account of a company commander's experiences
in Korea with the US 2nd Division. Describes the use of
machine guns, 75-MM Rifles and 81-MM Mortars. Calls for
an increased size of the mortar platoon, an extra machine
gun platoon and a better tripod for the heavy machine gun.

785. "Napalm Attack." AIR UNIV Q R, 1950 4 (2):38-39.

A brief assessment, with photographs, of the use and
effectiveness of US napalm attacks in the early months of
the war.

786. "New M47 Medium Tank Ready for Armor Troops."
      ARMOR, 1952 61 (3):32-33.

Describes the characteristics and features of the new US
M47 medium tank which began coming off the assembly lines in
the spring of 1952.

787. Owen, Richard W. "AA Makes the Team." COM FOR J,
      1953 3 (10):27-29.

Survey of the use of Anti-aircraft Artillery by the US
during the first year of the war. Gives examples of its
effectiveness in specific engagements and notes that it
was used more for ground operations than its primary
mission to shoot down enemy aircraft.

788. "Paramunitions in the Korean War." AIR UNIV Q R,
      1951-52 5 (1):19-23.

The US Air Force made widespread use of general purpose
bombs equipped with a device that snapped open in para-
chute fashion to slow the fall enabling the pilot to
climb up and away from the dangers of detonation and
reducing the "skip" effect. The use of such para-
demolition and parafragmentation bombs and the advantages
and disadvantages of using them is covered. Photographs.

789. Parr, Robert J. "The Big Bazooka." INF SCH Q, 1951
      38 (1):5-13.

Describes the characteristics and operation of the 3.5
inch rocket launcher, the Big Bazooka, which appeared in
large numbers in late 1950 and was an effective tank killer
which enabled US units to more readily halt the enemy's
T-34 tank.

790. Patterson, James A. "The New 2 1/2 Ton GMC." INF SCH
      Q, 1952 41 (2):46-52.

      Describes and illustrates some of the major characteristics
      of the new M135 truck which rapidly replaced the WWII model
      M34 in the latter stages of the Korean War.

791. "The Patton 48." ARMOR, 1952 61 (4):14-17.

      Details the development of the US Patton 48 Tank, unveiled
      July 1, 1952. This was the first completely new medium
      tank developed after WWII. Describes the characteristics
      of this four-man weapon in the 45-50-ton class. Also covers
      production facilities and problems. Illustrated.

792. Pick, Lewis A. "Forward Observer in Korea." COM FOR J,
      1951 2 (5):31-32.

      Tells the importance of the artillery forward observer
      whose instructions enable his unit to support the infantry.
      Tells of the problems experienced in the rough terrain and
      difficult weather of Korea and how he overcomes those
      obstacles.

793. Pickett, George B. "Tanks in Defense: Kapyong." ARMOR,
      1951 60 (4):14-17.

      Account of an April 23-25, 1951, battle of Company A,
      72nd Tank Battalion in which it fought in support of
      British, Canadian, Australian and ROK forces. Good
      example of UN Command combined operations.

794. Pickett, George B. "Tanks in Korea." ARMOR, 1950
      59 (6):6-9.

      Analysis of US tank operations in Korea during the early
      months of the war by the Chief of the Armored Section, IX
      Corps. Claims many US officers did not realize the mobility
      of tanks in rice paddies and mountainous terrain, nor did
      they understand the need for teamwork between infantry and
      tank units. Critical of lack of training of tank crews
      being sent into battle. Claims US tank M4A3 was inferior to
      the Russian made T-34.

795. Pickett, George B. "Tanks in Korea: 1950-1951."
      ARMOR, 1951 60 (6):12-16.

      Analysis of US tank operations by an Army officer of IX
      Corps. Examines such things as methods of attack, night
      combat, employment in snow and extreme cold and tank
      maintenance. Among his conclusions are that: tank-borne
      infantry cannot perform the armored infantry role;
      rapidly advancing tank units cannot be accompanied by

standard infantry and rocket launchers are relatively
ineffective against tank attacks in open terrain.

796. Pickett. Theodore R., Jr. "The Tank-Infantry Team at
      Work." ARMOR, 1951 60 (3):9-11.

      Observations of a combat tank platoon leader of the 72nd
      Tank Battalion in Korea. Follows the unit in eight
      consecutive days of engagements.

797. Potts, John O., and Harold L. Wheeler. "Infantry Weapons
      in Korea." INF SCH Q, 1952 40 (1):27-30.

      Two US Army combat officers compare views on the
      performance of infantry weapons under combat conditions.
      Frequently critical of US weapons. Evaluations on the M1
      Rifle, carbine, BAR, 45 cal. pistol, 3.5 inch rocket
      launcher, machine guns and recoilless rifle.

798. Rand, H.P. "Meet the FA Battalion." COM FOR J, 1953
      3 (7):24-27.

      Describes the organization, mission and operations of the
      Field Artillery Observation Battalion in Korea. Tells how
      the unit locates the enemy's guns by sound, flash and
      radar ranging.

799. Rathbun, Frank F. "Cold-Wet Weather Tips from Korea."
      INF SCH Q, 1952 40 (2):43-46.

      Based on the experiences of men in the US 25th Infantry
      Division who had spent at least one winter in Korea. This
      report tells how men, weapons, equipment and vehicles can
      be prepared to cope with the extreme cold.

800. Richter, Henry J. "Battle Without Darkness." ARMY INFO
      DIG, 1954 9 (5):10-20.

      Maintains that the Korean fighting experience shows the
      importance of night fighting and thus the need for adequate
      battlefield illumination. In Korea US forces made good use
      of flares and illuminating shells as well as searchlights.

801. Stapleton, Bill. "Fire a Round for Collier's." COLLIER'S,
      1951 127 (5):18-19.

      Describes an artillery engagement by the 78th AAA Gun
      Battalion. Shows use of anti-aircraft guns as artillery.
      Excellent color photographs of a battery in combat.

802. Stapleton, Bill. "Napalm--Canned Hell." COLLIER'S, 1951
      128 (5):32-33.

      One of the US's best and most fearsome weapons in Korea--
      Napalm--is explained and its use discussed. Photos show how

a white powder is converted into the glue-like jelly that
burns fiercely and clings to everything it touches.

803. Tracy, George. "Meet Sergeant Mulrooney." INF SCH Q,
      1953 42 (1):104-110.

      Explains the use of barbed wire as a tactical device in
      Korea. The story is told by the mythical Mulrooney, who
      represents the experienced noncommissioned officer in the
      US Army.

804. Voss, Charles W. "Men and Vehicles in Korea." ARMY INFO
      DIG, 1952 7 (10):17-22.

      Examines the operations of the US Army's 60th Ordnance
      Group, the unit which operated 60% of the vehicles in the
      forward combat areas of Korea. The terrain and roads in
      Korea were among the world's worst, thus making it extremely
      tough on army vehicles; however, the 60th was up to the task.

805. Watson, F.M., and Bennie R. Ridges. "Who Are We Fooling?"
      INF SCH Q, 1955 45 (3):17-22.

      Mines were used extensively in Korea both by UN and
      communist forces. This article utilizes WWII and Korean
      combat experiences to show how mines were utilized
      effectively.

806. Webel, James B. "Scratch Two T-34's." COM FOR J, 1952
      3 (2):32-34.

      Relates details of a September 29, 1950, attack when
      Company K, 3rd Battalion, 7th Cavalry Combat Team was sent
      out from Pyongtaek to halt an advancing North Korean force of
      ten T-34 tanks. In the ensuing engagement the rifle company
      destroyed two of the tanks, three were destroyed by air
      strikes and five were abandoned.

807. Withers, William P. "Report From Korea." ARMOR, 1951
      60 (2):23.

      Controversial assessment of the performance of the US
      M4A3 tank in the early days of the Korean War. Claims that
      the tank proved superior to the enemy's T-34 in every tank-
      versus-tank engagement and that US crews liked the tank.

                    F. THE SOLDIER IN COMBAT

808. Anders, Curtis L. "Of Hills and Hell Raisers." INF SCH Q,
      1952 41 (1):13-22.

      Answers a number of questions frequently asked by US
      soldiers headed for combat assignments in Korea. Answers

such questions as how long will I be there, how much
money will I need, what is morale like, and what will the
fighting be like? By a company commander who served with
the 7th Division.

809. Berkum, Mitchell, and Tor Meeland. "Sociometric-Effects
      of Race and of Combat Performance." SOCIOMETRY, 1958
      21 (2):145-149.

      Major study of fighters and nonfighters, as identified by
      their peers, who served in US infantry units in Korea. A
      racial mix was achieved and the men, unaware of why they had
      been chosen, spent a week together before they were asked
      about the comrades they liked most and least. Each racial
      subgroup picked its own members as most suitable except in
      the selection of leaders where whites were predominant.

810. Blair, Melvin R. "I Send Your Son Into Battle."
      SAT EVE POST, 1951 223 (52):26-27, 111-113, 116.

      A US Infantry officer, who commanded units in Korea,
      describes what combat is like and tells the character-
      istics young men need to perform well.

811. Blair, William D., Jr. "Journey Beyond Fear." READ
      DIG, 1951 59 (352):1-4.

      A war correspondent who was wounded while covering the
      September 1950 battle for Seoul gives an account of men
      in combat and the fear and anxiety that is involved in
      fighting.

812. Cannon, Jimmy. NOBODY ASK ME. New York: Dial, 1951.

      Well-known NEW YORK POST columnist Jimmy Cannon was in
      Korea during the early weeks of the war and wrote a number
      of eyewitness accounts of the US fighting man in that
      period. Very good in dealing with company and platoon
      level activity. Includes many of his columns from that
      period as well as subjects far removed from the war.

813. Chester, David J., and Niel J. Van Steenberg. "Effect
      On Morale of Infantry Replacement and Individual
      Replacement Systems." SOCIOMETRY, 1955 18 (4):587-597.

      Details a US Army research project which contrasted the
      morale and combat efficiency of replacements sent to Korea
      as four-man teams and individual replacements. Concludes
      the former led to higher morale and, probably, higher
      combat efficiency.

814. De Reus, C.C. "The Perimeter Pays Off." COM FOR J,
      1952 3 (5):31-34.

      Utilizes the experiences of the 3rd Battalion, 7th

Infantry, 3rd Infantry Division to show how patrols
operated out of patrol bases. Those bases, virtually
behind enemy lines, enabled patrols to make deep forays
into enemy territory.

815. Dodd, Stephen. "Control of Pay of the Army in Combat
      Areas." Master's Thesis. Pennsylvania, 1955.

      The Korean War is covered in this work dealing with
      problems and procedures of paying US soldiers in the combat
      zone.

816. Egbert, Robert L. "Profile of a Fighter." INF SCH Q,
      1954 44 (4):46-55.

      Report of a summer 1953 study by three US Army
      psychologists who interviewed many infantry combat soldiers
      to determine the characteristics that made for a good
      fighter. The study concluded that the fighter was more
      intelligent, leadership-prone, stable, masculine and socially-
      oriented than his counterpart. Uses combat examples.

817. Flynn, John R. "Combat Tips From Korea." COM FOR J,
      1951 1 (7):14-16.

      Hints from an infantry company commander who served in
      Korea with the 1st Cavalry Division. Stresses use of all
      officers and noncoms, the need for realistic weapons
      training, dangers of enemy infiltration and the need for
      physical conditioning.

818. Hughes, John. "A Combat Captain Speaks." INF SCH Q,
      1953 42 (1):78-88.

      Combat lessons based on Korean War experience. Stresses
      the importance of fire power and fire control in offensive
      and defensive operations. Presents the author's views on
      specific US weapons, defensive and offensive tactics and
      tactics of the enemy.

819. "Ingenuity in the Field." AIR UNIV Q R, 1951-52 5
      (1):38-41.

      The American soldier has long demonstrated an uncanny
      ability to improvise to meet certain problems. The Korean
      War was no different, and examples of such ingenuity are
      described and illustrated. These include using a jeep
      engine's vacuum to draw blood from a collapsed lung and
      the use of old napalm tanks as a survival capsule for
      pilots downed in rough terrain in cold weather.

820. Janowitz, Morris. THE PROFESSIONAL SOLDIER: A SOCIAL AND
      POLITICAL PORTRAIT. Glencoe, IL: Free Press, 1960.

      This classical sociological study of the development of

the US military profession during the first half of the 20th
century ends with 1950 and thus gives a composite of the
military man on the eve of the Korean War. Does not,
however, get to the war itself.

821. Kemp, Harry. "Get There ... Get It ... Get Back!"
      INF SCH Q, 1955 45 (3):62-69.

      Relates the role of different echelons of US Army
      commanders in planning and carrying out successful patrols.
      Concerning patrols in the Korean conflict, it discusses
      the role of the battalion commander, company commander and
      patrol leader.

822. "Korea's Winter." COM FOR J, 1953 3 (7):20-21.

      Photographs of Army activities in the Korean winter.

823. Long, Fred. "Fire As Maneuver." INF SCH Q, 1953
      43 (1):6-14.

      Stresses the importance of reconnaissance by fire, fire
      for deception and ambush by fire in infantry action in
      Korea. Uses US Army experiences from early 1951.

824. McCaffrey, William J. "Combat Tips--Report on Korea."
      INF SCH Q, 1952 41 (1):68-73.

      Assessment of the US Army fighting experiences in Korea is
      a mixture of positive and negative comments. Praised are the
      performance of non-commissioned officers and junior officers
      and communications. Tells of need for such things as gun
      powder that does not put forth so much smoke and muzzle
      flash, napalm packaged for delivery by the Infantry or
      artillery, and new uniforms.

825. Marshall, S.L.A. BATTLES AT BEST. New York: Morrow,
      1964.

      The master writer of men at war writes of a number of
      episodes in WWII and Korea when individuals and small units
      played major roles in the outcome of military engagements.
      The fighting man up close is his primary subject. From
      battles at Suwon to the Chosin Reservoir.

826. Michener, James A. "The Way It is in Korea." READ DIG,
      1953 62 (369):1-6, 139-144.

      After spending time with US troops, this well-known author
      claims that the Army is gambling that the enemy will not be
      able to mount a sustained offensive; thus, it is maintaining
      a relatively small force. Tells why morale should be low
      but isn't because of: excellent food, medical care, good
      shoes, mail, and rotation.

827. Mulvey, Timothy J. THESE ARE YOUR SONS. New York:
      McGraw, 1952.

      The author, a Catholic priest with movie-writing
      experience, went to Korea where he spent several months
      living with combat soldiers. His accounts of the impact
      of war on the fighting men are unusual from most on-the-
      scene accounts in that he frequently follows the story
      through to the end even if it takes many months.

828. Rosenberg, Anna, and James C. Derieux. "This I Saw in
      Korea." COLLIER'S, 1952 129 (5):20-21, 66-67.

      Observations of Mrs. Rosenberg, Assistant Secretary of
      Defense, on her fall 1951 trip to visit American soldiers
      on the front lines. Comments positively on their morale
      and efficiency. Talks a good deal about the wounded and
      their treatment.

829. Rowny, Edward L. "Going To Korea?" INF SCH Q, 1953
      43 (1):99-103.

      The Commanding Officer of the 38th Infantry uses his
      Korean experience as the basis for a "letter" to
      infantry officers headed into combat. Considerable
      attention is given to the enemy and the methods he
      uses in fighting.

830. Sampson, Francis L. LOOK OUT BELOW!: A STORY OF THE
      AIRBORNE BY A PARATROOPER PADRE. Washington: Catholic
      University of America, 1958.

      Recollection of a Catholic Chaplain who served with the
      101st Airborne Division during WWII and the 187th Airborne
      Combat Team in Korea. In September 1950 he went to Korea
      with the 187th and was involved in the fighting around Seoul
      and shortly thereafter jumped behind enemy lines at Sunchon.
      Tells of the advance North and the retreat. On February
      1951, surgery ended his Korean service. Good account of what
      a combat chaplain and the men ministered to went through.

831. Sevareid, Eric. "Why Did They Fight." READ DIG, 1953
      63 (378):1-2.

      The noted CBS news commentator speculates as to why US
      boys fought so willingly and so well in an unpopular war
      and finds the answer "deep in the heart and tissues of
      American life and none among us can unravel all its
      threads."

832. Standish, A. "Crisis in Courage: I. Fighters and
      Nonfighters." COM FOR J, 1952 2 (9):33-37; 2 (11):31-34.

      Maintains that ground combat soldiers in Korea who were
      determined by their peers to be aggressive fighters and

interceptor pilots who were aces were well above average
in social adaptability. Based on psychological scales
developed to determine traits predictive of successful
combat performance.

833. Vollmer, John P. "The Rifle Platoon Below Zero."
      INF SCH Q, 1951 39 (2):61-64.

      A platoon leader in the 17th Infantry, 7th Division
      describes the problems of keeping a combat unit functioning
      in extremely cold weather. Tells of encounters with the cold
      from October 1950 through the remainder of the year as it
      fought its way to the Yalu River and then retreated. Tells
      of the suffering and hardships brought on by the cold.

834. Westover, John G. COMBAT SUPPORT IN KOREA. Washington:
      Combat Forces, 1955.

      Cites more than 140 experiences of individual soldiers and
      small units of the US Army during the Korean conflict.
      Intended purpose is to use those experiences to instruct
      others on what they should and should not do in certain
      combat situations.

835. Wilkinson, Allen B. UP FRONT KOREA. New York:
      Vantage, 1968.

      Recollections of young infantryman who served with the
      2nd Infantry Division in Korea in 1950-1951. While it
      is autobiographical, the characters are fictitious
      composites of men he knew in battle. The author entered
      the Army at the age of 19, just prior to the Korean War.
      Tells of his training and noncombat activities.

836. Worden, William L. "What Good Can Come Out of Korea?"
      SAT EVE POST, 1951 24 (20):36-37, 66-72.

      Defends the process of claiming it has provided excellent
      combat experience that will enable American troops to meet
      future military challenges. Looks at the progress made by
      black soldiers when put in integrated units.

VIII.   US AIR FORCE
A.   OVERVIEW OF AIR ACTIVITIES

837.   Albright, Joseph G.   "Two Years of MIG Activity."   AIR UNIV
       Q R, 1953 6 (1):83-89.

       An examination of MIG operations between November 1, 1950,
       and October 31, 1952.   claims those were four distinct phases
       in the enemy's operations: (1) November 1950 to August 1951,
       a build up of aircraft; (2) September 1951 to April 1952, mass
       training by sending combat flights over North Korea; (3) May
       to July 1952, reduced activitiy while doing more training
       over Manchuria; (4) August 1952 until early 1953, another
       training program over North Korea.

838.   Baer, Bud.   "Three Years of Air War in Korea."   AM AVI,
       1953 17 (3):20-21.

       Brief summary of the role of air power from the beginning
       of the war until the final days of the conflict.

839.   Bauer, Eddy.   "Trial of Strength in Korea."   INTV, 1950
       5 (11):567-573.

       A Swiss air analyst looks at the first several months of
       the Korean War and concludes that US air power was the key
       factor in keeping the North Koreans from completely over-
       running the South.

840.   Bunker, William B.   "Organization for an Airlift."   MIL
       R, 1951 31 (1):25-31.

       Discusses the organization and operations of airlift
       activities of the US Air Force operating out of Japan
       in support of units in Korea.

841.   Coble, Donald W.   "Air Support In the Korean War."
       AERO HIST, 1969 16 (2):26-29.

       Coverage of Air Force activities in the first war in
       which it operated as a separate service.   Tells of the
       Far East Air Force which maintained air superiority,
       The Fifth Air Force which provided air support to ground
       forces and the Combat Cargo Command which airlifted
       supplies.   Also tells of airlifting troops to the front
       and evacuating wounded.   Good overall view.

842.   Craigie, Laurence C.   "The Air War in Korea."   AERON
       ENG R, 1952 11 (6):26-31, 40.

A brief review of US air activities during the first
two years of the war.

843. Daoust, George A. "The Role of Air Power in US Foreign
      Policy in the Far East, 1945-1958." Doctoral Dissertation.
      Georgetown, 1967.

      In the Far East in the late 1940's and 1950's, American
      foreign policy relied primarily on air power for military
      support. Such was the case in Korea (1950-53), Indochina
      (1954) and Taiwan (1958).

844. DeSeversky, Alexander P. AIRPOWER: KEY TO SURVIVAL.
      New York: Simon, 1950.

      The famous air power advocates makes his pitch for an
      invincible air force as the means to world peace. Puts forth
      the view shared by many Americans at the time war broke out
      in Korea, that air power was the answer to the nation's
      future military needs.

845. "The Expanding Air Force: 1 January to 1 August 1951."
      AIR UNIV Q R, 1951 4 (4):97-110.

      Heavy demands on the USAF during the Korean War resulted
      in tremendous expansion which in turn led to major
      reorganization. As a result, the first seven months of
      1951 saw the establishment of two new major commands, six
      new air forces, eighteen more air divisions and twelve
      auxiliary units. There follows a listing of commands and
      brief accounts of the upper-echelon Air Force organizations
      in the midst of the conflict in Korea. Covers such things
      as Strategies, Air Command, Air Defense Command, Air
      Training Command, Tactical Air Command and Military Air
      Transport Service.

846. Futrell, Robert F., and Albert F. Simpson. "Air War in
      Korea: II." AIR UNIV Q R, 1951 4 (3):47-72.

      A series of articles by US Air Force historians on air
      operations in Korea from June 25 to November 1, 1950.
      Topics covered include: The Far East Air Force and the
      outbreak of hostilities; early command problems; close-
      support control and operations; interdiction; the Inchon
      landing and Naktong break-out and the performance of the
      F-80 and F-51.

847. Futrell, Robert F., Lawson S. Moseley, and Albert F.
      Simpson. THE UNITED STATES AIR FORCE IN KOREA, 1950-
      1953. New York: Duell, 1961.

      Official account of the US Air Force's role in the
      Korean War. A well-written, definitive account based

on primary documents and extensive interviews. Very
good bibliography, especially on air activities.

848. Futrell, Robert F. US AIR FORCE OPERATIONS IN THE KOREAN
       CONFLICT: VOLUME I, JUNE 25-NOVEMBER 1, 1950. USAF
       Historical Study No. 71. Washington: Government Printing
       Office, 1952. VOLUME II NOVEMBER 1, 1950-JUNE 30, 1952.
       USAF Historical Study No. 72. Washington, 1955. VOL III
       JULY 1, 1952-JULY 27, 1953. USAF Historical Study No. 127.
       Washington, 1956.

       Studies originally published as classified documents.
       These accounts of Air Force activities in the war, which
       are based on official records, are quite detailed.
       Futrell's classic one volume work on the subject was
       based on these works.

849. Glines, Carroll V., Jr. THE COMPACT HISTORY OF THE
       UNITED STATES AIR FORCE. New York: Hawthorn, 1963.

       Brief survey of the growth of American air power from
       Civil War reconnaissance baloons to the early 1960's
       has a very sketchy, laudatory look at the US air
       activities in Korea.

850. Goldberg, Alfred, ed. A HISTORY OF THE UNITED STATES
       AIR FORCE 1907-1957. Princeton, NJ: Van Nostrand, 1957.

       Includes a chapter on The Korean War by Robert F. Futrell.
       Narrative account of the activities of the Far East Air
       Force includes tactical air warfare and the Pusan peri-
       meter, strategic bombing of the North, Inchon invasion,
       advance to the Yalu and the retreat and the air campaign
       after the stalemate. Good overview of events but little
       analysis.

851. Gray, Robert L. "Air Operations Over Korea." ARMY
       INFO DIG, 1952 7 (1):16-23.

       Overview of US air operations in North Korea during
       the first year of the war. Emphasis is put on the fact
       that the Far East Air Forces did not need to be
       concerned with extensive enemy air opposition and that
       geographical limits on the war made it impossible to
       attack the enemy's war potential at its source.

852. Grogan, Stanley J., Jr. "Lightning Lancers: Combat
       Highlights of the 68th Squadron in Korea." AIRP HIST,
       1962 9 (4):249-252.

       Activities of the USAF unit credited with the first air to
       air kill; first to begin interdiction and escort evacuees
       and first to use night fighters and all weather jet fighters
       in combat. Tells of the use of the North American F-82 "Twin
       Mustang" and E-94B all weather fighter.

853. Jackson, Robert. AIR WAR OVER KOREA. London: Allan,
      1973.

      Good narrative and excellent photographs mark this work
      on the role played by the Allied Air Force contingents
      in the conflict. Focus is on the first two years of the
      war and attention is given to aircraft other than the
      F-86. Fine reference work but lacks index and documenta-
      tion.

854. Katzaman, Jim. "To Stem the Tide." AIRMAN, 1983 27
      (7):24-30.

      An assessment of the role played by US airpower in the
      Korean War. Puts the conflict in its political setting
      before discussing the key aircraft of US and enemy forces
      and their respective contributions. Tactics are also
      covered. Includes many statistics on size of US Air Force,
      aircraft, sorties, destruction, kill ratios and accomplish-
      ments of US aces.

855. Key, William G. "Air Power in Action: Korea, 1950-51."
      PEG, 1951 17 (4):1-16.

      Good overview of US air operations during the first
      full year of the Korean War.

856. Knight, Charlotte. "Air War in Korea." AIR FORCE,
      1950 33 (8):21-25.

      A woman war correspondent writes on US air operations
      trying to halt the North Korean advance south of
      the 38th Parallel in the first month of the war.

857. Knight, Charlotte. "Korea: A Twenty-Fifth Anniversary."
      AIR FORCE, 1975 58 (6):59-63.

      Describes the performance of the US Air Force during the
      first month of the war. Based on an August 1950 field
      report.

858. Mason, Herbert M. THE UNITED STATES AIR FORCE: A
      TURBULENT HISTORY. New York: Mason, 1976.

      This general history includes an overview of air
      operations during the Korean War. Strategic and
      tactical activities are covered as are the types of
      aircraft used and a comparison of the MIG and F-86
      Sabrejet.

859. Ruestow, Paul E. "Air Force Logistics in the
      Theater of Operations." AIR UNIV Q R, 1953 6
      (2):46-56.

With the coming of war in Korea the Air Force Air
Logistic Force had its workload multiplied five
fold in the first year and continual growth after
that. This account tells how the problems of supply,
maintenance, training and communications were met.

860. Rust, Kenn C. "Not By Arms Alone." AIRP HIST,
     1964 11 (3):71-77.

     A history of the Army Surveillance Group (3rd
     Bombardment Group and later the 3rd Bomb Wing) from
     1919 to the 1960's with emphasis on its service in
     occupied Japan and the Korean War.

861. Stewart, James T. AIRPOWER: THE DECISIVE FORCE
     IN KOREA. Princeton, NJ: Van Nostrand, 1957.

     Contains twenty articles on US airpower in the Korean War
     which appeared in the AIR UNIVERSITY QUARTERLY REVIEW between
     1950-1954. Subjects covered include: air-to-air combat,
     enemy aircraft, debriefings, role of bombers, tactics, air
     rescue, photo reconnaissance, and airfield construction.
     Concludes with a good analysis of air operations and lessons
     to be learned.

862. US Aerospace Studies Institute. GUERRILLA WARFARE AND
     AIRPOWER IN KOREA, 1950-1953. Maxwell Air Force Base,
     AL: Air University, 1964.

     In-depth study of US anti-guerrilla warfare with
     particular emphasis on the use of air operations.

863. US Secretary of Defense. "Air War In Korea." AIR
     UNIV Q R, 1950 4 (2):19-39.

     An official US government assessment of US Air Force
     operations in Korea from June 25 to November 1, 1950.
     Concludes, as would be expected, that it performed well.
     Good statistics on number of sorties flown, what they
     delivered and accomplished. Includes examination of
     ground support and supply activities.

864. Vandenberg, Hoyt S. "The Truth About Our Air Power."
     SAT EVE POST, 1951 223 (34):20-21.

     The US Air Force Chief of Staff during the Korean War
     compares US and Soviet air capabilities and discusses
     the importance of air power in Korea.

865. Weyland, Otto P. "The Air Campaign in Korea."
     AIR UNIV Q R, 1953 6 (3):3-28.

The American commander of the Far East Air Forces in
Korea discusses the problems and accomplishments of
air power in the conflict. Recapitulates the main
phases of the fighting and maintains that the role of
air power, be it in combat support or interdiction,
was crucial to the success of the US-UN defense of
South Korea.

866. Wykeham-Barnes, P.G. "The War in Korea With Special
      Reference to the Difficulties of Using Our Air Power."
      J ROY UNI SER INST, 1952 97 (586):149-163.

      A recounting of problem areas in the use of air power
      in Korea by a Royal Air Force officer who served on the
      staff of several Fifth Air Force Commanders during the
      Korean conflict.

867. Zimmerman, Don Z. "FEAF: Mission and Command
      Relationships." AIR UNIV Q R, 1951 4 (4):95-96.

      The coming of war in Korea placed heavy responsibilities
      on the Far East Air Force. This is a brief explanation of
      FEAF's various missions and the changes in organization to
      meet the problems. Tells of joint services planning and
      the command structures for air units contributed by
      various nations to the UN Command.

                        B.   TACTICAL SUPPORT

868. "The Air-Ground Operation in Korea." AIR FORCE, 1951
      34 (3):19-58.

      Nearly the entire issue of this magazine is devoted to
      the ground support role played by the US Air Force in the
      first six months of the Korean War.

869. "Air Strike." ARMOR, 1951 60 (1):28-29.

      Sequences of combat film mounted in US tactical planes
      as they hit at five different targets in late 1950
      fighting.

870. Air University Quarterly Staff. "The Bridges of Sinanju
      and Yongmidong." AIR UNIV Q R, 1954 7 (1):15-34.

      An in-depth look at a January 1953 US air operation which
      entailed the occupation and control of a two mile by four
      mile area, one hundred miles behind enemy lines, completely
      by the use of air power. This operation which went on for
      eleven days showed the ability to control any segment of
      enemy territory that it desired.

871. Barcus, Glenn O. "Tally for TAC." FLY, 1953 53 (1):17, 65.

An evaluation of the effectiveness of US tactical air power
during the last year of the war by the Commander of the Fifth
Air Force. Tells of the characteristics and role of the
Republic F-84 Thunderjet. Also contains statistics on the
destruction inflicted by tactical air units between September 1,
1950, and February 1, 1953.

872. Black, Charles L. "The Truth About Air Support." FLY,
        1951 48 (2):11-15, 57-59.

        Examination of close air support of US combat troops by
        the different branches of the armed services.

873. "Close Air Support." FLY, 1951 49 (5):56-58, 176.

        A look at the successful use of air support for US ground
        forces stresses the importance of close cooperation between
        air and ground observers and pilots.

874. Dolan, Michael J. "What's Right and Wrong With Close Air
        Support." COM FOR J, 1951 1 (12):24-30.

        Claims that close tactical air support of ground forces has
        come of age in Korea. Describes the functions of the TACP,
        Tactical Air Control Party, and the problems it encounters.
        Discusses the communications equipment being used by US
        forces and is very critical of its ability to perform.

875. Fricker, John. "Air Supremacy in a Limited War." AEROP,
        1951 80 (2074):473-475.

        In Korea the tactical air power of the US enabled the UN
        Command to successfully oppose numerically superior enemy
        forces; however, air power had its effectiveness limited by
        the nature of the mountainous terrain and the immunity
        of the enemy's industrial, transportation and military
        facilities.

876. Hotz, Robert. "The Jet War in MIG Alley: First Time in
        World History Jet Fighters ..." US AIR SER, 1952
        37 (5):7-8.

        A comparison of the air battles taking place between US
        and Chinese Communist aircraft over North Korea and the
        WWII Battle of Britain. Examines the forces, strengths,
        weaknesses and objectives of both nations. Contends that
        whichever side achieves air superiority will win in Korea.

877. Kohn, Richard, and Joseph Harahan, eds. AIR SUPERIORITY
        IN WORLD WAR II AND KOREA. Washington: Office of Air
        Force History, 1983.

        Four US Generals who were instrumental in the development
        of the doctrine of air superiority discuss its evolution
        and its real taking of shape in WWII. There follows a

consideration of the concepts as they applied to the Korean War.

878.   McDowell, Donald. "Fourth But First." AERO AL, 1971 4 (2):2-9.

   "Fourth But First" was the motto of the US 4th Fighter Group which accounted for the destruction of 502 Communist aircraft during the Korean War. This is an operational account of that Group which covers service in WWII and Vietnam as well as Korea.

879.   McNitt, James R. "Tactical Air Control in Korea." AIR UNIV Q R, 1953 6 (2):86-92.

   Relates how the tactical air control system impacts operations of the tactical air forces of the US. The system relies on tactical air control parties (TACP's) as airborne spotters ("Mosquitoes") to guide strike aircraft and warn them of approaching enemy aircraft. Although the system was saddled with obsolete communication equipment from the WWII era, it achieved a high degree of efficiency.

880.   Nelson, Carl G. "REMCO, A Korean War Development." AIR UNIV Q R, 1953 6 (2):78-85.

   To meet the maintenance needs of tactical air units of the US Air Force in Korea, there was created, shortly after the war began, the Rear Echelon Maintenance Combined Operation (REMCO). Under the concept maintenance facilities were established at stable rear-area bases in Japan and the aircraft were flown to that location. This worked far better than those units which carried their heavy maintenance equipment along with the Wing.

881.   Owens, Elmer G., and Wallace T. Veaudry. "Control of Tactical Air Power in Korea." COM FOR J, 1951 1 (9):19-21.

   Analysis of tactical air power by an author with firsthand experience of combined air-ground cooperation. Praises the practice of using pilots for ground control work because they better understand the nature of targets when they return to flying. Points to a number of problems such as radios that are too delicate and bulky, air charts not made available to infantry regiments, and abuses of requests for support by claiming exaggerated threat by the enemy.

882.   Risedorph, Gene. "Mosquito." AM AVI HIST SOC J, 1979 24 (1):45-51.

   In early July 1950, T-6 Trainers were brought by US forces to Korea for use as airborne tactical air coordinators who "talked" fighters and fighter-bombers

to ground targets. Initially they were given
radio call signs which started "Mosquito ... " The
name caught on and afterwards the unit was called the
"Mosquito" squadron, and the airborne controllers and
their planes were called "Mosquitoes." Their
contribution in directing air strikes for ground units
was significant on numerous occasions.

883. Simpson, Albert F. "Tactical Air Doctrine: Tunisia
      and Korea." AIR UNIV Q R, 1951 4 (4):5-20.

      A study of the lessons of command of air power that were
      learned in the Tunisian campaign during WWII and how
      they were applied to Korea. The main concept that came
      out of North Africa was the idea that tactical air should
      not provide a "defensive umbrella" for US ground troops
      but must be centralized through the air commander. Korea
      saw a mixture of both, but the author asks that the clock
      not be turned back and that command of air power remain
      with air commanders and not be turned back to army
      commanders.

                    C.   STRATEGIC OPERATIONS

884. Air University Quarterly Staff. "The Attack on Electric
      Power in North Korea." AIR UNIV Q R, 1953 6 (2):13-30.

      In June 1952 in the biggest air raid of the war, 500 US
      aircraft attacked four electric power sites in North
      Korea. This led to considerable controversy from those
      who condemned the action to those who asked why the
      targets had not been hit earlier. This account examines
      the attacks, assesses their impact and tells why they
      were hit. Many photographs.

885. Air University Quarterly Staff. "The Attack on the
      Irrigation Dams in North Korea." AIR UNIV Q R, 1953
      6 (4):40-61.

      In May 1953, US aircraft attacked five major irrigation
      dams in North Korea, in what was one of the most important
      air actions of the war. This study looks at the tactical
      and political considerations that went into the decision
      to attack those targets. Also included is an account of
      the attacks and their impact.

886. "Bomb Damage." AIR UNIV Q R, 1950 4 (2):81-87.

      A photo essay which shows the effectiveness of US
      bombing raids on a North Korean chemical-industrial
      complex in August of 1950.

887. "The Cumulative Effect of Interdiction." AIR UNIV
      Q R, 1953 6 (3):74-78.

Statistics of the US Air Force on the destruction heaped
upon North Korean railroads (bridges, tunnels and rolling
stock) during the war. Includes photographs.

888. DuPre, Flint O. "Night Fighters in MIG Alley." AIR
      FORCE, 1953 36 (11):29-30, 70.

      Night-time air operations by US Air Force units in
      the latter stages of the war.

889. Folson, S.B. "Korea--A Reflection From the Air."
      US NAVAL INST PROC, 1956 82 (7):733-735.

      A US Marine Corps Colonel maintains that the US air
      interdiction campaign in Korea was a failure, not
      because we lacked the power and technology to separate
      the enemy from his supplies but because the enemy made
      use of darkness to transport supplies, and the US was
      too inflexible to pursue him. Calls for development
      of doctrine and training to perform the night function.

890. Hotz, Robert. "Can We Win in MIG Alley?" AIR FORCE,
      1952 35 (4):23-27.

      US fighter pilots discuss techniques used in fighting
      MIG 15's piloted by Red Chinese pilots in Korea.

891. Hotz, Robert. "Jet War in MIG Alley." BEE-HIVE,
      1952 27 (1):4-9.

      Personal accounts of air combat by pilots of the US
      Air Force 4th and 5th Fighter Wings.

892. Hotz, Robert. "Working on the Railroad." BEE-HIVE,
      1952 27 (1):10-13.

      Describes "Operation Strangle," a US Air Force inter-
      diction campaign against supply lines in North Korea.

893. "Industry." AIR UNIV Q R, 1951 4 (3):32-37.

      Pictorial essay on the effectiveness of US Air Force
      attacks on North Korean industrial sites in August and
      September 1950. Targets included: Chinnampo ore
      smelter, Konan ore refinery, Sunchon Chemical Works,
      Pyongyang Arsenal and Wonsan Locomotive Works.

894. "Interdiction." AIR UNIV Q R, 1950 4 (2):56-61.

      Photo essay on the US Air Force's August 1950 air
      interdiction campaign against North Korean transportation
      facilities.

895. Johnson, Robert S. "Working on the Railroads." AIR

FORCE, 1952 35 (3):25-29.

Account of US air interdiction campaign against
communist supply routes in North Korea.

896. "Marshalling Yards." AIR UNIV Q R, 1951 4 (3):101-107.

One of the primary targets in the US Air Force's attacks
on North Korea were the railroad marshalling yards. Because
the road system in Korea was so poor, the use of rail
transportation was of great importance. This brief photo
essay shows the impact of air attacks on marshalling yards
at Songjin, Wonsan, Pyongyang and Sunchon.

897. Martin, Harold H. "How Our Air Raiders Plastered Korea."
SAT EVE POST, 1950 223 (6):26-27, 88-90.

Traces events in the different Far East Commands from
June 25 through July 4, 1950. Emphasis is given to US
air and naval operations in Korea in the first week and
a half of hostilities. The author was a war correspondent with the US 7th Fleet.

898. "Precision Bombing." AIR UNIV Q R, 1951 4 (4):58-65.

Precision bombing became extremely important to US
forces during the Korean War because of the political
decision to confine bombing to vital military targets.
Through unit training and technological advances
(especially radar), the results were much improved over
WWII. Discussion of hitting area and constricted
targets. Contains many fine photos to demonstrate
the effectiveness of different types of bombing.

899. Quester, George H. "The Impact of Strategic Warfare."
ARM FOR SOC, 1978 4 (2):179-206.

A broad look at indiscriminate strategic bombing by
the US Air Force from WWII through Vietnam. Examines
use of such bombing in North Korea during the Korean
War and concludes it was very effective in limiting
the communist ability to wage war in the south.

900. Scholin, Allan R. "On the Graveyard Shift." AIR
FORCE, 1973 56 (9):102-106.

Discusses night bombing missions by the US Air Force,
using B-26 bombers, to hit convoys, supply dumps and
transportation facilities to prevent the communists
from supplying their ground forces.

901. Shingledecker, Richard S., ed. TRUCK-BUSTERS: 18TH
FIGHTER BOMBER WING ... ITS SAGA OF THE KOREAN CONFLICT
IN THE FAR EAST. Toyko: Toppan, 1951.

Yearbook style work on the military and social activities
of the 18th during the first year of the war.

902. Sleeper, Raymond S. "Korean Targets for Medium
      Bombardment." AIR UNIV Q R, 1951 4 (3):18-31.

      An assessment of strategic bombing by US Air Force B-29's
      in the first five months of the Korean War. Maintains that
      industrial targets were effectively neutralized when an
      opportunity to attack was given, but many important strategic
      targets were placed, for political reasons, "out of bounds"
      thus enabling the enemy to continue the fight.

                              D. PILOTS

903. Brooks, James L. "That Day (Over the Yalu)." AERO
      HIST, 1975 22 (2):65-69.

      Personal account of an F-86 Sabre jet pilot who was
      in the first group of F-86 fighters transferred to Korea
      in November 1950. Tells of one of the first engagements
      between US and North Korean fighter aircraft.

904. Dille, John. "The Jets' First Ace." LIFE, 1951
      30 (23):135-142.

      Exploits of US Air Force Captain James Jabara as
      he shot down five MIG's to become America's first jet
      ace and first ace of the Korean War.

905. Eagleston, Glenn T., and Bruce H. Hinton. "Eyes,
      Speed, and Altitude." AIR UNIV Q R, 1951 4 (4):83-84.

      The tasks of the fighter pilot in air combat in Korea
      was much more difficult than in past wars because of
      several factors: speed--which made enemy aircraft hard
      to spot and difficult to react to; and altitude--which
      also made sighting difficult because of the background
      of dark sky. The limitations of the eyes in such
      combat is emphasized.

906. Evans, Douglas K. "I Fight the Red Jets." SAT EVE
      POST, 1952 225 (3):30, 90, 92.

      A pilot with the 4th Fighter-Interceptor Group and
      a veteran of 100 combat missions who shot down three
      MIG's recounts a number of his experiences over MIG
      Alley.

907. Frisbee, John L. "MIG Hunter." AIR FORCE, 1984
      67 (5):207.

Details the engagements that enabled US Air Force
Major George A. Davis of the 4th Fighter Interceptor Wing
to shoot down fourteen enemy aircraft over Korea in
less than three months before being shot down in
February 1952. Medal of Honor was presented posthumously.

908. Gurney, Gene. FIVE DOWN AND GLORY. New York:
        Putnam's, 1958.

Well-researched and -written account of American
air aces in WWI and II and Korea. Includes coverage
of Air Force, Navy and Marine aces and the development
of air tactics and command.

909. Heinecke, Roy E. "Jet Ace #1." LEATHERNECK, 1953
        36 (10):70-71.

Major John F. Bold, a Marine Corps pilot attached to
an Air Force interceptor squadron during the Korean
War shot down six MIG's.

910. Hess, William N. THE AMERICAN ACES OF WORLD WAR II
        AND KOREA. New York: Arco, 1968.

The exploits of American jet aces are set forth in
adventure story form in this book for juvenile readers.

911. Jabara, James. "Air War in Korea." AIR FORCE,
        1951 34 (10);53, 60.

Comments from the US Air Force Captain who in May 1951
became the world's first jet ace after shooting down his
fifth and sixth enemy aircraft. Includes Jabara's views
on enemy aircraft, pilots and tactics.

912. Maurer, Maurer. USAF CREDITS FOR DESTRUCTION OF ENEMY
        AIRCRAFT, KOREAN WAR. USAF Historical Study No. 81.
        Washington: Government Printing Office, 1963.

Lists the official credits awarded to US Air Force
pilots for enemy aircraft destroyed during the Korean
War.

913. Meyer, John C. "What Makes a Jet Ace?" AIR TR,
        1952 39 (1):20-21.

A former commander of the US 4th Fighter Group in
Korea, who was an ace during WWII, discusses such air
activities as fighter tactics, aerial gunnery and the
importance of air discipline and aggressiveness.

914. Reed, Boardman C. "First Korean Kill of the USAF."
        AM AVI HIST SOC J, 1957 April-June:72.

Maintains that in all likelihood the first US pilot to
shoot down an enemy plane in Korea was 1st Lt. William G.
Hudson of the 68th Fighter Squadron. Acknowledges
several others who might possibly have been the first.

915. Schoeni, Arthur L. "Tall Tales From Korean Skies."
      POP MECH, 1952 97 (5):104-109, 254-256.

      Accounts of unusual situations that combat pilots found
      themselves in and tells how they got out of the situations.
      Attests to the training, skill and ingenuity of US pilots.

916. Sheldon, Walt. "MIG's Are Down His Alley." COLLIER'S,
      1952 129 (7):27, 68.

      Tells the exploits of US jet ace George A. Davis, Jr.
      of the 4th Fighter Interceptor Wing who shot down twelve
      enemy aircraft in a seventeen-day period, including four
      in one day. Includes an interview with Davis and a look at
      his homelife and background.

917. Taylor, L.G. "Flying Training in Fifth Air Force."
      AIR UNIV Q R, 1953-54 6 (4):111-117.

      During the Korean War the US Fifth Air Force conducted
      continuous training in Korea even at the height of
      hostilities. Training varied considerably from unit to
      unit and pilot to pilot because readiness was determined
      by pilot proficiency as determined by the unit commander.
      This was necessary because the pilots varied from
      experienced WWII pilots to virtual novices. The combat
      record attests to the success of this program.

918. Thyng, Harrison R. "Air-to-Air Combat in Korea."
      AIR UNIV Q R, 1953 6 (2):40-45.

      The commander of the US 4th Fighter-Interceptor Wing
      and 16th jet ace of the Korean War describes the air
      war on the sweep to the Yalu, the merits and short-
      comings of the Sabrejet and MIG-15 and the impact of a
      mix of veteran WWII pilots and new pilots right out
      of school.

919. Tregoskis, Richard. "Gabreski, Avenger of the Skies."
      SAT EVE POST, 1952 225 (24):17-19, 76-77, 80-88.

      Exploits of US Air Force Colonel Francis S. Gabreski, who
      shot down thirty-one planes during WWII and was taken
      prisoner. When war broke out in Korea, he joined and later
      led the 51st Fighter Interceptor Wing, flew more than 120
      missions and shot down 6.5 MIG's--making him second to Major
      Dick Bong as the all-time American ace.

920. Ulanoff, Stanley M., ed. FIGHTER PILOT. New York:

Doubleday, 1962.

This collection of combat experiences of fighter pilots,
told in their own words. Covers from WWI through the Korean
conflict--with several accounts from the latter.

E. AIRCRAFT

921. "Air Pipeline to Korea." LIFE, 1951 30 (10):62-66.

The role of "Flying Boxcars" in supplying US combat
troops in Korea is examined. Looks at preparation and
delivery.

922. Amody, Francis J. "We Got Ours at Night: The Story of
the Lockheed F-94 Starfire in Combat." AM AVI HIST SOC J,
1982 27 (2):148-150.

Recounts the experiences of the 319th Fighter Interceptor
Squadron, which flew Lockheed F-94 Starfires.

923. "Battle Damage." AIR UNIV Q R, 1951-52 5 (1):51-53.

US jets returning from combat over North Korea
frequently demonstrated an ability to sustain serious
battle damage and still remain flyable. This photo
essay shows the extent of damage some craft suffered
and still returned to their base.

924. "The C-124." AIR UNIV Q R, 1951-52 5 (1):82-85.

In September 1951 the C-124 aircraft joined the US airlift
command in Korea. This craft, with its ability to carry
70,000 pounds of cargo 2,000 miles without refueling, soon
became a major means of moving personnel and heavy equipment.
Describes the payload capabilities on trips from 2,000 to
6,000 miles and the airplane's ability to operate easily on
5,000-foot runways.

925. Cole, James L. "Lamplighters and Gypsies." AERO HIST,
1973 20 (1):30-35.

Describes the role played by the C-47 "Gooney Bird" in
US operations during the Korean conflict.

926. Davis, Larry. AIR WAR OVER KOREA. Carrollton, TX:
Squadron/Signal, 1982.

Excellent photo history of US air activities during the
Korean War. Includes pictures, sketches and specifications
on the different US aircraft that saw action.

927. Davis, Lou. "Korea: Air War Report." A SUPPLEMENT TO
      PEGASUS. January, 1954.

      Firsthand observations of the air war by a man sent to
      Korea to evaluate the effectiveness of air weaponry.

928. DeRoos, Robert. "Safety Gadgets--Do They Kill Our
      Fighter Pilots?" COLLIER'S, 1953 131 (12):15-18.

      Controversial article that claims the number of
      gadgets being put on US combat aircraft is becoming, and
      in fact may already be, so excessive and so heavy that they
      are endangering American pilots. Maintains that gadgeting
      may weaken the nation's defenses by weakening the capa-
      bilities of American combat air power.

929. Dolan, Michael J. "Mosquito and Horsefly." COM FOR J,
      1952 2 (7):35-36.

      Tells of the work performed by US Army aviators flying
      the Horsefly (L-5) liaison aircraft and the Air Force
      pilots manning the Mosquito (T-6) plane, in controlling
      close air support strikes for ground forces.

930. Doolittle, James H. "Safety Gadgets--They're Helping
      Out Fighter Pilots." COLLIER'S, 1953 131 (22):14-17.

      A counter to Robert DeRoos' charges in COLLIER'S, 1953
      131 (12):15-18, that gadgets are weighing down US combat
      aircraft so much that they are endangering pilots. General
      Doolittle explains many of the new safety devices and
      gives examples of how they have saved and will continue to
      save many pilot's lives.

931. Far East Air Force Bomber Command. "Heavyweights Over
      Korea: B-29 Employment in the Korean Air War."
      AIR UNIV Q R, 1954 7 (1):99-115.

      This study examines day and night offensive air operations
      against North Korean and Chinese units and the development
      of night defensive tactics.

932. "The Flyaway Kit." AIR FORCE, 1950 33 (9):26-27.

      Within days of the US decision to intervene in Korea,
      the Strategic Air Command deployed B-29 bombers to Japan
      for use in Korea. Then, on July 12, 1950, those aircraft
      undertook their first combat mission. This is the story
      of the deployment and the mission.

933. Hassakarl, Robert A., Jr. "Every Inch a Fighter."
      AIRP HIST, 1962 9 (3):180-184.

      Traces the development of the Lockheed F-80 "Shooting
      Star" from the end of WWII to its emergence as the major

US warplane in the early days of the Korean War.

934. "Heavyweights Over Korea: B-29 Employment in the Korean
      Air War." AIR UNIV Q R, 1954 7 (1):99-115.

      Nearly all attention in the Korean air war is focused on
      MIG-Sabrejet confrontations; consequently, the very
      significant role played by the WWII vintage B-29 is
      frequently ignored. Heavy bombers hit strategic targets in
      North Korea in all but twenty-six days of the three-year war
      and successfully neutralized the eighteen key targets
      designated by the Joint Chiefs of Staff. Discusses day and
      night operations.

935. Keenan, Richard M. "The Aircraft That Won a War: The
      Last of the Superfortresses." AERO HIST, 1970
      17 (1):20-27

      The B-29 is best known for the role it played in helping
      bring WWII to an end against Japan, but it also played a
      significant role in the Korean War.

936. Knight, Charlotte. "The New Air War--Sabres vs MIG's."
      COLLIER'S, 1951 127 (16):26-27, 68-72.

      In Korean air engagements US aircraft, especially the F-86
      Sabre jet, lost only one aircraft for every eight MIG 15's,
      the Russian counterpart aircraft with Chinese Communist
      markings, which were shot down. Claims the two aircraft
      themselves are quite even in capabilities, but the US
      superiority results from the tactics, training and gunnery
      accuracy.

937. Lanham, Harvey P. "The Jet Comes of Age." US NAVAL
      INST PROC, 1951 77 (4):371-377.

      The commander of Air Group Five, the first carrier borne
      jets to engage in combat in a July 3, 1950, raid against
      the North Korean capitol of Pyongyang tells of the
      success of that mission and the training and development
      of doctrine prior to the attack. The jets were F9F
      Grumman Panther's flying off the USS VALLEY FORGE.

938. Martin, Harold H. "How We Blasted the Enemy's Life Line
      to Russia." SAT EVE POST, 1950 223 (9):30, 105-106.

      Account of B-29 raids against the transportation center
      at Wonsan, North Korea, in the early weeks of the war.
      These raids originated from US-held Okinawa.

939. Martin, Robert P. "Sabres Still Rule Skies Over MIG
      Alley." AVI WK, 1952 57 (18):13-15.

      Discusses superior performance of US F-86 Sabre jets
      over Russian built MIG's in Korea. Attributes advantage

primarily to skill and training of US pilots.

940. "MIG Maneuvers." AIR UNIV Q R, 1953 6 (4):8-13.

In Korean air combat the US shot down 802 MIG's while
losing only fifty-six Sabrejets, this was due primarily to
pilot skill rather than aircraft superiority. This article
discusses the advantages of the MIG and then looks at the
tactics utilized by the communist pilots.

941. Nigro, Edward H. "Early Troop Carrier Operations in
      Korea." AIR UNIV Q R, 1954 7 (1):86-87.

Troop carrier activities were extremely important to
the US military in the early phases of the war. Using
C-46's, C-47's, C-54's and C-119's, American pilots
landed and took off from crude airstrips to evacuate
Americans from Korea in June 1950, drop paratroopers
of the advancing Eighth Army in the fall of that year,
evacuate Army and Marine troops from Kimpo and Yonpo
in the setback of December and the resupply of the
spring 1951 offensive. All four phases of the air war
are described.

942. "One Air Power." AIR UNIV Q R, 1951 4 (14):21-30.

A look at the contributions of fighter aircraft, light
bombers and medium bombers in the activities of the US
Air Force in Korea. The F-86, F-80 and F-84 not only
helped achieve air superiority but were also useful
in ground support. The B-26, a light bomber and B-29,
a medium bomber, were used primarily in interdiction
activities and hitting industrial targets. Good
photographs to support story.

943. Putt, Donald L. "Air Weapon's Development Systems."
      ARMY INFO DIG, 1953 8 (8):8-13.

Maintains that the steadily climbing ratio of MIG-15
kills per F-86 losses (which stood at 11 to 1 in April
1953) in the Korean War is due to the superior well-
balanced weapons system. Examines other factors such
as training of US pilots.

944. Roth, Michael J. "Nimrod--King of the Trail." AIR
      FORCE, 1971 54 (10):30-35.

Evolutionary study of the Douglas B-26 aircraft first
used in WWII then modified and used in Korea and ultimately Vietnam.

945. Teschner, Charles G. "The Fighter-Bomber in Korea."
      AIR UNIV Q R, 1954 7 (2):71-80.

During the war, more personnel were involved in the use

of the Fighter-Bomber than with any other weapon except
the rifle. That aircraft, which was utilized by all the
US military services, was the primary weapon involved in
taking the war to the enemy during the last two years of
the war. Discusses the role of the Fighter-Bomber in the
various phases of the war.

946. "Where $1,600,000,000 of Your Taxes Went: Korea, the
      First Jet-Age Air War." FORTUNE, 1953 48 (4):55-56,
      59-65.

      Discusses the high economic costs involved in the loss of
      US aircraft and Soviet built MIG's during the conflict. US
      Air Force lost about 1,750 aircraft most in ground support
      missions, the Navy and Marines 1,250 aircraft, the North
      Korean and Chinese probably lost about 2,400 aircraft. Tells
      of the use of the MIG and later in the war the IL-28. Based
      on information supplied by Colonel Robert H. Orr, Fifth Air
      Force's chief of combat operations.

947. Winchester, James H. "Report on Korean Air Losses."
      AVI AGE, 1951 16 (5):38-39.

      The record of the US Air Force F-84 and F-86 aircraft
      against the Soviet built MIG-15 during the first fifteen
      months of the war.

948. Worden, William. "The Flare Plane Dares the Reds."
      SAT EVE POST, 1951 223 (39):30-31, 119-120.

      The use of the Lamplighter, aged C-47's, used by the US Air
      Force's 3rd Bomb Wing in Japan to drop flares to guide B-26
      bombers on their night time attacks in Korea.

IX. US NAVY
A. OVERVIEW OF NAVAL ACTIVITIES

949. AMPHIBIOUS CONSTRUCTION BATTALION ONE. Tokyo: Toppan,
      1952.

      Brief history of a US Naval Battalion that was called upon
      several times during the Korean conflict to handle difficult
      projects such as airfield construction. Covers the period
      from 1947 to mid-1952.

950. Cagle, Malcolm W., and Frank A. Manson. THE SEA WAR IN
      KOREA. Annapolis, MD: US Naval Institute, 1957.

      Definitive work on the role of the US Navy in the Korean
      War. Makes extensive use of official records and inter-
      views.

951. Coletta, Paolo E. THE AMERICAN NAVAL HERITAGE IN BRIEF.
      Washington: University Press of America, 1978.

      This overview of the Navy includes a short section on the
      Korean War, but the focus is on land and air
      operations as well as those on the sea.

952. Coletta, Paolo E. "The Defense Unification Battle,
      1947-50: The Navy." PROL, 1975 7 (1):6-17.

      When the Korean War broke out in 1950 the US Navy and
      Marines were considerably understrength and lacking in
      equipment because of the turmoil that resulted from the
      attempts to unite the Army, Navy and Air Force under the
      Secretary of Defense.

953. Fane, Francis D. THE NAKED WARRIORS. New York:
      Appleton, 1956.

      Authoritative work on the US Navy Underwater Demolition
      Teams in WWII and Korea. Covers make-up of the team,
      training and sketches of their wartime activities.

954. Field, James A., Jr. HISTORY OF UNITED STATES NAVAL
      OPERATIONS: KOREA. Washington: Government Printing Office,
      1962.

      A thorough examination of naval strategy, tactics and
      operations during the war. Looks at the military and
      political decision-making process as revealed by official

US Naval Records. Although an official account, it
represents solid historical scholarship.

955. "Frogmen In Korea." COLLIER'S, 1953 131 (8):50-51.

Activities of US Navy frogmen are described using Operation
Fishnet as an example. In July 1952 personnel of Underwater
Demolition Team Five successfully located and destroyed the
fishing nets of North Korean Communists of Wonsan in order
to keep them from catching fish for their soldiers. The
mission was successful.

956. Griffin, Harry K. "The Navy in Korean Waters." ARMY
      INFO DIG, 1951 6 (12):12-22.

An examination of the US Navy's role during the first
year of the Korean conflict. During that time the tasks
of minesweeping, amphibious supply, off-shore bombardment
and aerial strikes on inland targets were successfully
undertaken. Mentions the activities of many US naval
ships by name and includes many statistics.

957. Hayes, John D. "Patterns of American Sea Power,
      1945-1956: Their Portents for the Future." US NAVAL
      INST PROC, 1970 96 (5):337-353.

Sees the Korean War as being a pivotal point in US
maritime history because in deciding not to blockade China
or take other naval action against it, the US abrogated
the idea of the importance of control of the sea.
Consequently, the Navy stopped being a major force in
warfare and was relegated to status below that of the Army
and Air Force.

958. Ingram, M.D. "The United States Navy in Japan, 1945-
      1950." US NAVAL INST PROC, 1952 78 (4):379-383.

While much has been written about the US Army in Japan
from the end of WWII through the outbreak of war in Korea
not much has appeared on the Navy. This brief article
helps fill that void, but it concentrates primarily on
1945-1946.

959. Karig, Walter, et al. BATTLE REPORTS VOL. VI. THE WAR IN
      KOREA. New York: Rinehart, 1952.

Focuses on US naval operations in Korea during the first
six months of the war--based on official sources. Sketchy
account of land warfare during that period. Many eyewitness
accounts of key actions are included.

960. Lovell, Kenneth C. "Navy Engineer Support in Korea."
      MIL ENG, 1952 44 (302):413-417.

Examines the direct support role of the Seabees in Korean

operations during the first eight months of the conflict.
The Seabees' role in the Inchon invasion, establishment of
supply bases at Sasebo and Yokosuka, Japan, the assault on
Wonsan and withdrawal from Hungnam and Inchon and the
retaking of Inchon in February 1951 are all covered.

961. McGraw, Harry. "The Seabees--1952." MIL ENG, 1952
      44 (298):81-84.

      This overall assessment of Seabee activities focuses on
      their contributions to the Korean conflict. The importance
      of reservists is covered--within several months of the
      outbreak of war, 60% of the Seabees on active duty were
      reservists.

962. McMaster, Donald. "The Evolution of Airpower--With
      Particular Emphasis Upon its Application by the US Navy
      and US Marine Corps in Korea, June 1950-July 1953."
      Master's Thesis. Maryland, 1954.

      Examines initial use of air support of ground troops in
      Korea and shows how those tactics were modified after the
      war developed into a stalemate.

963. Miller, Max. I'M SURE WE'VE MET BEFORE: THE NAVY IN
      KOREA. New York: Dutton, 1951.

      Misleading title since this is not an account of naval
      combat but is an account of a naval reserve officer who
      returns to duty and travels via surface ship and aircraft
      to areas such as Pusan, Inchon and Wonsan but not in time
      of naval action. Tells of life of the sailor and the
      marine and concludes they are doing a good job. Light
      reading.

964. Millis, Walter. "Sea Power: Abstraction or Asset?"
      FOR AFF, 1951 29 (3):371-384.

      A top US military affairs expert puts down those
      Americans calling for the nation to confine its
      contribution to the common defense to sea power and air
      power. Argues that while sea and air strength can be
      of value, it can be so only in support of land forces.
      Uses the early months of the war in Korea to provide
      support for his claims.

965. "Naval Air War." NAV AVI N, 1952 December:1-7.

      Traces the role of naval aviation from the beginning of
      the Korean War through June 1952. Claims that over one-
      third of US Combat air strikes in Korea were by the US
      Navy. Covers aircraft carriers, tactical air support
      and interdiction role. Includes many statistics on
      damage inflicted. Lists the carriers, air groups and
      air groups commanders.

966.   "Navy Air Power in Korea" and "Korean Air War." NAV
       AVI N, December 1950 through July 1953.

       Series of news type items with human interest stories of
       navy pilots and their support personnel. A regular feature
       in the news from December 1950 through the end of the
       war.

967.   Pratt, Fletcher. THE COMPACT HISTORY OF THE UNITED
       STATES NAVY. New York: Hawthorn, 1957.

       Popular history of the American sailor and the Navy from
       the Revolution through the Korean War. No bibliography
       or footnotes. For the generalist or young reader.

                         B.   FLEET ACTIVITIES

968.   Edwards, Harry W. "A Naval Lesson of the Korean Conflict."
       US NAVAL INST PROC, 1954 80 (12):1337-1340.

       The US Marines scheduled assault landing at Wonsan in
       October 1950 had to be delayed a week because it took so long
       to clear the enemy mines from the harbor. Explains the
       problems the US Navy had in clearing more than 2,000 mines.
       Calls for a new approach and new technology to prevent such
       delays of amphibious operations in the future.

969.   Finan, James. "Voyage From Hungnam." READ DIG,
       1951 59 (355):111-112.

       A story of the SS MEREDITH VICTORY and its skipper
       Leonard P. Larue who evacuated more than 10,000 Koreans
       from Hungnam in December 1950 after encircled US troops
       had withdrawn. At risk to his ship and crew, Larue
       undertook the action which undoubtedly saved the lives
       of those evacuated because the communists had pledged
       death to traitors. Condensed from NAVAL AFFAIRS,
       September 1951.

970.   "Iowa-Class Battleships Off Korea." US NAVAL INST
       PROC, 1952 78 (7):785-789.

       Pictorial section which pays tribute to the roles played
       by the US Battleships: MISSOURI, NEW JERSEY, WISCONSIN
       and IOWA. Focus is on the IOWA, which was activated in
       early 1952, and her support action for US ground forces.

971.   Keighley, Larry. "Four Dead--Three Wounded." SAT EVE
       POST, 1950 223 (17):32-33, 157.

       Human interest story which focuses on Landing Craft,

Vehicle and Personnel (LCVP) No. 8 as it picks up US
Marines from the USS HENRICO and transports them to the
shore in the Inchon invasion. As soon as they stepped
off the boat, four were killed and three wounded. Good
photographs.

972. Kinney, Sheldon. "All Quiet at Wonsan." US NAVAL INST
PROC, 1954 80 (8):859-867.

Details the longest siege in US Naval history, the 861-day
bombardment of the North Korean port city of Wonsan. From
February 16, 1951, until the halt of hostilities July 1953,
navy destroyers fired on the industrial and transportation
centers as Task Force 95 blockaded the port. Tells of the
various attacks and counterattacks on the city.

973. Knight, Charlotte. "Men of the Mine Sweeper." COLLIER'S,
1951 128 (19):13-15, 66-68.

Unsung heroes of the US Navy whose mission was to clear
the seas for UN shipping off the coast of Korea. Although
these men constituted only two percent of the naval
personnel in the Far East, they accounted for twenty
percent of the dead, thus, revealing the hazardous nature
of their task.

974. KOREAN CRUISE USS ST. PAUL CA-73. Berkeley, CA: Lederer,
1951.

One of the first heavy cruisers to arrive in Korean
waters, its cruise lasted from August 12, 1950, to
May 21, 1951.

975. THE KOREAN CRUISE OF THE USS TINGEY DD539. San Diego, CA:
Davidson, 1951.

Brief narrative of the destroyer's contribution to the
Korean cause early in the conflict.

976. Lott, Arnold S. MOST DANGEROUS SEA. Annapolis, MD:
US Naval Institute, 1959.

A history of mine warfare and accounts of US naval mine
warfare operations in both WWII and Korea. Focuses on the
men who conducted such warfare. Cites numerous ships
involved in Korean operations.

977. Marcus, J.W. USS ROCHESTER CA-124 OPERATION KOREA.
New York: Yearbooks, 1951.

Tells of the 1950-51 cruise of this heavy cruiser.

978. Phillips, Richard B. "The Siege of Wonsan." ARMY INFO
DIG, 1953 8 (11):39-47.

On February 16, 1951, US forces began a siege of the North Korean port of Wonsan on the east coast of the country. This siege, which was still underway when the article was written, was the longest active siege in naval history and to sustain it, UN forces utilized air, naval and land forces. The operation neutralized what had been the enemy's main supply route on the east coast.

979. Rairden, P.W., Jr. "The Junior Officer in Mine Warfare." US NAVAL INST PROC, 1953 79 (9):977-979.

During the Korean War young, inexperienced US naval officers frequently were placed in command of mine-sweepers. Mine Division Thirty-One had five AMS's, four commanded by lieutenants and one by a lieutenant junior grade. Those officers learned much about command very early in their careers.

980. Worden, William L. "The Trick That Won Seoul." SAT EVE POST, 1950 223 (20):29, 146-148.

Relates the feats of the USS COLLETT and five other destroyers that played a major role in taking Wolmi Island thus making possible the successful invasion at Inchon. Traces the movement of the ship from the outbreak of war through Inchon.

C. CARRIERS AND AIR SUPPORT

981. "Air War in Korea." NAV AVI N, 1950 October:20-21.

Naval aviation activities are examined in the early months of the war. Jet Panthers and F4V's furnished close air support from aircraft carriers, and helicopters played an important role in evacuating the wounded. Photographs.

982. Amador, Richard. THE UNITED STATES SHIP ESSEX CRUISE BOOK, 1950-51. Tokyo: Toppan, 1952.

Tells of the conversion of this WWII Carrier (CV-9) for duty in Korea and its first cruise in the conflict.

983. ANTIETAM. New York, 1952.

Photo-narrative of the aircraft carrier USS ANTIETAM (CV-36) in action in Korean waters from September 8, 1951-May 2, 1952.

984. Burns, Harry A. "The Case of the Blind Pilot." SAT EVE POST, 1952 225 (22):41, 66-67, 69.

Account of a pilot from the Yellow Devil Squadron from
the carrier USS VALLEY FORGE who was hit by antiaircraft
fire over Wongsong-ni, North Korea, and blinded by the
hit. A fellow pilot then successfully talked him down
at an abandoned US airfield just inside friendly lines.

985. "Carrier Strike." MIL R, 1953 32 (10):57-62.

Narrative and photographs are used to cover the
activities of carrier-based planes of the US Seventh
Fleet as they supported UN forces by giving close air
support to ground forces.

986. CRUISE BOOK OF THE USS ESSEX (CVA-9) AND CARRIER AIR
      TASK GROUP TWO: SECOND KOREAN CRUISE. Nashville: Benson,
      1953.

Narrative and photographic account of the carrier's
support of the conflict in 1952.

987. Denson, John. "Captain Thach's Phantom Carrier."
      COLLIER'S, 1950 126 (16):18-19, 52-56.

Describes the US Navy operations of the escort carrier
USS SICILY and a handful of destroyers operating off the
coast of Korea in the first two months of the Korean War.
The small task force used its carrier based Corsairs to
provide close air support for ground troops, give cover to
British warships shelling the coast and raise havoc with
advancing North Korean troops.

988. "Flares Light the Way for Fighters." NAV AVI N, 1953
      January:14-15.

Describes the procedures where Navy patrol bombers would
drop huge flares behind enemy lines to light supply targets
for Marine fighter pilots who followed closely behind.

989. Hill, Arthur S. "Flight of the Filliboo Bird." US NAVAL
      INST PROC, 1953 79 (1):45-49.

Observations and recollections by a Naval Captain who
served as a tail gunner on a B-29 which flew combat
missions over Korea from its base in Japan. Describes
bombing missions and encounters with enemy fighters in
missions flown in late 1950 and early 1951.

990. King, D.L. KOREAN ENCORE: THE STORY OF THE USS PHILIPPINE
      SEA. Berkeley, CA: Lederer, 1952.

Details the activities of the carrier and Carrier Air
Group Eleven on the ship's second tour in Korea,
31 December 1951 to 9 August 1952.

991. Matt, Paul R. UNITED STATES NAVY AND MARINE CORPS
     FIGHTERS, 1918-1962. Letchworth, England: Harleyford,
     1962.

     Includes photos, descriptions and brief histories of
     land- and sea-based fighter aircraft used in the Korean
     conflict.

992. Metzner, Franklin. "I Fly the Night Skies Over Korea."
     SAT EVE POST, 1952 225 (26):26-27, 48.

     A US Navy carrier pilot from the USS PRINCETON tells what
     it is like to fly night attacks against enemy targets in
     a Skyraider dive bomber.

993. Michener, James A. "All For One: A Story From Korea."
     READ DIG, 1952 61 (363):1-2.

     Tells of the concerted effort by planes and crew from the
     carrier USS VALLEY FORGE to rescue three fellow crewmen
     downed behind enemy lines. The attempts were futile, and
     the fate of the three is unknown, but the account demon-
     strates the dedication of men in combat to their comrades.

994. Michener, James A. "The Forgotten Heroes of Korea."
     SAT EVE POST, 1952 224 (45):19-21, 124-128.

     Recalls a number of acts of heroism by US Navy pilots
     serving off the coast of Korea in Task Force 77. Includes
     a good look at a pilot's life when not flying combat
     missions.

995. PHOTO NARRATIVE OF THE AIRCRAFT CARRIER USS ANTIETAM
     (CV-36) IN ACTION AGAINST THE COMMUNIST AGGRESSORS IN
     NORTH KOREA. Berkeley, CA: Lederer, 1952.

     Photographs and brief narrative of carrier's activities
     off the coast of Korea from September 8, 1951, to May 2,
     1952.

996. Polmar, Norman. AIRCRAFT CARRIERS. Garden City, NY:
     Doubleday, 1969.

     Covers the development of the aircraft carrier from 1911
     to the present. Contains a chapter on the Korean war that
     not only looks at the US role but the contributions of
     Australian and British carriers to the UN command.

997. READY DECK: THIS IS THE USS PRINCETON, 1952. Tokyo:
     Toppan, 1952.

     Very detailed history of this carrier's (CV-37) extensive
     involvement in the Korean conflict with three cruises in
     the war zone.

998. "Salute to the Essex." US NAVAL INST PROC, 1953 79
      (12):1337-1345.

      Pictorial tribute to the aircraft carrier USS ESSEX looks
      at her WWII contributions and her modernization and
      recommissioning after the outbreak of war in Korea. Shows
      the sea and air crews as they undertake operations in support
      of the UN Command.

999. Shane, Patrick C., III. "The 13 Wild Weeks of the USS
      Princeton." SAT EVE POST, 1953 225 (37):28-29, 74-76, 80.

      Saga of a US aircraft carrier which was in mothballs when
      war broke out in Korea and in slightly over three months was
      in action off the Korean coast. Tells of that action plus
      life aboard the craft in the first year of the conflict.
      Includes the Inchon invasion and the evacuation of Marines
      from Hungnam.

1000. Small, Dorothy L. "Catapults Come of Age." US NAVAL
      INST PROC, 1954 80 (10):1113-1121.

      Traces the development and use of catapults on US
      aircraft carriers from 1911 through the Korean War. By
      the time of Korea, the device had become a vital piece
      of machinery. Describes the types of catapults and how
      they worked.

1001. Smith, M.S. THE KOREAN CRUISE USS PHILIPPINE SEA
      CV-47. Berkeley, CA: Lederer, 1951.

      The July 1950 to June 1951 support activities of its
      first combat tour off the coast of Korea. Includes action
      in the Chosin theater.

1002. Suffrin, Mark. "Incident At Chosin Reservoir."
      MANKIND, 1973 4 (1):52-59.

      Lieutenant Thomas J. Hubner was the first naval officer to
      receive the Congressional Medal of Honor in Korea. In
      December 1950 Hubner landed behind enemy lines and attempted,
      unsuccessfully, to save a fellow pilot, Ensign Jesse L.
      Brown, a black naval officer. Hubner was evacuated by
      helicopter thus avoiding capture. A vivid account of an act
      of heroism.

1003. "Three Very Long Minutes." US NAVAL INST PROC, 1950
      76 (12):1365-1369.

      Photographic essay which contains a remarkable sequence
      of photos showing the abortive take-off, crash and
      subsequent rescue of a US Navy Corsair pilot aboard an

unidentified aircraft carrier of Task Force 77. The
aircraft was supporting the Inchon invasion. The title
comes from the time the plane's engine malfunctioned
until a helicopter delivered the pilot from the sea back
onto the carrier deck.

1004. USS BON HOMME RICHARD CVA-31 SECOND KOREAN CRUISE.
Tokyo: Toppan, 1952.

Photos and brief narrative of this aircraft carrier's
second combat tour in the war zone.

1005. USS PRINCETON (CV-37) KOREA, 1950-51. Berkeley, CA:
Lederer, 1951.

Tells of this mothballed ship which was activated in
July 1950 and manned primarily by reservists. Reached
Korean waters on December 5 to begin her first of three
Korean cruises.

1006. Van Fleet, Clark. "Carrier Air Over Korea." NAV AVI
MUS FD, 1984 Spring:56-61.

Overview of the role of US aircraft carriers and the role
of naval aircraft in providing ground support to UN forces
throughout the conflict.

1007. Vernor, W.H., Jr. "Standby Squadron." US NAVAL INST
PROC, 1952 78 (7):729-739.

Traces the contribution of the US Navy's Attack Squadron
702, a reserve unit from Dallas, Texas, from its activation
on July 20, 1950, through its combat activities in Korea in
the spring of 1951. Shows problem of activating a unit,
the training and combat activities as carried out, with
three other activated reserve units, from the aircraft carrier
USS BOXER.

1008. "War is Hard Work." NAV AVI N, 1952 September:1-7.

While the land war in Korea in 1952 saw some lulls, the
naval air war did not, since carriers cruising the coasts sent
aircraft to strike against the enemy everyday. This article
examines the various aspects of that naval air contribution.

1009. Weber, M.L. USS ROCHESTER CA-124: OPERATION KOREA,
1951-1952. San Diego, CA: Book, 1952.

Account of its fine support mission for US ground troops
in Korea.

1010. Weems, John E. "Black Wings of Gold." US NAVAL INST
PROC, 1983 109 (7):35-39.

Account of the Korean War experience of Ensign Jesse L. Brown, the first Black aviator in the US Navy who died after being shot down over North Korea in October 1950. Valiant efforts to rescue him were unsuccessful.

1011. Wheeler, Gerald E. "Naval Aviation in the Korean War." US NAVAL INST PROC, 1957 83 (7):762-777.

Carrier based aircraft strike at Korean targets from aboard the USS BADOENG STRAIT and USS SICILY. Well illustrated.

1012. Canzona, Nicholas A. "Reflections on Korea." MARINE CORPS
      GAZ, 1951 35 (11):56-65.

      A Marine Corps officer looks critically at his service as
      he focuses on shortcomings of weapons, equipment and tactics
      during the Korean War.

1013. Donavon, James A. "The FMF in Korea." LEATHERNECK,
      1952 35 (11):16-23.

      Brief accounts of operations of the 1st Marine Division
      and 1st Marine Aircraft Wing from September 1951 to
      September 1952.

1014. Duncan, David D. THIS IS WAR. New York: Harper, 1951.

      An excellent photographic account of US Marines fighting
      in Korea. Short text with uncaptioned photographs that
      conveys the emotions of men at war.

1015. Feningo, William G. "Letter From Korea." MARINE CORPS
      GAZ, 1951 35 (1):20-21.

      A Marine Corps Master Sergeant reflects on his Korean
      experience with observations on such diverse topics as
      ambushes, battlefield illumination, the poncho and
      shelter tent.

1016. Gardella, Lawrence. SING A SONG TO JENNY NEXT. New York:
      Dutton, 1981.

      Supposedly a personal narrative of a group of half-a-dozen
      US Marines who are dropped behind enemy lines in Manchuria
      during the Korean War for the purpose of destroying a nuclear
      research facility. Only time will tell whether this account
      tells of one of the war's most bizarre covert operations or a
      hoax.

1017. Geer, Andrew. THE NEW BREED: THE STORY OF THE US MARINES
      IN KOREA. New York: Harper, 1952.

      Traces the activities of the First Marine Division from the
      time they are thrown into the Pusan Perimeter to the Inchon
      Invasion and the drive north to the Yalu and subsequent
      retreat. The author, a Marine Reserve Officer who went to

Korea in 1950, is overly partial to the Marines. Reads like
a propaganda tract for the Corps.

1018. Gray, Bob. "Seoul Liberty." LEATHERNECK, 1952 35 (8):43-45.

Activities of combat Marines on three days of rest and
rehabilitation liberty in Seoul.

1019. Heinl, Robert D. SOLDIERS OF THE SEA: THE US MARINE
CORPS 1775-1962. Annapolis, MD: US Naval Institute, 1962.

An extremely pro-Marine history of the Corps. The author
attacks politicians and leaders of the other services for
supposedly trying to destroy the Corps. One of the first
general works to cover the Marines in Korea.

1020. Johnstone, John H. A BRIEF HISTORY OF THE 1ST MARINES.
Washington: Historical Branch, G-3, US Marine Corps, 1968.

Contains extremely brief overview of activities throughout
the Korean War.

1021. Kalischer, Peter. "The Marines Remarkable Foreign Legion."
COLLIER'S, 1952 130 (17):96-101.

Looks at the 1st Marine Reconnaissance Company in Korea
and focuses on the varied backgrounds and nationalities of
its personnel. These US fighters came from such countries as
China, Germany, Russia, Spain, Poland and Latvia.

1022. Lederer, William J. "Our Hilarious Heroes: 'Them US
Marines!" CORONET, 1952 31 (3):96-103.

Tongue-in-cheek assessment of why the US Marines are such
good forces. Uses examples allegedly from Korea to
substantiate the Marines' claim to be innovative, show
initiative and be the best fighters in the world.

1023. Martin, Harold H. "Toughest Marine in the Corps."
SAT EVE POST, 1952 224 (38):40-41, 105-110.

Human interest story on Brig. Gen. Lewis B. "Chesty"
Puller, commander of the 1st Marine Regiment in Korea and one
of the Corps' most decorated soldiers. Recaps his long career
and focuses on his service in Korea, from the taking of Seoul
through early 1952. Puts forth many of Puller's views on
what makes for good leaders, good soldiers and a good
fighting force.

1024. Millett, Allan R. SEMPER FIDELIS: THE HISTORY OF THE
UNITED STATES MARINE CORPS. New York: Macmillan, 1980.

The best single volume yet written on the history of the
US Marine Corps. Well-written and thoroughly researched.

Has an excellent chapter on the US Marines in the Korean War
and a good essay on historical sources.

1025. Montross, Lynn. "Fleet Marine Force Korea, I." US
       NAVAL INST PROC, 1953 79 (8):829-841.

       Evolution of the Fleet Marine Force from its inception in
       1933 through WWII with major focus being on the Force in the
       early Korean War especially the Inchon invasion. Goes into
       considerable detail on the planning and execution of the
       Inchon and Seoul operations.

1026. Montross, Lynn. "Fleet Marine Force Korea, II." US
       NAVAL INST PROC, 1953 79 (9):995-1005.

       Excellent examination of US Marine operations from the
       September 1950 Seoul operation through the March 1951
       Operation RIPPER which took Hongchon and Chunchon and ends
       with the summer 1951 armistice talks. Detailed account of
       the Chosin Reservoir breakout and evacuation from Hungnam.

1027. Nicholson, Dennis D. "SOP: Night Raids." MARINE CORPS
       GAZ, 1955 39 (3):20-27.

       Describes the techniques used by the US Marines in making
       night raids against enemy positions. Examines the lessons
       learned in such tactics and tells of the Standard Operating
       Procedures that were developed.

1028. Prickett, W.F. "Why We Fought." US NAVAL INST PROC,
       1954 80 (7):751-753.

       A US Marine Corps Colonel who served in Korea reflects
       on the reason Americans fought so well in Korea.
       Maintains he and others fought because it was decent and
       right. Critical of the US homefront where, he claims,
       the purpose of the war was lost.

1029. Renfrow, Frank. "24 Hours in Korea." AM LEG MAG,
       1952 53 (5):41-43.

       Traces a typical day in the life of a US Marine major
       who commanded a detachment of armored amphibious tractors.

1030. Russ, Martin. THE LAST PARALLEL: A MARINE'S WAR
       JOURNAL. New York: Rinehart, 1957.

       Inciteful and informative account of a 21-year old
       corporal in the First Marine Regiment, First Marine
       Division who describe life on the front in the last
       seven months of the fighting. Good look at social
       life on the front and on leave.

1031. Scott, Jay. MARINE WAR HEROES. Derby, CT: Monarch, 1963.

This book, which covers all US wars, includes a chapter on the Marines who won the Medal of Honor in Korea.

1032. Simmons, Edwin. THE UNITED STATES MARINES 1775-1975. New York: Viking, 1976.

This brief popular history of the Marine Corps includes a chapter on the war in Korea.

1033. Third Marine Division. FLEET MARINE FORCE PACIFIC. Dallas: Taylor, 1953.

A privately published, illustrated souvenir book of the Force's activities throughout the Korean War.

1034. 3rd Marine Division Public Information Office. 3RD MARINE DIVISION. Dallas: Taylor, 1952.

Brief survey of the activities and engagements of the Division during the first two years of the Korean War. Includes sketches.

1035. US Marine Corps, Historical Branch, G-3. OUR FIRST YEAR IN KOREA. Quantico, VA: Marine Corps Gazette, 1954.

Collection of articles from the MARINE CORPS GAZETTE on Corps activities in Korea from July 1950 through November 1951.

1036. Wells, H.B. "They Double in Brass." LEATHERNECK, 1953 36 (1):26-29.

Describes the life and duties of members of the 1st Marine Division Band while in the combat zone.

B. GROUND OPERATIONS

1. PUSAN PERIMETER

1037. Canzona, Nicholas A. "A Hill Near Yongsan." MARINE CORPS GAZ, 1955 39 (6):55-59.

Account of the taking of Hill 91 in the Second Naktong River campaign, September 3, 1950, by four companies of the 1st and 2nd Battalions, 5th Marines.

1038. Chung, Ul Mun. "Letters From Almond." LEATHERNECK, 1953 36 (4):34-35, 74, 79.

Observations of a Korean who served as an interpreter with the 7th Marines in the early months of the war.

1039. Conner, John. "The New Breed." COLLIER'S, 1950 126 (15):13-15, 71-72.

Traces the military activities of the 1st Marine Brigade in the first two months of the war.

1040.   Denson, John. "What Hurt Was to See Us Retreat."
        COLLIER'S, 1950 126 (10):17, 58.

One of the first Marine casualties of the war, Sergeant Leonard Smith, tells of one of the first contacts between US and North Korean forces. Describes his shock at the strong showing of the enemy and laments over the fact that he had never seen Americans thrown back. Relates some of the early activities of the enemy.

1041.   Fenton, Francis I. "Changallon Valley." MARINE CORPS
        GAZ, 1951 35 (11):48-53.

Operations of Company B, 1st Battalion, 5th Marines in the Sachon Ambush on August 12, 1950.

1042.   Martin, Harold. "The Epic of Bloody Hill." SAT EVE
        POST, 1950 223 (16):19-21, 50-54, 59-60.

Describes the bloody August 17-19, 1950, engagement of the 5th Regiment, 1st Provisional Marine Brigade near the Naktong River. After bitter fighting the North Korean forces were driven from mountainous terrain but at a heavy cost.

1043.   Martin, Harold H. "The Ordeal of Marine Squad 2." SAT
        EVE POST, 1950 223 (20):24-25, 126-130, 133.

Follows a US Marine squad of the 5th Marine rifle regiment from the time they arrived in Korea in late July until August 17. In that brief period of heavy fighting, the thirteen-man squad saw four of its number die and five seriously wounded, leaving only four to join the September push on Seoul.

1044.   Montross, Lynn. "Development of Our Body Armor."
        MARINE CORPS GAZ, 1955 39 (6):10-16.

Reviews the development of body armor at the Naval Medical Field Research Laboratory and its use in Korea by US Marines.

1045.   Montross, Lynn, and Nicholas A. Canzona. THE PUSAN
        PERIMETER. Vol. I of US MARINE OPERATIONS IN KOREA
        1950-53. Washington: Historical Branch, G-3, Headquarters,
        US Marine Corps, 1954.

Official account of the operations of 1st Provisional Brigade and Marine Air Group 33 during the fighting in the Pusan Perimeter from the date of their landing on August 2, 1950 until their withdrawal on September 13, 1950. All books in the series have excellent maps.

1046. Montross, Lynn. "The Pusan Perimeter: Fight for a
       Foothold." MARINE CORPS GAZ, 1951 35 (6):30-39.

       Follows the operations and engagements of the 1st
       Provisional Marine Brigade in South Korea from August 7
       to September 7, 1950 as it helped establish the UN
       Command's Pusan Perimeter.

1047. Montross, Lynn, and Norman W. Hicks. "They Were There."
       LEATHERNECK, 1960 43 (12):48-53; 1961 44 (1):48-53.

       Personal experiences of Marine officers and enlisted
       men involved in operations through the Chosin Reservoir
       Campaign.

1048. Murray, R.L. "The First Naktong." MARINE CORPS GAZ,
       1965 49 (11):84-85.

       Brief account of the fighting between North Koreans
       and US Marines along the Naktong River from August 17
       through 19, 1950.

1049. Tallent, Robert W. "Pusan--a Stop Enroute."
       LEATHERNECK, 1950 33 (12):14-17.

       Traces the activities of the 1st Provisional Marine
       Brigade from the time it was pulled from the Pusan
       Perimeter until it was involved in the Inchon
       Invasion. During the period the Marines rested and
       were re-equipped for the surprise operation.

                    2.   INCHON AND THE DRIVE NORTH

1050. Aguirre, Emilio. WE'LL BE HOME FOR CHRISTMAS: A TRUE
       STORY OF THE UNITED STATES MARINE CORPS IN THE KOREAN WAR.
       New York: Greenwich, 1959.

       Recollections of a member of Company G, 3rd Battalion,
       7th Marines from the Inchon invasion, the march north to
       the Yalu and the retreat from the Chosin Reservoir.

1051. Alsop, Joseph. "Matter of Fact." LEATHERNECK, 1950
       33 (12):33.

       Observations by a well-known American news columnist on
       the Marine advance from Inchon to Seoul in September 1950.

1052. Campigno, Anthony J. A MARINE DIVISION IN NIGHTMARE
       ALLEY. New York: Comet, 1958.

       Brief account (by an enlisted man) of the 11th Marines
       from September through December of 1950. Includes the
       advance to the Yalu and the Chosin Reservoir operation.

1053. Canzona, Nicholas A. "Dog Company's Charge." US NAVAL
          INST PROC, 1956 82 (11):1203-1211.

          Describes the bitter fighting of two rifle companies, but
          especially D Company of 2nd Battalion, 5th Regiment in the
          September 1950 battle for Seoul. In the successful battle
          for Hill 56 and Smith's Ridge, the Company had six of its
          seven officers killed or wounded, and the enlisted
          ranks experienced the loss of more than half its personnel.

1054. Halloran, B.F. "Inchon Landing." MARINE CORPS GAZ,
          1972 56 (9):25-32.

          Analysis of the US Marines, successful amphibious landing
          at Inchon in September 1950. Concludes the attack was
          masterfully conceived and carried out.

1055. Heinl, Robert D. "Inchon." MARINE CORPS GAZ, 1967
          51 (9):20-28 and 51 (10):45-50.

          A look at the Inchon Invasion from planning to successful
          operation with focus on the US Marines' role. A short
          version of the in-depth study published in book form in
          1968.

1056. Heinl, Robert D. "The Inchon Landing: A Case Study in
          Amphibious Planning." NAV W C R, 1967 39 (9):51-71.

          Examination of the background, planning and execution of
          the September 1950 invasion of Inchon by US forces -
          Operation CHROMITE - by the top expert on the subject.
          Given as a lecture at the Naval War College.

1057. Heinl, Robert D. VICTORY AT HIGH TIDE: THE INCHON-SEOUL
          CAMPAIGN. Philadelphia: Lippincott, 1968.

          The best work on the Inchon landing and the subsequent
          reconquest of Seoul, in spite of the author's pro-
          US Marines bias. Covers the planning as well as carrying
          out of the operations. Based on official and other primary
          sources. Well-written.

1058. Kimp, Jack W. "The Battle for Seoul: Marines and MOUT."
          MARINE CORPS GAZ, 1981 65 (11):79-82.

          Utilizes the Marine Corps fighting to take Seoul
          (20-28 September 1950) as the basis for describing
          military operations on urbanized terrain (MOUT).
          Covers not only fighting concepts in cities and
          villages but the rural areas surrounding them.

1059. Lavine, Harold. "Inchon: 'A Helluva Gamble' That Paid
          Off." NEWSWEEK, 1950 36 (13):25.

A war correspondent's eyewitness account of the Inchon landing.

1060. McMullen, Robert A., and Nicholas A. Canzona. "Wolmi-do: Turning the Key." US NAVAL INST PROC, 1956 82 (3):290-297.

The key to the success of the Inchon invasion was the successful taking of the small island of Wolmi-do in Inchon harbor. This study describes the Communist defense of the island, the plans for its capture and the September 10-15 operation which resulted in its capture.

1061. Mainard, Allen G. "Sea Wall." LEATHERNECK, 1957 40 (9):42-45.

Account of the scaling of the high harbor sea wall by US Marines during the Inchon landing.

1062. Marcus, Steven. "In the Highest Tradition ... Henry Alfred Commiskey." LEATHERNECK, 1954 37 (5):50-52, 75.

Relates the exploits which won the Congressional Medal of Honor for 1st Lieutenant Commiskey, 1st Marines, at Yongdung-po on September 20, 1950.

1063. Marshall, S.L.A. "Into the Alligator's Jaws." MARINE CORPS GAZ, 1956 40 (10):12-16.

An account of a 1950 engagement between US Marines and North Korean troops in the Yokkokchon Valley.

1064. Montross, Lynn. "The Capture of Seoul: Battle of the Barricades." MARINE CORPS GAZ, 1951 35 (8):26-37.

Follows the movement of the 1st Marine Division from Inchon to Seoul, the capture of Seoul and the advance to Uijongbu from September 18 to October 3, 1950.

1065. Montross, Lynn. "The Inchon Landing: Victory Over Time and Tide." MARINE CORPS GAZ, 1951 35 (7):26-35.

The 1st Marine Division's build-up prior to the invasion, the planning required to overcome the numerous problems, the invasion and the day after.

1066. Montross, Lynn. "Majon-ni, Perimeter of Expediency." MARINE CORPS GAZ, 1956 40 (11):58-62.

Narrative account of successful defensive operation in which the 3rd Battalion, 1st Marines defended a key road junction west of Wonsan, North Korea, from October 30 until November 14, 1950.

1067. Montross, Lynn. "Trouble in Hell Fire Valley." MARINE CORPS GAZ, 1957 41 (3):53-57.

Tells of an ambush by Communist forces on Marine Task
Force Drysdale between Hagaru-ri and Koto-ri, North Korea,
in late November, 1950.

1068. Montross, Lynn, and Nicholas A. Canzona. THE INCHON-SEOUL
       OPERATION. Vol. II of US MARINE OPERATION IN KOREA
       1950-1953. Washington: Historical Branch, G-3,
       Headquarters US Marine Corps, 1955.

       Detailed operations of the 1st Marine Division and the 1st
       Marine Aircraft Wing during and immediately after the Inchon
       invasion on September 15, 1950. Includes, mobilization of
       the reserves to augment the Division and Wing, movement to
       the staging area, the invasion and activities at Kimpo, the
       Han, Yongdungpo and Seoul. Covers the period to October 7,
       1950.

1069. Montross, Lynn, and Nicholas A. Canzona. "Large Sedentary
       Targets on Red Beach." MARINE CORPS GAZ, 1960 44 (9):44-50.

       Tells the key role played by LST's (Landing Ship Tanks) in
       the Marines successful amphibious landing at Inchon.

1070. "Operation 'Load-Up." QM R, 1950 30 (3):40-41, 109-110.

       The story of an operation unofficially known as "Load-Up"--
       the backbreaking twelve-day operation at Kobe Base, Japan,
       which set the stage for the First Marine Division's
       invasion at Inchon in September 1950. The load-up was
       accomplished under a unified command made up of Army, Navy
       and Marine troops.

1071. Smith, O.P. "The Inchon Invasion. MARINE CORPS GAZ,
       1960 44 (9):40-41.

       Personal account of the invasion by the commander of the
       First Marine Division. Focuses on the planning and
       preparation of the operation.

1072. "Spearhead." LEATHERNECK, 1950 33 (12):34-49.

       Photographic account of the September 1950 capture of
       Seoul by US Marines.

1073. Stanford, N.R. "Road Junction." MARINE CORPS GAZ,
       1951 35 (9):16-21.

       Describes a US Marine Corps Company's successful assault
       of the Duk Soo Palace in Seoul on September 26, 1950.
       Account is by the company commander, Company E, 2nd
       Battalion, 1st Marines.

1074. Tallent, Robert W. "Inchon to Seoul." LEATHERNECK,
       1951 34 (1):12-17.

Account of the US Marines September 1950 advance from
Inchon, after the successful invasion, to Seoul. Author
was a noncommissioned officer who relates the operation from a dog face's perspective.

1075. Tallent, Robert W. "Street Fight in Seoul." LEATHERNECK,
1951 34 (1):20-24.

Illustrated story on operations of units of the 1st Marine
Division as they fight their way through Seoul in September
1950.

1076. Walker, Stanley L. "Logistics of the Inchon Landing."
ARMY LOG, 1981 13 (4):34-38.

Focuses on the virtually ignored topic of the logistical
aspects of the Inchon invasion. Tells how the logistics
support planning, preparation and execution of the landing
was accomplished in only 33 days. The supply efforts in
the several days following the assault were instrumental
in the attack on Seoul.

3. CHOSIN RESERVOIR

1077. Chandler, James B. "Thank God, I'm a Marine." LEATHERNECK,
1951 34 (6):24-27.

A US Marine Lieutenant of the 1st Battalion, 7th Marines,
describes his unit's withdrawal from Hagaru to Koto in early
December 1950 in the Chosin operation. Stresses the
importance of discipline and training in holding the unit
together under trying conditions.

1078. Davis, William J. "The Bloody Breakout." US NAVAL INST
PROC, 1953 79 (7):737-739.

A Marine Captain of the 7th Marines, First Marine Division
recounts the suffering experienced and the obstacles overcome
in the withdrawal from the Chosin Reservoir.

1079. Davis, W.J. "Fire for Effect." MARINE CORPS GAZ, 1954
38 (7):16-21.

Tells of the importance and effectiveness of mortar fire
in support of the Chosin Reservoir withdrawal.

1080. Drysdale, D.B. "41 Commando." MARINE CORPS GAZ, 1951
37 (8):28-32.

Joint operation of the 41st Independent Commando, Royal
Marines and personnel of the 1st US Marines Division in
the Chosin Reservoir breakout.

1081. FIRST MARINE DIVISION, NOVEMBER 1-DECEMBER 15, CHOSIN
RESERVOIR. Washington: Government Printing Office, 1951.

Very brief account of the US Marines in the Chosin
Campaign. Taken from Marine Corps Gazette. Focuses
on the gallantry of men and units.

1082. Hammel, Eric. CHOSIN: HEROIC ORDEAL OF THE KOREAN WAR.
        New York: Vanguard, 1981.

Extremely detailed account of the late 1950 withdrawal of
US military units from North Korea. Focuses on the men
who fought, died, suffered and escaped from that Chinese
onslaught. Little analysis of the various engagements and
the entire operation.

1083. Higgins, Marguerite. "The Bloody Trail Back." SAT EVE
        POST, 1951 223 (31):30-31, 117-120.

Firsthand account of how the First Marine Division battled
its way out of he icy trap at Changjin Reservoir in
November-December 1950. Describes how they fought back the
fanatical Chinese Communists and brought their wounded
comrades to safety.

1084. Leckie, Robert. THE MARCH TO GLORY. Cleveland, OH:
        World, 1960.

The author used many interviews along with official records
to develop this account of the First Marine Division at the
Chosin Reservoir. Well-written account which focuses on
the ordeal of men in combat fighting for survival.

1085. Montross, Lynn. "Hagaru: Perimeter of Necessity."
        MARINE CORPS GAZ, 1958 42 (12):20-30.

Tells of the fighting of the 3rd Battalion, 1st Marines
against Communist Chinese troops in the Chosin Reservoir
from November 28 to December 5, 1950.

1086. Montross, Lynn. "Wonsan to the Reservoir: Red China
        Enters the Fight." MARINE CORPS GAZ, 1951 35 (10):30-39.

General account of the fighting by US forces from the
time the Chinese Communists entered the fighting in large
numbers, in late October 1950, until their first major
victory over US forces at Yudam-ni a month later.

1087. Montross, Lynn, and Nicholas A. Canzona. THE CHOSIN
        RESERVOIR CAMPAIGN. Vol. III of US MARINE OPERATIONS IN
        KOREA 1950-1953. Washington: Historical Branch, G-3,
        Headquarters US Marine Corps, 1957.

In-depth examination of 1st Marine Division and 1st Marine
Aircraft Wing from October 26, 1950, the date of the landing
at Wonsan, to December 24, 1950, when the final troops were
evacuated from Hungnam. Examines why the Marines were in

northeast Korea, the Chinese intervention and the Marines'
heroic fight through twelve Chinese divisions over eight
miles of rough terrain in sub-zero weather.

1088. Owen, Joseph R. "Chosin Reservoir Remembered." MARINE
       CORPS GAZ, 1980 64 (12):52-58.

       A retrospective look at the Chosin Reservoir Campaign
       thirty years after the event.

1089. Parry, F.F. "Fat Cats." MARINE CORPS GAZ, 1963 47
       (12):28-34.

       A firsthand account of the role of US Marine artillery
       in the Chosin Reservoir campaign. The author was an
       artillery officer in the 3rd Battalion, 11th Marines.

1090. Read, Benjamin. "Our Guns Never Got Cold." SAT EVE
       POST, 1951 223 (41):32-33, 145-148.

       A US Captain with the 1st Marine Division recounts how
       his field artillery battery was surrounded at Hagaru, and
       the Changjin Reservoir in late November 1950 and for two
       weeks fought its way south through the communist hoardes
       to Koto-ri.

1091. Smith, O.P. "Looking Back at Chosin." MARINE CORPS
       GAZ, 1960 44 (12):30-31.

       Reflection on the Chosin withdrawal by the General who
       commanded the 1st Marine Division.

1092. "There Was a Christmas." LIFE, 1950 29 (26):8-15.

       Excellent photographs of US Marines fighting their way
       from the Changjin Reservoir in December 1950.

                          4. STALEMATE

1093. Averill, Gerald P. "Final Objective." MARINE CORPS GAZ,
       1956 40 (8):10-16.

       An account of a US Marine attack on North Korean positions
       near Inje and Yanggu, Korea, in August 1951. The author was
       the operations officer of the 2nd Battalion, 5th Marines,
       the unit which led the attack.

1094. Averill, Gerald P. "Run the Ridges and Win." COM FOR J,
       1952 3 (3):24-25.

       Contends that the original emphasis which the US Army in
       Korea placed on corridors as the way to enter battle is
       unsound. Argues that the best tactic is to stick to the
       high ground. Cites the operation of 2nd Battalion, 5th

Marines in the spring of 1951 to prove his point.

1095.   Fugate, Robert T. "Vegas, Reno, and Carson."
        LEATHERNECK, 1953 36 (6):16-21, 74.

        Details the March 25, 1953, battle by US Marines for
        three strategic hills near Panmunjom.

1096.   Gray, Bob. "A New Kind of War." LEATHERNECK, 1952
        35 (7):16-21.

        Development of trench warfare on the eastern front in
        Korea in late 1951 and early 1952.

1097.   Heinecke, Roy E. "The Last 12 Hours." LEATHERNECK,
        1953 36 (10):22-25, 64, 66.

        Describes the activities of a Company of the 2nd Battalion,
        5th Marines in the twelve hours preceding the July 27, 1953,
        cease-fire.

1098.   Hicks, Norman W. "US Marine Operations in Korea, 1952-
        1953." Master's Thesis. Maryland, 1962.

        Examines the problems of outpost warfare as experienced
        by US Marines during the last year of the war.

1099.   Hicks, Norman, and Truman R. Strowbridge. "Over the Hill."
        MARINE CORPS GAZ, 1962 46 (11):49-52.

        Description of US Marine operations against North Korean
        and Chinese troops on Bunker Hill, near Panmunjom in 1952.

1100.   Jordon, Curtis W. "Wonsan Marines." LEATHERNECK,
        1952 35 (6):24-29.

        Depicts the life of US Marines on shore fire-control
        party duty on islands in Wonsan harbor.

1101.   Meid, Pat, and James M. Yingling. OPERATIONS IN WEST KOREA.
        Vol. V of US MARINE OPERATIONS IN KOREA 1950-1953.
        Washington: Historical Branch, G-3, Headquarters, US
        Marine Corps, 1972.

        Detailed examination of 1st Marine Division and 1st Marine
        Aircraft Wing from March 1952 to the end of hostilities in
        July 1953. Covers key battles such as Bunker Hill, the Hook,
        and Boulder City.

1102.   Montross, Lynn, and Hubard D. Kuokka, and Norman W.
        Hicks. THE EAST-CENTRAL FRONT. Vol. IV of US MARINE
        OPERATIONS IN KOREA 1950-1953. Washington: Historical
        Branch, G-3, Headquarters, US Marine Corps, 1962.

        Examines Marine activities along the static front in

central and east Korea from December 1950 through December
1951. Covers the guerrilla hunt, the Punchbowl and other
lengthy operations. Shows the new-found importance of the
helicopter in combat operations.

1103.   Reissner, P.D., Jr. "The Victors at Boomerang."
        MARINE CORPS GAZ, 1958 42 (8):8-13.

        Tells of a brief, but bitter engagement between US
        Marines (1st Battalion, 1st Marines) and Chinese
        Communist forces near Hwachon, South Korea, on April
        23-24, 1951.

1104.   Woessner, H.J., II. "Strongpoints?" MARINE CORPS GAZ,
        1955 39 (2):26-33.

        Citing successful Chinese Communist attack on US Marine
        positions near Ch'unch'on in the spring of 1951, the
        author is critical of the strategy of concentrating troops
        in isolated strongpoints for the purpose of defending
        territory against the enemy.

                    C.   MARINE AIR SUPPORT

1105.   Braitsch, Fred G., Jr. "Air Strike." LEATHERNECK, 1953
        36 (4):16-20.

        US Marine air support for ground troops, focusing on the
        importance of coordination between forward air controllers,
        Tactical Air Direction Centers and pilots.

1106.   Braitsch, Fred G., Jr. "Flying Sergeants." LEATHERNECK,
        1952 35 (2):14-19.

        Little known fact that US Marines utilized some enlisted
        men as pilots during the Korean War.

1107.   Braitsch, Fred G., Jr. "Marine Air War." LEATHERNECK,
        1951 34 (11):30-35; 1952 35 (11):30-35.

        These two articles present an overview of Marine air
        activities in Korea in the first year and first two years
        of the war, respectively.

1108.   Braitsch, Fred G., Jr. "Photos by Banshee." LEATHERNECK,
        1952 35 (10):26-30.

        Shows how the McDonnel F2H2P "Banshee" was utilized by the
        US Marines to secure aerial reconnaissance photos that were
        of great value to intelligence officers. This was done by
        the Marine Photographic Squadron 1 over North Korea.

1109.   Condit, Kenneth W., and Ernest H. Giusti. "Marine Air
        Over Inchon-Seoul." MARINE CORPS GAZ, 1952 36 (6):18-27.

Narrative of the activities of the 1st Marine Aircraft
Wing in providing air support to ground troops following
the successful invasion at Inchon.

1110.   "Land Based Marine Air Hammers Reds." NAV AVI N,
        1952 September:10-13.

        While much of US Marine air activity in Korea was conducted
        from carriers much was carried on from land bases. This
        account looks at Marine Aircraft Group 12's activities in
        mid-1952.

1111.   Phillips, C.A., and H.D. Kuokka. "1st MAW in Korea."
        MARINE CORPS GAZ, 1957 41 (5):42-47 and 41 (6):20-26.

        Two-part account of the activities of the US Marine Corps'
        1st Marine Aircraft Wing against North Korean and Chinese
        forces from August 1950 to July 1953. Covers both ground
        and carrier-based action.

1112.   Reinburg, J.H. "Night Fighter Squadron." ORDNANCE,
        1965 49 (268):416-418.

        A Marine Corps pilot relates the problems involved in
        flying night air support operations.

1113.   Saxon, Thomas J. "Cook's Tour for Pilots." MARINE CORPS
        GAZ, 1953 37 (11):37-39.

        Describes the briefings and indoctrination of replacement
        pilots for Marine Attack Squadron 323 in Korea.

1114.   Thach, John S. "Right On the Button: Marine Close Air
        Support in Korea." US NAVAL INST PROC, 1975 101 (11):54-56.

        Recollections of the Commander of the escort carrier SICILY
        which had the "Black Sheep Squadron," a wing of 24 F4V
        Corsairs. The Marine aircraft began flying close air support
        for ground troops on the west coast of Korea early in the
        war. Tells of the missions and the pilots who flew them.

                              D. HELICOPTERS

1115.   Barker, Edward L. "The Helicopter in Combat." US NAVAL
        INST PROC, 1951 77 (11):1207-1222.

        Detailed descriptions of specific instances in which the
        helicopter is proving its military value to the Navy in
        combat operations. Claims the Korean conflict pushed
        helicopter development ahead by at least five years.
        Good photographs.

1116.   Boesen, Victor. "The Copters Are Coming." CORONET,

1952 31 (5):60-63.

Describes in journalistic fashion the extensive use of helicopters in combat operations by US forces in Korea. Describes the first mass helicopter attack in history which took place in September 1951 using US Marines. Includes other combat uses plus a brief history of the aircraft's development.

1117.   Collins, William R. "The Helicopter in Marine Operations."
        ARMY INFO DIG, 1951 6 (6):47-53.

Traces the US Marines' interest in the use of the helicopter in the post-WWII period and its employment in the early months of the Korean War for reconnaissance flights and evacuation of wounded. Predicts a bright future for the helicopter in future Korean operations.

1118.   Crosby, Willard B., and Todd Wright. "Helicopters Cop the
        Collier Trophy." COLLIER'S, 1951 128 (25):30-31, 51-52.

In 1951 the American top aviation award went to the helicopter industry, Coast Guard and military services for development and use of the craft in air rescue. In the first year of the Korean War, 10,000 UN wounded were evacuated by the craft. Many examples of rescue operations in Korea.

1119.   Foley, Edward D. EQUITATUS CAELI 1952. Tokyo: Kasai,
        1953.

A history of US Marine Helicopter Transport Squadron 161 during the Korean War. This unit served with the First Marine Air Wing and later the First Marine Division.

1120.   Gahagan, Neil. "The Versatile Helicopter." MIL ENG,
        1952 44 (297):37-38.

Use of the helicopter in evacuation of US wounded, reconnaissance missions and tactical air assaults. Describes the September 1951 movement of 250 marines to the top of a 3,000-foot mountain--the first tactical assault in history. Two weeks later 1,000 troops were moved eighteen miles to the front.

1121.   Mahone, Nelson A. "A Tactical Role for Helicopters."
        ARMY INFO DIG, 1955 10 (9):33-38.

Emphasizes the versatility of the helicopter in combat support by examining the activities of the 6th Transportation Helicopter Company in Korea from October 1950 through the end of the war.

1122.   Montross, Lynn. CAVALRY OF THE SKY: THE STORY OF US
        MARINE COMBAT HELICOPTERS. Harper, 1954.

Covers the role that the helicopter played for the US Marines in Korea. Based on Official records, it actually covers developments from 1947 through 1954.

1123.   "Night Flying 'Choppers' Busy in Korea." NAV AVI N, 1952 October:13-15.

Traces the activities of VMO-6 in Korea from July 1950 through the summer of 1952. This helicopter unit (which also included some light fixed-wing aircraft) logged more flying time in Korea than any other Navy or Marine combat unit.

1124.   Strain, Joseph H. "Cavalry of the Air." MARINE CORPS GAZ, 1952 36 (3):30-35.

Operation SUMMIT, the first helicopter lift of combat troops, was undertaken by the US Marines, September 18-20, 1951. The HMR-161 was utilized.

1125.   Winkler, Robert. "Height of Battle." INF SCH Q, 1954 45 (1):93-101.

Korea marks the first war in which the helicopter was used extensively. Its first use in that conflict was to evacuate battlefield casualties. Next it was used in combat at the Hungnam Beachhead. Thereafter it served many purposes, and this article discusses them as well as early problems and techniques of employment.

1126.   Worden, William. "The War's Craziest Contraption." SAT EVE POST, 1950 223 (25):26-27, 94-96.

Notes that helicopters have no guns or speed, but they are being used extensively by the US Marines to evacuate wounded and trapped soldiers.

XI. MILITARY SUPPORT SERVICES
A. SUPPLY AND LOGISTICS ACTIVITIES

1127. "Air Drop." AIR UNIV Q R, 1951 4 (4):111-116.

Because of rough terrain, poor roads and limited rail
facilities in Korea, it quickly became apparent that air
drops could play a major role in supplying US and UN troops.
Not only small supplies but major items like jeeps, trucks
and howitzers. Many problems of this method of re-supply
surfaced but were overcome. C-119's and C-47's were the
aircraft most used in such operations. Tells of air
drops to troops at the Chosin Reservoir.

1128. Arrington, Leonard J., and Thomas G. Alexander. "Supply
Hub of the West: Defense Depot Ogden." UTAH HIST Q, 1964
32 (2):99-121.

A history of a key US Army supply depot in Utah during WWII
and Korea.

1129. Arrington, Leonard J., et al. "Utah's Biggest Business:
Ogden Air Material Area at Hill Air Force Base, 1938-1965."
UTAH HIST Q, 1965 33 (1):9-33.

This history shows the economic impact a major military
facility can have on an area, especially at times like the
Korean War.

1130. Baldwin, Coy W. "Food Service, United Nations Korea." QM R,
1953 32 (6):20-21, 116-120.

Meals served to US-UN troops in Korea were better than any
ever served under battle conditions. In fact, it was
generally acknowledged that the farther forward, the better
the food. It is not generally realized that the food that UN
forces received, except for non-perishable items of British
Commonwealth troops, was provided by the US Army Quartermaster Corps. Tells how the task was accomplished.

1131. Banks, Charles L. "Air Delivery in Korea." MARINE CORPS
GAZ, 1951 35 (11):46-47.

Air drop operations in support of US Marines during the
withdrawal from the Chosin Reservoir. Flying Boxcars were
used to deliver equipment and supplies as well as a nineteen
ton bridge.

1132.   Bennett, Gordon C. "They Wrote the Book!" QM R, 1953
         32 (4):50-53, 130.

         Tells how the 8081st Army Unit, Quartermaster Airborne Air
         Supply and Packaging Company, met the problems of supporting
         the Eighth US Army through sustained airdrop operations while
         lacking sufficient airdrop equipment. Includes discussion of
         airdrops to US forces encircled at the Chosin Reservoir.

1133.   "Big Pipeline Arms Troops for Big Push." LIFE, 1950
         29 (10):17-25.

         Photos and stories are used to show how the US was sending
         men, supplies and equipment from the states to the Korean
         battlefront.

1134.   Bondshu, Lowell T. "The Korean War: As Seen by a Chair-
         borne Soldier." QM R, 1953 32 (4):16-20, 134-135.

         Observations of a Quartermaster member of an Observer
         Team set up by the Chief of Army Field Forces to make an
         assessment of US Army activities throughout Korea in the
         winter of 1951-52. Tells how food, clothing and petroleum
         were provided to the men on the front lines.

1135.   Boyd, Ralph C. "Truck Platoon--Withdrawal From Taejon."
         COM FOR J, 1952 3 (2):26-27.

         Follows the activities of a Truck Platoon for the 24th
         Quartermaster Company from the day of its arrival in Pusan
         on July 5, 1950, to its complete destruction at Taejon
         two weeks later. Shows the confusion and setbacks
         suffered by US units in the early weeks of the war.

1136.   Bruce, A.D. "Tank Rebuild ... in Japan." ARMOR, 1952
         61 (2):10-14.

         Knocked out US tanks that could not be put in running
         order in Korea were sent back to Japan where they were
         completely rebuilt with parts from other incapacitated
         tanks. This photo essay tells how the complete rebuilding
         operation occurred. By early 1952 two tanks a day were
         being rebuilt at a cost of $700 each--quite a savings
         for the $245,000 weapons.

1137.   Burr, H.A. "What Flavor, Soldier." AM MERCURY, 1953
         77 October:34-37.

         A true account of how a Quartermaster Company of the 1st
         US Cavalry Division produced and delivered ice cream to
         front line units. The ice cream production facilities
         were later turned over to the 45th Division, which even
         resorted to delivery by helicopter.

1138.   Cocheu, S.D. "Hand Laundry, Korean Style." QM R,

1951 31 (2):29.

Tells how the Quartermaster of the 24th Infantry Division operating in the vicinity of Seoul in the spring of 1951 was able to improvise and provide laundry services to units even though it had only half its authorized equipment.

1139. "Comfort Items at the Front." QM R, 1952 31 (6):22, 94.

The development and distribution of ration supplement sundries pack, containing comfort items such as soap, toothbrushes, candy, razor blades and cigarettes, to US combat troops in Korea.

1140. Cook, John C. "Graves Registration in the Korean Conflict." QM R, 1953 32 (5):18, 131, 133, 135-144.

A history of the recovering, caring for and interring the remains of US and UN Command soldiers killed in action during the war in Korea--a Quartermaster responsibility. This was especially difficult early in the war when remains were buried in temporary graves pending return to their dependents only to have the area overrun by the enemy. This was the first US war in which the dead were returned during hostilities.

1141. Cooper, David M. "The QMC Buys for Defense." QM R, 1952 32 (3):10-11, 130-131.

Sets forth the procurement problems faced by the US Army Quartermaster Corps as it had to feed, clothe, house and equip American fighting forces in Korea and throughout the world. Many examples of the huge quantities of items such as socks, underwear, towels, and gloves secured in the period from July 1951 through June 1952.

1142. Dooley, Edward G. "Pon My Sole." QM R, 1952 31 (5):14-15, 110-112.

Problems of providing combat boots for US troops and ROK troops during the Korean War. After WWII many boots had been made available to Japanese civilians and many had to be reclaimed in 1950. To meet the needs of the ROK with their small shoe size, a Japanese manufacturer was given a contract for cutting larger sizes down to smaller sizes.

1143. Dorsett, Harold L. "Airborne Supply Operations." ARMY INFO DIG, 1951 6 (9):52-57.

Describes the activities of the 8081st Quartermaster Aerial Supply Company in Korea. This unit, the first of its kind, was activated in September 1950 and in its

first year dropped 45,000 tons of supplies to UN forces
in the combat zone. Describes different kinds of
missions undertaken, including airdrops of ammunition
to a specific gun.

1144. "Economy in the Air Force." AIR UNIV Q R, 1952
      5 (3):98-111.

      As the war heated up charges of economic waste were
      hurled at the US Air Force. Consequently, programs
      were launched at all levels to cut costs. The
      Management Improvement Program instituted to improve
      efficiency, especially manpower wise. Equipment
      Review Boards, Employee Suggestion Programs, and
      numerous entities did their part to save money.
      Scores of examples of big savings are cited.

1145. "FEALOGFOR and Japanese Labor." AIR UNIV Q R, 1953 6
      (2):93-97.

      During the Korean War the US's Far East Air Logistic
      Force (FEALOGFOR) met many logistical needs and saved
      American taxpayers more than $50 million a year by
      utilizing inexpensive Japanese labor to repair, reclaim
      and modify supplies and equipment necessary for US
      combat forces. More than 14,000 Japanese laborers and
      skilled craftsmen contributed to the US war effort by
      providing valuable salvage functions.

1146. "FEAMCOM." AIR UNIV Q R, 1951 4 (4):76-82.

      In the year following the outbreak of war, the US Far
      East Air Material Command led the awesome task of
      providing logistical support for the Far East Command
      and the ROK Air Force. Keeping the numerous aircraft
      flying was a monumental task but by modification and
      engineering development, structured repair advances
      and parachute repair, all of which are discussed, they
      were quite successful. Also discusses supply problems
      with a 10,000-mile supply line.

1147. Feldman, Herman. "Partners in a Tough Fight." QM R,
      1950 30 (3):6-7, 90-94.

      The Quartermaster General of the US Army sets forth
      the major problems facing the Corps as a result of the
      war in Korea. Looks at matters such as single service
      procurement, standardization, research and the need for
      flexibility in planning.

1148. Gosorn, Louis M. "The Army and Foreign Civilian
      Supply." MIL R, 1952 32 (2):27-42.

      Discusses the US Army's responsibility to supply
      foreign civil populations and focuses on such aid to

Korea in the post-WWII period and through 1951. Notes
that it is an integral part of military operations and,
if properly carried out, helps achieve them. Also
covers UN supply efforts to Korean civilians in the
early phases of the war.

1149. Haggard, John V. PROCUREMENT OF CLOTHING AND TEXTILES,
1945-1953. Washington: Government Printing Office, 1958.

A history of clothing procurement for the US Army
by the Army Quartermaster from the end of WWII through
the Korean War. The war in the Far East put heavy
demands on clothing supply, but the experience gained
during WWII enabled the military to meet its needs.

1150. Hospelhorn, Cecil W. "Aerial Supply in Korea." COM
FOR J, 1951 1 (10):28-30.

Account of the activities of the US 2348th Quartermaster
Aerial Supply Company in the first six months of the war.
Notes that early in the conflict, parachutes were in such
short supply that recovery teams were sent out to retrieve
them. Tells of the November-December 1950 airdrop to
Marines in the Chosin Reservoir area. Even bridges, in
sections weighing 4,500 pounds each, were airdropped.

1151. Hospelhorn, Cecil W. "Quartermaster Aerial Supply in
Korea." QM R, 1951 30 (5):4-7, 141-142, 145.

Story of how the 2348th Quartermaster Airborne Air
Supply and Packaging Detachment supported UN ground
troops in Korea during the first six months of the
war. The unit dropped 1,500 tons of supplies to
Marines in the Chosin Reservoir area, including a
treadway bridge.

1152. Houston, James A. THE SINEWS OF WAR: ARMY LOGISTICS,
1775-1953. Washington: Government Printing Office, 1966.

A general history of US Army supply from the Revolutionary
War through Korea. The final portion of the book deals
with the problem of moving supplies by sea and air from
the American west coast to the mountains and valleys of
Korea.

1153. Kaye, Frank A. "Operational Rations." QM R, 1951
30 (4):4-7, 120-121.

During the first six months of the Korean War, US troops
were continually on the move, thus making operational rations
of utmost importance. Such rations were pre-cooked,
ready-to-eat meals that contained as many calories as the
meals prepared in garrison or mobile kitchens. Tells of
their development, importance and use.

1154. Kujawski, Joseph S. "Feeding the Army." ARMY INFO
       DIG, 1953 8 (8):40-47.

       Describes the feeding of US soldiers in Korea. Notes
       that most soldiers were fed two hot meals a day and
       tells how they are prepared. Explains the various Army
       field rations as well as the training given US mess
       personnel.

1155. "Life Line To Korea." MIL R, 1953 33 (2):33-39.

       Describes the tremendous logistical problems that had
       to be met to supply US and UN troops in Korea. Each
       infantry division needed 17,000 tons of equipment to
       begin an offensive and 580 tons a day to keep it going.
       The photographic essay shows how the Navy's Military
       Sea Transport Service and Army Transportation moved
       goods from the States to the front.

1156. Lucas, Jim G. "Operation Roll Up." READ DIG, 1951
       59 (355):5-7.

       Tells of the biggest salvage drive the US military ever
       undertook. In the early days of the Korean War with
       combat equipment sorely lacking the US Army gathered
       WWII surplus left rotting throughout the Pacific to
       equip American forces. Military leaders were convinced
       that without those supplies the US would not have been
       able to remain in Korea in 1950.

1157. Mattia, Hugh J. "Air Force Procurement in Japan."
       AIR UNIV Q R, 1953 6 (3):123-127.

       The coming of war in Korea put heavy logistical stress
       on the Far East Command. Because of production and
       transportation bottlenecks in the US and the long
       shipping time to Korea, it was necessary to procure
       many goods from Japanese manufacturers, many of whom
       had to be taught US production techniques.

1158. Moore, F.W. "Class II and IV Supply in the ROK
       Army." QM R, 1953 32 (5):12-13, 126-127.

       The Republic of Korea Army was approximately 90%
       dependent on the US for its support of quartermaster
       items. Support was furnished in several ways primarily
       as end items, such as clothing, blankets, etc., or
       raw material components for the manufacturer of end
       items in Korea.

1159. Norman, R.G. "Tokyo Quartermaster Depot." QM R,
       1952 31 (4):24, 110-115.

       Background of the US depot in Tokyo which, beginning
       in the summer of 1950, had the primary responsibility

of providing the logistical support required of US and
UN forces in Korea as well as occupation units of Japan.
Tells the problems of operating a large depot near a
combat zone.

1160. "Oil For the Machines of War." COM FOR J, 1953
       3 (9):34-35.

       The petroleum requirements of US armed forces in Korea
       were unbelievable. Tells of the various products needed
       and gives examples of the amounts of fuel required. For
       example, an armored battalion required 17,000 gallons of
       gasoline to travel 100 miles while a B-29 might use
       10,000 gallons for one long-range round trip.

1161. "Operation Rebuild." MIL R, 1953 32 (11):51-62.

       The Japan Logistical Command, later redesignated US
       Army Forces, Far East, utilized Japanese personnel to
       rebuild thousands of vehicles thereby saving a great
       deal of money and making trucks and jeeps available
       when they could not be secured from other sources.
       Photographs detail the rebuilding process from
       beginning to end.

1162. Peifer, William H. SUPPLY BY SKY: QUARTERMASTER
       AIRBORNE DEVELOPMENT, 1950-1953. Washington: Government
       Printing Office, 1958.

       Historical study of the techniques developed by the
       US Army Quartermaster to prepare, pack and deliver
       food and supplies to combat troops in Korea via air.

1163. Rogers, Carmon A. "Three Million For Dinner." ARMY
       INFO DIG, 1951 6 (4):54-59.

       Describes the various field rations provided US
       troops, including those in Korea, in the early 1950's.

1164. Rogers, Charles A. "QM Operations, 1st Cavalry Division,
       Korea." QM R, 1951 31 (1):4-5, 143-150.

       Discusses the history, problems and accomplishments of
       1st Cavalry's Quartermaster section in Korea. Examines
       supply operations in the July-August 1950 holding action,
       Inchon invasion and breakout, the advance north and retreat
       and the stabilization of early 1951. Transportation
       difficulties made supply of clothing, food and petroleum a
       real challenge.

1165. Smith, Merwin H. "Petroleum Supply in Korea." QM R,
       1951 31 (3):35, 116-121.

       Problems of meeting the tremendous petroleum demands of
       UN forces in the first year of the war. Fortunately,

storage facilities in Japan were full when the war broke
out (except for jet fuel), but when the conflict became
extended, the long supply line from the US became a major
problem. To the credit of the US Army Quartermaster,
serious fuel shortages never became a major problem.

1166. US Senate, Committee on Armed Services. AMMUNITION
      SHORTAGES IN THE FAR EAST. 83rd Cong. 1st Sess.
      Washington: Government Printing Office, 1953.

      April 1953 testimony of US Army and Pentagon leaders
      concerning reasons for shortages of ammunition
      experienced by the Eighth Army in Korea over a two-year
      period. Procurement bottlenecks and problems of
      getting ammunition plants operational following the
      outbreak of war were among the reasons for the shortages.

1167. Warner, W.W. "Arsenals in Action." ARMY INFO DIG,
      1951 6 (9):39-44.

      Examines the mission, organization and operation of the
      US Army's Rock Island (Illinois) Arsenal just prior to
      and in the month after war broke out in Korea. Tells
      about the development and production of the 3.5 inch
      rocket launcher which was rushed to the front to halt
      advancing North Korean tanks in the early days of the
      fighting.

1168. Weaver, John O. "Stock Number 56-C-13065-H." QM R,
      1953 32 (4):45-46, 131-132.

      The strange and interesting account of the US Quarter-
      master's entry into the field of psychological warfare by
      printing pro-UN propaganda in Chinese and Korean on
      cigarette packages distributed to prisoners of war.
      56-C-13065-H was the stock number for the propaganda
      cigarette.

1169. Whittle, Aubrey C. "Jeffersonville Quartermaster
      Depot." QM R, 1952 32 (1):12-15, 121-122.

      Traces the history of the Indiana depot from its
      beginnings in 1864 through the first two years of the
      Korean War. In the latter conflict its activity more
      than doubled from its pre-June 1950 level and nearly
      reached its peak WWII level. Explains functions of
      such areas as: Maintenance Division; Parachute
      Department; Mechanical Products Division; Textile
      Production Division; Photographic Branch and the
      Storage Division.

1170. Williams, Alex N. "Subsistence Supply in Korea."
      QM R, 1953 32 (4):29-30, 132-133.

The food provided US combat troops in Korea, even those
on the front lines, was better than that provided any
soldiers at anytime in history. The meals served were
quite different from WWII and breakfasts of fresh oranges,
fried eggs and bacon and milk and suppers with fried
chicken and ice cream were not uncommon. Tells how and
why those changes came about.

B. TRANSPORTATION AND COMMUNICATION

1171. Akin, S.B. "Signal Problems In the Far East." ARMY
         INFO DIG, 1951 6 (2):27-31.

Maintains that the communications problems that plagued US
troops in the early phases of the Korean War were not based
so much on poor equipment as they were on the lack of trained
personnel to use it. Looks at the problems in the early
months of the fighting.

1172. Atkins, Ollie, and Sylvia Myers. "The World's Worst
         Railroad Headache." SAT EVE POST, 1951 224 (2):26-27, 126.

Pictorial story about the 3rd Transportation Military
Railway Service (TMRS) which ran a railway service
throughout Korea to bring supplies to UN forces and
evacuate the wounded. The service saw its railway
system destroyed four times and in each case rebuilt it.
The unit moved 95% of the US Eighth Army's supplies.

1173. Deyo, William J., Jr. "Gateway to the Orient." ARMY
         INFO DIG, 1953 8 (2):42-47.

Most of the manpower and supplies utilized by the UN
Command during the Korean War went through the 2nd
Transportation's major port in Yokohama, Japan; thus,
making it one of the busiest ports in the world. This
article explains the organization, operation and
efficiency of this military-run transportation center.

1174. Griffin, William. "Typhoon at Kobe." MARINE CORPS
         GAZ, 1951 35 (9):60-65.

US shipping of soldiers and supplies from the Japanese
port of Kobe to Korea was disrupted in the first week of
September 1950 when typhoon "Jane" struck Kobe.

1175. Holliday, Kate. TROOPSHIP. New York: Doubleday,
         1952.

A woman reporter's account of her eleven-day trip
aboard a US Navy troopship headed for Korea with 3,000
soldiers. A daily account of what the men experienced
on the journey and, more importantly, descriptions of
the feelings and frustrations being experienced by men
headed for combat.

1176. Howard, David S., and John G. Westover. "Everyone
       Wants a Telephone." COM FOR J, 1952 2 (12):16-17.

       US Signal Corps units were immediately besieged upon
       arriving in Korea for telephones, especially for staff
       headquarters. Tells how those requests were met and
       the problems that were encountered. Based on after-
       action reports.

1177. Key, William G. "Combat Cargo: Korea, 1950-51." PEG,
       1951 17 (5):1-15.

       The operation of the Combat Cargo Command during the
       period from July 1950 through the summer of 1951.
       Includes the problems and accomplishments involved in
       airlifting combat supplies to combat zones in Korea.

1178. Knight, Clayton. LIFELINE IN THE SKY: THE STORY OF
       THE US MILITARY AIR TRANSPORT SERVICES. New York:
       Morrow, 1957.

       Overview of the establishment of MATS during the post-WWII
       years and its valuable service in the Berlin Airlift, the
       Korean War and post-war era. Looks at WWII era antecedents
       of the service.

1179. "Korea-Captured Communist Communications Equipment."
       TELE-TECH, 1953 12 (47):62-64.

       Photographs and descriptions of Russian-made transmitters,
       receivers, telephone and telegraph equipment that were
       captured from North Korean and Chinese forces in Korea.

1180. Koyen, Kenneth. "MATS Builds Another Air Bridge."
       BEE-HIVE, 1950 25 (4):24-29.

       Tells the role of the Military Air Transport Service
       in transporting men and equipment from the US and Japan
       to supply points in Korea.

1181. Mallman, Margaret A. "Korean Brawn Backs the Attack."
       ARMY INFO DIG, 1951 6 (12):47-49.

       Beginning in early 1951 the US Army began the first large-
       scale employment of Korean natives to carry vital supplies to
       frontline units. Because spring rains made roads frequently
       impassable, the UN Command requested South Korea to organize
       and equip a Civilian Transportation Corps. By June 1951
       eighty-five such units of 250 men each were in operation, and
       they performed extremely well.

1182. "Military Air Transport Service." MIL R, 1953 33 (9):37-43.

Traces the first five years of MATS from the time of its
establishment on June 1, 1948. Considerable attention
to activities connected with the Korean War, including
statistics on flights and men and supplies delivered to
combat zones. Illustrated.

1183. "Military Sea Transport Service." US NAVAL INST
       PROC, 1951 77 (12):1327-1336.

Describes the mission, organization and accomplishments of
the Military Sea Transport Service (MSTS) during the first
sixteen months of the fighting in Korea. During that period
the service delivered twenty-six million tons of cargo, two
million passengers, and 120 million barrels of petroleum.
This was done by utilizing more than 200 ships only
twenty-six of which were US naval vessels.

1184. Milliken, Morton E. "The World's Biggest Little
       Airline." ARMY INFO DIG, 1951 6 (11):59-60.

Tells of the use of the Mosquito, the light L-5
aircraft, by the US Signal Corps to airdrop small light
items, like maps, records and orders, to remote units.
Such activities were very important in Korea where the
terrain was so difficult. The unit examined is the
Air Section of the 304th Signal Operations Battalion.

1185. Morrow, Hugh. "He's the Stingiest Admiral!" SAT
       EVE POST, 1952 225 (2):26-27, 105-106, 108.

Vice Admiral Bill Callaghan, Commander of the Military
Sea Transportation Service (MSTS) is the focus of this
article. The MSTS Task Force of 273 ships was hard
pressed to supply US troops in Korea with the mountains
of material needed to carry on the war, but it met the
challenge.

1186. Shiflet, Kenneth E. "Communications Hill." SIG,
       1964 18 (10):32-33.

Cooperation between US Army and Marine personnel in
protecting communications during the Chosin Reservoir
retreat.

1187. Sigel, Clinton H. "The Reserve Fleet." US NAVAL INST
       PROC, 1951 77 (7):681-689.

Stresses the importance of maintaining a US reserve fleet
in the post-WWII period because it was that mothballed fleet
which provided so much of the amphibious transport force and
supporting ships when war came to Korea. Relates a number
of the problems, mechanical and personnel, in getting the
ships ready for active duty.

1188.   Stringfellow, Donald, and Paul B. Lowney. "I See
        Them Kiss and Cry." COLLIER'S, 1951 128 (20):20-21,
        52-54.

        A Military Police sergeant at the Seattle Port of
        Embarkation describes the joys and sorrows of working
        at a spot where US troops leave for combat assignments
        in Korea, many to never return, and others return having
        survived the horrors of war and receiving a warm welcome
        from family members.

1189.   Thompson, Annis G. THE GREATEST AIRLIFT: THE STORY
        OF COMBAT CARGO. Tokyo: Dai-Nippon, 1954.

        An extremely well-written and -illustrated history of
        the activities and accomplishments of the 315th Air
        Division, Combat Cargo, during the Korean War. The
        author, a command pilot and historian, tells of the
        greatest airlift of men and material ever undertaken
        into a combat zone. Very thorough.

1190.   Towne, Raymond L. "Yonpo Evacuation." AIR UNIV Q R,
        1951 4 (3):15-17.

        An account of the US Cargo Command's air evacuation of
        surrounded UN and South Korean troops from the Yonpo
        Airfield in North Korea on December 13-17, 1950. In
        the final three days air transports lifted 2,400 tons
        of men and equipment from the position deep in Communist
        territory. The author was a pilot involved in the
        evacuation.

1191.   Van Fleet, James A. RAIL TRANSPORT AND THE WINNING
        OF WARS. Washington: Association of American Railroads,
        1956.

        Contains a chapter on the importance of rail traffic in
        the Korean War. Tells how the Communist armies managed
        to maintain their supplies in the face of heavy air attacks
        by UN forces. Interesting look at the logistics of
        warfare.

1192.   Winston, Waldon C. "Mobile Maintenance Made'em Roll."
        COM FOR J, 1953 3 (8):18-21.

        Relates the maintenance problems facing the 52nd
        Transportation Truck Battalion in Korea from January
        through March 1951. Because of operation over rough
        terrain in extremely bad weather, army trucks frequently
        broke down, but innovative maintenance personnel kept
        them running through hard work and innovative techniques
        of repair.

C. ENGINEERING

1193. Albert, Joseph L., and Billy C. Wylie. "Problems of
       Airfield Construction in Korea." AIR UNIV Q R, 1951-52
       5 (1):86-92.

       Problems facing US Air Force engineers in constructing
       airfields in Korea during the first year of the war were
       monumental. Initially, there were serious shortages of
       construction equipment and trained personnel. In addition
       there were physical problems such as rugged terrain and
       waterlogged land, all of which were successfully overcome.

1194. Colvocoresses, Alden P. "Flood Prediction in Korea."
       MIL ENG, 1954 46 (312):266-270.

       In 1951 and 1952 the US Eighth Army experienced serious
       losses of life, equipment and facilities, especially bridges,
       from floods. To reduce such losses, the Army instituted, in
       1952 and 1953, a program to minimize flood damage. One of
       the keys of the program was a flood prediction service which
       warned of approaching floods and their intensity, thus
       reducing losses.

1195. "Fighting Floods in Korea." MIL ENG, 1952 44
       (302):445.

       Heavy rains and mountainous terrain frequently led to
       flooding in Korea. This presented a special problem to
       US Army engineers who had to see that the flood waters
       would not destroy key bridges. This shows some of the
       techniques used to prevent debris from destroying the
       bridges.

1196. Fortson, Eugene P. "Mock-up for Test of Korean
       Mountain Pass." MIL ENG, 1952 44 (297):20.

       Good example of innovativeness of US Army Engineers as
       they built an iron-frame mock-up of a 20-ton tractor to
       move over newly constructed mountain roads to assure
       the real 20-ton tractors could traverse the roads.
       Photos on its testing.

1197. Fortson, Eugene P. "Railroad Bridge Reconstruction
       in Korea." MIL ENG, 1954 46 (314):410-413.

       In the summer of 1950 retreat of South Korean and US
       troops to Pusan, the US Air Force and Engineers destroyed
       most of the bridges in hope of slowing down the enemy.
       After the breakout in the fall, it became necessary to
       repair those bridges. This tells of the 1950 temporary
       repairs and 1951 permanent repairs that were made and the
       obstacles that were overcome.

1198. Fowler, Delbert M. "Bailey Bridge Across the Pukhan."

MIL ENG, 1952 44 (298):86-87.

The steel structure Bailey bridge played an extremely important role in US Army engineer operations with hundreds being installed. Traces the destruction and rebuilding of a bridge over the Pukhan River at Mojin.

1199. Fowler, Delbert M. "Bridging the Han River." MIL ENG, 1951 43 (296):414-416.

During the US withdrawal across the Han River in 1951, all bridges were destroyed but with a forward advance a month later, a treadway bridge had to be constructed across the ice-filled river. During construction a heavy rain and thaw complicated things. Describes the engineering problems and tells how they were overcome.

1200. Fowler, Delbert M. "Operations at the Hwachon Dam, Korea." MIL ENG, 1952 44 (297):7-8.

In early April 1951 the Chinese Communists released massive amounts of water from the Hwachon Dam in order to destroy US bridges downstream; however, the floating bridges were cut loose, swung and thus saved. Later the dam gates were destroyed to deny the enemy the opportunity to again use the flood as a weapon.

1201. Godsey, James P. "Soyang River Bailey Bridge." MIL ENG, 1951 43 (296):395-397.

Traces the construction of the longest bridge built by US Army Engineers (772 feet) north of the 38th Parallel and the longest Bailey bridge in Korea. The feat was quite remarkable because the project was accomplished in fourteen days by two small engineer combat companies of the 185th Engineer Combat Battalion.

1202. Hall, W.C. "Maps For Combat." COM FOR J, 1952 2 (6):24-27.

Maps are essential to military leaders at all levels. Unfortunately, at the start of the Korean War, maps were not as available as would have been desired. Tells the problems of securing proper maps, lead time required and how they can be used more effectively when they are received.

1203. Hyzer, Peter C. "Third Engineers in Korea, July-October 1950." MIL ENG, 1951 43 (292):101-107.

Traces the 3rd Engineer Combat Battalion of the 24th Infantry Division from its July departure from Japan through October 1950. Provides a good picture of the organic engineer component of an infantry division on

combat operations. Tells of building roads, bridges
and airfields and the laying and destruction of mine
fields. All of this occurred in a situation of rapid
movement.

1204. Hyzer, Peter C. "Third Engineers in Korea, Part II,
       November 1950-February 1951." MIL ENG, 1952 44 (300):
       252-259.

       Week by week, month by month account of the activities
       of the 3rd Engineer Battalion in the critical period
       following the US Army's rapid withdrawal following the
       entry of the Chinese Communists into the conflict.

1205. Hyzer, Peter C. "Third Engineer in Korea, Part III,
       March-April 1951." MIL ENG, 1952 44 (301):356-361.

       In March and April 1951 the 3rd Engineer Combat Battalion
       accompanied the 24th Infantry Division as it advanced
       northward to the 38th Parallel over extremely rough terrain.
       Road and trail construction was the primary task of the
       engineers.

1206. Itschner, Emerson C. "Engineers in Operation 'BUG-OUT.'"
       MIL ENG, 1951 43 (294):255-258.

       Role of US Army Engineers in the Chosin Reservoir
       operation. In the retrograde movement of December 1950,
       engineers were busy keeping at least one good route of
       withdrawal open to each Corps, executing demolitions to delay
       the enemy, and destroying all military equipment and supplies
       that might fall into enemy hands.

1207. Itschner, Emerson C. "The Naktong River Crossings in
       Korea." MIL ENG, 1951 43 (292):96-100.

       Account of the role of US Engineer units in the September
       1950 assault crossings of the Kumho and Naktong Rivers.
       In a period of one week, four US divisions and a brigade
       were involved in four independent crossings. The
       accomplishments were especially remarkable when one
       considers the relative lack of equipment and inexperience
       of the personnel.

1208. Kalischer, Peter. "They Call It Jane Russell Hill."
       COLLIER'S, 1953 131 (7):30.

       Early in the Korean War hills were designated by their
       height, but numbers were too impersonal for soldiers and
       reporters, thus, they began naming the hills. This practice
       taxed the innovative soldiers, but they rose to the occasion
       with such designations as Old Baldy, T-Bone, Pork Chop,
       Arrowhead and Jane Russell Hill, the latter for reasons
       obvious to any red-blooded American soldier.

1209.   "Korean Engineer Specialists." MIL ENG, 1952 44 (301):
        372.

        In spite of the language barrier, members of the 185th
        Engineer Combat Battalion taught ROK soldiers to operate
        heavy equipment such as bulldozers and road graders,
        thereby overcoming the shortage of such skilled personnel.

1210.   Kozaczka, Felix. "Enemy Bridging Techniques in Korea."
        AIR UNIV Q R, 1952 5 (4):49-59.

        A major reason that air interdiction against the Communist
        forces had a limited impact was the enemies' ability to
        repair rail and highway bridges at such a rapid rate. The
        speed of repairs was not due to new techniques but the fact
        that large supplies of lumber and labor were close at hand.
        Furthermore, the construction workers were well organized
        and directed. Many excellent photographs.

1211.   Ladd, J.G. "Maps for Korea." MIL ENG, 1950 42 (290):
        448-450.

        The invasion of Korea brought on immediate demand for maps
        of the country from all staff echelons in the US Army. The
        Army Map Service was able to meet those demands, which
        amounted to 750,000 maps, during the first two weeks of
        hostilities. Also tells of preparation of a gazette of place
        names and three dimensional terrain models.

1212.   Lay, Kenneth E. "Roads-Transport-Firepower, in Korea."
        MIL ENG, 1951 43 (296):389-394.

        One of the major obstacles to US operations in Korea was
        the poor road system which existed throughout the country.
        This challenge was most effectively met by the US Army
        Engineer. Tells the problem of road building, use of
        Korean labor, construction techniques and the importance of
        improvisation and salvage. Focuses on road building in the
        East-Central front in early 1951.

1213.   Lepke, Richard P., and John G. Westover. "Three River
        Crossings." COM FOR J, 1952 3 (1):33-35.

        Details how C Company, 3rd Engineer Combat Battalion, 24th
        Infantry Division received orders, planned and executed three
        assault river crossings of the Naktong River near Taegu in
        September 1950.

1214.   Love, Robert W. "Engineers in Operation Touchdown."
        MIL ENG, 1954 46 (313):325-331.

        Utilization of the Divisional Engineer Battalion, 2nd
        Division, is described in a late summer 1951 operation which
        was the decisive blow in the struggle for Heartbreak Ridge.
        The engineer activities reveal the wide variety of tasks

which they had to perform in support of an armored attack
in extremely difficult terrain.

1215. McCallam, William, Jr. "The Evacuation of Hungnam."
        COM FOR J, 1951 2 (1):32-35.

        Examines the role of the 2nd Engineer Special Brigade in
        the December 1950 evacuation of 100,000 US troops and their
        equipment from the North Korean port of Hungnam. In spite
        of the urgency of the departure and continual enemy attack
        on the port, the operation was quite orderly and no usable
        equipment was left behind. Details the planning and
        implementation of the evacuation plan.

1216. McCallam, William, Jr. "Raising the Tidal Basin Lock
        Gates at Inchon." MIL ENG, 1952 44 (298):96-101.

        When US troops evacuated the port of Inchon in January
        1951, they demolished the lock gates at the tidal basin.
        On their return a month later they were faced with the
        difficult task of repairing those locks. Describes that
        difficult repair job.

1217. Malkin, Lawrence. "Pipe Lines in Korea." MIL ENG,
        1953 45 (306):273-274.

        Explains how the 82nd Engineer Pipe Line Company supplied
        the US Eighth Army with fuel for their tanks, trucks and
        aircraft. The unit continually laid pipe lines behind
        advancing troops to assure that combat operations would
        not be hampered by a lack of fuel. Traces the flow of
        petroleum from the US to Korean ports to frontline units.
        Tremendous problems of supply and maintenance of facilities
        were overcome.

1218. Mann, Frank L. "Operation 'Versatile.'" MIL ENG, 1952.
        44 (299):168-173.

        Operations and accomplishments of the 2nd Engineer
        Special Brigade from the landing at Inchon through the
        evacuation of Hungnam and the subsequent departure, return
        and departure (October of 1951) from Inchon. During that
        thirteen-month period, the Brigade opened, operated and
        developed two major ports and two minor ones. Also undertook
        extensive road building and construction projects.

1219. Martin, Paul G. "Tramway to Hill 1220." MIL ENG,
        1953 45 (305):181-183.

        One way that US Army Engineers were able to minimize the
        negative impact of the mountains was by construction of
        tramways which were able to transport ammunition and supplies
        up long, steep grades with a minimum of effort and a savings
        of manpower that would otherwise have been needed to move the
        goods. Examines tramway construction.

1220. "Memorial to Sergeant George D. Libby, Corps of Engineers."
       MIL ENG, 1954 46 (313):372.

       Tells of the courage and valor which won for a US Army
       Engineer the Congressional Medal of Honor. On July 20, 1950,
       Libby's patrol was ambushed by North Koreans and all except
       him were wounded or killed. He held back the attackers and
       loaded all the wounded on an artillery tractor which evacuated
       them. In the ensuing action he was killed. On July 4, 1953,
       a bridge across the Imjin was dedicated to Libby.

1221. Millberry, R.I. "Engineer Aviation Forces in Korea."
       AIR UNIV Q R, 1953 6 (3):114-119.

       Problems and construction techniques in building airfields
       and airstrips in the rugged South Korean terrain. The
       problems were basically different from WWII because of the
       need for runways that could handle jet aircraft and the heavy
       C-124 cargo aircraft.

1222. Miller, M. Clare. "High Steel in Korea." MIL ENG,
       1951 43 (295):332-333.

       In late 1950 when the US withdrew from the Yalu, it was
       necessary to destroy a rail bridge at Kiba-chon, seven
       miles south of Wonju. In April 1951 as US troops advanced
       north again, the bridge had to be reconstructed by the
       439th Engineer Construction Battalion. Details that
       repair job.

1223. "PSP Runway Repair in Korea." MIL ENG, 1952 44
       (301):328.

       The Pierced Steel Plank (PSP) was used extensively in
       construction of airfields in Korea. Repair of the plank
       had to be undertaken in such a way as to not interfere
       with operational flights.

1224. Pickett, Evan S. "Twinnan River Bridge, Korea." MIL ENG,
       1952 44 (297):43-45.

       The spring of 1951 reconstruction of a major concrete bridge
       at Hoengsong, South Korea, by US Army Engineers. An extremely
       difficult repair job on this bridge which was important in
       providing ammunition to stop a May communist offensive.

1225. Reppert, Leonard B. "The Installation Squadron in Korea."
       AIR UNIV Q R, 1952 5 (2):87-97.

       Korea was the first time the Air Force did not depend on
       the Army Corps of Engineers for construction and maintenance
       of real estate. Assuming that responsibility was the AF
       Installation Squadron. This article describes the unit's
       organization and function along with the problems it

experienced in constructing buildings and airfields in Korea.

1226. Rowny, E. L. "Engineers in the Hungnam Evacuation."
      MIL ENG, 1951 43 (295):315-319.

      Engineering aspects of the withdrawal of US troops from the
      Chosin Reservoir and subsequent evacuation from Hungnam.
      Covers the air drop of a treadway bridge which was essential
      in the withdrawal, demolition of bridges and destruction of
      US military supplies and the dock facilities at Hungnam
      harbor.

1227. Sawin, C. Van. "Air-Raid Shelter in Korea." MIL ENG,
      1952 44 (299):197.

      The design, construction and characteristics of air-raid
      shelters as constructed for the IX Corps by Korean labor
      under the supervision of US Army Engineers.

1228. "The Seoul Bridge Complex." AIR UNIV Q R, 1950 4
      (2):72-73.

      Examines the efforts of the US Air Force to knock out the
      railroad bridges crossing the Han River in Seoul in July
      and August 1950. Includes photos of destruction but notes
      how the North Koreans were able to quickly repair the
      destroyed spans.

1229. "Steel Planking." AIR UNIV Q R, 1952 5 (2):128-132.

      Early in the Korean War it became evident that runway
      problems were monumental. To solve those problems engineers
      turned to pierced steel planking which had been utilized
      successfully on Pacific island airstrips during WWII.
      Because of plank shortages, plants in Korea and Japan were
      set up to rehabilitate bent, torn and corroded planks.
      Such activity was very cost-effective.

1230. Stowall, Michael. "Spring Means Mud." MIL ENG, 1953
      45 (306):263.

      Spring in Korea meant thaws and rain which turned the
      dirt roads to pools of mud, thus, creating a major
      challenge to US Army Engineers. Tells how the mud
      problem was tackled by the 10th Engineer Combat
      Battalion of the 3rd Division.

1231. Strong, Paschal N. "Army Engineers in Korea." MIL ENG,
      1952 44 (302):405-410.

      Follows US engineer operations during the first year of the
      conflict. Discusses Korean geography, the campaigns,
      operations of US and allied engineers and tells the lessons
      learned, which were actually basic, time-honored principles.

1232.   Strong, Paschal N.   "Engineers in Korea--Operation
        'Shoestring.'"   MIL ENG, 1951 43 (291):11-14.

        Traces US Army Engineer activities in Korea from the
        beginning of hostilities until the communist counter-
        attack in late November 1950. Most time and energy
        during the period was devoted to laying minefields,
        clearing enemy mines and obstacles and the
        restoration of bridges and railways.

1233.   Strong, Paschal N.   "The Korean Builder."   MIL ENG,
        1951 43 (295):336-338.

        The rebuilding projects facing the US Army Engineers
        were so numerous that they could not undertake them
        all; thus, many jobs were undertaken by Korean
        civilians. Although the natives lacked construction
        knowledge they utilized their labor intensive methods to
        rebuild bridges, lay railroad track, build roads
        and unload bulk cargo.

                        D.   USE OF ANIMALS

1234.   Barthelme, Donald.   "York--Army Scout."   ARMY INFO DIG,
        1954 9 (10):56-59.

        Recounts many of the Korean War exploits of a scout dog
        named "York," who was engaged in 148 combat missions as a
        part of the 2nd Division's 26th Infantry Scout Dog
        Platoon. Explains the training, use and problems
        encountered by use of scout dogs.

1235.   Deringer, Clifton H, Jr.   "The Infantry Goes to the
        Dogs."   INF, 1958 48 (4):57-62.

        Briefly tells of the accomplishments of the 276th Infantry
        Scout Dog Platoon in the Korean War and tells the techniques
        that were used and would in the future, if the need arose,
        to train the dogs.

1236.   Geer, Andrew.   RECKLESS: PRIDE OF THE MARINES.   New York:
        Dutton, 1955.

        Tells of a horse purchased by a Marine platoon leader in
        Korea and used to carry 75 mm ammunition to its recoilless
        rifle position. Its reputation grew first in Korea and
        then in the US as the press helped spread its fame. After
        the war veterans of the 1st Marine Division brought it
        back to the states for its reunion and gave it the royal
        treatment.

1237.   Geer, Andrew.   "Reckless the Pride of the Marines."
        SAT EVE POST, 1954 226 (42):31, 184-186.

Brief story of the most famous animal to come out of the Korean War--a horse named "Reckless" which carried ammunition for a Marine Recoilless Rifle Platoon of the 1st Marine Division.

1238.   Geer, Andrew. "Red Carpet for Sergeant Reckless." SAT EVE POST, 1955 228 (17):22-23, 48-56.

Relates the journey of the famous war animal from Korea to the US and its reunion with the men of the 1st Marine Division.

1239.   Gorman, Paul F. "Scout Dogs on Patrol." INF SCH Q, 1954 44 (3):60-69.

Attempts to dispel the many myths that grew up over the use of dogs on combat patrols in Korea. Tells of the experiences of the 26th Infantry Scout Dog Platoon which was activated in mid-1952. The use of dogs went from an initial period of extreme skepticism about their value to a belief they could do miracles on a patrol. Shows the truth was somewhere in between.

1240.   Stapleton, Bill. "Hoss Marines." COLLIER'S, 1951 128 (16):10.

Some Americans were quite amused when they learned some Chinese Communist cavalry were utilizing horses and mules in Korea. However, members of the First Marine Division were pleased because those captured animals served a most useful function in transporting supplies over the mountainous terrain to isolated units.

E.   PSYCHOLOGICAL WARFARE

1241.   Avedon, Herbert. "War For Men's Minds." MIL R, 1954 33 (12):53-60.

Maintains that truth is the best weapon the US and UN forces have in the psychological war against the communists in Korea. Discusses the mission of propaganda, its tactics and use in Korea. Tells of use of leaflets and loud speakers.

1242.   Davison, W. Phillips. "Air Force Psychological Warfare in Korea." AIR UNIV Q R, 1951 4 (4):40-48.

Examination of US Air Force psychological warfare which concludes that in terms of conventional operations, i.e., dropping leaflets, radio broadcasts and use of loudspeakers, there was minimum activity. Discusses the personnel and technological problems that made this true. There were, however, things the Air Force did which contributed to

psychological warfare in other ways. Those factors
included visibility of aircraft over enemy positions and
harassing raids, both of which demoralized the enemy.

1243. Hall, Donald F. "Organizing for Combat Propaganda."
       ARMY INFO DIG, 1951 6 (5):11-16.

       Briefly looks at Pentagon activities for planning and
       administering psychological warfare activities. Examines
       closely the operations of strategic group units such as the
       Radio Broadcasting and Leaflet Group with its Reproduction
       Company and Mobile Radio Broadcasting Company and tactical
       propaganda units including the Loudspeaker and Leaflet
       Company and the Propaganda Platoon.

1244. Hall, Donald F. "Psychological Warfare Training."
       ARMY INFO DIG, 1951 6 (1):40-46.

       Maintains that psychological warfare which the US
       aimed at the enemy was very effective, but the
       enemy's efforts failed miserably when they tried to
       imitate such tactics. Tells of early uses of
       psychological warfare by the US Army in Korea.

1245. Kalishcher, Peter. "We're Asking the Reds to
       Surrender--Please!" COLLIER'S, 1952 130 (24):15-18.

       Efforts of the UN Command to convince enemy soldiers to
       surrender by using psychological warfare. Tells of the
       600 "Psywarriors," military and civilian planners, writers,
       directors, actors, broadcasters, artists and printers and
       how they carry out their mission. More than 130 Koreans
       and Chinese served the UN cause, including some at the
       radio stock company in Japan and others, especially Korean
       WAC's, on loud speakers mounted on aircraft.

1246. Linebarger, Paul. PSYCHOLOGICAL WARFARE. New York:
       Arno, 1972.

       Although the book focuses on WWII it contains an
       extended appendix on US Military Psychological Warfare in
       Korea from 1950-1953. Examines such things as: leaflet
       delivery, loudspeaker activities, propaganda policy, the
       Psy War officer, radio operations and radio propaganda.

1247. "Psychological Warfare in Korea." PUB OP Q, 1951 15
       (1):65-75.

       An account of UN psychological warfare activities during
       the first six months of the war in Korea. Tells of its use
       of leaflets, radio and other forms of propaganda aimed at
       North Korean soldiers and civilians. Goes into the
       preparation, production and distribution of materials by
       the Psychological Warfare Branch of the Far East Command.

1248. Story, Dale. "Psywar in Korea." COM FOR J, 1952 2
          (12):25-27.

       Describes the goals and methods of psychological warfare
       used by the US Eighth Army in Korea. Examines the use of
       loudspeakers and leaflets to convince the enemy to surrender.
       The most stressed theme was the good treatment afforded
       POW's. Distributed leaflets were used as Safe Conduct
       Passes. Examples of propaganda messages used.

1249. Wilmot, Fred W. "The Infantry and Psychological Warfare."
          INF SCH Q, 1952 41 (2):100-104.

       Describes the principles of psychological warfare as they
       apply to the US Army situation in Korea. Tells of the use
       of leaflets and loudspeakers. Makes clear that such warfare
       is a supporting weapon, not a "high level trick."

                  F. THE CHAPLAINCY AND RELIGION

1250. Bare, Paul W. "A Chaplain Writes Home." CHAP, 1952
          9 (3):9-11.

       Recollections of a US Army Chaplain serving with the 24th
       Division in Korea. Human interest stories involving wounded
       soldiers.

1251. Bennett, Ivan L. "The ROK Army Chaplaincy." KOREAN SUR,
          1955 4 (4):3-4, 13.

       The Chief Chaplain of the UN Command details the
       establishment, in the summer of 1950, of chaplaincy
       services for ROK soldiers. Only Koreans were used and
       their salaries were paid for by their religious
       denominations.

1252. "Casualties Among Protestant Chaplains in Korea."
          CHAP, 1951 8 (4):1-2

       List of US Army and Navy chaplain killed, missing and
       wounded in action in Korea. In some instances an account of
       how they were killed or wounded is included.

1253. "Chaplains in Korea." CHAP, 1950 7 (6):35-37.

       Tells of the service of more than half a dozen chap-
       lains in Korea in the early stages of the fighting.
       Gives accounts of two chaplains killed in combat and
       several others caught behind enemy lines but who ultimately
       escaped. Tells of their positive influence on morale.

1254. Craven, John H. "Marines in Combat Remember Fallen
          Comrades." CHAP, 1951 8 (6):16.

Tells of US Navy Chaplains serving with the First Marine
Division having memorial services for the men who were lost
in each engagement. Gives account of one such service.

1255. Dowe, Ray M. FATHER KAPAUN: THE ORDEAL OF KAPAUN AS
      TOLD TO HAROLD H. MARTIN. Notre Dame, IN: Ave Maria,
      1954.

      In-depth account of the Korean experiences of US Army
      chaplain of Roman Catholic faith who ministered extensively
      to US troops before dying in the line of duty.

1256. Dowe, Ray M. "The Ordeal of Chaplain Kapaun."
      SAT EVE POST, 1954 226 (29):20-21, 60, 63.

      Exploits of a noncombant American hero of the Korean War,
      Captain Emil J. Kapaun, a Roman Catholic chaplain of the
      8th Cavalry Regiment. He won the Bronze Star for his
      heroism in an engagement along the Naktong River and a
      Distinguished Service Cross for heroism at the time of
      his capture by the Chinese in November 1950. He died in
      a POW camp the following May.

1257. Graham, Billy. I SAW YOUR SONS AT WAR. Minneapolis,
      MN: Billy Graham Evangelistic Assoc., 1953.

      Brief, illustrated account of the famous evangelist's
      visit to American soldiers on the battlefields of Korea.
      This diary account looks at the subject of meeting soldiers'
      spiritual needs in wartime.

1258. Hershey, Scott, and Harry Tennant. "Are the Churches
      Failing our G.I.'s?" AM MERCURY, 1953 76 (351):3-13.

      Claims that American churches, primarily the Protestant
      sects, have failed to meet the needs of American service-
      men mobilized to meet the Korean crisis. Furthermore, they
      have refused to make their best young ministers available
      for chaplain duty. Tells of some of the programs being
      initiated to solve those problems.

1259. Hess, Dean E. BATTLE HYMN. New York: McGraw, 1956.

      Recollections of a Protestant minister who entered WWII as
      a fighter pilot rather than a chaplain. When war came in
      Korea, he again became a combatant but also became involved
      in aiding Korean war orphans, including an orphanage on
      Cheju Island. Stresses importance of religious faith and
      attempts to apply religious teachings in time of war.
      This book was ultimately made into a movie.

1260. Jaeger, Vernon. "Experiences in Korea." MIL CHAP,
      1950 October:1-2.

A US Army Chaplain makes some observations on what took place the first few months of the war and predicts a UN victory and a great interest in Christianity following hostilities.

1261. Jorgensen, Daniel B. AIR FORCE CHAPLAINS, 1947-1960. Washington: Government Printing Office, 1961.

This first volume in the history of the chaplaincy of the US Air Force covers from its establishment through the Korean War and beyond. Tells of the organization, activities, problems and contributions of the chaplains to the effort in Korea as well as to units and troops elsewhere.

1262. Mainard, Allen S. "First Chapel With First Marine Division." CHAP, 1951 8 (6):29-30, 40.

Describes the dedication of a permanent chapel built by the First Combat Service Group in Korea and tells of its initial services and how it became a reality.

1263. Martin, Harold H. "The Pious Killer of Korea." SAT EVE POST, 1951 224 (3):26-27, 87-90.

Examines the life and military career in Korea of a US-ordained minister, Lt. Col. Dean E. Hess, who served as a combat pilot with the 5th Air Force. The veteran of more than 250 missions also trained South Korean pilots and provided major support for an orphanage of 800 Korean children.

1264. Muller, John H. WEARING THE CROSS IN KOREA. Redlands, CA: The Author, 1954.

Recollections of a US naval chaplain who served with the 1st Marines from the spring of 1952 until February 1953. Details his work with combat troops and his humanitarian efforts with South Korean refugees.

1265. Pardue, Harry A. KOREAN ADVENTURE. New York: Morehouse, 1953.

A well-known Episcopal Bishop and writer of religious faith tells of his visit to Korea and the role of religion for the US fighting man.

1266. Parker, Roy H. "Religion at Work." CHAP, 1952 9 (1):9-10.

Describes some of the humanitarian and religious services performed by US Army chaplains serving in Korea during the war.

1267. Rayburn, Robert G. FIGHT THE GOOD FIGHT: LESSONS FROM THE KOREAN WAR. Pasadena, CA: Covenant, 1956.

Shows how war can strengthen the religious beliefs of
individuals caught up in it. Covers religious aspects of
the Korean War for US servicemen.

1268.   "A Salute to the Chaplain." CHAP, 1951 8 (6):1-5.

Tribute to the 200 US chaplains serving in Korea beside
combat troops as well as those serving at hospitals in
Japan where many of the wounded are taken. Traces a day
in the life of Far East Command Chaplain Lt. Col. Julian S.
Ellenberg serving at the Tokyo Army Hospital.

1269.   Singer, Howard D. "Your Kids Taught Me About
        Religion." SAT EVE POST, 1953 226 (10):30-31, 63, 66,
        68-69.

The only Air Force Jewish chaplain in Japan and Korea
reflects on his experience serving men in combat. Notes
that the religious needs and growth of individuals are the
same whether they are Jewish, Protestant or Catholic.
Talks about the successes and shortcomings of chaplains
ministering to the needs of soldiers.

1270.   Sizoo, Joseph R. "Report on Korea and Japan." CHAP,
        1953 10 (3):1-4.

Describes the service being rendered by US military
chaplains serving in Korea. Notes the suffering being
inflicted on the civilian populace by the fighting and
the efforts of many military personnel to alleviate the
hardships.

1271.   Tonne, Arthur. THE STORY OF CHAPLAIN KAPAUN:
        PATRIOT PRIEST OF THE KOREAN CONFLICT. Emporia, KS:
        Didde, 1954.

US Army Chaplain Emil J. Kapaun of the 3rd Battalion,
8th Regiment, 1st Cavalry Division became one of the
popular heroes of the Korean War after he died in a
Chinese Communist prisoner of war camp in May 1951.
Kapaun chose to remain with a group of fifty wounded soldiers, rather than escape a November 1950 attack. The
group was taken prisoner and he ministered to their
needs for six months before succumbing to pneumonia
and dysentery.

1272.   US Navy Department. THE HISTORY OF THE CHAPLAIN CORPS,
        UNITED STATES NAVY. Vol. 6, DURING THE KOREA WAR, 27
        JUNE 1950-27 JUNE 1954. Washington: Government Printing
        Office, 1960.

Organization of the chaplaincy, along with procurement,
training and assignment of combat clergy ministering to
US Naval and Marines personnel in Korea during and after

the conflict.

1273. Venzke, Rodger R. CONFIDENCE IN BATTLE, INSPIRATION
       IN PEACE: THE UNITED STATES ARMY CHAPLAINCY, 1945-1975.
       Washington: Office of the Chief of Chaplains, Department
       of the Army, 1977.

       This volume (V) of the history of the Chaplaincy in the
       US Army includes a chapter on the Korean War. Focuses on
       individuals and the services they rendered. Looks at the
       various phases of the war and shows how the chaplains
       attempted to meet the spiritual needs of soldiers
       experiencing the nation's first limited war.

1274. Whitman, Howard. "What Soldiers Believe: A Reporter
       in Search of God." COLLIER'S, 1951 127 (22):18, 68-71.

       Men in the military, like others, often search for the
       nature and purpose of God, but the search frequently
       becomes more intense to soldiers experiencing the
       horrors of war. Uses many examples of US soldiers
       wounded or captured in Korea to show the importance
       of religious faith when facing such hardships.

1275. Wildman, Albert C. "The Work of Chaplains in Korea."
       CHAP, 1952 9 (2):28-29.

       Description of problems, mental and physical, facing
       chaplains serving US Army troops in the combat zone.
       The author, who served with I Corps, noted that chaplains
       served South Korean as well as American troops.

                    G. RECREATION AND EDUCATION

1276. Fisher, Kenneth E. "A Comparative Analysis of Selected
       Congressional Documents Related to Educational Benefits
       Legislated for the Veterans of WWII, the Korean Conflict,
       and the Vietnam Era Under the G.I. Bill." Doctoral
       Dissertation. Florida State, 1975.

       An examination of congressional debates concerning
       veterans' educational benefits during these wars. Includes
       analysis of the actions of the 82nd Congress, 2nd Session
       which in 1952 passed legislation for Korean War veterans.

1277. Mattila, J. Peter. "G.I. Bill Benefits and Enrollments:
       How Did Vietnam Veterans Fare?" SOC SCI Q, 1978 59
       (3):535-545.

       Comparative analysis of benefits and enrollment rates of
       the WWII, Korean and Vietnam GI Bill programs. Concludes
       that Korean War and Vietnam veterans did not take
       advantage of educational opportunities to the extent that

WWII veterans did.

1278. Riley, Nelson J. "Red Cross Clubmobiles Roll in
       Korea." ARMY INFO DIG, 1954 9 (2):11-17.

       Within three months of the ending of hostilities in Korea,
       Red Cross personnel, including many young women, began
       visiting remote US Army units to provide programs of
       recreation and entertainment. Notes that the service
       was an extension of services offered during the war
       and tells what some of those services were.

1279. Schless, George B. "Hospitality Through Associated
       Services." ARMY INFO DIG, 1951 6 (1):47-53.

       Describes the role of Associated Services established in
       April 1950 as the successor to the United Service
       Organization (USO) in helping to make off-duty hours more
       pleasant for members of the US Armed Forces. The
       organization was a coordinating and financing agency for
       the programs of the Young Men's Christian Association,
       National Catholic Community Service and the National
       Jewish Welfare Board.

1280. Smith, John C. "The Red Cross in the Field."
       ARMY INFO DIG, 1953 8 (2):35-41.

       Describes the services offered to US military personnel
       serving in Korea and their families at home by the American
       Red Cross. The combat field office, its personnel and
       functions are described as is the role played by the 3,700
       local chapters. Explains the unique way in which the
       independent agency works with the government to meet the
       serviceman's needs.

1281. Stevenson, Charles. "G.I. University." ROTARIAN,
       1952 80 (1):29-31.

       During the Korean War thousands of US soldiers found
       time, even when serving in combat zones to take academic
       classes and study, with their homework being graded via
       correspondence. Many earned the equivalent of a high
       school diploma while many others earned the equivalent
       of a year of college during their combat tour.

1282. US Veterans Administration. ADMINISTRATOR OF VETERANS
       AFFAIRS ANNUAL REPORT, 1951, 1952, 1953. Washington:
       Government Printing Office, 1952-1954.

       Sets forth the Korean War period legislation impacting
       US veterans. Very good information on such things as
       activities of Veterans Hospitals, education programs and
       veterans' benefits.

1283. US Veterans Administration. REPORT OF EDUCATIONAL

TESTING SERVICE ON EDUCATIONAL ASSISTANCE PROGRAMS FOR
VETERANS: A COMPARATIVE STUDY OF THREE G.I. BILLS.
Washington: House Committee on Veterans' Affairs, 1975.

An analysis, comparison and evaluation of the G.I.
Bills for WWII, Korea and Vietnam. Includes the scope
of the Korean program, degree of participation, outreach
efforts, abuses and administration. Extensive bibliography.

H. AWARDS AND HONORS

1284. ARMY TIMES, eds. AMERICAN HEROES OF ASIAN WARS.
New York: Dodd, 1968.

Stories of Americans involved in combat during the
Korean War and in Vietnam. For Korea it looks at the
exploits of General Walton "Bull Dog" Walker, Colonel
John H. "Iron Mike" Michaelis, Sergeant Connie Charlton,
Colonel James Jabara (Jet Ace), and war correspondent
Marguerite Higgins.

1285. "Award of the Medal of Honor." ARMOR, 1951 60
(3):5.

Tells of the heroics of three US Army soldiers who
received the Medal of Honor for acts performed in 1950
and early 1951. Those individuals were: Carl H. Dodd,
5th Infantry Regiment; John A. Pittman, 23rd Infantry
Regiment and Ernest R. Kouma, 72nd Tank Battalion.

1286. Colton, Willard A. "The Hero of Hill 543." SAT EVE
POST, 1953 226 (5):17-19, 52, 54-55.

Details the exploits that posthumously won Sergeant
Cornelius H. Charlton the US Medal of Honor. In a June 2,
1951, engagement, Charlton, a black from West Virginia
and a member of the 24th Regiment, 25th Division, knocked out
two Chinese Communist machine gun positions before losing his
life.

1287. Costello, Michael. "The Army Thinks He's Earned a
Rest." READ DIG, 1952 60 (357):12-15.

Lt. Carl H. Dodd of the Fifth Infantry won the Medal of
Honor for forty-eight hours of heroic acts near Inchon in
January 1951. In that period he killed many of the enemy,
silenced a number of machine guns and inspired his comrades
to continue fighting. Condensed from VFW MAGAZINE, December
1951.

1288. Detzer, Karl. "Einor Wins His Medal." READ DIG,
1951 59 (356):1-4.

The exploits of US Army Corporal Einor H. Ingman who

stormed two enemy machine gun emplacements near Maltrai,
Korea, on February 26, 1951, and killed twenty enemy
soldiers before being seriously wounded. For his acts
he received the Congressional Medal of Honor. Condensed
from VFW MAGAZINE, November 1951.

1289. Detzer, Karl. "No Push Buttons For Cap'n Easy."
       READ DIG, 1952 60 (361):61-62.

       Captain Lew Millett led a patrol of eleven men against
       communist forces near Soam-ni, Korea, on February 7,
       1951. The group ran into an enemy stronghold which it
       attacked and in the ensuing engagement killed 97 enemy
       soldiers. For his leadership Millett won the Medal of
       Honor. Condensed from VFW MAGAZINE, April 1952.

1290. Herbert, Anthony B. HERBERT--THE MAKING OF A SOLDIER.
       New York: Hippocrene, 1982.

       A personal account of the experiences of the most decorated
       US soldier in the Korean War--thirty-one citations. This
       story, by the professional soldier whose later critique of
       the US war in Vietnam (in the book SOLDIER) caused
       considerable controversy, details the gallantry he showed in
       fighting with the 23rd and 38th Infantry. This work is
       far superior to Herbert's 1955 book on his experiences.

1291. Herbert, Anthony B., and Robert Niemann. CONQUEST TO
       NOWHERE. Herminie, PA: Keystone, 1955.

       America's most decorated soldier in the Korean War
       collaborates on an account of the military exploits that
       won him thirty-one combat citations while serving with
       the 23rd and 38th Infantry Divisons.

1292. Jacobs, Bruce. HEROES OF THE ARMY: THE MEDAL OF HONOR
       AND ITS WINNERS. New York: Norton, 1956.

       Popular history of the US's highest military honor from
       its inception in the Civil War through the Korean War.
       Includes an appendix that has the names of the Korean
       conflict recipients.

1293. Jacobs, Bruce. KOREA'S HEROES: THE MEDAL OF HONOR
       STORY. New York: Lion, 1953.

       In-depth look at the exploits that won the Medal of Honor
       for twenty US servicemen in Korea. The range of individuals
       from private to general shows that heroism knows no rank.
       Also includes individuals from various phases of the war,
       thus, giving the reader an overview of the conflict and
       the key engagements.

1294. Johnson, Martin H. "Above and Beyond the Call of Duty."
       AIR FORCE, 1951 34 (9):34-35.

Tells of the action which won the US Medal of Honor, posthumously, for Major Louis J. Sebille, the first Air Force man to earn the medal in the Korean War. He flew his disabled fighter into a group of enemy armored vehicles on August 5, 1951. The author was Sebille's wingman.

1295. Kerrigan, Evans E. AMERICAN BADGES AND INSIGNIA. New York: Viking, 1967.

The author, himself a decorated Korean War Marine, has prepared an encyclopedic guide of American military badges and insignias. More than 1,000 drawings are used to identify the decorations. National Guard Units as well as regular units are included.

1296. Kerrigan, Evans E. AMERICAN WAR MEDALS AND DECORATIONS. New York: Viking, 1964.

A guide to US medals, decorations, badges and awards conferred upon servicemen and civilians from 1780 to 1963. Includes awards authorized during the Korean War.

1297. Marshall, S.L.A. "Death of a Hero." COM FOR J, 1951 2 (4):14-22.

Vividly recounts the November exploits that won for Captain Reginald B. Desiderio, E Company, 27th Infantry Regiment, the Medal of Honor and for his company a Distinguished Unit Citation. One of the first major engagements between US and Communist Chinese forces.

1298. Marshall, S.L.A., and Bill Davidson. "Do the Real Heroes Get the Medal of Honor?" COLLIER'S, 1953 131 (8):13-15.

Marshall, one of the top analysts of the US Army, contends that while worthy soldiers sometimes receive the decorations they deserve, the selection system is very unfair and many worthy acts of heroism go unrewarded. Uses many examples from the Korean War to prove his contentions.

1299. Reynolds, Quentin. KNOWN BUT TO GOD. New York: Day, 1960.

Half non-fiction, half fiction, this book tells of the founding of Arlington National Cemetery and the choosing of the unknown soldiers from WWI and II and the Korean War. The author then gives fictional accounts of the last days of the men who could be the men selected.

1300. Shores, Christopher. AIR ACES. Novoto, CA: Presidio, 1983.

Brief sketches of all US air aces from WWI through
Vietnam including a chapter on aces from the Korean
War.

1301. Stevens, Paul D., ed. THE CONGRESSIONAL MEDAL OF HONOR:
THE NAMES AND DEEDS. Forest Ranch, CA: Sharp, 1984.

This massive work describes the heroic deeds of all
recipients of the Medal of Honor from the American Civil
War through Vietnam, including the Korean War.

XII. THE UNITED NATIONS AND THE WAR
A. POLITICAL COMMITMENT

1302. Bloomfield, Lincoln P. "The Department of State and
the United Nations." DEPT STATE BUL, 1950 23 (594):
804-811.

Praises the UN for quickly coming to the defense of
South Korea. Says the period of uncertainty as to the
effectiveness of the UN is over. Goes on to explain the
manner by which the US State Department works with and
through the UN.

1303. Boen, Sharon E. "The Leadership Role of the Secretary-
General in Times of International Crisis." Doctoral
Dissertation. Virginia, 1965.

One chapter focuses on UN Secretary-General Trygve Lie's
role in the collective security action in the Korean crisis.

1304. Deyo, M.L. "How Far Can the Bear Walk?" US NAVAL
INST PROC, 1951 77 (11):1203-1205.

Maintains that the US and UN must be willing to make
the commitment to halt the communist take-over of South
Korea because if not Russia will have control of a
strategic area she has wanted for a long time. If
Russia encounters strong US resolve to defend Korea,
she will probably back down.

1305. Dille, John. SUBSTITUTE FOR VICTORY. New York:
Doubleday, 1954.

Contends that the US-UN effort in Korea was justified,
necessary and wise. Also claims that the settlement was
as good as could be expected, and it was, in reality, a
victory for democracy over communism. Critical of
MacArthur, whose ideas of victory were archaic by the
time of war in Korea.

1306. Douglas, Paul H. "United to Enforce Peace." FOR AFF,
1951 30 (1):1-16.

Relates the problems the UN had between 1945 and 1950 in
moving to halt aggression but was able to act in Korea
because of two accidents: Russia's temporary walkout of the
Security Council; and the availability of US troops in Japan
that could be moved quickly to Korea. Maintains that the UN

must, in the future, move quickly to halt aggression whenever it occurs.

1307.   Everett, John T., Jr. "The United Nations and the Korean
        Situation, 1947-1950: A Study of International Techniques
        of Pacific Settlement." Doctoral Dissertation. Cincinnati,
        1955.

        This study focuses on the Korean problem as it emerged from
        the Japanese defeat in WWII, proceeds through the US-Russian
        conflict, the US appeal to the UN and the UN's role in
        establishing the ROK. Details the establishment and
        operation of the UN Commission on Korea.

1308.   Ferwerda, Vernon L. "The United Nations Role in the
        Maintenance of Peace." Doctoral Dissertation. Harvard,
        1954.

        A look at the various efforts of the UN to build machinery
        to assure peace. A chapter is included on the military
        response to North Korean aggression, citing it as a major
        departure from earlier attempts to meet problems by
        non-military means.

1309.   Goodrich, Leland M. "Korea: Collective Measures
        Against Aggression." INTER CON, 1953 494:131-192.

        A condensed version of the author's in-depth study of
        US relations with the UN as applied to Korea between
        1947 and 1953. Sees the US-UN action as a clear signal
        to the Communist world that aggression would not be
        tolerated and believes that in acting as they did, they
        kept the conflict from escalating into a world war.

1310.   Goodrich, Leland M. KOREA: A STUDY OF US POLICY IN
        THE UNITED NATIONS. New York: Council on Foreign
        Relations, 1956.

        Examines the UN's involvement in Korea from 1945 until
        1953. Considerable emphasis is placed on the United
        States' use of the UN to carry out its Korean policy.
        Numerous UN documents.

1311.   Great Britain Foreign Office. FURTHER SUMMARY OF
        EVENTS RELATING TO KOREA, OCTOBER 1950 TO MAY 1951.
        London: Her Majesty's Stationery Office, 1951.

        Brief summary of the political and military actions of
        the British Government as it worked through the UN in Korea.

1312.   Great Britain Foreign Office. SUMMARY OF EVENTS
        RELATING TO KOREA, JUNE 25, 1950 TO OCTOBER 9, 1950.
        London: Her Majesty's Stationery Office, 1950.

Brief chronological account of political and military
actions of the British Government during the first
three and a half months of the conflict.

1313. Hamilton, Thomas J. "The UN and Trygve Lie."
       FOR AFF, 1950 29 (1):67-77.

       Examines the first four and a half years of Lie's service
       as Secretary General of the UN. The Norwegian Socialist is
       generally criticized for failure to assert his power but
       praised for his push for intervention in the face of North
       Korean intervention in June 1950. Describes the
       expectations, authority and restrictions placed on the
       Secretary and admits to the magnitude of the problems facing
       him.

1314. HOW THE UNITED NATIONS MET THE CHALLENGE OF KOREA.
       New York: UN, Department of Public Information, 1953.

       Brief illustrated history of the role of the UN in
       Korea from 1950-1953. Includes a chronology of the
       Korean issue plus a text of the armistice agreement.

1315. Kahng, Tae Jin. "A Handling by the Security Council of
       Legal Questions Involved in International Disputes and
       Situations." Doctoral Dissertation. Columbia, 1962.

       Analysis of the UN Security Council's handling of the
       Korean crisis and war as both legal and political
       questions.

1316. Kahng, Tae Jin. LAW, POLITICS AND THE SECURITY COUNCIL.
       The Hague: Nijhoff, 1969, 2nd ed.

       This study of the interplay between international law
       and politics in the UN Security Council includes an
       analysis of that body's role in the Korean crisis and war.

1317. Keeton, G.W. "International Law in the Far Eastern
       War." TWEN CENT, 1951 149 (888):95-108.

       Examines a number of thorny questions of international
       law that appeared with the development of war in Korea.
       Looks at problems such as abstentions in the UN Security
       Council, UN intervention in a Civil War and establishment
       of the ROK. Does not really answer those questions but
       maintains they are complex issues with no clear cut
       answers.

1318. KOREA AND THE UNITED NATIONS. New York: UN, Department
       of Public Information, 1950.

       A history of the debates and actions taken by the Security
       Council on the North Korean aggression against South Korea
       from June 25 to September 7, 1950.

1319. Lee, Tong Won. "The United Nations and Korea, 1945-1953."
       Doctoral Dissertation. Oxford, 1958.

       Traces UN policies and involvement in the Korean issue.
       Maintains that while some mistakes were made in handling
       the Korea issue initially, the organization's response to
       North Korean aggression showed its ability to respond to
       a real crisis in a positive way.

1320. Lie, Trygve. IN THE CAUSE OF PEACE: SEVEN YEARS WITH
       THE UNITED NATIONS. New York: Macmillan, 1954.

       Memoirs of the man who was UN Secretary-General during
       the Korean War. Gives details of behind the scenes
       maneuvering in the UN as that body met what was until
       that time its most serious challenge. Lie saw the
       conflict in Korea as a "War against the United Nations."

1321. Lowe, Herbert S. "United Nations in Korea." Master's
       Thesis. Tulane, 1952.

       Sees the UN decision to intervene in Korea as a major
       test of the concept of international security. Cannot
       determine its outcome since the war was still going on
       when this was written.

1322. Lyons, Eugene M. "The Decline of a Multilateral
       Policy for Korean Reconstruction." Doctoral Dissertation.
       Columbia, 1958.

       A case study of the relationship between the UN and US
       foreign policy as it concerned the UN Korean Reconstruction
       Agency (UNKRA), a body created in late 1950 to provide a
       program of relief and rehabilitation to war-racked Korea.

1323. Mazuzan, George T. "America's UN Commitment, 1945-
       1953." HISTORIAN, 1978 49 (2):309-330.

       Warren R. Austin of Vermont, the first US Ambassador
       to the United Nations, was serving when war broke out
       in Korea. This details his actions in putting forth the
       US position and having to justify it before the world
       body.

1324. Panikkar, K. M. IN TWO CHINAS: MEMOIRS OF A DIPLOMAT.
       London, Allen, 1956.

       Recollections of the Indian ambassador to Communist China
       at the time of the Korean War. Chinese officials warned
       Panikkar that they would enter the war if UN forces crossed
       the 38th Parallel, and he echoed that message, but it was
       ignored or discounted by top US and UN officials.

1325. Perrin, Kwan Sok. "The Problem of Korean Unification
        and the United Nations, 1945-1955." Doctoral Dissertation.
        Utah, 1971.

        Sees the problem of Korean unification as a complex
        political phenomenon that developed because of the power
        politics of Russia and the US and the ineffectiveness of
        the UN because of weaknesses in its charter.

1326. Raitt, Walton A. "American Ideology and the United
        Nations: A Study in Ambivalence." Doctoral Dissertation.
        Claremont, 1968.

        An analysis of the relationship between American idealogy
        and the UN, with the UN and the Korean War being one of the
        case studies.

1327. Riggs, Robert E. "The Policy of the United States With
        Respect to Political Questions in the General Assembly of
        the United Nations." Doctoral Dissertation. Illinois, 1956.

        One of the issues addressed is the political maneuvering
        within the UN General Assembly that led to condemnation of
        the Chinese Communist intervention in Korea.

1328. Romulo, Carlos P. "The United Nations and the New
        States of Asia." YALE R, 1950 40 (2):193-200.

        Claims the UN response to aggression in Korea is a major
        turning point in the life of the organization because it
        took a stand in ways other than words. Says the UN must
        not only stick to its position but will face another test
        when it comes time to rebuild the country.

1329. Schwebel, Stephen M. THE SECRETARY-GENERAL OF THE
        UNITED NATIONS. Cambridge: Harvard University, 1953.

        Puts forth the difficulties that the Secretary-General
        has in carrying out his responsibilities. Maintains that
        success hinges in large part on interpersonal skills.
        Looks at Secretary-General Lie's situation and lauds his
        performance in handling such difficult problems as the
        Korean crisis.

1330. Stairs, Denis. "The United Nations and the Politics
        of the Korean War." INTER J, 1970 25 (2):302-320.

        It is widely held that the US did pretty much as it pleased
        in the Korean conflict and then informed the UN of its
        decisions. This challenges that view and shows that
        intervention under UN auspices significantly impacted
        American decision making during the war.

1331. Weissberg, Guenter. "The International Personality
        of the United Nations." Doctoral Dissertation. Columbia,

1959.

Shows how the Korean conflict and the UN response to it had
a major impact on the development and personality of the
organization.

1332. Wolfers, Arnold. "Collective Security and the War
        in Korea." YALE R, 1954 43 (4):481-496.

A study of the UN-US response to North Korean aggression
maintains that the decision to intervene was not based on the
importance of collective security but on the need to
implement the containment policy.

1333. Yoo, Tai-Ho. THE KOREAN WAR AND THE UNITED NATIONS: A
        LEGAL AND DIPLOMATIC HISTORICAL STUDY. Louvain, Belgium:
        Institute for Political and Social Sciences, 1965.

Examines UN involvement in Korea from the end of WWII
through the Korean War and concludes that both the US and
Soviet Union were pursuing their own interest rather than
those of Korea and the UN. Based on French and English
sources.

1334. Yoon, Young Kyo. "North Korean Regime's Rejection of
        the Competence and Authority of the United Nations."
        KOREAN AFF, 1963 (2):247-263.

North Korea, at the direction of the Soviet Union, did all
it could to discredit the UN and its efforts to establish an
independent government in South Korea.

1335. Yoon, Young Kyo. "United Nations Participation in
        Korean Affairs, 1947-1951." KOREANA, 1960 2 (Spring):22-54.

Overview of the role of the UN in the establishment of the
Republic of Korea, extension of recognition and the response
to North Korean aggression. Russian opposition to the
establishment of the ROK is also covered.

B. UN COMMAND

1336. Amody, Francis J. "The Sabre Tooth Cheetahs of Osan."
        AM AVI HIST SOC J, 1980 25 91):42-44.

Discusses the air activities of the UN Command in Korea.
The planes used were F-86F Sabres, which were converted from
F-51D Mustangs, and were piloted by members of the South
African Air Force. The flights were made from Osan Air Base
near Korea from late 1950 until the end of the war.

1337. Burk, Richard J. "The Organization and Command of
       United Nations Military Forces." Master's Thesis. Yale,
       1956.

       Includes problems encountered by the UN in establishing the
       UN Command at the outbreak of war and the continuing
       difficulties involved in having a multinational force conduct
       a united military effort.

1338. Carver, George A. "Military Support of the United
       Nations." MIL R, 1950 30 (8):3-9.

       Maintains that the military support of South Korea by the
       collective military forces of members of the UN has become a
       reality and thus the weakness which spelled the doom of the
       League of Nations has been avoided. Goes into background of
       UN activities in Korea from 1946 until after the outbreak of
       war.

1339. Cooling, B. Franklin. "Allied Interoperability in
       the Korean War." MIL R, 1983 63 (6):26-52.

       The UN Command quickly learned that if interoperability was
       to be a reality in pursuing the war in Korea, two things were
       needed: (1) standardization of weapons and ammunition; and
       (2) language commonality for adequate communication. Making
       those factors a reality greatly increased combat efficiency
       of UN Forces.

1340. Goodrich, Leland M. "Collective Action in Korea:
       Evaluating the Results of the UN Collective Action."
       CUR HIST, 1960 38 (226):332-336.

       Maintains the UN played a key role in keeping the Korean
       War limited and aided the US government in its desire to keep
       from fighting a major war in the Far East. Sees significance
       in the fact that the US assisted the ROK within the UN frame-
       work.

1341. Hayler, W.B. "Hail, Hail, the Gang's All There."
       US NAVAL INST PROC, 1953 79 (7):749-751.

       Covers the operations and contributions of Task Force 95,
       the UN Blockading and Escort Force, composed of ships from
       Britain, Holland, Canada, Columbia, Australia, Thailand, New
       Zealand, South Korea and the US. Shows the extent of
       cooperation and coordination of the navies in the UN Command.

1342. Hume, Edgar E. "United Nations Medical Service in
       the Korean Conflict." MIL SURG, 1951 109 (2):91-95.

       The Medical Director General, UN Forces in Korea, presents
       observations and analysis of UN activities during the first
       eight months of the war. Compares the casualties of all

previous US wars and notes that only the Civil War and WWII
saw more casualties. Examines treatment of diseases and
preventative medical measures. Praises the service being
provided by UN personnel.

1343. "Liberation of South Korea." US NAVAL INST PROC,
        1951 77 (1):73-83.

        Photo section pays tribute to the accomplishments of the
        nations of the UN Command during the first six months of the
        Korean War. Shows contribution of ground, naval and air force
        personnel. Brief introduction recaps the war up to January
        1951 and indicates it is already a frustrating conflict.

1344. "Responses of Governments to Action By Security
        Council on Korean Attack." UN BUL, 1950 9 (2):50-53.

        Excerpts of replies of more than forty UN members to the
        Secretary-General's inquiry as to the type of assistance each
        country would be able to provide.

1345. "Turning of the Tide in Korea and the Meeting of 'A
        New Foe." UN BUL, 1950 9 (10):528-535.

        Three reports from UN Commander-General MacArthur cover
        the period from September 15 to November 1, 1950, along with
        a special report dated November 5. Recounts the Inchon
        invasion, capture of Seoul, crossing of the 38th Parallel, the
        move north and entry of the Chinese Communists into the war.

1346. UNITED ACTION IN KOREA. New York: UN, Department
        of Public Information, 1951.

        Short photographic account of the UN commitment of men and
        material to the defense of South Korea during the first year
        of the conflict.

1347. "United Nations Allies in the Korean War." ARMY INFO
        DIG, 1953 8 (9):57.

        Listing of the UN ground force contingents and their dates
        of arrival in Korea. Also lists UN flying and sea
        contingents as well as medical support elements.

1348. UN, Secretary-General. REGULATIONS: UN SERVICE
        MEDAL, KOREA. New York: UN, 1951.

        Defines eligibility for receiving the UN medal for serving
        in the Korean conflict. Tells of the history of the award,
        which was authorized by the General Assembly in December
        1950.

1349. Yoon, Young Kyo. "United Nations Participation in
        Korean Affairs: 1945-1954." Doctoral Dissertation.
        American, 1959.

Reviews the achievements of the UN in the establishment and recognition of the Republic of Korea and studies the UN collective security action against communist aggression in Korea in June 1950.

C. UN FORCES

1350. "Casualties of UN Forces in Korea." DEPT STATE BUL, 1951 24 (616):656.

Casualties of UN forces in Korea from July 1950 through March 9, 1951, are listed by country. Includes those killed in action, wounded and missing.

1351. Darragh, Shaun M. "Hwanghae-do: The War of the Donkeys." ARMY, 1984 34 (11):66-75.

During the Korean War the UN Command supplied, trained and supported North Korean guerrilla bands fighting the North Korean Government. The guerrilla bands, which operated primarily in Hwanghae Provinance, called themselves "donkeys."

1352. DeVaney, Carl N. "Know Your Allies." MIL R, 1953 32 (12):11-19.

The UN military effort in Korea was the greatest combined operation in history with twenty nations fighting to accomplish a single mission. Discusses problems of language, orders, cultures and customs. Concludes that the allied nations must gain an understanding of military doctrine, customs, manner of living and temperament and personalities as well as the art of warfare.

1353. "Diary of the War in Korea." ROY UNI SER INST J, 1950 95 (579) to 1954 99 (593).

Successful issues carry a general chronology of key events covering UN forces involved in military action during the Korean War. Covers the period from June 25, 1950, through January 26, 1954.

1354. Jennings, Gary. "The KCOMZ Story." ARMY INFO DIG, 1953 8 (10):56-60.

In July 1952 the UN forces in Korea were divided into two commands, one of those was to fight, the other, The Korean Communications Zone, was to provide logistical and administrative support and exercise territorial control in support of combat operations. The new command, which had four subordinate commands: Korean Base Section; Third Transportation Military Railway Service; Prisoner of War Command and Taegu Military Post, has as its top priority procuring, importing and delivering supplies to UN forces throughout Korea. It was best known, however, for handling the repatriation of US POW's.

1355. Kahn, Eli Jacques, Jr. THE PECULIAR WAR. New York: Random, 1952.

Focuses on human interest aspects of the war especially as brought about by the international character of the UN fighting force. Tells of some of the unusual features of such forces as the Greeks, Turks and Thais. Deals with relationships between Koreans, civilians and members of the ROK, and Americans.

1356. Kahn, Eli Jacques, Jr. "United Nations Army." COM FOR J, 1951 2 (1):12-14.

Describes the make-up and contribution of the UN ground forces that were part of the Eighth US Army in Korea. Sixteen nations contributed 35,000 men to the force during the first year of the war. During that time 5,000 troops from those nations died in combat. The British Commonwealth contributed 20,000 while Turkey provided 5,000. After that the numbers fell off sharply down to the 50-man force from Luxembourg.

1357. Kirby, Pierre. "Supplying United Nations Troops in Korea." MIL R, 1953 33 (1):21-26.

Explains the operations and accomplishments of the Japan Logistical Command (JLC) whose responsibility was to provide a programmed movement of military supplies to Korea. After initial problems of supplying UN combat forces, a sophisticated and efficient system was established.

1358. Lyons, Jake. "Feeding the United Nations in Korea." QM R, 1951 31 (1):6-7, 150-154.

Problems of supplying food to UN forces in Korea was complicated by the fact that the men of the multi-national force had very different tastes; thus, what was pleasing to an American soldier was not acceptable to a Greek, a Turk or a Thai. Also examines the preparation of rations for US soldiers and enemy prisoners.

1359. Royal Netherlands Navy, Historical Section, Naval Staff. "On the Way From Tread! ..." US NAVAL INST PROC, 1952 78 (9):969-971.

Relates the cooperation between US Navy helicopter pilots who served as spotters for the Netherlands warship H.N.M.S. EVERTSON. Tells particularly about the contribution of an unidentified American pilot who spotted during the bombardment of Wonsan, before losing his life.

1360. "United Nations Forces in Korea." MIL R, 1952 32
       (3):30-33.

       A brief photographic essay on the UN commitment to meet
       Communist aggression in Korea. Tells of the different
       nations sending troops and supplies and the contributions
       they are making to the military effort.

1361. Wells, H.B. "Kimpo Provisional Regiment." LEATHERNECK,
       1953 36 (7):14-19, 72.

       Tells of the organization, problems and activities of a
       composite combat force composed of US Army, Navy and
       Marine personnel and ROK Army, Marines and National
       Police.

D. CONTRIBUTING NATIONS

1. AUSTRALIA

1362. Bartlett, Norman, ed. WITH THE AUSTRALIANS IN KOREA.
       Canberra: Australian War Memorial, 1954.

       Brief story of the Australian contribution to the UN
       military action in Korea. Tells the various forces that
       were involved and their contribution to the fighting.

1363. KOREA.   Canberra: Australia, Department of External
       Affairs, 1950.

       Brief account of Australia's support of the UN call for
       assistance to repel aggression in Korea. Tells of early
       military commitment to the UN effort.

1364. McLeod, Alan L. "Australian-Korean Relations."
       KOREAN SUR, 1955 4 (2):5-7.

       Summarizes official Australian actions in respect to the
       ROK from 1947 through 1954. Lists books and pamphlets
       published relevant to the war. Includes chronology of
       important events.

1365. McLeod, Alan L. "Australia and the War in Korea."
       KOREAN SUR, 1953 2 (7):6-7.

       Describes Australia's political and military commitments
       to the defense of South Korea. The various Australian
       fighting units serving in Korea are described and
       statistics on casualties through February 1953 are
       cited. Also contains an assessment of the average
       Australian's view of the war.

1366. Millar, Thomas B. "Australia and the American Alliance."
       PAC AFF, 1964 37 (2):148-160.

The Korean War had a major impact on US-Australian
relations as it brought the two nations closer together.
As they fought together in the UN force, they also saw
a need to protect each other's interest and thus, in
1952, they signed the ANZUS Pact.

1367. Odgers, G. ACROSS THE PARALLEL: THE AUSTRALIAN 77TH
       SQUADRON WITH THE US IN KOREA. Sidney: Heinemann, 1953.

       The organization and activities of the Australian
       Fighter Air Squadron that was attached to the Far East
       Air Force, as part of the UN Command, throughout the war.

1368. O'Neill, Robert. AUSTRALIA IN THE KOREAN WAR, 1950-
       1953. Vol. I, STRATEGY AND DIPLOMACY. Canberra:
       Australian Government, 1981.

       The first volume in a projected multi-volume work on
       Australia and the war in Korea looks at the decision
       to join the UN Command and the extent of the military
       commitment.

2. CANADA

1369. Canada, Army Headquarters, General Staff Historical Section.
       CANADA'S ARMY IN KOREA: A SHORT OFFICIAL HISTORY. Ottawa:
       Queen's Printers, 1956.

       Overview of the Canadian military commitment in Korea.
       Examines the political context of involvement and shows
       the advantages and disadvantages of being part of the UN
       Command.

1370. Canada, Army Headquarters, General Staff Historical
       Section. CANADA'S ARMY IN KOREA: THE UNITED NATIONS
       OPERATIONS, 1950-1953, AND THEIR AFTERMATH. Ottawa:
       Queen's Printers, 1956.

       Official account of the Canadian Army's contributions
       to the UN's military effort.

1371. CANADA AND THE KOREAN CRISIS. Ottawa: King's Printer,
       1950.

       Official Canadian explanation of the political and
       military response to the UN's move to halt North
       Korean aggression in the summer of 1950.

1372. "Canada's Army in Korea." CAN ARMY J, 1955 9
       (1):5-29; (2):20-42; (3):20-42; (4):16-34; (5):21-34.

       A five-part history of Canadian military operations in
       Korea from June 30, 1950, when three destroyers were
       dispatched to the Far East, until the armistice and

beyond. Written by the Historical Section, Army
Headquarters. Includes good analysis of operations and
illustrations. Brief bibliography of Canada and the
Korean War.

1373. Dayal, Rajeshwar. "The Power of Wisdom." INTER J,
1973-74 29 (1):110-121.

Traces the efforts of Canadian Prime Minister Lester B.
Pearson to back the UN position of support to South Korea.
Influenced by his commitment to self-determination,
Pearson led his nation to maintain support through the UN.

1374. Harbron, John D. "Royal Canadian Navy at Peace 1945-
1955: The Uncertain Heritage." QUEEN'S Q, 1966 73 (3):
311-334.

The Royal Canadian Navy had problems after WWII as it
attempted to break away from its British traditions.
With the coming of the war in Korea friction developed
because there was considerable division among the top
officials as to what role Canada should play. Consequently, the service, like the country, performed a
balancing act as it maneuvered between complete
commitment and no role at all.

1375. McDougall, C.C. "Canadian Volunteers Prepare for
Combat." ARMY INFO DIG, 1951 6 (6):54-57.

Describes the formation and training of the Canadian Army
Special Force, an all-volunteer brigade formed to fight
in Korea as part of the UN Command. Tells of part of the
training at Ft. Lewis, Washington, as a cooperative venture
between the US and Canadian Governments.

1376. McNair, Charles T. "The Royal Canadian Navy in Korea."
ARMY INFO DIG, 1951 6 (11):50-53.

A month after the Korean War began, three Canadian naval
vessels joined other UN ships in the action against the
invading forces. In the months that followed, the three
ships, the CAYUGA, SIOUX and ATHABASKON, often served with US
naval groups and at times led UN naval forces. They were
active in the Inchon invasion and evacuation of Chinnampo.

1377. Melady, John. KOREA: CANADA'S FORGOTTEN WAR.
Toronto: Macmillan, 1983.

Examines the military contributions of Canada to the
UN effort in Korea with special emphasis on the role
and experiences of ground troops, specifically the
Princess Patricia's Canadian Light Infantry, the
Vandoos and the Royal Canadian Regiment. Strong on
military aspects but not on diplomatic story or
analysis.

1378. Newman, Peter. "The Royal Canadian Navy." US NAV
          INST PROC, 1954 80 (3):295-299.

          Brief survey of the Canadian Navy in the 20th century,
          includes the role it played as part of the UN Command in
          Korea. Tells of cooperation between the Canadian and
          US navies.

1379. Pearson, Lester B. "The Development of Canadian
          Foreign Policy." FOR AFF, 1951 30 (1):17-30.

          The Canadian Secretary of State for External Affairs
          notes the support, material and verbal, to the UN
          Command in Korea. Claims that Canada is making a
          major contribution and doing so as quickly as is
          politically possible.

1380. Pearson, Lester B. MIKE: THE MEMOIRS OF THE RIGHT
          HONORABLE LESTER B. PEARSON. VOLUME 2, 1948-1957. New
          York: Quadrangle, 1973.

          Account of Canada's Secretary of State for External
          Affairs from 1948 through 1957. Pearson claims the
          Korean War was the most important international
          situation he dealt with. Includes Canada's position
          on Korea prior to the war plus its response to the
          UN's call for assistance in halting aggression.
          Considerable attention is given to the war effort and
          the search for peace.

1381. Preston, Richard A. "Toward a Defense Policy and
          Military Doctrine for Canada." ARM FOR SOC, 1977
          4 (1):127-141.

          A review article which focuses on Canadian foreign and
          defense policies in the post-WWII period, especially the
          development of NATO and the Korean War. Notes that
          Canada had reservations over its contribution to the
          Korean War and sought to maximize the UN role as a way
          of limiting the US role. This was done because of a
          desire to offset the US tendency to shape UN strategy
          to achieve unilateral goals.

1382. Stairs, Denis. "Canada and the Korean War: The
          Boundaries of Diplomacy." INTER PER, 1972 (6):25-32.

          During the Korean War, Canada continually attempted to
          alter the diplomatic behavior of the US by pressing it
          to pursue its ends through the UN. Examines US-
          Canadian relations as they were impacted by the war in
          Asia and Soviet-American friction.

1383. Stairs, Denis. THE DIPLOMACY OF CONSTRAINT:
          CANADA, THE KOREAN WAR AND THE UNITED STATES. Toronto:
          University of Toronto Press, 1974.

Scholarly study of Canada's involvement with Korea from 1947 through 1954 with primary emphasis on the Korean War. Canada was caught up in the pressures of her neighbor to the south to make international commitments and her somewhat different views of her obligations. When war came Canada was more concerned it might trigger a war in Europe and thus it did not want the US to react in a way that might bring about such an event. Shows that while support was given to the UN effort it was done largely to minimize US unilateral action that might spread the war.

1384.   Stairs, Denis W. "The Role of Canada in the Korean War." Doctoral Dissertation. Toronto, 1969.

Analysis of Canadian policy as it relates to the Korean War from its onset to the armistice. Also includes discussion of Canadian policy to: UN Temporary Commission on Korea (1947-48); the UN military command and role in the 1954 Geneva Conference.

1385.   Stevenson, John A. "Canada, Free and Dependent." FOR AFF, 1951 29 (3):456-467.

This look at Canadian foreign policy in the 20th century focuses on the post-WWII period with a good examination of the Canadian response to the Korean War. Praises the immediate Canadian endorsement of the US-UN stand against North Korean aggression but is critical of the slow response to meet its UN military obligations.

1386.   Thorgrimsson, Thor, and E.C. Russell. CANADIAN NAVAL OPERATIONS IN KOREAN WATERS, 1950-1955. Ottawa: Department of National Defense, 1965.

Account of the operations and activities of eight Canadian destroyers that served in the UN Command during and after the Korean War.

1387.   Wood, Herbert F. STRANGE BATTLEGROUND: THE OPERATIONS IN KOREA AND THEIR EFFECTS ON THE DEFENSE POLICY OF CANADA. Ottawa: Queen's Printer, 1966.

The official account of the operations of the Canadian Army during the Korean War. Covers the political and military considerations that being part of the UN Command had.

3. COMMONWEALTH ACTIVITIES

1388.   Carew, John M. KOREA: THE COMMONWEALTH AT WAR. London: Cassell, 1967.

Regimental histories of the Commonwealth nations
serving in Korea as part of the UN Command.

1389.   Goswami, Birendra N. "The Policies of Some Commonwealth
        Countries Toward the Korean Crisis, 1950-1953."
        Doctoral Dissertation. Indian School of International
        Studies, New Delhi, India, 1963.

        Compares and contrasts the positions of various
        Commonwealth nations on the Korean War. While those
        positions may have varied in some respects, they
        shared in common efforts to assure that the conflict
        did not spread.

1390.   Gottlieb, Paul H. "The Commonwealth of Nations at
        The United Nations." Doctoral Dissertation. Boston, 1962.

        Includes an examination of the position taken by the
        British Commonwealth nations on the Korean War issue.

1391.   Great Britain, Battles Nomenclature Committee. OFFICIAL
        NAMES OF THE BATTLES, ACTIONS AND ENGAGEMENTS FOUGHT BY THE
        LAND FORCES OF THE COMMONWEALTH, THE KOREAN CAMPAIGN, 1950-
        1953. London: Her Majesty's Stationery Office, 1958.

        The final report of the British Army Council assigning
        official titles for Korean War actions.

1392.   Linklater, Eric. OUR MAN IN KOREA. London: Her
        Majesty's Stationery Office, 1952.

        A brief book, with illustrations, which explains the part
        played in Korea by British Commonwealth Forces from the
        beginning of the war until July 1951. This straight
        narrative is based, in large part, on the author's
        observations on visiting Commonwealth units in 1951.

1393.   New Zealand, Department of External Affairs. NEW
        ZEALAND AND THE KOREAN CRISIS. Wellington: Owen, 1950.

        Brief tract describing the New Zealand Government's
        decision to support the UN Security Council's call for
        help to stop aggression in Korea. Tells of initial
        military commitment and justifies action in terms of
        need for world order.

1394.   Scott-Moncrieff, A.K. "Naval Operations in Korean
        Waters." MIL R, 1953 33 (7):103-109.

        The Commander of the Commonwealth Navy in Korea from
        April 1951 to September 1952 relates the organization of
        the UN naval setup, blockade, areas of responsibility,
        island protection, bombardment of shore batteries and
        combined air and gun strikes. Digested from the May

1953 JOURNAL OF THE ROYAL UNITED SERVICE INSTITUTION.

1395.   Soward, F.H. "The Korean Crisis and the Commonwealth."
        PAC AFF, 1951 24 (2):115-130.

        Describes the attitude of the Commonwealth nations (United
        Kingdom, India, Pakistan, New Zealand, Australia, Ceylon,
        South Africa and Canada) toward Communist China the
        outbreak of the Korean War and the intervention of the
        Chinese Communists. While those countries were generally
        supportive of the US and UN, their official actions were
        not always looked upon favorably by US officials.

4.   GREAT BRITAIN

1396.   Barclay, C.N. THE FIRST COMMONWEALTH DIVISION: THE
        STORY OF BRITISH COMMONWEALTH LAND FORCES IN KOREA,
        1950-1953. Aldershot: Gale, 1954.

        A general history of British Army units which served
        throughout the conflict.

1397.   "The British Centurion Tank." ARMOR, 1951 60
        (2):32-33.

        Photo essay on the performance of the British Centurion
        Tank which was used by the King's Royal Irish Hussans
        to cover the UN withdrawal from the Pyongyang area in
        December 1950.

1398.   "British Commonwealth Naval Operations During the
        Korean War." ROY UNI SER INSTI J, 1951 96:250-255,
        609-616; 1952 97:241-248.

        A three-part series which traces the contribution of
        the British Navy to UN Command naval operations during
        the first two years of the conflict.

1399.   Carew, Tim, pseudonym (John M. Carew). KOREA: THE
        COMMONWEALTH AT WAR. London: Cassell, 1967.

        General but useful overview of the military activities of
        the British Commonwealth in the Korean conflict.

1400.   Davies, S.J. IN SPITE OF DUNGEONS. London: Hodder,
        1954.

        The chaplain to the British First Battalion, the
        Gloucestershire Regiment, writes of his experiences with the
        unit and as a prisoner of war of the Chinese Communists.
        Conditions, physical and psychological, are discussed.

1401.   "The Destruction of the Royal Heavy Tank Battalion."
        ROY ARM CORPS J, 1951 5 (3):137-141.

A look at the Chinese Communist use of war propaganda
during the Korean War. The focus is on a Communist
newspaper account of a battle between Chinese and
British forces.

1402. Farrah-Hockley, Anthony. THE EDGE OF THE SWORD.
London: Muller, 1954.

A British Army Captain recounts his experiences in Korea
as a member of the Gloucestershire Regiment. A good look at
the April 1951 battle of the Imjin River and his capture
and confinement as a prisoner of war. Very critical of
the Communists' treatment of prisoners.

1403. Geer, Andrew. "Eight Perilous Hours Inside Red Lines."
SAT EVE POST, 1951 224 (23):26-27, 92-96.

Describes the activities of the British 41st Independent
Commandos, who entered the war as part of the UN command
shortly after hostilities began and specialized in hit
and run attacks behind enemy lines. Goes into detail on
one operation that attacked a railroad 150 miles behind
enemy lines.

1404. Gilby, Thomas. BRITAIN AT ARMS. London: Eyre, 1953.

An anthology which covers from the time of Marlborough
through the Korean War uses recollections and reflections
to portray war and the fighting of wars as seen by the
British. Brief coverage on Korea.

1405. Gladwyn, Hubert M. THE MEMOIRS OF LORD GLADWYN.
New York: Weybright, 1972.

The distinguished British diplomat, who served as his
country's UN ambassador during the Korean crisis of 1950,
gives his inside account of the attitudes and actions of
his government in the UN and at home. His memorable
speeches made during the Korean debates are included in
an appendix.

1406. Holles, Robert O. NOW THRIVE THE ARMOURERS. London:
British book Centre, 1953.

Describes the combat experiences of a British platoon of
the 1st Battalion, The Gloucestershire Regiment, a unit of
the 29th Brigade. This account, written by a member of
the unit, relates the infantryman's war as fought at Hills
327 and 235 and the Imjin battle, where after suffering
heavy losses, they were rotated home.

1407. James, A.G. Trevenen. THE ROYAL AIR FORCE: THE PAST
30 YEARS. London: MacDonald, 1976.

This examination of the British Air Force from the end of
WWII through 1974 includes two chapters on the air
contribution to the UN Command in Korea. Also discusses
training, supply and organization.

1408. Malcolm, George I. THE ARGYLLS IN KOREA. London:
         Nelson, 1952.

         A brief account of the Argyll and Sutherland Highlanders
(Great Britain) military activities in Korea from 1950 to
1952.

1409. Owens, P.J. "A History of the 41 Commando, Korea,
         1950-1952." GLB LAU, 1960 68 (4):148-201.

         Brief history of a Royal Marine unit that served as part
of the UN Command and saw considerable combat, much of it
in cooperation with US Marines.

1410. Porter, Brian E. "British Opinion and the Far Eastern
         Crisis, 1945-1954." Doctoral Dissertation. London, 1962.

         Shows that the Korean War presented a dilemma not only for
British policy makers but her citizens as well, especially
after Communist China entered the fighting. While this
work looks at several Far Eastern issues, three chapters
examine opinion on the Korean War.

1411. Thomas. R.C.W. "The Campaign in Korea." BRAS AN, 1953:
         222-238.

         Brief account of the activities of the British Common-
wealth Division in Korea from May 1952 through April 1953.
Covers military operations, the peace talks, Koje POW
Camp uprisings, analysis of the enemy soldier and exchange
of prisoners.

1412. Tunstall, Julian. I FOUGHT IN KOREA. London:
         Lawrence, 1953.

         A British soldier who fought in Korea tells of the
hardships and suffering experienced in the brutal war.
Tells of atrocities committed by the enemy.

1413. Worden, William L. "Britain's Gallantry is Not Dead."
         SAT EVE POST, 1951 223 (34):28-29, 94-96.

         Heroic efforts of the 27th British Brigade, a 1,500-
man force, that fought quite effectively against
advancing North Korean troops in August and early
September, advanced rapidly northward only to be driven
back in November when the Chinese entered the war.
Ends in January 1951 as they fought to stabilize the
front.

5. INDIA

1414.   Austin, Henry. "India in Asia, 1947-1954." Doctoral
        Dissertation. American, 1957.

        Gives considerable attention to Indian-Korean relations
        in the 1940's, India's role in the Korean War and their
        support of UN efforts to achieve peace. Includes Nehru's
        efforts to end the fighting.

1415.   Chang, David W. "A Comparative Study of Neutralism
        of India, Burma and Indonesia." Doctoral Dissertation.
        Illinois, 1960.

        Examines the efforts of the governments of the three
        nations to steer a path of neutrality during the Cold
        War. Looks at those efforts in response to several
        international crises, including the Korean War.

1416.   Dayal, Shiv. INDIA'S ROLE IN THE KOREAN QUESTION.
        Delhi: Chand, 1959.

        Examination of India's policy toward Korea before, during
        and after the war. Stresses India's initial commitment
        to halt aggression and defends its subsequent policy of
        being mildly supportive of the UN but trying to steer a
        middle course between the East and West.

1417.   Doody, Agnes G. "Words and Deeds: An Analysis of
        Jawaharlal Nehru's Non-alignment Policy in the Cold
        War, 1947-1953." Doctoral Dissertation. Pennsylvania
        State, 1961.

        Includes an examination of Nehru's tight-rope act
        which enabled him to lead India in such a way that it
        supported the UN stand against aggression in Korea yet
        succeeded in aligning his country with neither the
        East or the West as the war progressed.

1418.   Feer, Mark C. "India's China Policy, 1949-1954."
        Master's Thesis. Fletcher, 1954.

        In spite of the title, this study gives considerable
        attention to India's policy toward Korea during the
        period examined and the Chinese-Indian conflict over
        the Korean issue.

1419.   Gogate, Rajaram V. "How India Looks at Korea."
        KOREAN SUR, 1953 2 (2):7-8.

        Claims that Korea has become a political football
        for the Russians and Americans, and India does not
        want to get caught between them. Explains that while

Nehru wants to expel North Korean aggressors, he will
not support any UN plans that he feels will expand the
war.

1420.   Gupta, Karunakar. INDIAN FOREIGN POLICY IN THE
        DEFENSE OF NATIONAL INTEREST. Calcutta: World, 1956.

        Brief study on Indian policy during the Korean War
        period shows how the government tried to follow an
        independent route considered most beneficial to the
        nation rather than following a policy designed to
        please either the East or the West.

1421.   Gupta, Karunakar. "The Korean Crisis and the Indian
        Union." Doctoral Dissertation. London, 1954.

        Traces Indian foreign policy toward the Korean issue
        during the war, including the government's position in
        the UN on the conflict.

1422.   Heimsath, Charles H. "India's Role in the Korean War."
        Doctoral Dissertation. Yale, 1957.

        India's primary goal in the Korean War was to assist the
        warring nations in reaching a peaceful settlement. Attempts
        to mediate were not always effective, but its major
        success, that of settling the POW dispute, was
        hailed internationally. India also achieved its goal of
        improving relations with China.

1423.   Kaushik, Ram P. THE CRUCIAL YEARS OF NON-ALIGNMENT:
        USA, THE KOREAN WAR AND INDIA. New Delhi, India:
        Kumar, 1972.

        Traces India's reaction to the Korean War and the impact
        the conflict had on Indian-US foreign relations. Shows
        how India attempted to pursue policies which were supportive
        of the UN and walked the middle ground between the US and
        China.

1424.   Kaushik, Ram P. "India's Role in the Korean War: The
        Initial Phase." J UNI SER INST IND, 1971 101 (424):
        245-254.

        When trouble came in Korea in 1950, India, a nonaligned
        nation, supported the UN resolutions condemning the North
        but then refused to provide military support. After the
        Chinese entered the war, India continually attempted to
        play the role of mediator. The West was generally critical
        of India's response to the war.

1425.   Mahoney, James W. "India in the Commonwealth." Doctoral
        Dissertation. Fletcher, 1957.

In-depth study of India's foreign policy stands in the
Commonwealth from 1949 through 1954 with considerable
attention given to the matter of Korea. Looks at India's
reaction to aggression, Chinese intervention, POW exchanges
and her stand in the 1954 Geneva Conference.

1426. Sheean, Vincent. "The Case For India." FOR AFF,
      1951 30 (1):77-90.

      Traces India's foreign policy as it related to the UN and
      the war in Korea during the first year of the conflict.
      It defends Nehru's policy of non-alignment with any of the
      major powers. Notes the areas in which India has been
      supportive of UN and areas in which it has not. Condemns
      the US position that those not with us are against us.

1427. Varma, Shanti N. "India's Policy in the United Nations
      With Special Respect to the Maintenance of International
      Peace and Security." Doctoral Dissertation. Columbia,
      1952.

      This broad study includes an evaluation of the Indian policy
      on the Korean issue from initial aggression until after the
      Chinese intervention.

6. OTHER NATIONS

1428. Abu-Diab, Fawzi. "Lebanon and the United Nations,
      1945-1958." Doctoral Dissertation. Pennsylvania, 1965.

      This study includes a description and analysis of the
      Lebanese stand in the UN on the Korean War.

1429. Brecher, Michael. ISRAEL, THE KOREAN WAR AND CHINA:
      IMAGES, DECISIONS AND CONSEQUENCES. Jerusalem:
      Jerusalem Academic Press, Hebrew University, 1974.

      A study of Israel's failure in 1950 to establish
      diplomatic relations with Communist China. In hopes of
      furthering its own situation, Israel moved to extend
      recognition to the People's Republic; however, the
      coming of war in Korea forced abandonment of recognition
      plans as Israel was forced to support the US and UN
      stands. After the war, relations were so strained that
      the original policy could not be implemented.

1430. Brown, Janet W. "Burmese Policy in the United Nations:
      an Analysis of Five Selected Political Questions, 1948-
      1960." Doctoral Dissertation. American, 1964.

      One of the questions analyzed is the Burmese stand on
      Korea. Looks at the motivations, deliberations and

decisions reached.

1431. Gonlubol, Mehmet. "A Critical Analysis of Turkish
      Participation in the United Nations." Doctoral
      Dissertation. New York, 1956.

      Looks at Turkey's interest in and support of the UN
      including reaction to North Korean aggression and
      military participation in the UN Command.

1432. McGregor, P.M.J. "History of No. 2 Squadron, SAAF,
      in the Korean War." MIL HIST J, 1978 June:82-89.

      The story of the men and activities of a squadron of
      the South African Air Force which joined with similar
      units from Canada and Australia as part of the UN
      Command. An important part of the Far East Air
      Forces, this unit has been overlooked because of the
      prominence of the USAF.

1433. Martin, Harold H. "The Greeks Know How to Die."
      SAT EVE POST, 1951 224 (1):26-27, 83-84.

      Human interest story on the Greek Battalion that fought as
      part of the UN Command in Korea. The Greeks were battle
      experienced soldiers who had fought communist guerrillas in
      their own country in the post-war period. The unit was
      attached to the US 7th Cavalry Regiment.

1434. Martin, Harold H. "Who Said the French Won't Fight."
      SAT EVE POST, 1951 223 (45):19-21, 107-108.

      Assessment of the French Battalion, an all-volunteer
      unit, which served as part of the UN Command in Korea.
      Concludes that the Battalion, which worked closely with US
      Army and ROK Army troops, is a spirited and effective
      fighting force.

1435. Moore, D.M. "SAAF in Korea." MILTA, 1980 (4):
      24-34.

      Contributions of the South African Air Force, which sent a
      fighter squadron to the UN Command in Korea. It's service
      was as part of the US Far East Air Force.

1436. Ozselcuk, Musret. "The Turkish Brigade in the Korean
      War." INTER R MIL HIST, 1980 (46):253-272.

      When the UN call went out for nations to halt North
      Korean aggression, Turkey responded by sending a 5,000-
      man Brigade. That unit fought valiantly but suffered very
      heavy losses, especially in an engagement near Wawon in late
      November 1950. It later fought at such spots as Yangwan-ni
      and Kunu-ri. Tells of its problems, setbacks and acts of

heroism by Turkish soldiers.

1437. Plotkin, Arieh L. "Israel's Role in the United Nations:
       an Analytical Study." Doctoral Dissertation. Princeton,
       1955.

       Analysis of Israel's role in the first five years of its
       membership in the UN. In-depth examination of its stand
       and votes on Korean conflict issues brought before the
       General Assembly.

1438. Royal Greek Embassy. INFORMATION SERVICE ON GREECE'S
       STAND ON THE KOREAN QUESTION. Washington, 1951.

       Official Greek explanation of the need to support the
       UN's response to aggression in South Korea. The action
       was driven by a desire to halt communist expansion and a
       need to show support for the fledgling UN.

1439. Skordiles, Komon. KAGNEW, THE STORY OF THE ETHIOPIAN
       FIGHTERS IN KOREA. Tokyo: Radio Press, 1954.

       The military organization and contributions of Ethiopian
       armed forces to the UN Command.

1440. Villasanta, Juan F. DATELINE KOREA: STORIES OF THE
       PHILIPPINE BATTALION. Bacolod City, P.I.: Nalco, 1954.

       Human interest stories and accounts of the fighting
       engaged in by the men of the Philippine 10th Infantry
       Battalion Combat Team which saw action from September
       1950 on.

1441. Worden, William. "The Terrible Hours of the Turks."
       SAT EVE POST, 1951 223 (32):28-29, 68.

       Tells of the performance of a Turkish Brigade, which was
       part of the UN Force in the fall of 1950. Accounts of
       their performance against the advancing Chinese are
       extremely mixed, some saying they fought valiantly, others
       claiming they disintegrated. Supporters respond to the
       latter charge by blaming the language difficulties.

XIII. NON US-UN FORCES
A. ROK FORCES

1442. Balmforth, Edward E. "Getting Our ROKS Off."
COM FOR J, 1951 1 (7):22-25.

Describes the problems encountered in August 1950 when,
due to manpower shortages, one thousand Republic of Korea
soldiers were integrated into the US 17th Infantry of the
7th Division. Many problems were encountered with matters
such as language difficulties and an attempt to use the
"buddy system" to integrate the foreign soldiers. US
soldiers kept asking when they would get rid of the ROKS.
Criticizes the US Army for improper orientation and
training procedures.

1443. Berbert, Henry. "Engineer Field Notes--Korea: Delaying
the Advance in the First Few Days." MIL ENG, 1950 42
(290):433-434.

Describes the roles played by ROK Army engineers and their
American advisors from June 30-July 5, 1950. Destruction of
key bridges and cratering of roads were about all that could
be done because mines and items such as barbed wire were
often in short supply or not available.

1444. Braitsch, Fred, Jr. "The Korean Marine Corps."
LEATHERNECK, 1953 36 (1):30-33.

Operations of the Korean Corps during the early war period.

1445. Buckler, Phillip J. "An Introduction to the Medical
Field Service School, Republic of Korea Army." MIL SURG,
1953 112 (5):364-367.

Less than a year before the Korean War began, the South
Korean Army established a medical field school and when
war came the school began providing combat medical
support. In November 1950 it resumed its mission of
training ROK Army medical, dental and nursing personnel.

1446. Cameron, Robert C. "The Last Corps." MIL R, 1953
33 (2):9-18.

Maintains that the complete destruction of the Third
Division II Corps of the Republic of Korea Army in a
twenty-four hour period in the last week of November, 1950
was the result of the Chinese Communist expert

261

application of time-honored tactics of war. Details the
setting and Chinese operations.

1447.   Duncan, David. "The Durable ROKS." LIFE, 29 (11):
         52-54.

         Photo essay which shows South Korean Army's shortcomings
         as evidenced in an unsuccessful attack on an enemy held
         hill. Not only did they get rebuffed but they also
         abandoned their wounded on the field of battle in this
         early September 1950 engagement.

1448.   Edwards, Spencer P., Jr. "KATUSA--An Experiment in
         Korea." US NAVAL INST PROC, 1958 84 (1):31-37.

         Details the successful US experiment known as KATUSA
         (Koreans Attached To US Army) whereby South Koreans were
         drafted into the ROK Army then processed, trained and sent
         into battle with US units. Their performance was better
         than expected. Points out that there were a number of
         problems, many surrounding personal communications. US
         training was provided by the Seventh Division.

1449.   Eliot, George Fielding. "Asian Wars Need Asian Soldiers."
         AM MERCURY, 1953 76 (350):20-22.

         A top military analyst argues that the US must make
         heavy use of South Korean soldiers to fight the communists
         in Korea because no Western Army has ever fought a
         successful war in Asia without using Asian soldiers.

1450.   Eye, Ralph F.W. "Private Kim Mans the OP." COM FOR J,
         1952 2 (7):25.

         Tells how US Army was able to use ROK soldiers for
         observation duty, in spite of an inability to speak
         English, by using simple math and military symbols and
         plotting activity on acetate grids on maps.

1451.   "Free Koreans Meet the Test of Battle." ARMY INFO DIG,
         1950 5 (11):25-31.

         This pictorial section shows the contribution which the
         South Koreans made to the UN effort during the early months
         of fighting and the suffering which the fighting brought
         to the populace.

1452.   Heinecke, Roy. "Korean Boot Camp." LEATHERNECK,
         1953 36 (9):12-18.

         Describes the operation of the Korean Marine Corps
         Training Center at Chinhae. Includes the training the
         soldiers received and the role played by US Marine
         advisors.

1453. Henderson, Lindsey P. "My Roks Were Good." COM FOR
       J, 1952 3 (5):35-37.

       A US Army Lieutenant of Company L, 21st Infantry, 24th
       Division, who commanded a "Gimlet" platoon, as attached
       Republic of Korean troops were called, praises them as
       good soldiers. Maintains they trained hard and
       performed well in combat.

1454. Holly, David C. "The ROK Navy." US NAVAL INST PROC,
       1952 78 (11):1219-1225.

       Examines the development, organization, training and
       activities of the South Korean Navy from the end of WWII
       through the first two years of the Korean conflict.
       During that period the US provided virtually all the
       equipment and training for the Korean personnel. The
       ROK Navy played a major role in key operations such as
       the Inchon invasion and Hungnam evacuation.

1455. Hutchin, Walter J. "Little Belvoir (Konglyung
       Hakkyo)." MIL ENG, 1951 43 (296):401-403.

       Describes the training center for ROK Army Engineers.
       During the conflict 350 specialists--riggers, demolition
       experts and construction foremen were graduated every
       two weeks; 300 soldiers completed branch training each
       week and every month fifty-two new engineer officers were
       graduated. Includes a history of the training of ROK Army
       engineer personnel.

1456. Jeung, U.H. "ROK Marines: Battle Hardened Heroes."
       KOREAN SUR, 1957 6 (8):6.

       In April 1949 three hundred members of the ROK Coast
       Guard were activated as the ROK Marine Corps. This
       brief account tells of their initial training, attempts
       to delay the North Korean advance south, Inchon
       invasion and service during the subsequent stalemate.

1457. King, Helen B. "The WAC's of Korea." KOREAN SUR,
       1955 4 (4):10-11.

       Brief history of the Republic of Korea Women's Army Corps
       (WAC's) from their creation in 1948 through 1954. Tells of
       Korean War service.

1458. Kramer, Don. "The Pride of the Corps." KOREAN SUR,
       1953 2 (3):4-5.

       Brief account of the history of the ROK Marine Corps
       and the cooperation between it and the US Marine Corps
       in the early part of the Korean conflict.

1459. Limb, Ben C. "The Pacific Pact: Looking Forward or

Backward?" FOR AFF, 1951 29 (4):539-549.

Claims that South Korea wants to play a major role in a
Pacific collective security pact when the war is over. In an
attempt to show that the nation will be a strong military
ally and viable nation, it tells of the ROK Government's
wartime activities to handle refugees, rebuild its industry,
upgrade its agricultural production and educate its citizens.

1460. Mapp, Thomas H. "Engineer Training for Koreans."
       ARMY INFO DIG, 1952 7 (12):9-16.

In February 1951 the US Army helped establish the
Engineer School, Korean Army. The purpose of the facility
was to train Korean officers and enlisted men in every
phase of combat engineering from mine laying to bridge
building. Virtually all instruction was done by
American soldiers.

1461. Randolph, John. "When Can the ROK's Take Over in
       Korea." COLLIER'S, 1953 131 (10):28-31.

By the spring of 1953 the US was heavily involved in
helping the Republic of Korea build and strengthen its
Army so it could assume more responsibility for taking
control of the front lines. Tells of US training
activities and the savage discipline being used by
South Koreans to make their army an effective fighting
force. Maintains that the South Koreans are good soldiers
who will be able to defend their country.

1462. Republic of Korea Army, Office of Information HQ.
       REPUBLIC OF KOREA ARMY. Vol. I. Seoul: ROK Office of
       Information, 1954.

Pictorial history of the Korean War with emphasis on the
role and contributions of the ROK Army. Color plates of
insignia and medals.

1463. Rodgers, Gordon B. "ROK's Forge the Thunderbolt!"
       ARMOR, 1954 63 (3):42-45.

While discussing the training of ROK Armor units, brief
attention is given to the establishment of the armored
school in South Korea in 1951 and the role of ROK tankers
in the January 1953 raid on "Big Nori."

1464. Skaggs, David C. "The KATUSA Experiment: The Integration
       of Korean Nationals Into the US Army, 1950-1965." MIL AFF,
       1974 38 (2):53-58.

Because of a manpower shortage in the early months of the
Korean War, General MacArthur assigned Republic of Korea
(ROK) troops to American Army units, especially the 7th

Division. As filler troops the experiment was a disaster
while as a supplier of trained South Korean soldiers it
had limited success.

1465. Sneider, Vern. A LONG WAY FROM HOME AND OTHER STORIES.
New York: Putnam's, 1956.

Collection of essays on the Far East, by the author of
The Teahouse of the August Moon," include several works
on the Korean War, including one on the valor of Korean
recruits, who fought with US troops in the bitter early
days of the war.

1466. Van Fleet, James A. "Who Says Our Allies Won't Fight?"
READ DIG, 1953 62 (370):23-25.

The Commander of the US Eighth Army tells of the major role
being played by other than US forces in Korea. Notes that by
late 1952 60% of the front was held by ROK forces, 15% by other
UN forces and 25% by US troops. Describes how the ROK Army
has been turned into an effective fighting force. Condensed
from THIS WEEK, November 23, 1952.

1467. Wright, John M. "Military Bargain Basement." US NAVAL INST
PROC, 1954 80 (7):773-775.

The story of Yodo Island, a scant ten miles off the key North
Korean port city of Wonsan, where Korean Marines headed by a
small group of US Marines and Navy men held out against
communist forces throughout the war. The island was a thorn
in the enemy's side because it provided forces of the UN
Command with a spot from which to launch guerrilla attacks
and a place where UN pilots could land crippled aircraft.

1468. Yanik, Anthony J. "Chinhae-An Old Korean Port Gone
Modern." US NAVAL INST PROC, 1954 80 (2):163-167.

Focuses on the South Korean port city of Chinhae which
served as the headquarters of the Republic of Korea Navy.
Tells of the activities of the ROK Naval Academy, Recruiting
and Training Center, Supply Department, Shiphand and Naval
Hospital. Describes the contribution of the US Naval
Advisory Group, Chinhae Detachment to the ROK naval base.

B.   DPRK ARMY

1469. "Battle Facts For Your Outfit." COM FOR J, 1951
1 (10):27-28.

Analysis of the military capabilities and effectiveness of
North Korean and Chinese forces in Korea by two Infantry
officers who served there. Also examines US military tactics,
firepower effectiveness, defense against night attacks and
impact of airpower.

1470. Bok, Ju Yeoung. "I Was in the Invading Army in Korea."
       KOREAN SUR, 1958 7 (8):3-4, 11.

       A North Korean POW who refused repatriation at the end of
       the Korean War describes life in North Korea from 1945
       through the invasion of 1950. As a member of the Army, he
       tells of Soviet training and supplies, buildup for the
       attack on the South and the attack itself.

1471. Davenport, Marshall. "Why Are Russian Tanks Better
       Than Ours?" SAT EVE POST, 1950 223 (15):30-31, 155-157.

       Blames the fact that American light tanks were pounded to
       pieces by Russian-built medium tanks in the first two months
       of the war on Pentagon decision-makers who put all their
       faith in mobility and thus fostered the light and faster
       Patton Tank rather than develop a medium tank that could
       slug it out.

1472. Edwards, Harry W. "Danger! Mines." MARINE CORPS GAZ,
       1952 36 (4):38-41.

       Communist forces made extensive use of land mines and
       inflicted heavy casualties on UN troops. Tells of the
       dangers of those weapons to US-UN soldiers.

1473. Karig, Walter. "Korea--Tougher to Crack than Okinawa."
       COLLIER'S, 1950 126 (13):24-25, 69-70.

       Warns that the war in Korea will be a most difficult one
       for the US because the North Korean forces scorn all rules of
       civilized warfare and hide behind the civilian populace
       knowing we will not attack. A seasoned military observer,
       the author concludes that winning in Korea will be "nastier
       and more tedious" than taking Okinawa.

1474. Loesch, Robert J. "Profile of the Enemy Soldier."
       ARMY INFO DIG, 1951 6 (9):9-15.

       Very biased profile of the typical North Korean and
       Chinese Communist soldier fighting in Korea. This article,
       written by an Eighth US Army public information officer,
       would lead one to conclude that the enemy were all agents
       of the devil himself. Good example of US propaganda.

1475. Nicholson, Dennis D. "Creeping Tactics." MARINE CORPS
       GAZ, 1958 42 (9):20-26.

       Describes the Chinese Communist and North Korean use of
       the tactics of creeping in on American positions and then
       launching devastating attacks. This tactic was used
       extensively in 1950-1951.

1476. "Portrait of a North Korean Spy" in Donald Robinson, ed.

THE DIRTY WAR. New York: Delacorte, 1968, pp. 214-219.

North Korea used guerrillas behind enemy lines to gather information. A US Army intelligence report shows the kind of men utilized for such assignments and the functions they performed by giving a profile of one such spy who was captured.

1477. Riley, John W., Jr., and Wilbur Schramm. THE REDS TAKE A CITY: THE COMMUNIST OCCUPATION OF SEOUL, WITH EYEWITNESS ACCOUNTS. New Brunswick, NJ: Rutgers University, 1951.

The authors were part of a team sent by the US Air Force to Seoul after its liberation in September 1950 to assess Communist activities during the ninety days of occupation. Based on extensive interviews, the authors tell of the propaganda activities, administrative techniques, and functioning of People's Committees. Also included are eleven extensive accounts of individuals who suffered great personal agony during the occupation.

1478. Segal, Julius. A STUDY OF NORTH KOREAN AND CHINESE SOLDIERS' ATTITUDES TOWARD COMMUNISM, DEMOCRACY, AND THE UNITED NATIONS. Chevy Chase, MD: Operations Research Office, The Johns Hopkins University, 1954.

The pro-communist, anti-Democratic and anti-UN attitudes of Communist soldiers fighting in Korea are examined in this study which was based on interviews with several thousand Communist POW's.

1479. Soltys, Andrew T. "Enemy Antiaircraft Defenses in North Korea." AIR UNIV Q R, 1954 7 (1):75-81.

During the Korean War the North Korean and Chinese Communist forces made a major commitment to protecting key targets from air attack by use of antiaircraft guns. Those efforts were not effective primarily because the antiaircraft guns supplied were obsolete WWII models that were no match for the new jet aircraft.

1480. Stelmach, Daniel S. "The Influence of Russian Armored Tactics on the North Korean Invasion of 1950." Doctoral Dissertation. St. Louis, 1973.

Stresses the Soviet role in training and equipping of the North Korean Army. While the role of armor is central, the study looks at the triangular base of armor-infantry artillery. The experience of North Korean tankers in July and August 1950 is closely examined.

1481. Steward, Hal D. "Rise and Fall of an Army." MIL R, 1951 30 (11):32-35.

Examines the reasons behind the complete collapse of the
North Korean Peoples Army between June and October 1950.
Concludes that the fall of the fifteen divisions is due
to the ruthlessness and cruel and inhuman treatment of
civilians and forced conscriptees.

C.   COMMUNIST CHINA

1.   LEADERS AND POLICIES

1482.   Baldwin, Hanson W.   "China As a Military Power."   FOR
        AFF, 1951 30 (1):51-62.

        A top military analyst concludes that Red China will not
        be a major threat for decades because she lacks the air and
        sea power which can only come with industrialization.   Notes,
        however, that progress is being made in improved
        transportation and Russianization of the army.   Examines the
        Chinese soldier and his military equipment, pointing out
        strengths and weaknesses of each.

1483.   Burchett, Wilfred G.   THIS MONSTROUS WAR.   Melbourne,
        Australia: Waters, 1953.

        An Australian newspaperman turned socialist gives his
        account of the Korean War with an extremely Red Chinese-
        North Korean bias.   Critical of the US and UN for waging
        an immoral and cruel war of aggression, complete with the
        use of germ warfare, in Korea.

1484.   Chen, Wen-hui.   WARTIME "MASS" CAMPAIGNS IN COMMUNIST
        CHINA: OFFICIAL COUNTRY-WIDE "MASS MOVEMENTS" IN PROFESSED
        SUPPORT OF THE KOREAN WAR.   Lackland Air Force, TX: Air
        Research and Development Command, 1955.

        Once the Chinese Communists got involved in the Korean War,
        the government launched several successive country-wide
        propaganda campaigns designed to mobilize mass support for
        the war effort.   Looks at those campaigns--their goals,
        techniques and effectiveness.

1485.   Cleveland, Harlan.   "The Closed Door in China."
        REPORTER, 1953 9 (4):8-9.

        Maintains that if the US extends technical aid and
        political agreements with friendly nations in the Far
        East, the Chinese Communists will realize it is better
        to cooperate with the US rather than fight it.   Sees the
        US as working closely with the UN to show the Chinese
        that they should work with them to develop their nation.

1486.   DeConde, Alexander.   "Is China a Great Power?"
        US NAVAL INST PROC, 1953 79 (1):29-37.

Urges the American public and leaders to awaken to the fact that Communist China is not a weak, undeveloped country but a nation of 500 million people unified under an efficient totalitarian regime. Says the 1949 takeover by the communists marks a major turning point in China's history and that when she harnesses her potential, which she will, the US will need to deal with her as a major military, diplomatic power. Cites military accomplishments and shortcomings in the Korean conflict.

1487. Devane, Richard T. "The United States and China: Claims and Assets." ASIAN SUR, 1978 18 (12):1267-1279.

In response to Chinese military intervention in Korea the US pressed claims previously ignored and announced that they would be revoked when Red China behaved "properly." The People's Republic replied by placing all American assets in their country under their control. Some two decades after the war, the situation still was not resolved.

1488. Elegant, Robert S. CHINA'S RED MASTERS. London: Bodley Head, 1952.

Covers the careers of leaders of the Communist Chinese from 1921 through the beginning of Red involvement in Korea. Looks at political figures such as Lin Shao-ch'i, Chou En-lai and Ting Ling and military persons such as Chu Teh, Lin Piao and P'eng Te-huai.

1489. Gilliland, William S. "Roots of Red China's Strategy in the Korean War." Master's Thesis. Stanford, 1960.

Examines factors and leaders in Russia and China that helped shape the Chinese Communist strategy in Korea. Notes the obscurity of Red strategy but then shows the influence of Mao's strategic objectives. Includes analysis of Red Chinese military geography, military history, strengths and weaknesses.

1490. Gittings, John. "Military Control and Leadership, 1949-1964." CHINA Q, 1966 26:82-101.

A look at Communist China's military leadership and the philosophy that guided it for a fifteen-year period, including the Korean War years.

1491. Griffith, Samuel B., trans. MAO TSE-TUNG ON GUERRILLA WARFARE. New York: Praeger, 1961.

Translation of Mao's important work on guerrilla warfare. Although written during the war with Japan, the principles were followed in the Civil War and in Korea.

1492. Griffith, Samuel B. "Mao Tse-Tung--'Sun in the East'"
       US NAVAL INST PROC, 1951 77 (6):615-623.

       Brief but very good look at Mao, his life and his political
       and military thought. Notes his confidence in guerrilla units,
       self-defense corps, intelligence and propaganda. Warns that
       Mao is not a Soviet puppet but an able, intelligent man whose
       primary commitment is to his own country, China.

1493. Hanrahan, Gene Z. "Red China's Three Top Field
       Commanders." MARINE CORPS GAZ, 1952 36 (2):54-61.

       Discussion of the political and military backgrounds and
       views of Generals P'eng Teh-huai, Lin Piao and Ch'en Yi.
       All have written on strategy and tactics and their thinking
       is very evident in the conduct of the fighting in Korea.
       Attention is given to their views on guerrilla warfare.

1494. Hittle, J.D. "Background of Chinese Action." US NAVAL
       INST PROC, 1952 78 (8):821-830.

       Puts forth the idea that Red China is making a deliberate
       effort to re-establish the country as the dominant power of
       East Asia and that she is a Communist nation which is working
       with the Soviet Union to help bring about world conquest.
       The bulk of the study is a historical and cultural look at
       China and her people from about 200 B.C. to intervention in
       Korea. Sees the war as an attempt to help reconstruct a
       China that for so long had dominated East Asia.

1495. Hittle, J.D. "The Basis of Sino-Soviet Accord."
       US NAVAL INST PROC, 1953 79 (4):373-381.

       Describes the background, provisions and significance of
       the February 14, 1950, Sino-Soviet Treaty of Friendship,
       Alliance and Mutual Assistance and the March 27, 1950,
       Sino-Soviet Economic Agreements. The two agreements,
       which were so instrumental in leading to Soviet aid to
       Red China when the latter entered the Korean conflict,
       showed that China was turning her base of power away
       from the sea and toward the interior of Asia.

1496. Huang, William Y. "China's Role With Respect to Major
       Political and Security Questions Under Consideration by
       the United Nations." Doctoral Dissertation. Michigan, 1954.

       Gives attention to Nationalist Chinese efforts to work with
       the UN in condemning Red Chinese intervention in Korea and
       blocking Peking's membership in the UN.

1497. Iriye, Akira. ACROSS THE PACIFIC: AN INNER HISTORY OF
       AMERICAN-EAST ASIAN RELATIONS. New York: Harcourt, 1967.

       This survey of US foreign policy toward China and Japan from

1780 to the present includes a dozen pages on the US-Chinese Communists military contest in Korea. Notes that the US response to North Korean aggression was ideologically clear but strategically ambiguous.

1498. Kalicki, J.H. THE PATTERN OF SINO-AMERICAN CRISES: POLITICAL INTERACTION IN THE 1950'S. New York: Cambridge University, 1975.

This attempt to give some semblance of order to Chinese-American relations in the 1950's devotes nearly one-fourth of its attention to the Korean War and Chinese intervention. Primarily recounts the events that occurred. Tends toward simplistic explanation of complex events. Attempts to show that lessons learned in Korea influenced later US relations with Red China.

1499. Lawrance, Alan. CHINA'S FOREIGN RELATIONS SINCE 1949. London: Routledge, 1975.

Collection of documents to help describe Chinese foreign policy. Part I examines the era of Soviet-Chinese friendship from 1944-1955. Includes Chou En-Lai's warning to the US not to cross the 38th Parallel and charges that President Rhee launched the June 25th attack.

1500. Levi, Werner. MODERN CHINA'S FOREIGN POLICY. Minneapolis: University of Minnesota, 1953.

A comprehensive examination of Chinese Communist diplomacy covers its policy during the Korean War as well as an account of the "Hate America" campaign that was launched prior to intervention.

1501. Lifton, Robert J. "Thought Reform of Chinese Intellectuals: A Psychiatic Evaluation." J SOC IS, 1957 13 (3):5-20.

Describes the process of thought reform which the Chinese Communist regime imposed on the intellectuals. Shows the intensity with which the new government resorted to indoctrination of large segments of society in order to assure support.

1502. Lindner, Kenneth R. "Military Geography of China." MIL R, 1953 33 (4):42-56.

Overview of China's geography looks at factors such as terrain, climate, transportation and economic factors and concludes that because of its large population and area, China could, by influencing the political alignments of her periphery states, tip the balance of world power between the East and West. Claims the Chinese involvement in Korea is part of a pattern of a campaign for the domination of Asia.

1503.   Mao Tse-Tung. MAO TSE-TUNG, SELECTED WORKS, VOLUME FIVE:
        1945-1949. New York: International, 1962.

        While the earlier five volumes of Mao's works are important
        to understanding his military and political views, this
        volume is especially important because it takes the story
        from the surrender of Japan to the eve of the Korean War.

1504.   Melby, John F. "The Origins of the Cold War in China."
        PAC AFF, 1968 41 (1):19-33.

        Traces US actions and policies toward China from 1945-1950.
        This brief account helps to understand Chinese Communist
        policies in Korea during the Korean War.

1505.   Patterson, Richard O. "The Masters of War." US NAVAL
        INST PROC, 1952 78 (7):751-755.

        Presents the views of two Chinese students of war, Sun-tzu
        and Wu-tzu, whose concepts of war were very important to the
        Chinese Communists as they carried out the war against US-UN
        troops in Korea some 2,500 years after Sun and Wu set forth
        their views. The two men believed that wars should be
        concluded quickly and that both the defensive and offensive
        should be used to achieve victory.

1506.   Payne, Robert. MAO TSE-TUNG, RULER OF RED CHINA.
        New York: Schuman, 1950.

        A biography of Mao that covers the period up to the Korean
        War. The focus is upon his mind--his thinking, values,
        attitudes, goals and philosophies. Sees Mao as a very
        complex person who heads the Peking regime in a most
        impressive fashion. This work is of major importance to
        anyone wanting to understand the man who led the Chinese
        Communists during the Korean War.

1507.   Reday, Joseph Z. "The Economic War Potential of Asia."
        US NAVAL INST PROC, 1951 77 (11):1137-1147.

        Warns that the US should not be overly impressed by the
        military impact of manpower being put forth by the Chinese
        Communists in Korea. Claims that it is commodities that
        ultimately wins wars and such key items as food, fuel and
        fertilizer are in short supply, consequently so is
        industrial potential in all countries except Japan. If
        Japan remains out of the Communist camp, the war potential
        of Communist Asia would be extremely limited.

1508.   Rifkin, Sylvia. "The 1951 Resist-America--Aid-Korea
        Campaign in Communist China." Master's Thesis.
        Columbia, 1962.

        Tells of the Red Chinese government's domestic propaganda
        campaign designed to get popular support for waging war

against US imperialism in Korea.

1509. Shuo, Yang. A THOUSAND MILES OF LOVELY LAND. Peking:
       Foreign Languages Press, 1957.

       A Chinese Communist account of the Korean Conflict puts the
       Reds in the position of trying to defend the North Koreans
       against US aggression.

1510. Tucker, Nancy B. "An Unlikely Peace: American Missionaries
       and the Chinese Communists, 1948-1950." PAC HIST R, 1976
       45 (1):97-116.

       In 1948 and 1949 when the Communists took over in China,
       they tolerated different religions in their country,
       including the activities of foreign missionaries; however,
       when war came to Korea and the nation became involved,
       religious toleration came to an end.

                2. THE RED ARMY AND OTHER MILITARY FORCES

1511. Alsop, Joseph. "The Shocking New Strength of Red China."
       SAT EVE POST, 1954 226 (37):19-21.

       Describes the impact of the Korean War on the Communist
       Chinese Armed Forces. Tells of Russian help to the Red
       Army and Air Force before and during the conflict and the
       advantages gained from the truce. Speculates on the likely
       consequences of its new-found military strength.

1512. "The CCF's AAA." COM FOR J, 1953 3 (10):20-21.

       The Chinese Communists had a very effective Antiaircraft
       Artillery force in spite of the fact that it was armed
       primarily with WWII vintage weapons from various nations.
       Describes the AAA organization of the Communist forces.

1513. Campbell, James W. "Combat Efficiency and Fire Power."
       ARMY INFO DIG, 1953 8 (3):35-50.

       Contends that while Communist units may have more firepower
       than similar US units, the latter has more killing power
       because of its communications, training and skill. While
       much of the comparison is made with Russian units, there is
       much discussion of Chinese Communist firepower and efficiency
       in Korea. Tells of medical service, food and shelter the
       US troops are receiving in Korea.

1514. Chang, Yukon. "The Man Who Makes Red China Tough."
       SAT EVE POST, 1951 223 (31):36-37, 84-85, 88.

       An American-Chinese living in China at the time of the
       Communist takeover describes the Red soldier:
       what he thinks and believes, what his life in the army

is like, and why he is willing to give his life in
battle. Compares the older, seasoned veterans of WWII
with the young, inexperienced soldiers.

1515.   Cheng, J. Chester. "The Dynamics of the Chinese
         People's Liberation Army: Regularization and
         Revolutionization, 1949-1959." MIL R, 1974 54
         (5):78-89.

         Involvement in the Korean War found the Chinese
         Liberation Army sadly lacking in organization and the
         primary responsibility for correcting that flaw fell on
         the Minister of National Defense, P'eng Te-Huai, who
         did an excellent job of implementing reorganization
         during the war and after.

1516.   Chinese People's Army. A VOLUNTEER SOLDIER'S DAY.
         Peking: Foreign Languages Press, 1961.

         Recollections from Chinese Communist soldiers of their
         combat experiences in North Korea during the Korean War.
         Maintains morale of troops was high because they were
         involved in a just war to aid their North Korean allies
         against US aggression.

1517.   THE CHINESE PEOPLE'S LIBERATION ARMY. Peking:
         Foreign Languages Press, 1950.

         Official Chinese Communist account of its army. Sets
         forth its history, objectives in peace and war, and its
         role in national and political life. Some of its
         pronouncements, such as the rule "Do not ill-treat
         prisoners of war," are interesting in view of what was
         done when fighting in Korea. Includes photographs of
         Red political and military leaders.

1518.   Chu, Te. THE BATTLE FRONT OF THE LIBERATED AREAS, 3rd
         ed. Peking: Foreign Languages Press, 1969.

         Brief assessment of conditions for Communist Chinese
         soldiers on the Korean front in late 1951 and early 1952.
         Portrays the noble efforts of the Reds to halt American
         aggression in North Korea.

1519.   Colwell, James. "Korea: Are We Teaching More Than We
         Learn?" REPORTER, 1953 8 (3):24-26.

         Points out that while there is some validity to the claim
         that the US is gaining valuable military experience in Korea,
         the fact is that the Chinese Communist forces are benefiting
         much more because they had no previous experience in regular
         military operations. US has many trained leaders from WWII
         while Korea is giving the Chinese Reds the opportunity to
         develop them.

1520. "Communist Camouflage and Deception." AIR UNIV Q R,
       1953 6 (1):90-100.

       Although it was not widely publicized, the Chinese
       Communists did an outstanding job of using camouflage
       and deception to circumvent the US interdiction campaign.
       This study makes good use of photographs to show the
       effectiveness of the enemy's techniques.

1521. "Communist Weapons Captured in Korea." COM FOR J,
       1951 1 (6):6-9.

       Photographs of weapons captured from North Koreans early
       in the war reveal that the Soviets supplied them with WWII
       vintage and post-war models but not with their latest
       models. Weapons include Goryunov M 1943 heavy machine
       gun, Maxim M 1910 machine gun, M 1943 120-mm mortar,
       M 1891/30 bolt action rifle, and 7.62-mm Soviet sub-
       machine gun, T 34 tank and various anti-tank guns.

1522. "Conditions in the British and Communist Armies Compared."
       UNI SER EM R, 1951 April:2-3.

       A comparative study of the British, Russian and Communist
       Chinese Armies. Comparison of pay, allowances, living
       conditions, discipline and relationships between officers
       and enlisted men. Of value is understanding the Chinese
       military performance in Korea.

1523. Corr, Gerard H. THE CHINESE RED ARMY: CAMPAIGNS AND
       POLITICS SINCE 1949. New York: Schocken, 1974.

       Popular account of the military activities of the Red
       Army by an American journalist. Based on non-Chinese
       sources, this work has limited coverage of the Korean War.

1524. Deutscher, Isaac. "Stalin's Stake in Mao's Army."
       REPORTER, 1952 6 (10):27-29.

       Although the Soviet Union diverted considerable supplies
       to the Chinese Communists for the war effort in Korea, it did
       gain some benefits in return--specifically it was able to
       entrust the Chinese Army with the role previously played by
       the Soviet Far Eastern Army. By the resulting manpower
       savings, the Russians were able to divert their reserves to
       Europe.

1525. Farrah-Hockley, Anthony. "A Reminiscence of the Chinese
       People's Volunteers in the Korean War." CHINA Q, 1984
       98 (June):287-304.

       Looks at the training of Red Chinese soldiers on the eve of
       the conflict and tells of the decision to commit "volunteers"
       to help their friends in Korea. Looks at the early activities
       of the XIII Army Group in the fall of 1950 and spring of 1951.

Maintains that the intervention led to factionalism in the
military leadership and hastened the rift with the Russians.

1526.   "Fortified Hill--Communist Style." COM FOR J, 1952 2
        (8):18-20.

        Examines the Communist Chinese use of emplacements, bunkers
        and trenches in fortifying their positions. Uses photos and
        diagrams to show construction techniques and demonstrate the
        effectiveness of such fortifications.

1527.   Gavin, P.M. "Random Observations, Korea." INF SCH Q,
        1952 40 (2):95-99.

        Evaluation of Chinese Communists and UN forces by a battle-
        experienced US Army non-commissioned officer. Examines tactics,
        camouflage, supply, mines and booby traps. Critical of UN
        forces on such matters as giving orders and defensive
        tactics.

1528.   George, Alexander L. THE CHINESE COMMUNIST ARMY IN
        ACTION: THE KOREAN WAR AND ITS AFTERMATH. New York:
        Columbia University, 1967.

        An examination of why the Chinese fought so well in Korea,
        based on interviews of 300 prisoners of war. Describes the
        political organization and practices of the army along with
        its problems of morale and motivation. Initially the
        political officers and military commanders were able through
        criticism and self-criticism to keep morale up, but as the
        war waned so did the enthusiasm of the Chinese soldiers.●

1529.   Griffith, Samuel B., II. THE CHINESE PEOPLE'S
        LIBERATION ARMY. New York: McGraw, 1967.

        A history of the Chinese Army from its origins, covers
        the Long March, the war against Japan and the Korean War.
        Discusses the development of the army in the post-WWII
        era and its organization, training and leadership just
        prior to and during the fighting in Korea. Aimed at the
        general reader.

1530.   Grunther, Richard L. "This Is What It Is Like."
        POINTER, 1951 28 (17):2-4.

        An examination of the tactics used by the Chinese Communists
        in Korea. Deals with such things as night attacks, defensive
        positions, use of camouflage, and reliance on superior
        numbers to overrun UN forces. Recommends ways to counter
        those tactics.

1531.   Hanrahan, Gene Z. "The Chinese Red Army and Guerrilla
        Warfare." COM FOR J, 1951 1 (7):10-13.

        Examines the basic ideas behind the guerrilla warfare

developed by Mao Tse-tung and Red Army Commander Chu Teh.
Their warfare consists of three phases: intelligence
gathering, movement and action. Tells why they are so adept
at that kind of warfare. Urges serious study of their way of
fighting.

1532. Hanrahan, Gene Z. "How Strong is Red China." COM FOR J,
       1952 2 (6):34-38.

       Analysis of Communist China by a top American expert
       concludes that while the Reds are strong politically and
       defensively they are not a first line military offensive
       power because of economic and geographical problems. Claims
       that limitations make it impossible to do any more in Korea
       than it has.

1533. Hanrahan, Gene Z. "Report on Red China's New Navy."
       US NAVAL INST PROC, 1953 79 (8):846-854.

       The involvement of the Chinese Communists in the Korean
       conflict led to a major strengthening of its Navy, whose
       strength rose to more than four hundred craft. Its
       strength is in submarines and patrol boats, and its
       weakness is in heavy surface vessels. Major assistance
       comes from the Russian Naval Advisory Mission.

1534. Harris, Frank J. (J.F.?). TRAINING THE COMBAT RIFLEMAN IN
       THE CHINESE COMMUNIST FORCES AND NORTH KOREAN ARMY. Chevy
       Chase, MD: Johns Hopkins University, Operations Research
       Office, 1954.

       Describes the military training and political
       indoctrination of infantrymen of the Communist Forces
       during the Korean War.

1535. Kai-Yu, Hsu. "Behind Red China's Human Sea Tactics."
       COM FOR J, 1952 2 (11):14-18.

       Discusses the fanaticism of Red Chinese soldiers fighting
       in Korea, including their willingness to use human sea
       tactics to overrun UN positions, even at such a heavy cost.
       Examines how that level of commitment is achieved. By
       using "speak bitterness" sessions, complaint and revenge
       education, publicly proclaimed self-criticism and battle
       challenges, the Communist Chinese succeeded in turning
       peasants into fanatical fighters.

1536. Kim, Hung Il. THE EXISTING CHINESE COMMUNIST FORCES:
       A REPORT BY MAJOR GENERAL KIM HUNG IL, REPUBLIC OF KOREA
       ARMY. Santa Monica, CA: Rand, 1951.

       Utilizes interviews with Chinese Communist officers taken
       prisoner in Korea to set forth the organization, training
       and performance of Chinese forces in Korea. Explains how
       the Communists get soldiers to resist UN psychological
       warfare.

1537. Liu, F.F. A MILITARY HISTORY OF MODERN CHINA, 1924-
       1949. Princeton: Princeton University, 1956.

       Sound study of the role of the military in the affairs of
       China by a former Nationalist Army officer. Provides
       valuable insight into the Chinese (Nationalist and
       Communist) soldier's characteristics of patience, courage
       and commitment as well as his problems, such as disregard
       for human life and lack of education.

1538. "Mig Alley." AIR UNIV Q R, 1952-53 5 (4):18-21.

       Photographs and a brief account of the large Chinese
       Communist airfields that lay immediately north of the
       Yalu River. UN restrictions on the area of military
       operations permitted these enemy bases to function
       without restriction in clear view of American pilots.

1539. RACING TOWARDS VICTORY: STORIES FROM THE KOREAN FRONT.
       Peking: Foreign Languages Press, 1954.

       A collection of short articles on the suffering and
       heroism of Chinese Communists fighting in Korea.

1540. Rigg, Robert B. RED CHINA'S FIGHTING HORDES. Harrisburg,
       PA: Military Service, 1951.

       An in-depth look at the Chinese Communist Army. Examines
       the development and evolution of the army as well as its
       training, organization and discipline. Objective
       assessment of the military's strengths and weaknesses.

1541. Rigg, Robert B. "The Red Enemy." ARMY, 1960 12
       (11):67-73.

       Looks at the Chinese Communist military involvement in
       the Korean War and speculates on lessons that can be
       learned from that experience. Notes the logistical
       shortcomings of the Chinese but shows how the use of
       manpower and willingness of leaders to sacrifice their
       forces enabled them to make a strong showing.

1542. Ryder, Wilfred. "China--A New Military Power." EAS
       WORLD, 1952 6 (4):15-16.

       A status report on the Communist China military machine as
       of early 1952. Army strength stood at 5,000,000 with a
       militia of nearly 13,000,000. The Navy was very small, and
       the Air Force had a thousand aircraft, half of which were
       Russian-built MIG 15's. Tells of the October 1951 decision
       to postpone general industrial development in order to create
       a heavy industrial war machine.

1543. Sterne, Paul J. "The Build-Up of Enemy Air Potential."
         AIR UNIV Q R, 1951 4 (4):84-89.

         The first two months of the war saw the US Air Force
         virtually wipe out the North Korean Air Force, but after Red
         China entered the war, that situation began to change
         rapidly. Traces the development of the CCAF from 1949 to
         late 1951 and concludes that while it has not been committed
         to all-out air warfare, it is a formidable force. Discusses
         kinds of aircraft and numbers in both CCAF and NKAF.

1544. Tallent, Robert W. "New Enemy." LEATHERNECK, 1951
         34 (2):12-15.

         An assessment of the Chinese Communist soldier based on
         information gained from prisoners captured by US Marines.
         While they are not as well-equipped, trained or fed as US
         troops, they have received considerable Communist
         indoctrination and are well-disciplined. Concludes they
         are good fighters, far better than the North Koreans.

1545. Thomas, R.C.W. "The Chinese Communists Forces in
         Korea." ARMY Q, 1952 65 (1):35-41.

         An assessment of the fighting capabilities of the forces
         as of June 1952. Looks at tactics, weapons, organization,
         strength, propaganda and an evaluation of the Chinese
         soldier as a fighter. Concludes that the Communist Army
         fighting in Korea is a "powerful machine."

1546. Wilson, Paul E. "What Makes Luke Run." MIL R, 1954
         36 (5):40-45.

         An assessment of the fighting abilities of Communist
         Chinese soldiers which concludes that they performed very well.
         The experience they gained in fighting during the Civil War
         was very valuable. Discusses the army's strengths.

3. THE CHINESE DECISION TO INTERVENE

1547. Bernstein, Barton J. "The American Road to War With
         China: A Reconsideration." USA TODAY, 1979 108 (2410):
         47-49.

         Critical account of the Truman Administration, which pursued
         policies in Korea in the Fall of 1950 that led to the crisis
         caused by Chinese Communist intervention. Says too much
         blame is placed on MacArthur because it was the
         administration that accepted a policy of unification which
         led to Chinese intervention.

1548. EIGHT YEARS OF RESISTANCE TO AMERICAN AGGRESSION AND
         AIDING KOREA. Peking: Foreign Languages Press, 1958.

Propaganda tract from the People's Republic which tells of
their efforts to help their neighbor, North Korea, halt the
aggression of US-UN forces from 1950-1953. In the post-war
period they gave economic and technical aid to help North
Korea rebuild from the destruction of war.

1549.   Foot, Rosemary. "The Sino-American Conflict in Korea:
        The US Assessment of China's Ability to Intervene in the
        War." ASIAN AFF, 1983 14 (2):160-166.

        Examines the US assessment of the likelihood of Red China
        intervening in Korea during the early months of the conflict.
        Military officials believed that China was too weak politically
        and militarily to enter the war. That miscalculation was
        accepted by the President and his civilian advisors.

1550.   Meyers, Gilbert L. "Intervention By Chinese Communists."
        AIR UNIV Q R, 1951 4 (4):89-95.

        The impact of the intervention of Chinese Communist forces
        upon the air and ground operations of the UN forces from
        November 1, 1950, through mid-March 1951 is examined.
        Statistics on air losses suffered by both sides during the
        period and as would be expected from the source, these
        figures are suspect. Looks at Operation Killer--General
        Ridgway's March 1951 effort to destroy the enemy forces and
        make geographical gains--but does not put it forth as the
        failure that it was.

1551.   Rostow, Walter W. PROSPECTS FOR COMMUNIST CHINA.
        Cambridge: Massachusetts Institute of Technology, 1954.

        Looks at China from 1949-1954. Examines the reasons behind
        the Chinese Communist decision to intervene in Korea and
        concludes the most important factors were: loss of prestige
        if the UN was able to unify Korea on a democratic basis; loss
        of North Korea would mean the loss of an important buffer
        zone; and if the UN effort was not turned back, their position
        vis-a-vis Russia in Manchuria would be weakened.

1552.   Simon, Nancy S. "From the Chinese Civil War to the
        Shanghai Communique: Changing US Perceptions of China as
        a Security Threat." Doctoral Dissertation. Johns Hopkins,
        1982.

        Shows how Red China's intervention in Korea drastically
        altered the US perception of that government. Until
        intervention Mao's regime was seen as impotent, but the
        war ushered in more than a decade and a half of
        considerable friction.

1553.   Whiting, Allen S. CHINA CROSSES THE YALU: THE DECISION
        TO ENTER THE KOREAN WAR. New York: Macmillan, 1960.

A top expert on Chinese foreign relations concludes that
Red China played no role in planning the North Korean attack
nor did they agree to make any commitments there. The
decision to enter the conflict came only after UN troops
crossed the 38th Parallel, and it soon became evident that
North Korea would be crushed, thereby threatening their
security.

1554. Zelman, Walter A. CHINESE INTERVENTION IN THE KOREAN
      WAR. Los Angeles: University of California, 1967.

      The US misgauged the Chinese Communist willingness to
      intervene in the war in Korea because it overestimated
      the deterrence value of a united US-UN commitment to halt
      communism.

4. GERM WARFARE AND OTHER CHANGES

1555. Bardendsen, Robert D. "The Chinese Communist Germ
      Warfare Propaganda Campaign, 1952-53: A Case Study of the
      Use of Propaganda in Domestic and Foreign Policies."
      Doctoral Dissertation. Yale, 1957.

      Examines how the Red Chinese utilized the charges of
      germ warfare against the US to gain support for their
      policies at home and to gain sympathy from the inter-
      national community.

1556. "Bodies of American Soldiers Murdered by Communists
      in Korea." COM FOR J, 1954 4 (6):37.

      Pictures from the US Department of Defense show US and
      UN soldiers who allegedly died as the result of Communist
      atrocities.

1557. Clews, John. THE COMMUNIST'S NEW WEAPON--GERM WARFARE.
      London: Prager, 1953.

      Claims that the Communists fabricated charges that the US
      resorted to the use of germ warfare in fighting the North
      Korean and Chinese in Korea. Looks at the methods and
      means employed by the Communists to put forth the myth.
      Rejects the findings of an International Scientific
      Commission, which found the US guilty, because the
      Commission members were Communist sympathizers.

1558. Commission of the International Association of
      Democratic Lawyers. REPORT ON US CRIMES IN KOREA.
      Peking, 1952. Supplement to PEOPLE'S CHINA.
      June 1, 1952.

      This report from a Communist front organization charges
      that the US not only engaged in bacteriological and
      chemical warfare via the air but also, along with ROK

troops, murdered civilians and committed other atrocities
against civilians and Communist soldiers.

1559.   Cooke, Alistair. "The Evil Truth Behind the Germ-
        Warfare Confessions." READ DIG, 1954 64 (383):43-46.

        Tells of the Communist-sponsored International Scientific
        Commission which investigated and concluded that the US
        was using germ warfare in Korea. Explains how the Reds
        identified US Air Force personnel whom they forced to
        admit to acts of germ warfare. Describes filmed
        "confessions" and tells how they were secured.

1560.   Endicott, Stephen L. "Germ Warfare and 'Plausible
        Denial': The Korean War, 1952-1953." MOD CHINA, 1979
        5 (1):79-104.

        Examines Chinese and North Korean charges of 1952-53
        that the US used bacteriological warfare in Korea.
        Testimony before a 1976 Senate Committee may, the author
        claims, "lend credence" to the charges. The basis of the
        contention is germ agents and delivery systems were being
        developed and US policy of denial was part of US diplomacy.
        No hard evidence to support the contention is cited.

1561.   Ginneken, Jaap van. "Bacteriological Warfare."
        J CONT ASIA, 1977 7 (2):130-152.

        During the war the North Koreans and Chinese Communists
        charged that the US was using bacteriological warfare.
        These allegations came as a result of major outbreaks of
        disease in North Korea along with the appearance of
        unusual insects and "confessions" of captured US airmen.
        The US government denied the charges, and a 1952 inter-
        national fact-finding body could come to no conclusion.
        Maintains a serious examination of the issue is needed.

1562.   Gittings, John. "Talks, Bombs and Germs: Another
        Look at the Korean War." J CONT ASIA, 1975 5 (2):205-217.

        Rejects Communist claims that the US did not negotiate
        in good faith at Panmunjom, treated prisoners poorly,
        attacked civilians and considered use of chemical and
        germ warfare.

1563.   Gross, Ernest A. "Germ Warfare in Korea." CUR HIST,
        1952 23 (133):172-178.

        A speech made to the UN Security Council on June 18, 1952,
        by Deputy US Representative to the UN, Ernest Gross. Not
        only does he castigate the Soviet Union for its continual
        charges of germ warfare but absolutely denies ever using
        or wanting to use them. Claims the US is willing to
        eliminate such weapons if the Soviets do too.

1564.   International Scientific Commission. FOR THE
          INVESTIGATION OF THE FACTS CONCERNING BACTERIOLOGICAL
          WARFARE IN KOREA AND CHINA. Peking, 1952.

          Communist Chinese propaganda piece which provides
          "evidence" that the US resorted to the use of germ warfare
          in Korea.

1565.   "Investigation of Charges of Use of Bacteriological
          Warfare by UN Forces." QM R, 1954 33 (4):8-9.
          33 (4):8-9.

          Major portions of a speech by Dr. Charles W. Mayo,
          alternate US delegate to the UN General Assembly, in
          which he denies the Communist charges that the US used
          germ warfare in Korea. Cites "evidence" that the
          Communists forced US prisoners of war to confess to use
          of germ warfare.

1566.   Mayo, Charles W. "The Role of Forced Confessions in
          the Communist 'Germ Warfare' Propaganda Campaign." DEPT
          STATE BUL, 1953 29 (750):641-647.

          Statement from the US Representative to the UN General
          Assembly examines the history of Communist charges of
          biological warfare against the US, notes that the so
          called confessions by American prisoners were gained by
          coersion. Denounces the entire affair as a propaganda
          ploy.

1567.   Stevenson, Charles. "The Truth About 'Germ Warfare'
          in Korea." READ DIG, 1953 62 (372):17-20.

          Rejects the idea that the US engaged in germ warfare in
          Korea and argues that Communist lies to that effect were
          put forth out of a sense of guilt because they had done
          nothing to combat a major outbreak of disease. Tells of
          US efforts to help South Koreans combat illness and disease.
          Condensed from PATHFINDER, April 1953.

1568.   Stockholm International Peace Research Institute.
          THE PROBLEM OF CHEMICAL AND BIOLOGICAL WARFARE. 6 vols.
          New York: Humanities, 1971.

          Volumes four and five contain an introduction to the charges
          and countercharges made by the Communists and the US over
          the matter of chemical and germ warfare during the Korean
          War.

1569.   STOP US GERM WARFARE. Peking: Chinese People's Committee
          for World Peace, 1953.

          Chinese charges against US for conducting biological warfare
          are set forth in essays, lectures, news releases and speeches
          from leading Communist officials.

1570. US Senate, Committee on Government Operations. REPORT OF
      THE SUBCOMMITTEE ON KOREAN WAR ATROCITIES. Senate Report 848,
      83rd Cong 2nd Sess Washington: Government Printing Office,
      1954.

      This government report examines the history and operations
      of The War Crimes Division in Korea. Topics covered include:
      types of war atrocities committed against US prisoners,
      killings of American prisoners after capture, forced marches,
      treatment in POW camps and statistics. Concludes that North
      Korea and the Chinese Communists violated or ignored virtually
      every provision of the Geneva Convention governing prisoners.

1571. Winnington, Alan. I SAW THE TRUTH IN KOREA: FACTS AND
      PHOTOGRAPHS THAT WILL SHOCK BRITAIN. London: People's,
      1950.

      Pamphlet by the reporter of the LONDON DAILY WORKER which
      shows pictures of civilians and Communist soldiers supposedly
      murdered by US aggressors in Korea. Charges that US-UN
      troops are committing war atrocities.

XIV. THE TRUMAN-MACARTHUR CONTROVERSY
A. TRUMAN

1572. Hamby, Alonzo L. BEYOND THE NEW DEAL: HARRY S. TRUMAN
AND AMERICAN LIBERALISM. New York: Columbia University,
1973.

An excellent one-volume study of the Truman presidency
focuses on liberalism but has very fine chapters on the
Korean War, including the decision to intervene and the
difficulties of command, the domestic ramifications of the
stalemate and the problems of economic and military
mobilization.

1573. Hamby, Alonzo L. "The Vital Center, The Fair Deal,
and the Quest for a Liberal Political Economy." AM HIST R,
1972 77 (3):653-678.

President Truman's Fair Deal economic policy was aimed at
spreading the benefits of abundance throughout American
society by stimulating economic growth. Although the
Korean War greatly curtailed the Fair Deal social legislation,
it did lead to increased economic growth.

1574. Haynes, Richard F. THE AWESOME POWER: HARRY S. TRUMAN
AS COMMANDER-IN-CHIEF. Baton Rouge: Louisiana State
University, 1973.

A must for anyone wanting to understand Truman's actions
in Korea. Follows performance as Commander-in-Chief
throughout his years in the White House. Very informative,
scholarly work which gives considerable attention to Korea.
Generally favorable to Truman.

1575. Heller, Francis H., ed. THE TRUMAN WHITE HOUSE: THE
ADMINISTRATION OF THE PRESIDENCY, 1945-1953. Lawrence:
Regents Press of Kansas, 1980.

Examines the administrative operation of the Truman
presidency by presenting personal reflections of twenty-two
key associates. Based on a May 1977 conference which brought
the participants together to discuss, among other things,
policy making in the areas of national security and foreign
affairs. Of importance on the Korean War are views of
special assistant W. Averell Harriman, special counsel,
Charles S. Murphy, naval aide Robert L. Dennison, and
economic advisor Leon H. Keyserling.

1576.   Hoare, William W., Jr. "Truman" in Ernest R. May, ed.
            THE ULTIMATE DECISION. New York: Braziller, 1960, pp.
            179-210.

            Examines Truman's position in the controversy with
            MacArthur over Far Eastern policy, the conduct of the
            war and the decision to relieve him.

1577.   Kirkendall, Richard S., ed. THE TRUMAN PERIOD AS A
            RESEARCH FIELD. Columbia, MO: University of Missouri,
            1967.

            Papers from a 1966 conference at the Truman Library
            examine the key works that have been done on different
            aspects of the Truman presidency and suggests topics
            that need to be covered. An excellent section on
            foreign and military policies. Covers the key
            works on the Korean War up to 1965.

1578.   Kirkendall, Richard S., ed. THE TRUMAN PERIOD AS A
            RESEARCH FIELD: A REAPPRAISAL, 1972. Columbia, MO:
            University of Missouri, 1974.

            A look at the scholarship on the Truman Administration
            that was emerging in the period 1966-1972 with primary
            emphasis on foreign policy including the growing
            controversy between the traditionalists and revisionists.
            Relatively little is included on the Korean War itself.

1579.   Miller, Merle. PLAIN SPEAKING: AN ORAL BIOGRAPHY OF
            HARRY S. TRUMAN. New York: Berkeley, 1973.

            Reflections of his life by Truman some eighteen years
            after he left the White House. Based on long interviews
            with the author. Two chapters are especially pertinent:
            one on the decision to intervene and another on the
            decision to fire MacArthur. Other references to the
            war are included.

1580.   PUBLIC PAPERS OF THE PRESIDENTS OF THE UNITED
            STATES, HARRY S. TRUMAN, 1950. Washington: Government
            Printing Office, 1965; 1951 Volume, Washington, 1965;
            1952-53 Volume, Washington, 1966.

            These volumes, which contain the public messages,
            speeches and statements of President Truman are extremely
            valuable when studying the Korean War. Includes all his
            White House press conferences. Indexed.

1581.   Sander, Alfred D. "Truman and the National Security
            Council: 1945-1947." J AM HIST, 1972 59 (2):369-388.

            Background on the establishment of the National Security
            Council, which was formalized in 1947. Truman, fearful
            the Council might limit his prerogatives, tended to ignore
            it until the Korean War after which he relied on it
            considerably.

1582. Seltzer, Robert V. "The Truman-Johnson Analog: A Study
         of Presidential Rhetoric in Limited War." Doctoral
         Dissertation. Wayne State, 1976.

         Studies President Truman's use of analogues in his
         rhetoric to justify US entrance into and sustained
         effort in the Korean conflict. Analyzes speeches and
         speaking of Truman during the war and of President
         Johnson during the Vietnam War.

1583. "A Trace of Walter Mitty?" NAT R, 1980 32 (18):1064-1065.

         Assesses statements made by President Truman in a private
         journal on January 27 and May 18, 1952, that he was
         considering ultimatums to the Russians and Red Chinese
         telling them to stop supporting the war in Korea or face
         all out destruction at the hands of the US. Historian
         Francis Loewenheim concludes they were in the realm of
         fantasy and not real policy considerations.

1584. Truman, Harry S. MEMOIRS: YEARS OF TRIAL AND HOPE
         Vol. II. Garden City, NY: Doubleday, 1956.

         Truman's memoirs are among the best presidential memoirs
         written. Extensive consideration is given to the decision
         to intervene, the move north of the 38th Parallel, conduct
         of the war, domestic considerations and the frustrating
         peace negotiations. Also Truman's side of the MacArthur
         controversy. Absolutely essential to any serious student
         of the war.

1585. Truman, Margaret. HARRY S. TRUMAN. New York: Morrow,
         1973.

         A much better biography than would generally be expected
         from the daughter of a subject, this work gives considerable
         inside information on such aspects of the Korean War as
         the decision to intervene and the dismissal of General
         MacArthur.

1586. Twedt, Michael S. "The War Rhetoric of Harry S. Truman
         During the Korean Conflict." Doctoral Dissertation. Kansas,
         1969.

         An analysis of President Truman's efforts, through his
         rhetoric, to unify the American people behind the war
         effort, concludes that he was not successful. Also
         maintains he did not use radio and television to his
         advantage.

B. MACARTHUR

1587. Cagle, Malcolm W. "Errors of the Korean War." US NAVAL
       INST PROC, 1958 84 (1):31-35.

       A critical account, by a well known naval historian, of
       General MacArthur's military strategy after the Inchon
       Invasion.

1588. Cagle, Malcolm W. "Inchon--The Analysis of a Gamble."
       US NAVAL INST PROC, 1954 80 (1):47-51.

       This analysis is a rare critical account of General
       MacArthur's role in the planning of the Inchon Invasion.
       Maintains that the landing site was arbitrarily chosen
       by the General who then proceeded to develop justifica-
       tion for that decision--a procedure that runs counter to
       sound military planning.

1589. Dupuy, R. Ernest, and Trevor N. Dupuy. BRAVE MEN AND
       GREAT CAPTAINS. New York: Harper, 1959.

       Extols the valor of US military leaders from George
       Washington to MacArthur in Korea. The authors attempt to
       make the General a martyr.

1590. Falk, Stanley L. "Comments on Reynolds: 'MacArthur
       as Maritime Strategist.'" NAV WC R, 1980 33 March/April:
       92-99.

       Critical assessment of Clark G. Reynolds' contention that
       MacArthur was a great maritime strategist. Claims maritime
       strategy was grand strategy while MacArthur's concepts were
       "petty and parochial." Critical of the General's decision
       to attack at Inchon. Solid analysis of the decision.

1591. Flint, Roy K. "The Tragic Flaw: MacArthur, the Joint Chiefs
       and the Korean War." Doctoral Dissertation. Duke, 1976.

       A study of military leadership as reflected in the members
       of the Joint Chiefs of Staff and Far East and UN Commander,
       General MacArthur. Sees the decision to cross the 38th
       Parallel as a poor one which led to a widening of the war.
       Claims that weaknesses in command structures and MacArthur's
       shortcomings led to a blotched policy.

1592. Gunther, John. THE RIDDLE OF MACARTHUR: JAPAN, KOREA
       AND THE FAR EAST. New York: Harper, 1951.

       Journalistic account focuses on MacArthur's occupation
       policies in Japan. Goes into the occupation policies and
       problems of the US in post-WWII Korea, outbreak of war and
       early conflicts in the war between MacArthur and Truman.
       Ends with the October 15, 1950, meeting at Wake Island.

1593. Hunt, Frazier. THE UNTOLD STORY OF DOUGLAS MACARTHUR.
       New York: Devin, 1954.

An extremely long and laudatory biography of MacArthur
which includes considerable coverage of the Korean War.
Felt the General could do no wrong. The book is poorly
researched and contains many inaccuracies.

1594. Kenney, George C. THE MACARTHUR I KNOW. New York:
         Duell, 1951.

A superficial and laudatory account of MacArthur by the
air commander who helped the General turn the tide in the
Pacific during WWII. Considerable attention is given to
the Korean War and the General's dismissal.

1595. Langley, Michael. INCHON LANDING: MACARTHUR'S LAST
         TRIUMPH. New York: Times, 1979.

Maintains that the Inchon Invasion's success was due
largely to General MacArthur's leadership. A brief,
superficial account by a British author.

1596. Lee, Clark, and Richard Henschel. DOUGLAS MACARTHUR.
         New York: Holt, 1952.

Author Lee was an Associated Press correspondent who was
probably closer to MacArthur over a longer period of time
than any other reporter. Covers not only the WWII years
but the occupation period, war in Korea, Wake Island
meeting and dismissal in a relatively objective fashion.
More than 400 photographs.

1597. MacArthur, Douglas. REMINISCENCES. New York: McGraw,
         1964.

MacArthur recounts some of the major events in his long
career, including Korea. This work is a major disappointment
because it relies heavily on quotations from his speeches,
declarations and reports to let the reader know how
infallible the author was. Also draws heavily on material
taken from other pro-MacArthur publications.

1598. Manchester, William. AMERICAN CAESAR, DOUGLAS MACARTHUR,
         1880-1964. Boston: Little, 1978.

This generally favorable account of the General's career is
a very readable and interesting work that was well received
by the public; however, professional historians divided
sharply over its merits. Gives considerable attention to
MacArthur's role in the early months of the war and the
growing friction with the President and Washington policy
makers. Feels the General was primarily a victim because
he was misunderstood.

1599. Norman, John. "MacArthur's Blockade Proposals Against
         Red China." PAC HIST R, 1957 26 (2):161-174.

Examines General MacArthur's late 1950 call for the
intensification of a US economic blockade of China and
application of a naval blockade against China's coast. Looks
at the controversy as brought out in the MacArthur hearings
and concludes that the General was unaware of what was being
done on the economic front and was impractical in his demands
for a naval blockade.

1600.   Reynolds, Clark G. "MacArthur as Maritime Strategist."
        NAV W C R, 1980 33 March/April:79-91.

        Maintains that MacArthur matured into a maritime-
        strategist of the first order as evidenced by his maritime
        strategy during the Korean War. His goals were to overcome
        the allied reverses early in the war, which he did with the
        Inchon Invasion, and keep the war from expanding into Red
        China, which he attempted to achieve by a naval blockade of
        China.

1601.   Ruetten, Richard T. "General Douglas MacArthur's
        'Reconnaissance in Force': The Rationalization of a
        Defeat in Korea." PAC HIST R, 1967 36 (1):79-93.

        Analyzes General MacArthur's claims that the ill-fated
        US-UN offensive of November 1950 was in reality a
        "reconnaissance in force to probe the intentions of the
        Chinese" by arguing it was a rationalization of a defeat.
        Maintains the decision was MacArthur's alone and went
        against the advice of many of his own field officers.

1602.   Ryan, Cornelius. "MacArthur: Man of Controversy."
        AM MERCURY, 1950 71 (322):425-434.

        This account of MacArthur, which was written very early in
        the Korean War, shows that the General was already involved
        in controversy with the President, some members of Congress
        and the press.

1603.   Sebald, William J., and Russell Brines. WITH MACARTHUR
        IN JAPAN: A PERSONAL HISTORY OF THE OCCUPATION. New York:
        Norton, 1965.

        Sebald was the top ranking US diplomat in Japan from 1947
        through 1952 and at times worked closely but not smoothly
        with MacArthur. Good firsthand account of the political
        maneuvering that took place when war came to Korea and in
        the months that followed. Generally critical of MacArthur.

1604.   Sheldon, Walt. HELL OR HIGH WATER: MACARTHUR'S LANDING
        AT INCHON. New York: Macmillan, 1968.

        Well-written narrative of Inchon from inception to the
        invasion and after. Lauds MacArthur for selling the idea
        to a reluctant President and Pentagon and then executing
        the extremely difficult operation in near perfect fashion.
        Good at explaining the tactical, logistical and geographical

problems that had to be dealt with.

1605.   Sondern, Frederic. "Right Man in the Right Place."
        READ DIG, 1951 58 (345):1-5.

        Contemporary account of General MacArthur and the Inchon
        Invasion from inception to planning to implementation.
        Shows how the General's knowledge of military history
        influenced his thinking.

1606.   Story, Anthony F. "My Air Adventures With General
        MacArthur." COLLIER'S, 1951 127 (24):13-15, 38-41.

        MacArthur's personal aide during the Korean War period
        tells a great deal about the General's movements and
        visits to the front during the first ten months of the
        war. During that period he made seventeen visits to
        Korea. Provides some good insights into MacArthur and his
        military bearing.

1607.   Timmons, Bascom M. "MacArthur's Greatest Battle."
        COLLIER'S, 1950 126 (25):13-15, 65-66.

        Contemporary journalistic account of MacArthur's conception
        of, planning and execution of the Inchon invasion. Very
        laudatory of the General and an operation the author calls a
        classic of amphibious warfare. Good on MacArthur's military
        background and thinking. Photographs.

1608.   Tomlinson, H. Pat. "Inchon: The General's Decision."
        MIL R, 1967 47 (4):28-35.

        Favorable look at General MacArthur's role and key
        decisions in the planning and carrying out of the Inchon
        amphibious invasion. Sees MacArthur as the master mind
        behind the operation.

1609.   Wheeler, Gerald E. "A Commentary on Dr. Clark Reynolds'
        Paper: 'MacArthur as Maritime Strategist." NAV W C R, 1980
        33 March/April:98-102.

        Challenges Reynolds' claim that MacArthur was a superior
        maritime strategist. Goes on to question General MacArthur's
        proposal for using the Nationalist Chinese Army of Chiang Kai
        Shek in Korea. The author asks if such a move would have
        been politically wise and whether the army would have
        performed any better than it did when it fled the mainland
        two years before.

1610.   Whitney, Courtney. MACARTHUR: HIS RENDEZVOUS WITH
        HISTORY. New York: Knopf, 1956.

        The author was MacArthur's closest confidant from 1941
        through 1954 and served as Chief of the Government Section
        of SCAP from 1945 to 1951. While the book lacks objectivity,

it gives many inside accounts of what was going on in Korea from the time of the attack through the dismissal.

1611. Willoughby, Charles A., and John Chamberlain. MACARTHUR, 1941-1951. New York: McGraw, 1954.

Throughout the period examined, author Willoughby served on MacArthur's intelligence staff, and there is no question of his admiration for the General. Nevertheless, this is a solid account of MacArthur which closely examines and analyzes key decisions of strategy, including those in Korea.

C. THE CONTROVERSY AND DISMISSAL

1612. Bradley, Omar N. SUBSTANCE OF STATEMENTS MADE AT WAKE ISLAND ON OCTOBER 15, 1950. Washington: US Senate, 1951.

The Chairman of the Joint Chiefs of Staff transcripts of the controversial meeting between President Truman and General MacArthur. Supportive of Truman's claims that he was led by MacArthur to believe that the Chinese Communists would not intervene.

1613. Fredericks, Edgar J. MACARTHUR: HIS MISSION AND MEANING. Philadelphia: Whitmore, 1968.

Ties the failure of the US to defeat the Chinese in Korea to the US situation in Vietnam and maintains that if MacArthur would have been permitted to achieve victory, the Communists in Asia might not have been willing to fight the US there later. Claims MacArthur saw the need for a clear-cut victory in Korea to convince Communists of US determination to resist expansion.

1614. Harris, Merne A. "The MacArthur Dismissal: A Study in Political Mail." Doctoral Dissertation. Iowa, 1966.

Analysis of the mail coming to President Truman at the White House regarding his dismissal of General MacArthur. Based on a sample of the 84,000 telegrams and letters received, 55% were critical of the decision while 45% were supportive of the President. Examines the reasons given by the pro and con advocates.

1615. Henderson, Thomas G. "Editorial Reaction of Selected Major Indiana Daily Newspapers to a National Controversy-- The Truman, MacArthur Conflict." Doctoral Dissertation. Ball State, 1977.

Surveys editorial opinion and reaction of five newspapers to President Truman's dismissal of General MacArthur. Shows that rationality or a balanced approach was rare since newspapers took their position based on whether or not they were supportive of the President's foreign policy.

1616. Henn, Carl L., Jr. "Collective Security, Military
      Sanctions, and Sea Power." US NAVAL INST PROC, 1954
      80 (2):125-135.

      Examines the use of the UN blockade against North Korea
      during the Korean War plus consideration of General Mac-
      Arthur's proposal that a blockade be imposed against Red
      China. Believes that collective sanctions utilizing sea
      power can be a major tool in halting international
      aggression.

1617. Higgins, Trumbull. KOREA AND THE FALL OF MACARTHUR:
      A PRECIS IN LIMITED WAR. New York: Oxford University,
      1960.

      Sees the controversy as stemming from the inability of the
      President and General to come to an agreement on the strategy
      of the conflict. MacArthur, seeing victory in the military
      sense, wanted to achieve victory over China by means of a sea
      and air blockade, the bombing of China and use of Chinese
      Nationalist troops. Truman and the Joint Chiefs of Staff
      rejected the ideas, feeling they might lead to WWIII.
      Critical of MacArthur. Considerable attention to the
      domestic debate over the firing following MacArthur's return.

1618. Huff, Sid. "The General's Last Fight." SAT EVE POST,
      1951 224 (17):30, 136-139, 141-142.

      General MacArthur's aide-de-camp from 1936 until his
      firing in Korea gives a firsthand account of the coming
      of the Korean War, its conduct and the friction that led
      to being relieved. As expected, very pro-MacArthur.

1619. Jessup, Philip C. "The Record of Wake Island: A
      Correction." J AM HIST, 1981 67 (4):866-870.

      The author, himself a participant in the Wake Island
      conference, explains the note-taking processes that
      took place and explains what author William Manchester
      referred to as the "inexplicable" presence of a female
      eavesdropper at the session. The notes in question
      were taken by Jessup's Administrative Assistant,
      Vernice Anderson, whose role is explained. Mention is
      made that Jessup, General Bradley and Dean Rusk also
      took notes.

1620. Karp, Walter. "Truman Vs. MacArthur." AM HERT,
      1984 35 (3):84-94.

      Maintains that the President's dismissal of the General
      brought about one of the angriest outbursts in American History
      and provided the most severe test yet for the concept of
      civilian control of the military. This study is different
      from most other accounts of the controversy in that it
      concentrates on events after the dismissal.

1621.   "The Korean War: Who Was Right, Truman or MacArthur?" In
        Sidney Fine ed., THE AMERICAN PAST: CONFLICTING
        INTERPRETATIONS OF THE GREAT ISSUES. Vol. 2, 2nd ed.
        New York: Macmillan, 1965.

        Presents conflicting points of view over the issue of
        whether MacArthur's proposals for achieving victory
        were correct or not. Alvin F. Cottrell and James E.
        Dougherty defend the General, while John W. Spanier
        defends the Truman Administration.

1622.   Lowitt, Richard, ed. THE TRUMAN-MACARTHUR CONTROVERSY.
        Chicago: Rand McNally, 1967.

        Brief account of the growing conflict between the two
        leaders from their pre-war differences over China and
        Formosa through the firing. Uses public statements,
        memoirs, congressional investigations and scholarly
        studies.

1623.   MacArthur, Douglas. MACARTHUR'S ADDRESS TO CONGRESS,
        APRIL 19, 1951, WITH HIGHLIGHTS OF HIS CAREER.
        New York: Rand McNally, 1951.

        The General's famous speech to Congress following his
        return to the US following his relief of the UN Command
        by President Truman. Includes chronological survey of
        his career.

1624.   "MacArthur and Truman Tell About a War US Didn't Win."
        US NEWS W R, 1956 40 Feb.17:48-54, 168-175.

        In an article "Mr. Truman Yielded to Counsels of Fear,"
        MacArthur gives his ideas of why he was fired and why the
        President handled the Korean issue unsatisfactorily.
        MacArthur's views were written in response to Truman's
        account of the controversy which appeared in the Feb. 13,
        1956, issue of LIFE. That account, "The Recall of
        General MacArthur," is printed in full in this article.
        MacArthur suggests that British spies provided
        information that convinced Red China to enter the war.

1625.   McGovern, James. TO THE YALU: FROM THE CHINESE
        INVASION OF KOREA TO MACARTHUR'S DISMISSAL. New York:
        Morrow, 1972.

        A critical account of General MacArthur's activities from
        October 1950 to April 1951. Contends that MacArthur should
        not have continued to push north when it was evident the
        Chinese were ready to enter the war. The General wanted to
        push to the Yalu, and although the Joint Chiefs of Staff
        had reservations, they did not have the political clout to
        stop him after his successful Inchon invasion.

1626. Millis, Walter, et al. ARMS AND THE STATE: CIVIL
         MILITARY ELEMENTS IN NATIONAL POLICY. New York: Twentieth
         Century Fund, 1958.

         Contains a penetrating chapter on the Truman-MacArthur
         controversy. Maintains the clash was not so much one of the
         independent field general and the top Washington command but
         a clash between personalities and partisan political
         interests. Covers the period from the outbreak of war through
         the MacArthur Hearings.

1627. Millis, Walter. "Truman and MacArthur" in Allen
         Guttmann, ed. KOREA AND THE THEORY OF LIMITED WAR.
         Lexington, MA: Heath, 1967, pp. 44-51.

         Focuses on the December 1950-March 1951 conflict between the
         President and the General over the military conduct of the
         war. MacArthur's proposals to carry the war to the Chinese
         and the administration's opposition and the role of the Joint
         Chiefs of Staff are examined.

1628. O'Ballance, Edgar. "The MacArthur Plan." ROY UNI SER
         INST J, 1965 110 (639):248-253.

         Defends General MacArthur's 1951 plan to end the war by
         using atomic bombs to destroy Chinese supply lines and at
         the same time create a radioactive belt which could trap
         the enemy in North Korea. The plan was not accepted by
         Washington and the UN because of political considerations.
         The author contends that tactically the plan was a good
         one.

1629. "The President and General MacArthur Confer on Korean
         and Far Eastern Policies." DEPT STATE BUL, 1950 23
         (590):643-644.

         Includes President Truman's October 10 statement that he is
         going to confer with MacArthur and the President's
         official communique released on October 15, 1950, on the
         Wake Island Conference.

1630. Rovere, Richard H., and Arthur M. Schlesinger, Jr.
         THE GENERAL AND THE PRESIDENT: THE FUTURE OF AMERICAN
         FOREIGN POLICY. New York: Farrar, 1951.

         A hastily prepared account of MacArthur's life which
         focuses on Korea and his dismissal. Argues that Truman's
         position was infallible while MacArthur's was sadly
         lacking. Uneven account with good insights and
         accurate information alternating with glaring errors of
         fact and interpretation.

1631.   Ryan, Halford R.   "Harry S. Truman: A Misdirected
        Defense for MacArthur's Dismissal." PRES STUDIES Q,
        1981 11 (4):576-582.

        Analysis of President Truman's April 11, 1951, radio
        speech to defend his dismissal of General MacArthur.
        The author contends the President spent too much time
        defending Acheson's war policy and not enough defending
        removal. Traces the preparation of the speech and
        evaluates its effectiveness.

1632.   Schlesinger, Arthur M., and Richard H. Rovere. THE
        MACARTHUR CONTROVERSY AND AMERICAN FOREIGN POLICY.
        New York: Farrar, 1965.

        A revision of the authors' 1951 work, THE GENERAL AND THE
        PRESIDENT.

1633.   Smith, Robert. MACARTHUR IN KOREA: THE NAKED
        EMPEROR. New York: Simon, 1982.

        Focusing on MacArthur's role in the Korean War, the
        author attempts, unsuccessfully, to portray the General
        as an incompetent, ineffective leader. Poorly organized
        and researched, the work does not succeed in putting
        MacArthur in the villain's role that the author intended.

1634.   Spanier, John W. "The Truman-MacArthur Conflict, June
        1950-April 1951." Doctoral Dissertation. Yale, 1957.

        This dissertation of the running conflict between the
        President and the General over the Korean War was
        published in 1959 and became one of the standard works
        on the feud and the dismissal.

1635.   Spanier, John W. THE TRUMAN-MACARTHUR CONTROVERSY AND
        THE KOREAN WAR. Cambridge, MA: Belknap, 1959.

        A scholarly study of the controversy based on
        published documents. Maintains that Truman rightfully
        dismissed MacArthur because the General failed to clear
        his statements as ordered, challenged the President as
        molder of foreign policy, and was unable to accept the
        policy of limited war. Spanier says Korea signifies the
        need for Americans to abandon their traditional concept
        of military victory and think in terms of the best
        political settlement that can be achieved.

1636.   "Tatoo For a Warrior." LIFE, 1951 30 (17):29-37.

        Contemporary account of MacArthur's dismissal stresses
        the major differences between he and the President on
        basic strategy in the Far East.

1637. US Senate. MILITARY SITUATION IN THE FAR EAST.
       HEARINGS BEFORE THE COMMITTEE ON ARMED SERVICES AND
       THE COMMITTEE ON FOREIGN RELATIONS, UNITED STATES
       SENATE, EIGHTY-SECOND CONGRESS, FIRST SESSION, TO
       CONDUCT AN INQUIRY INTO THE MILITARY SITUATION IN THE
       FAR EAST AND THE FACTS SURROUNDING THE RELIEF OF GENERAL
       OF THE ARMY DOUGLAS MACARTHUR FROM HIS ASSIGNMENTS IN
       THAT AREA. Washington: Government Printing Office,
       1951, 5 Volumes. Not released until 1973.

       For eight weeks in May and June 1950, two Senate committees
       held secret hearings to determine why MacArthur was
       relieved. They called thirteen witnesses, including the
       top civilian and military leaders. Included were MacArthur,
       Secretary of State Acheson, Secretary of Defense George
       Marshall, and former Secretary Louis Johnson and all the
       members of the Joint Chiefs of Staff. The thousands of
       pages of testimony give the most thorough raw information
       available on the political and military decisions made
       from June 1950 through April 1951. Absolutely essential
       to anyone doing primary research on the period just before
       and the ten months after the outbreak of war.

1638. Wiltz, John E. "The MacArthur Hearings of 1951: The
       Secret Testimony." MIL AFF, 1975 39 (4):167-173.

       In May and June 1951 the Senate Committees on Armed
       Services and Foreign Relations held an eight-week secret
       hearing on the reasons behind the dismissal of General
       MacArthur. In 1973 the hearings were declassified and
       published. This article culls out certain controversial
       issues in the Korean War and reveals what information
       was brought to light in the 1951 testimony.

1639. Wiltz, John E. "The MacArthur Inquiry, 1951." In
       Arthur M. Schlesinger, and Roger Bruns, ed. CONGRESS
       INVESTIGATES: A DOCUMENTED HISTORY 1792-1974. Vol. V.
       New York: Chelsea, 1975, pp. 3593-3726.

       An overall account of the dismissal and its antecedents
       is followed by fifteen documents associated with the
       controversy. Also includes a bibliographical essay.

1640. Wiltz, John E. "Truman and MacArthur: The Wake Island
       Meeting." MIL AFF, 1978 42 (4):169-176.

       Scholarly account of the October 1950 meeting between
       Truman and MacArthur at Wake Island--at which time the UN
       Commander indicated he did not feel the Chinese would
       enter the war. In looking at the background, the author
       concludes the President's visit was primarily for public
       relations and thus not much came from the meeting nor was
       much expected.

XV. MILITARY MEDICINE
A. RESCUE AND EVACUATION

1641. "Air Rescue Service." MIL R, 1953 33 (8):23-28.

Describes the world-wide responsibilities of the Air
Rescue Service (ARS), including air search rescue coverage
for the ocean areas around Japan and Korea in support of
UN operations, rescue of pilots forced down behind enemy
lines and evacuation of wounded soldiers.

1642. Air University Quarterly Staff. "Tactical Air Rescue in
Korea." AIR UNIV Q R, 1953 6 (3):120-123.

In the immediate post-WWII period, new concepts of air
rescue were developed. In Korea these new procedures
were successfully utilized for the first time in combat.
This recounts the experiences of the 3rd Air Rescue Group
in Korea. Based on information supplied by USAF Captain
Norman F. Williams.

1643. Albert, Janice. "Air Evacuation From Korea--A Typical
Flight." MIL SURG, 1953 112 (4):256-259.

A US Air Force nurse describes the training and
responsibilities of a flight nurse as she aids in the
evacuation of soldiers wounded in Korea. Describes a
typical flight to show what she does.

1644. Butera, James L. "Rescue Concepts, Before and After."
AERO HIST, 1974 21 (1):8-11.

Looks at US military rescue concepts in three wars,
including Korea. During that conflict 9,680 men were
recovered by Air Rescue Service (ARS), including 996
from behind enemy lines.

1645. Churchill, Edward. "Selective Evacuation vs. Hitchhiking."
J AMA, 1951 145 (11):841.

Warns US Medical personnel in Korea that they must be
selective in the individuals they evacuate from Korea back
to the states. Caution must be used to assure that an
abundance of aircraft capable of evacuating military
personnel so readily does not lead to so many soldiers with
minimal wounds being drained from units so as to endanger
those who remain behind.

1646. Green, Edward M. "Ambulance Air Line." LEATHERNECK,
       1952 35 (3):36-39.

       Describes the air evacuation of wounded US Marines in
       Korea to medical facilities in Japan, then to Hawaii and
       the states.

1647. Shershun, Carroll S. "It's the Greatest Mission of
       Them All." AERO HIST, 1969 16 (3):13-15, 38-41.

       Story of the 3rd Air Rescue Group, the most decorated unit
       in the US Air Force during the Korean War. In that conflict
       the unit received 1,500 personal awards, higher than any
       other unit, and the first unit to receive the Presidential
       Unit Citation.

1648. Smith, Allen D. "Air Evacuation--Medical Obligation and
       Military Necessity." AIR UNIV Q R, 1953 6 (2):98-111.

       Although the US had utilized medical air evacuation in WWI
       and WWII, it was not until the Korean War that it became
       generally accepted. The major development in Korea was the
       use of helicopters to evacuate wounded and injured. Although
       there were contributing factors, air evacuation was the major
       reason behind fifty percent reduction in the death rate of
       combat casualties for similar circumstances in WWII.

1649. Smith, Allen D. "Medical Air Evacuations in Korea and
       Its Influence on the Future." MIL SURG, 1952 110 (5):
       323-332.

       Traces the use of frontline air evacuation of US personnel
       in Korea from the first time its use was directed by General
       E.E. Partridge of the Fifth Air Force through its adoption
       and subsequent use by the Marines and Army. Battlefield
       deaths in Korea were nearly 50% less than in WWII largely
       because of this development. Also tells of evacuation to
       medical facilities in Japan. Describes the medical
       advantages of air evacuation and includes many statistics
       on air evacuations during the first fifteen months of the
       war.

1650. Tilford, Earl H. "The Development of Search and Rescue:
       World War II to 1961." AERO HIST, 1977 24 (4):228-239.

       In 1946 the US Air Rescue Service was established to
       evacuate wounded military personnel and those trapped behind
       enemy lines. In Korea the use of the helicopter enabled
       the service to perform admirably and lay the basis for the
       techniques used so effectively in Vietnam.

B. MEDICAL UNITS AND FACILITIES

1651.   Britton, George T. "Clearing Companies Can Do Holding."
        MIL R, 1952 31 (11):17-19.

        Examines the US 629th Medical Clearing Company (Separate)
        in Korea. Concludes that because of its elastic organization,
        a clearing company was useful as a medical holding unit at
        an airhead to expedite the evacuation of patients. When
        this is done it relieves the mobile surgical hospital of
        evacuation responsibilities and increases its capacity.

1652.   Buerger, Paul T. "Medical Support For Mountain
        Fighting in Korea." MIL SURG, 1951 109 (6):694-700.

        Traces the activities of a US medical battalion involved
        in Operation "Killer," a bloody UN offensive in February
        1951. Examines the unit's personnel, equipment, the
        operation, supply and evacuations. Makes recommendations
        on things that should be done in similar operations in
        the future.

1653.   Burlage, George E. "Easy Med." LEATHERNECK, 1952
        35 (1):19-23.

        Describes the functioning of Company E, 1st Medical
        Battalion in providing medical support of the 1st Marine
        Division.

1654.   Coyl, E.B. "Hospital Ships in Korea." MIL SURG,
        1953 112 (5):342-344.

        Describes the role of hospital ships supporting US-UN
        operations in Korea. Tells of the one British ship,
        HMS MAINE and three US ships: USS CONSOLATION; USS
        REPOSE; and USS HAVEN and the Danish ship, MS JUTLANDIA.
        Relates how men are brought to the ships and the services
        performed on board. Admission statistics.

1655.   "Floating Hospitals." MIL R, 1952 32 (5):58-62.

        This photo essay focuses on the US naval hospital ship,
        USS CONSOLATION, in the early months of the Korean War,
        to show the role such ships played in the evacuation and
        treatment of wounded military personnel.

1656.   Ginn, L. Holmes, Jr., et al. "Surgery in Division
        Clearing Stations." MIL SURG, 1953 113 (6):443-447.

        In Korea US Division Clearing Stations gradually
        defaulted on their earlier function of providing surgical
        care to the wounded as they sent nearly all wounded to
        mobile surgical hospitals. When the fighting increased in
        October 1952, it became necessary for the division clearing
        stations to resume their earlier function.

1657. Jetland, Robert I. "Medical Service Corps Duties in
        Korea." MIL SURG, 1952 110 (5):350-353.

        A US Army doctor describes his September 1950 activities
        as a liaison officer with a 200-bed Mobile Field Red
        Cross Hospital offered to the UN Command by Sweden. Tells
        of equipping the hospital, administering it and maintaining
        patients' records.

1658. Kolansky, Harold, and Richard K. Cole. "Field Hospital
        Neuropsychiatric Service." US ARM FOR MED J, 1951 2 (10):
        1539-1545.

        Describes the activities of the neuropsychiatric service of
        the 4th Field Hospital which served as the main psychiatric
        treatment center for UN forces in Korea in November and
        December 1950. Tells of personnel assigned, types of
        patients, treatment and disposition.

1659. "Korean Medical Care." MIL SURG, 1951 108 (1):13-15.

        Observations of the Surgeon General, US Department of
        Army after a late 1950 visit to Korea to observe combat
        medical service. Looks at such things as efficiency of
        mobile surgical hospitals, treatment of diseases,
        effectiveness of the preventive medicine program, high
        sense of professionalism of medical personnel and research
        activity.

1660. Marsh, Walter. "Army Surgical Hospitals at Work in
        Korea." ARMY INFO DIG, 1953 8 (8):48-52.

        Traces the utilization and evolution of Army Surgical
        Hospitals in the Korean conflict from the first month of
        the war, when three were operational, until the spring of
        1953 when five were functioning. These hospitals which
        were usually located ten to twenty miles behind the
        front lines did most of the major surgery required by
        combat casualties.

1661. Miller, Lois, and James Monahan. "Veterans' Medicine:
        Back in the Doldrums." READ DIG, 1951 58 (350):89-93.

        Claims that the Veterans' Administration medical program
        is not capable of meeting the needs of WWII veterans and
        providing adequate care for the growing number of Korean
        casualties because of bureaucratic bungling between 1948
        and 1950.

1662. Montross, Lynn. "They Make Men Whole Again." MARINE
        CORPS GAZ, 1952 36 (12):42-49.

        Describes the role of the Medical Battalion and chaplains
        in meeting the medical and religious needs of US Marines
        in Korea.

1663.   Newbold, William G. "Trans-Medic Team." MIL SURG,
        1953 113 (3):208-211.

        Extremely interesting article on the eight hospital
        trains operated in Korea by the US Army. The 3rd
        Transportation Military Railway Service and 8138th AV
        Hospital Train Evacuation Service united to provide
        this medical evacuation service. Tells of the services
        provided on the trains and the support units that keep
        them going.

1664.   Thornton, W.H. "The 24th Division Medical Battalion
        in Korea." MIL SURG, 1951 109 (1):11-19.

        Traces the activities of the 24th Division Medical
        Battalion during the first two months of the war. Details
        the movement of the unit from its headquarters in Japan to
        Korea, operations at Taejon and its actions in the retreat
        back to Pusan. Discusses problems encountered and the
        responses to them.

1665.   Von Buskirk, Kryder E. "The Mobile Army Surgical
        Hospital." MIL SURG, 1953 113 (1):27-31.

        In-depth study of a US Mobile Army Surgical Hospital,
        the 8076th MASH, in Korea. Includes a look at its
        organizaton, function, source of patients and the way the
        hospital functioned.

                        C. TREATMENT

                    1. PHYSICAL INJURIES

1666.   Beecher, Henry K. "Field Use of Methadone and Levo-
        Iso-Methadone in a Combat Zone." US ARM FOR MED J, 1951
        2 (9):1269-1275.

        Describes field testing of methadones to see if they would
        be as effective a pain-relieving agent as morphine.
        Testing was done at a field hospital at Hamhung, North Korea,
        during the Chosin Reservoir operation and the Tokyo Army
        Hospital. The new agents were found to be as effective as
        morphine.

1667.   Bell, Luther G., et al. "Frostbite in Korean Casualties."
        US ARM FOR MED J, 1952 3 (1):35-42.

        During the massive US retreat in the Chosin Reservoir
        operation in late 1950, American soldiers suffered numerous
        casualties due to frostbite. This study examined 150 of
        those victims and drew conclusions on such things as
        causative factors, initial and late symptoms, and initial
        and late treatment.

1668. Blake, Hu A., et al. "Recent Experiences in the
       Treatment of War Wounds of the Chest." US ARMY FOR MED J,
       1951 2 (6):861-870.

       Written for the members of the medical profession, this
       article details the treatment utilized in the field and
       zone of interior for nearly 300 US servicemen receiving
       thoracic injuries during the first seven months of
       fighting in Korea.

1669. Brown, Robert B. "Chest Surgery in the Korean
       Campaign." MIL SURG, 1953 112 (6):417-423.

       Observations and data dealing with the treatment of
       chest wounds on a US Navy hospital ship. Written
       primarily for medical personnel but does make reference
       to the value of body armor being worn by Marines in
       combat.

1670. Clark, Gale. "Craniotomies in Korea." US ARM FOR MED
       J, 1951 2 (8):1235-1238.

       Enumerates the major problems encountered in primary
       craniotomies performed by US medical officers on the
       hospital ship, USS CONSOLATION, from September 1950
       to May 1951.

1671. Clarke, Burdick G. "Early Management for War Wounds
       of the Genitourinary Organs." US ARM FOR MED J, 1951
       2 (6):871-882.

       While focusing on methods of medical treatment of soldiers
       suffering kidney, ureter and bladder wounds, this article
       covers the major goals of medical personnel on the front
       lines.

1672. Cowie, William K. "Casualty? Be Sure!" MARINE CORPS
       GAZ, 1953 37 (4):36-39.

       Sets forth the procedures used by the Marines to report
       combat casualties in Korea.

1673. Crouch, Robert D., et al. "Nongonococcal Urethritus
       in Korean Rotatees." US ARMY FOR MED J, 1953 4 (8):
       1159-1165.

       Emphasizes the importance of and prevalence of the
       veneral disease, nongonorrheal urethritis, among US
       military personnel serving in Korea. Also relates the
       ways of diagnosing and treating the disease.

1674. Douglas, William M. "Management of Korean Frostbite
       Cases." MIL SURG, 1952 110 (5):333-337.

       Details the medical treatment used in the treatment of US
       Army frostbite victims in the Korean War. While written for

physicians, it does contain some accounts of the experiences
of soldiers suffering from frostbite.

1675. Farago, Peter J. "Clinical Aspects of Cold Injury."
        MIL SURG, 1952 110 (4):249-253.

        While this article is designed for medical doctors faced
        with frostbite victims, it does discuss the impact of
        extremely cold weather on US Army soldiers serving in
        Korea in the winter of 1950-1951. Tells where and how
        frostbite victims were treated.

1676. Fox, Ted. "Division Combat Medical Service." MIL
        SURG, 1951 108 (5):427-429.

        Observations of a US Army surgeon, with the 25th Division,
        on providing medical aid in the crossing of the Han River.
        Tells of the need for military personnel accompanying assault
        troops, problems of supply and evacuation of the wounded.

1677. Higgins, Alton R., et al. "The Effect of Cortisone on
        Frostbite Injury." US ARMY FOR MED J, 1952 3 (3):369-372.

        Tells of a very limited study to see the effect of
        cortisone on frostbite injuries and concludes there is no
        significant impact. Tells of the reasons for frostbite,
        describes sensations, degrees of severity and consequences.

1678. Hinman, Frederick J., and Mary C. Horak. "Diet and High
        Altitude Flying in Korea." AIR UNIV Q R, 1953 6 (2):57-63.

        During the war a number of fighter interceptor pilots
        flying at altitudes above 35,000 feet complained of severe
        abdominal pains which adversely affected their performance.
        Flight surgeons decided to change the diet by reducing
        gas-producing foods. This dietary change resulted in a
        marked improvement in the combat efficiency of the pilots.
        Describes the testing of the specimen squadron and regular
        squadrons.

1679. Irwin, John B. "Treatment of Frostbite of Toes."
        US ARM FOR MED J, 1951 2 (8):1161-1163.

        Explains how the 3rd Battalion, 15th Infantry Regiment
        treated frostbite victims in Korea. In very few cases
        were those affected evacuated; thus, the strength of
        the unit was virtually unaltered. This unit's
        hospitalized frostbite victims averaged only twenty days
        in the hospital while those evacuated out of Korea
        averaged forty-five days.

1680. Kalischer, Peter. "Winter Warfare." COLLIER'S, 1953
        131 (6):11-13.

        During the winter of 1950-51 more than 6,000 US troops

were hospitalized for frostbite or exposure and 20% of the
soldiers treated at aid stations had cold injuries. Cold
knocked out more troops than did the enemy. This occurred
because adequate clothing and cold weather items like
antifreeze for vehicles were not provided. Tells of newly
developed winter clothing and equipment.

1681. King, J.H. "Army Opthalmology, Past and Present."
       MIL SURG, 1953 112 (2):88-96.

       A survey of opthalmology in the US Army from the
       Revolutionary War on with the bulk of the information on the
       Korean War experience. Details the treatment of soldiers
       receiving eye injuries in combat. Statistics through June 1,
       1952.

1682. KOREAN WAR ERA CASUALTIES, 1950-1958. Columbus, OH:
       Division of Soldier's Claims, 1971.

       Register of Ohio soldiers killed in the Korean War, along
       with those dying of non-battle causes and those dying later
       as a result of the hostilities.

1683. Kupperman, Karen O. "Apathy and Death in Early Jamestown."
       J AM HIST, 1979 66 (1):24-40.

       Compares prisoner of war camps in Korea and the early
       settlement in Jamestown to show the relationship between
       nutritional diseases and psychological factors both of
       which lead to a withdrawal from life. Interesting
       relationship between malnutrition and the impact it has
       on prisoner-of-war behavior.

1684. LIST OF KOREAN WAR DEATHS, 1950-1953. Seoul: UN Korean
       War Allies Association, 1978.

       This multi-volume work contains the names of individuals
       in the UN Command who were killed in the conflict. Volumes
       cover particular nations with several volumes covering
       US Army, Navy, Marine Corps and Air Force dead. All
       participating UN nations are included.

1685. Meirowsky, Arnold M. NEUROLOGICAL SURGERY OF TRAUMA.
       Washington: Government Printing Office, 1965.

       Details the progress made in neurological surgery by
       US Army doctors in Korea. Written for people in the
       medical field not laymen. Covers diagnostic procedures,
       resuscitation, treatment and rehabilitation of those
       receiving severe head wounds.

1686. Orr, Kenneth D., and David C. Fainer. "Cold Injuries
       With Emphasis on Frostbite." US ARM FOR MED J, 1952
       3 (1):95-103.

       A preliminary report on the treatment of US soldiers

suffering cold injuries in Korea from December 1950 to April 1951. Examines the activities of 4,216 such victims treated at the Osaka Army Hospital in Japan. In discussing the problem one realizes the severity of the cold weather.

1687. Pleasants, John E. "Dental Service in an Infantry Division." US ARMY FOR MED J, 1952 3 (7):1089-1094.

A dental officer who spent eleven months with combat troops of the 7th Infantry Division early in the Korean War and another year in Korea describes the operations of a Division Dental Section. Helps explain the importance of proper dental care for frontline soldiers.

1688. Radke, Ryle A. "Incidence of Amebiasis in Korean Veterans." US ARM FOR MED J, 1952 3 (2):323.

Findings of a limited study which concludes that amebiasis, an infection of the colon, is a disease of military significance in the Korean campaign.

1689. Reister, Frank A. BATTLE CASUALTIES AND MEDICAL STATISTICS: US ARMY EXPERIENCE IN THE KOREAN WAR. Washington: Government Printing Office, 1973.

Extensive statistics and casualties suffered by American troops in Korea plus an explanation of medical practices and sanitary affairs at the front.

1690. Robinette, C.D., et al. "Effects Upon Health of Occupational Exposure to Microware Radiation (Radar)." AM J EPID, 1980 112 (1):39-53.

A safety study of nearly 20,000 US servicemen, primarily navy, who received maximum exposure to radar equipment during the Korean War. Conclusion is that there were no adverse effects.

1691. Segal, Henry A. "Iatrogenic Disease in Soldiers." US ARMY FOR MED J, 1953 4 (1):49-60.

Examines iatrogenic disease which is any disorder induced, intensified or prolonged in a patient because of the physician's failure to deal with the patient properly, as it applied to US military personnel in Korea. Looks at impact of anxiety, somatization-reaction, the inadequate or immature soldier and oversympathy of the medical officer.

1692. Shaw, Christopher C. "The National Blood Program." US NAVAL INST PROC, 1953 79 (1):51-57.

Traces the development of the American Red Cross program to provide blood in time of emergency. Efforts got under-

way in the late 1930's and were expanded during WWII only
to fall away to nothing in the post-war years. In 1947
the Red Cross established a National Blood Program which
really became operational because of the war in Korea.
Describes the organization, operations and accomplishments
of the program during the first two years of the Korean
War.

1693. Sivertson, Julian B. "Smallpox." US ARM FOR MED J,
       1952 3 (12):1777-1785.

       Between October 1950 and April 1951, twenty-one patients
       with smallpox were seen at a station hospital in Korea
       and eight died. Thirteen who contacted the disease were
       US soldiers and all had been vaccinated, but it had not
       taken. Describes the classification of the disease among
       those treated.

1694. Snyder, Francis C. "Wartime Dentistry." MIL SURG, 1953
       112 (3):182-189.

       Excellent study of dentistry services offered in the field
       during the Korean War. The author recounts his experiences
       as a dentist with the 1st Marine Division from July 1951
       through July 1952. Describes the functioning of such groups
       as: Mobile Dental Units; Division Dental Units and Division
       Prosthetic Clinic.

1695. Soderberg, Bernard N. "Facial Wounds in Korean Casualties."
       US ARM FOR MED J, 1951 2 (2):171-182.

       Examines some of the first US casualties from the Korean
       conflict having wounds about the face, mouth and jaw.
       Reviews the medical treatment of those suffering serious
       facial lesions from the front line through treatment at
       stateside military hospitals. Written primarily for
       medical personnel. Illustrations.

1696. Sproul, M.T. "A Report of the Distribution of Whole
       Blood to the Pacific Theater." US ARM FOR MED J, 1951
       2 (2):293-296.

       Sets forth the practices and procedures used to collect
       and distribute whole blood to members of the US Armed
       Forces in Korea. Starts with the collection of blood by
       the American Red Cross and follows it through to its use
       in the field.

1697. "United States War Losses in Korea." US ARM FOR MED J,
       1953 4 (9):1288-1290.

       An excellent statistical study on US battle deaths in the
       Korean War. Breaks down such categories as rates by branch
       of service, comparisons with WWII, and death rates from non-
       battle causes, including disease.

1698.   Waln, Nora. "The Wounded." SAT EVE POST, 1950 223
           (13):32-33, 144-146.

           Describes the care and treatment of wounded US Marines of
           the 1st Provisional Brigade at a battalion aid station near
           Masan during the early weeks of the fighting.

1699.   White, William L. BACK DOWN THE RIDGE. New York:
           Harcourt, 1953.

           Examines medical treatment of US soldiers seriously
           wounded on the Korean war front. Using interviews of
           the victims, it traces what happened from the time the
           individual was hit through his evacuation and treatment
           stateside. Shows how medical advances saved many who
           would have died in earlier wars.

1700.   Witsell, Edward F. "The Casualty Report Tells the
           Story." ARMY INFO DIG, 1950 5 (11):7-10.

           Explains the procedures for and importance of preparing
           accurate casualty lists and releasing them as quickly as
           possible. Relates the problems which the Pentagon
           encountered in gathering and disseminating such informa-
           tion. An excellent how-to piece for all nations since no
           country did a better job in handling casualty information
           than the US.

1701.   Wright, Paul E., and James H. Braatz. "Bombardier's
           Palsy." US ARM FOR MED J, 1953 4 (9):1359-1361.

           Bombardier's palsy was a term applied to an occupational
           illness characterized by a paralysis of muscles which
           resulted in foot drop. In Korea the malady occurred only
           in US Air Force bombardiers in the B-26 light bombers
           because that was the only aircraft in which a kneeling
           rather than a sitting position was utilized.

                         2. PSYCHOLOGICAL PROBLEMS

1702.   Arthur, Ransom J. "Reflections on Military Psychiatry."
           AM J PSY, 1978 135 July Supplement: 2-7.

           Traces developments in military psychiatry in 20th century
           US wars, including Korea. Utilizing lessons learned in the
           World Wars, the US Army utilized the techniques of early
           treatment in a setting close to the front followed by a
           relatively rapid return to duty, frequently within 24-48
           hours.

1703.   Drury, Michael. "Treat 'Em Up Front and Treat 'Em
           Early." COLLIER'S, 1952 130 (18):20-23.

Examines the use of US Army psychiatrists to treat
neuro-psychiatric casualties at the front lines in
Korea. Practice was to give them rest, not
hospitalization. This approach allegedly led to
recovery for 98% of shock victims.

1704. Edwards, Robert M., and Donald B. Peterson. "Korea:
       Current Psychiatric Procedure and Communication in the
       Combat Theater." AM J PSY, 1954 110 (10):721-724.

       Reveals the contribution of military psychiatry to the
       development of a firmer discipline designed to prevent
       manpower loss on the battle front in the Korean War.
       Discusses the function of the division psychiatrist.
       Includes some case studies.

1705. "First-Aid Post: Mental." TIME, 1951 58 (19):55-56.

       Traces several days in the life of a combat psychiatrist
       with the US 1st Cavalry Division. Exhibits importance
       of the Army's philosophy that soldiers suffering combat
       exhaustion should be sent forward to the front lines as
       quickly as feasible.

1706. Glass, Albert J. "Combat Exhaustion." US ARMY FOR
       MED J, 1951 2 (10):1471-1478.

       Uses the US experience in Korea to clarify the concept of
       combat exhaustion (a temporary psychological failure of the
       soldier to function adequately in a combat situation) and
       explain its complex cause, which frequently includes
       physical factors. Tells how the Chinese Communists would
       use fear tactics to bring on combat exhaustion.

1707. Glass, Albert J. "Preventive Psychiatry In The Combat
       Zone." MIL R, 1953 33 (7):9-17.

       Claims that if the attention of combat and medical officers
       is focused on preventive psychiatry, benefits in combat
       efficiency are inevitable. Maintains that a soldier's
       performance is determined by the struggle in which personality,
       physical stature, training, group unity and leadership are
       opposed to the effect of battle fear.

1708. Glass, Albert J. "Psychiatry in the Korean Campaign."
       US ARM FOR MED J, 1953 4 (10):1387-1401 and 1953 4 (11):
       1563-1583.

       An excellent two-part study of the creation and evolution
       of the psychiatric program established by the Far East
       Command during the first fifteen months of the war. Tells
       of organizational changes and the conditions that led to
       those changes.

1709. Glass, Albert J. "Psychotherapy in the Combat Zone."
       AM J PSY, 1954 110 (10):725-731.

Recaps developments in psychotherapy in the combat zones
during the World Wars and Korean conflict. In the latter
war, treatment in the battle zone by general medical officers
proved very effective and only in extreme cases were
personnel evacuated. Furthermore, psychiatrists' performances
in the handling of combat cases improved as they moved closer
to the front lines since they were better able to understand the
stresses that the soldiers were experiencing.

1710. Koontz, Amos R. "Psychiatry in the Korean War." MIL
        SURG, 1950 107 (6):444-445.

Expresses concern that many US soldiers might succumb to a
"psychiatric" escape from combat duty in Korea. The reasons
for concern are that we have a nation of men who feel
they owe the country nothing and that too much attention
has been focused on people with minor psychiatric
conditions. Critical of the separation of psychiatry
from departments of medicine.

1711. Lifton, Robert J. "Psychotherapy With Combat Flyers."
        US ARM FOR MED J, 1953 4 (4):525-532.

Contends that psychiatric difficulties among US Air Force
combat flyers in Korea fall into three areas: anxiety
reactions during early missions; undue external stress in
the course of the combat tour; and tension related to the
final ten or fifteen missions.

1712. Morgan, Ralph W. "Psychiatric Social Work in a Combat
        Zone." US ARM FOR MED J, 1953 4 (6):847-856.

A US Army Medical Corps Officer reflects on his 1951
experience at an evacuation hospital in Korea and concludes
that the function of a social caseworker in a psychiatric
setting in a combat zone is essentially the same as in
other medical settings. Uses examples in working with US
soldiers to back up his argument.

1713. Moskos, Charles C., Jr. THE AMERICAN ENLISTED MAN.
        New York: Sage, 1970.

Field observations of US forces serving overseas note
that in Korea medical personnel identified a "short
termer's syndrome" whereby combatants began to exhibit
various symptoms of stress as they approach the time that
they were scheduled to rotate back to the states. This
characteristic was not tied to the number of days in
combat.

1714. Ranson, Stephen W. "Psychiatric Treatment in Combat
        Areas." US ARM FOR MED J, 1950 1 (12):1379-1397.

Sets forth the methods of handling psychiatric casualties

among American combat personnel in the Korean War. Discusses
treatment within the combat unit at the battalion aid station,
division clearing station and army neuropsychiatric treatment
station.

1715.   Schwartz, Lionel A., and Eugene R. Inwood. "Psychiatric
        Casualties Evacuated From Korea." US ARMY FOR MED J, 1952
        3 (7):991-1002.

        A study of US Army and Air Force personnel who experienced
        serious psychological problems while fighting in Korea and
        thus had to be hospitalized for more than 120 days. Sixty
        patients were involved in the study which examined such
        things as length of time in service, in Korea, in front line
        combat, age, branch of service and rank. Of many pre-
        cipitating causes uncovered, seeing a buddy killed or
        wounded or having a shell land nearby were by far the
        leading factors.

                        D.   MEDICAL PERSONNEL

1716.   Armstrong, O.K. "The GI's Guardian Angel." READ DIG,
        1952 60 (357):135-138.

        Activities of US military nurses serving near the front
        lines in Korea. Focuses on the 8054th Evacuation Hospital,
        composed of 12 nurses and 11 doctors which was one of the
        first medical units on the scene. Tells of their service
        in the early weeks of fighting.

1717.   Atkins, John, et al. "Fighting Medics." COM FOR J,
        1952 2 (12):17, 29.

        Firsthand account of a May 27, 1951, Chinese Communist
        attack on the Medical Company, 21st Infantry. Although
        inadequately armed, a handful of medics joined with a
        guard force of twenty men to repel the attack.

1718.   Aynes, Edith A. FROM NIGHTINGALE TO EAGLE: AN ARMY
        NURSE'S HISTORY. Englewood Cliffs, NJ: Prentice, 1973.

        A US Army nurse traces her experiences from the pre-WWII
        years into the Korean War and relates a number of the changes
        that were brought about for the profession as a result of the
        Korean experience. Tells of the organization and activities
        of US Army Hospitals in Japan in 1950-1951.

1719.   Brzezinski, Stanley D. "My Dental Duty With the US
        Marines in Korea." MIL SURG, 1952 110 (3):191-194.

        Reflections of a US Navy dentist on his duties and
        experiences while serving with a Marine field medical
        unit in Korea from September 1950 through May 1951.
        Good descriptions of field hospital activities.

1720. Detzer, Karl. "The Nurse Who Forgot Fear." READ DIG,
          1952 60 (358):75-78.

          US Army nurse Jonita R. Bonham was on a transport plane
          going from Japan to Korea which went down at sea shortly
          after take-off. Although badly injured she assisted
          seventeen soldiers in getting aboard a life raft that she
          activated. Condensed from EVERYWOMAN'S MAGAZINE, February
          1952.

1721. Dick, Everett N. "The Adventist Medical Cadet Corps
          As Seen By Its Founder." ADV HERT, 1974 1 (2):18-27.

          The Adventist Medical Corps was established prior to WWII
          to provide Adventist boys with training to serve in the
          Medical Corps so they could serve their country but not
          have to bear arms. The group served in WWII and the Korean
          War thus serving a real military need.

1722. "Effects of Mobilization on 1950-1951 Residents and
          Interns at Approved Nonmilitary Hospitals." US ARM FOR
          MED J, 1952 3 (3):389-390.

          Report on the manpower pool of US physician in the first
          eight months of the Korean War as its effect upon both
          military and civilian doctors. Tells of Public Law 779, the
          "doctor-draft" law and how it worked.

1723. Ely, Helen. "The Most Wounded, the Most Sick, the
          Most Tired." READ DIG, 1951 58 (350):9-10.

          A US Air Force flight nurse recounts her experience in
          flying the sick and wounded US soldiers out of Korea during
          the first eight months of the war. Nearly 20,000 men were
          evacuated in that period, and the role of military nurses
          in that undertaking is explained. Condensed from MCCALL'S,
          March 1951.

1724. Engle, Eloise. MEDIC. New York: Day, 1967.

          This history of US medical personnel in the Army, Navy and
          Air Force in time of war and peace includes a section on
          the activities of medics during the Korean War.

1725. Fielding, Fred J. "About the Army Medical Service:
          Operation Nav Med." US ARMY FOR MED J, 1951 2 (2):
          335-340.

          The early months of the Korean War saw the US Army facing
          a serious shortage of medical doctors. To meet that essential
          need the Army requested and, in October 1950, received 570
          naval medical officers for temporary duty with the army.
          This explains the drafting, processing, orientation and

assigning of these navy doctors at Brooke Medical Center in Texas.

1726. Fielding, Fred J. "Naval Reserve Physicians Serve With Army." MIL SURG, 1951 109 (1):35-36.

A severe shortage of US Army doctors in the early months of the war forced the Secretary of Defense to call 570 Navy doctors to active duty for temporary service with the Army. Describes the processing, orientation and assigning of the doctors.

1727. Friedrich, R.H. "Conscription of Dental Personnel." MIL SURG, 1953 113 (2):79-83.

Criticizes the legislation and procedures of the US government in securing dentists for the armed forces during the Korean War. Describes the provision of Public Law 779 and the priority system.

1728. Fugate, Robert T. "Hey Doc." LEATHERNECK, 1953 36 (5):16-20.

Describes the demands placed on a Navy medical corpsman serving in Korea with Marine units at the front.

1729. Harris, John F. "Practice of Field Medicine on Operation 'Killer.'" MIL SURG, 1951 109 (6):683-688.

A Regimental Surgeon, 9th Infantry, 2nd Infantry Division describes the life of a combat surgeon traveling just two or three miles behind an advancing infantry force during heavy battle with Communist forces in a February 1951 operation. Tells of the bitter fighting, field treatment and means of evacuation.

1730. Kalischer, Peter. "Doctor Commando." COLLIER'S, 1951 128 (12):28, 60-64.

Story of US Brigadier General Crawford F. Sams, a medical doctor who landed behind enemy lines in March 1951 to determine the truth of reports that bubonic plague--"the black death"--was running rampant in North Korea. If so, US troops and South Korean civilians would have to be vaccinated. Sams determined it was not the plague. For his mission the General received the Distinguished Service Cross.

1731. Karig, Walter. "The Navy's Men of Mercy." CORONET, 1951 29 (5):104-108.

Lauds the medical teamwork being used in Korea to evacuate and save wounded US servicemen. Follows the trail of a wounded marine from the time he got hit to his evacuation, operation on the Navy Hospital Ship, CONSOLATION, and flight to a hospital in Japan--all within twenty-four hours.

1732.   Lederer, William J. "They Were the Bravest." READ DIG,
        1951 58 (347):36-38.

        Condensed from THIS WEEK magazine, December 10, 1950,
        this account tells of the heroic acts and valuable service
        performed by Army medics and Navy hospital corpsmen on the
        front lines of Korea.

1733.   Marlette, Robert H. "Dental Service in Korea." US ARMY
        FOR MED J, 1951 2 (12):1811-1814.

        A regimental dental surgeon with the US 5th regimental
        combat team tells of the problems and satisfactions that
        came with operating a dental clinic three miles behind the
        front lines in the early months of 1951.

1734.   Mason, James B. "The Army Medical Service Reserve
        Program." MIL SURG, 1952 111 (4):246-252.

        Examines the Armed Forces Reserve Act of 1952 in general
        and its specific provisions and implications for the US
        Army Medical Service Reserve Program.

1735.   "Navy Flight Nurses Care for Wounded." NAV AVI N,
        1951 August:19-23.

        Describes the training and duties of Navy and Air Force
        nurses involved in the air evacuation of battlefield
        casualties in Korea.

1736.   Phillips, Phillip B. "The Navy's Medical Problem."
        US NAVAL INST PROC, 1955 81 (4):391-399.

        Looks at the problem of retention of career naval officers
        in the Medical Corps between 1945 and 1953. What was a
        serious problem before the Korean War became critical when
        the fighting began because the shortage led to a refusal to
        accept resignations, which in turn kept young doctors from
        entering the service for fear that they might not be able
        to get out. Calls for more money and benefits to make the
        military doctor's position comparable to the civilian
        sector.

1737.   Pole, Eleanor C. "Flight Nursing in the Pacific With
        Military Air Transport Service." MIL SURG, 1951 109 (6):
        702-706.

        Describes the activities of the Military Air Transport
        Service's 1453rd Medical Air Evacuation Squadron as it
        returned wounded soldiers from Korea and Japan to the US.

1738.   Pugh, Lamont. "Notes From the Navy's Medical Log."
        MIL SURG, 1952 110 (1):14-17.

Describes the contributions of US Navy doctors to the conflict in Korea during the first fifteen months of fighting. During the period 935 doctors, 210 dentists and 417 nurses from the Navy served in the Korean theater. Discusses innovations such as a three-man surgical team, ships with epidemic control units, improved evacuation and a new blood collecting and shipment program.

1739. Robinson, Paul I. "About the Army Medical Service." US ARM FOR MED J, 1950 1 (11):1359-1365.

Contains two parts, one dealing with the drafting of Doctors of Medicine, Dentistry and Veterinary Medicine, and a second examining the US Medical Service in action during the first few weeks of the fighting in Korea.

1740. Robinson, Paul I. "About the Army Medical Service: Officer Medical Procurement." US ARMY FOR MED J, 1951 2 (3):513-515.

Relates the problem of securing properly trained medical personnel for the US Armed Forces early in the Korean War. Focuses especially on the difficulty of securing nurses.

1741. Robinson, Paul I. "About the Army Medical Service: The Physician in the Present Emergency." US ARMY FOR MED J, 1951 2 (4):691-695.

Sets forth the problems presented by the shortage of US Armed Forces doctors in the early months of the Korean War and explains why Congress passed legislation to solve that problem. Explains the law and the difficulties in carrying it out. Concludes the US Army is doing an excellent job of meeting its medical responsibilities at the battle front.

1742. Robinson, Paul I. "About the Army Medical Service: Procurement of Medical Officers." US ARM FOR MED J, 1951 2 (5):843-845.

Tells how the US Army secured doctors for the Regular Army Medical Corps in the early months of the Korean War. Talks of the benefits of such service to medical officers and emphasizes the increased opportunities for medical research by individuals in the army.

1743. Scoles, Peter S. "Anecdotes of a Combat Medic." MIL SURG, 1952 110 (5):356-358.

A US Medical Corps Officer serving in the 7th Cavalry recalls some experiences early in the Korean War. Observations on the battles at Pyongyang, Taegu, Naktong River and Pakchon.

1744. Smith, Tony S. "Our Wounded Win a Home Battle."
       CORONET, 1951 29 (6):59-63.

       Praises Army doctors and politicians whose efforts led
       to a major upgrading of Army Hospitals in the early months
       of the war. Blames the bad initial conditions at the
       facilities on the 1949-1950 economy drive of then-Secretary
       of Defense Louis Johnson. Focuses on Camp Atterbury,
       Indiana, as an example of the impact of false economy.

1745. Spiegel, Frederick S. "Problems of the Flight Surgeon
       in Korea." US ARM FOR MED J, 1953 4 (9):1321-1324.

       Focuses on the medical and nonmedical difficulties that
       a flight surgeon faced in serving with US Air Force units
       in Korea but does an excellent job of explaining combat
       tours for various types of pilots or crew members and the
       importance of such factors on morale.

1746. Watts, J.C. SURGEON AT WAR. London: Allen, 1955.

       Experiences of a British surgeon who saw a great deal of
       front line duty during WWII and Korea. Considerable
       anatomical descriptions interspersed with interesting
       anecdotes about medicine at the front.

                        E. MEDICAL ADVANCES

1747. Armstrong, George E. "Medical Advances in Korea."
       ARMY INFO DIG, 1952 7 (6):21-26.

       Describes the job that the Army Medical Service did in
       combating disease in the Korean War. Notes that while the
       enemy and refugees suffered considerably from disease, US
       soldiers did not, primarily because of research leading
       to the development of nutritionally sound field rations
       and the use of individual water sterilization. Also
       covers prevention of malaria, typhoid and cholera.
       Includes discussion of the role of mobile surgical
       hospitals.

1748. Armstrong, George E. "Military Medicine in Korea."
       MIL SURG, 1952 110 (1):8-14.

       The US Army's Surgeon General notes the significant
       contributions made on the medical front in Korea by UN
       contributors such as Sweden, Norway, Britain, India,
       and Denmark before examining US activities. Discusses
       the medical accomplishments and explains what makes them
       possible. Looks at battlefield treatment, evacuation,
       laboratory support, use and delivery of blood and
       treatment of diseases.

1749. Carle, Donald E. "Medical Experiences in Korea."
      US ARMY FOR MED J, 1951 2 (11):1623-1630.

      Selected observations of the Second Infantry Division
      Surgeon on the Army Medical Service as it functioned in
      the first seven months of the Korean War. Covers such
      topics as organization and equipment, field training,
      cold weather problems, use of helicopters, evacuation
      difficulties and logistical support.

1750. Hering, H.C. "Combat Medical Practice." MIL SURG,
      1952 110 (2):102-106.

      Praises the US medical accomplishments in Korea and
      attributes them primarily to the joint efforts of the
      three services and the care provided by the highly
      mobile medical units which gave definitive surgical
      care in close support of fighting forces. Uses medical
      support given to the First Marine Division during the
      December 1950 withdrawal from the Chosin Reservoir as
      an example.

1751. Link, Mae M. "Development of the Armed Services
      Blood, Blood Derivatives and Plasma Expanders
      Program." US ARM FOR MED J, 1953 4 (8):1221-1225.

      Although the US Department of Defense had studied blood
      needs for war before the outbreak of war in Korea, that
      conflict created an immediate need. Consequently, a
      whole blood program was established for the Far East
      Command and blood donor recruitment was stepped up.
      Those programs were most effective.

1752. Ludwig, Verle E. "Korea's Contribution to Medicine."
      MARINE CORPS GAZ, 1955 39 (6):40-43.

      Stresses the positive medical benefits that resulted from
      the war in Korea. Advances in evacuation, contributions of
      field hospitals and techniques of treatment developed to
      treat combat casualties will have far-reaching effects.

1753. US Army, Walter Reed Institute of Research. RECENT
      ADVANCES IN MEDICINE AND SURGERY BASED ON PROFESSIONAL
      MEDICAL EXPERIENCES IN JAPAN AND KOREA, 1950-1953.
      Washington: Government Printing Office, 1955.

      Medically-oriented publication examines methods of
      treatment and surgery that were developed or significantly
      altered as a result of experiences gained at US field
      hospitals in Korea and fixed installations in Japan.

XVI. PRISONERS OF WAR
A. US-UN PRISONERS

1. CONDITIONS

1754. Bess, Demaree. "The Prisoner Stole the Show in Korea."
       SAT EVE POST, 1952 225 (18):36-37, 52-55.

       Traces the POW issue in peace negotiations from the time
       they began, on July 10, 1951, until the summer of 1952.
       Critical of the Truman Administration for letting the issue
       become the most important issue of settlement. Maintains the
       communists engineered the Koje Camp uprisings to divert
       attention from their inhumane treatment of UN POW's.

1755. Blair, Clay, Jr. BEYOND COURAGE. New York: McKay, 1955.

       Lively account of what happened to four US pilots shot down
       behind enemy lines.

1756. Bouscaren, Anthony T. "Korea, Test of American Education."
       CAT WORLD, 1956 183 (4):24-27.

       Critical of the conduct of American POW's in Korea and
       contends the cause lies in the failure of American education
       to teach proper values.

1757. Brown, Michael D. "A Prisoner of War Speaks." KOREAN SUR,
       1954 3 (1):3-5.

       Brief account of the captivity of Kim Chang Su, Commander
       of the 2nd Bn, 7th Regiment, 6th ROK Division, captured early
       in the war near Kochon, North Korea, and held captive for
       thirty-three months. Tells of his experience at three
       different POW camps, including those at Usi and Uiju.

1758. Brown, Wallace L. THE ENDLESS HOURS: MY TWO AND A HALF
       YEARS AS A PRISONER OF THE CHINESE COMMUNISTS. New York:
       Norton, 1961.

       Personal account of the capture and confinement of a US Air
       Force Lieutenant who was captured in January 1953 and held in
       a Peking prison.

1759. Brumbaugh, Thoburn T. MY MARKS AND SCARS I CARRY.
       New York: Friendship, 1969.

The true story of Dr. Ernst Keisch an American Methodist missionary who was captured by the North Koreans shortly after war broke out and died in a POW camp in June 1951.

1760. Chinese People's Committee for World Peace. SHALL BROTHERS BE. Peking: Foreign Languages Press, 1952.

Propaganda piece made up of accounts allegedly by American and British POW's claiming they received favorable treatment at the hands of Chinese Communists and North Korea while being held prisoner.

1761. Colebrook, Joan. "Prisoners of War." COMM, 1974 57 (1):30-37.

Looks at the treatment of US prisoners of war in Korea and Vietnam and American public opinion on prisoners in the period from 1950 through 1974.

1762. Condron, Andrew M., Richard G. Corden, and Larance V. Sullivan, eds. THINKING SOLDIERS. Peking: New World, 1955.

The editors are three US servicemen, two Army and one Marine, who defected to the Chinese Communists. The work is allegedly a collection of articles written by American prisoners of war for camp magazines. Includes articles on combat and prisoner experiences. Subtle but mild Communist propaganda.

1763. Crosbie, Philip. MARCH TILL THEY DIE. Westminster, MD: Newman, 1956.

Father Crosbie, an Australian and a member of the Society of St. Columbian, relates the hardships experienced by himself and nearly fifty other civilian prisoners of the Communists in North Korea from July 1950 until May 1953. Very critical of the treatment meted out by his captors. This book was published in Melbourne, Australia, in 1954 (Hawthorn Press) under the title PENCILLING PRISONER.

1764. Crosbie, Philip. THREE WINTERS COLD. Dublin: Browne, 1955.

Father Crosbie, of the Society of St. Columbian, tells of his nearly three years of captivity at the hands of the Communists in North Korea. Arrested near Hongchon and taken to the Yalu River, he was put with fifty other civilian prisoners who were herded around to various locations until their release in May 1953. Tells of cruel and inhumane treatment by his captors.

1765. Cunningham, Cyril. "The Origins and Development of Communist Prisoner-of-War Policies." ROY UNI SER INST J, 1974 119 (1):38-43.

Shows how communist policies on the treatment of POW's
developed along different lines in Europe and Asia. During
the Korean War, Chinese policy differed greatly from that
of Russia as the Chinese followed a "lenient policy" which
permitted those captured to live provided they "accepted"
certain political thinking.

1766. Dean, William F. as told to William L. Worden.
      GENERAL DEAN'S STORY. New York: Viking, 1954.

An account of the capture and confinement of the Commander
of the 24th Infantry Division, General Dean--the highest
ranking US military man to become a prisoner of war in
Korea. Tells of the ordeal of being held captive for
nearly three years. Reflects on life as a prisoner, efforts
to escape, and the enemy's attempt to use psychological
warfare. Dean received the Medal of Honor, a decision
bitterly contested by some military and civilian observers.

1767. Dean, William F. "My Three Years as a Dead Man."
      SAT EVE POST, 1954 226 (30):17-19, 82-88; and the next
      five issues (31-35).

The most famous US prisoner of war during the Korean
conflict, General Dean, tells of the events leading up to
his capture and the thirty-seven months of captivity that
followed.

1768. Deane, Philip, pseudonym (Michael Gigantes).   I WAS A
      CAPTIVE IN KOREA. New York: Norton, 1953.

An account of a British war correspondent's thirty-three
months of captivity by the communists in North Korea. A
vivid recollection of the brutality, as well as acts of
kindness, that characterized life as a prisoner of war.
Recounts some examples of American brutality.

1769. Dowe, Ray M. "A Prisoner Can Profit." ARMY INFO DIG,
      1954 9 (6):41-47.

An infantry lieutenant who spent thirty-four months in
Communist prison camps reflects on the treatment he received,
the enemy's attempt at indoctrination and the Communist sense
of loyalty to the state. He concludes that out of all his
suffering came a deeper appreciation of the American way of
life.

1770. Great Britain Ministry of Defense. TREATMENT OF BRITISH
      PRISONERS OF WAR IN KOREA. London: Her Majesty's
      Stationery Office, 1955.

Indictment of North Korea and Chinese Communist treatment
of British soldiers taken prisoner in Korea. Critical of
physical and psychological abuse which was utilized.

1771.   Harrison, Charles L. "Twice Across the Rainbow." US
        NAVAL INST PROC, 1952 78 (5):515-517.

        Recollections of a US Marine Sergeant who was a POW of the
        Japanese for more than three and a half years during WWII and
        suffered a similar fate for six months at the hands of the
        North Koreans from November 1950 through May 1951. Escape
        for Harrison and eighteen other American prisoners came in
        the confusion caused by a US artillery attack as they were
        being moved from one area of confinement to another.

1772.   Harrison, Thomas D. with Bill Stapleton. "Why Did Some
        GI's Turn Communist?" COLLIER'S, 1953 132 (13):25-28.

        An American pilot who served twenty-seven months in various
        communist POW camps expresses bitterness against those
        prisoners who collaborated with the enemy and those who went
        over to the other side. Notes that 95% of prisoners
        resisted. Tells of inhumane treatment and suffering at camps
        at Chongsong and Pyoktong.

1773.   Heller, Edwin L. "I Thought I'd Never Get Home." SAT
        EVE POST, 1955 228 (8):17-19; 228 (9):34-35.

        Recollections of a US Air Force pilot whose F-86E aircraft
        was shot down in January 1953, and who was taken prisoner.
        He remained a POW of the Chinese Communists until his
        release in 1955.

1774.   "How Reds Tortured US Prisoners." US NEWS W R, 1955
        39 (10):26-27.

        Tells of the inhumane treatment of US prisoners of war at
        the hands of the Red Chinese. Gives accounts of beatings,
        torture and starvation which were experienced by eleven
        recently released airmen.

1775.   Jones, Francis S. NO RICE FOR REBELS. London: Bodley
        Head, 1956.

        Account of a Sergeant Matthews of the Gloucester Regiment
        who was taken prisoner of war by the Chinese Communists.
        Relates the harsh treatment, physical and psychological,
        he experienced at the hands of his captors.

1776.   Jones, Thomas T. "Two Hundred Miles to Freedom."
        MIL ENG, 1951 43 (295):351-354.

        A US Army Engineer taken prisoner in September 1950 and
        held prisoner for twenty-one days before escaping tells of
        his capture, treatment by the enemy, physical suffering and
        200-mile trek to freedom.

1777.   Kinne, Derek G. THE WOODEN BOXES. London: Muller, 1955.

        Recounts the author's experiences as a POW in a Communist

camp in North Korea. Describes conditions in the camps and
prisoners' reactions to their captivity.

1778. Lane, Raymond A. AMBASSADOR IN CHAINS: THE STORY OF
         PATRICK JOSEPH BYRNE, BISHOP, MISSIONARY. New York:
         Kennedy, 1955.

         Account of the Catholic Bishop who lost his life in the
         Communist "Death March" of the prisoners taken northward
         during the winter of 1950-1951.

1779. Lankford, Dennis. I DEFY! London: Wingate, 1954.

         Tells of the capture and captivity of British Lieutenant
         Langford who was taken prisoner in November 1951 while
         taking pictures on a North Korean island for the British
         Navy. He was held prisoner for eighteen months, and his
         account of that experience is told straightforwardly and
         without heroics.

1780. MacDonald, James A. "The Problems of US Marine Corps
         Prisoners of War in Korea." Master's Thesis. Maryland,
         1962.

         Examines the hardships faced by Marine POW's and compares
         and contrasts their experiences with those of prisoners
         from the other American services.

1781. MacGhee, David. "In Korea's Hell Camps Some of Us
         Didn't Crack." COLLIER'S, 1954 133 (2):82-88; 133 (3):
         68-75.

         Firsthand account of nearly three years of captivity by one
         of the first US Air Force officers to be taken prisoner by the
         Communists in Korea. Tells of the physical hardships and
         mental stress imposed on American POW's. Example of one of a
         majority who did not collaborate with the enemy.

1782. Mahurin, Walker M. HONEST JOHN. New York: Putnam's,
         1962.

         Personal story of a US pilot shot down in Korea and
         taken prisoner. Tells of the suffering inflicted to induce
         him to sign a germ warfare statement.

1783. Manes, Donald L. "Barbed Wire Command." MIL R, 1963
         43 (9):38-56.

         Survival of American prisoners of war in North Korean and
         Chinese Communist camps was dependent primarily on
         organizational patterns and leadership within the group,
         concludes this case study.

1784. Millar, Ward. VALLEY OF THE SHADOW. New York:
         McKay, 1955.

First person account by a US Air Force pilot shot down over
North Korea and taken prisoner by the Chinese. In spite of
two broken ankles, he succeeded with the help of a North
Korean and some friendly Chinese to escape--one of the few
Americans to do so.

1785. Milrod, Martin O. "Prisoners of War in Korea: The
       Impact of Communist Practice Upon International Law."
       Master's Thesis. Georgetown, 1959.

       Shows that the Chinese Communist treatment of prisoners
       had an impact not only upon the enemy but the whole
       meaning of international law as related to POW's.

1786. Murray, J.C. "The Prisoner Issue." MARINE CORPS GAZ,
       1955 39 (8):32-40.

       Tells of the treatment of US prisoners of war in North
       Korea during and after the Korean War. Includes a review of
       US efforts to secure the release of prisoners during the War.

1787. O'Connor, Father Patrick. FAITH BEHIND BARBED WIRE.
       Notre Dame, IN: Ave Maria, 1954.

       This small pamphlet contains reprints of articles written
       by Father O'Connor after interviewing American prisoners
       within several hours of their repatriation. Tells of
       considerable suffering at the hands of their Communist
       captors.

1788. Pate, Lloyd W. as told to B.J. Cutler. REACTIONARY.
       New York: Harper, 1956.

       Popular account of an American prisoner of war who actively
       resisted his subjugation by the enemy--those who did were
       called "Reactionaries" by their captors. Tells of
       "Progressives" who actively collaborated with the enemy--the
       most famous being Sgt. James Gallagher who was subsequently
       court-martialed. Maintains North Koreans treated prisoners
       more cruelly than the Chinese, who wanted to brainwash them.

1789. Quinn, James F. "Evasion and Escape." INF, 1957 47
       (2):66-75.

       Techniques for evading the enemy and escaping if captured
       are set forth using examples taken from US troops in Korea.

1790. "Real Story of Returned Prisoners." US NEWS W R, 1953
       34 (22):54-63.

       Several firsthand accounts of life as a prisoner of war by
       US soldiers held by the Chinese Communists in Korea. All
       accounts tell of suffering which was used to soften them up
       before indoctrination was begun. Tells of different classes
       for "reactionary" and "progressive" prisoners.

1791.   Rosser, Helen. "Christmas by the Yalu." KOREAN SUR,
        1955 4 (10):7, 10.

        The experiences of a group of Christian civilians who were
        taken prisoner by the North Koreans early in the war. Tells
        of their holiday experience in 1950 and 1952. Notes that
        they were better-fed after the Chinese assumed control of
        them.

1792.   Sharpe, Robert L. "God Saved My Life In Korea." SAT
        EVE POST, 1951 223 (29):26-27, 95-96.

        Personal account of a US Army private taken prisoner by the
        North Koreans in July 1950 just two weeks after arriving in
        Korea. Tells of the slaughter of many prisoners, long marches
        from one POW camp to another and his ultimate escape from his
        captors.

1793.   Spivey, Delmar, et al. "The Soldier and the Prisoner."
        MARINE CORPS GAZ, 1965 49 (5):36-44.

        An overview of the conduct of US prisoners of war in the
        Korean conflict.

1794.   Tassey, George. "Evasion." INF SCH Q, 1954 44
        (1):56-61.

        Uses experiences of US soldiers cut off behind enemy lines
        in Korea to show other soldiers how they can successfully
        avoid the enemy and return safely to friendly forces.

1795.   Thornton, John W. BELIEVED TO BE ALIVE. Middlebury,
        VT: Eriksson, 1981.

        The experiences of a US naval flyer taken prisoner by the
        North Koreans and Chinese for nearly three years. Tells of
        the mistreatment and suffering at the hands of his captors.

1796.   US Department of the Army. COMMUNIST INTERROGATION,
        INDOCTRINATION AND EXPLOITATION OF PRISONERS OF WAR.
        Washington: Government Printing Office, 1956.

        A US Army manual warning of the Chinese Communist use of
        leniency and brainwashing to lessen POW resistance. After
        warning how effective their techniques of controlling
        prisoners can be, it concludes that the large majority of
        US prisoners in Korea successfully resisted the enemy.

1797.   US House of Representatives, Committee on Un-American
        Activities. INVESTIGATION OF COMMUNIST PROPAGANDA AMONG
        PRISONERS OF WAR IN KOREA. 84th Cong. 2nd Sess.
        Washington: Government Printing Office, 1956.

Testimony in the June 1956 investigation of the Save Our
Sons Committee, a group allegedly exploiting the POW issue
in an attempt to promote Communist propaganda.

1798.   US Senate, Committee on Government Operations. COMMUNIST
        INTERROGATION, INDOCTRINATION, AND EXPLOITATION OF AMERICAN
        MILITARY AND CIVILIAN PRISONERS. Senate Report 2832 84th
        Cong. 2nd Sess. Washington: Government Printing Office, 1957.

        Rejects the popular idea of Communist "brainwashing" of
        American POW's in Korea. Claims the practices utilized are
        based on simple ideas of weakening an individual physically
        and mentally.

1799.   Victoria, Sister Mary. "I Was a Prisoner of the Chinese
        Reds." COLLIER'S, 1953 131 (19):68-73.

        American soldiers were not the only ones to suffer as
        prisoners of the Chinese Communists during the Korean War.
        This tells the experience of an American nun who was taken
        prisoner in 1951, as were many others, to discredit them
        in the eyes of other Chinese. In describing the treatment
        of Sister Mary, it appears that the civilians were treated
        as poorly as POW's.

1800.   Voelkel, Harold. BEHIND BARBED WIRE IN KOREA. Grand
        Rapids, MI: Zondervan, 1953.

        Account by an American missionary in Korea before the war
        who became a chaplain in the Far Eastern Command after the
        fighting began. His service consisted of ministering to
        POW's held by the UN Command. He found many North Korean
        prisoners who were Christians. Tells of the hazards and
        satisfactions of dealing with the "enemy" in the POW
        camps.

1801.   Warner, Denis. "Australian Lord Haw-Haw." NAT R,
        1975 27 (13):395-397, 410.

        Describes a 1971 libel trial in which Australian
        newsman, Wilfred Burchett, challenged claims he was a
        Communist agent. The trial produced witnesses that
        claimed Burchett openly collaborated with and aided the
        Chinese who were holding American POW's.

1802.   Witherspoon, John A. "International Law and Practice
        Concerning Prisoners of War During the Korean Conflict."
        Doctoral Dissertation. Duke, 1968.

        Maintains that the Communist authorities responsible for
        US and UN prisoners being held in North Korea during the
        war ignored the obligations set forth by the Third Geneva
        Convention. While the UN Command permitted delegates of
        the International Committee of the Red Cross to examine

its POW activities, the North Koreans and Red Chinese did
not.

2.   BRAINWASHING

1803.   Asprey, Robert B., ed.   "The Soldier and the Prisoner."
         MARINE CORPS GAZ, 1965 49 (5):36-44.

         The John A. Lejeune Forum focuses on the issue of Korean
         War POW's. Denounces Eugene Kinkead's contentions that
         behavior was deplorable and is sympathetic to Albert
         Biderman's defense of the prisoners. Followed by reaction
         to the POW issue by three seasoned US Marine Corps
         Officers.

1804.   Bauer, Raymond A., and Edgar H. Schein.   "Brainwashing."
         Special issue of J SOC IS, 1957 13 (3).

         Five articles on brainwashing with focus being on the Korean
         War. Of special interest are articles by Robert J. Lifton on
         Chinese "thought reform," Edgar H. Schein on POW reactions to
         stress and Julius Segal on correlates of collaboration of
         American POW's. Good introduction and conclusion give unity
         to the issue. From a symposium of the American Psychological
         Association.

1805.   Bauer, Raymond A.   "Brainwashing: Psychology or
         Demonology?" J SOC IS, 1957 13 (3):41-47.

         Rejects the idea that brainwashing is really a scientific
         use of psychology developed by the Soviets. Claims the
         techniques are rather ordinary ones of coercion and
         persuasion that have been used in many different places at
         different times in history.

1806.   Biderman, Albert D.   "American Prisoners of War in Korea:
         Reinterpretation of the Data." Doctoral Dissertation.
         Chicago, 1964.

         Challenges the generally accepted interpretation that
         the conduct of American POW's in Korea was disgraceful.
         Looks at such issues as collaboration and resistance,
         mortality, treatment and prisoner organization.

1807.   Biderman, Albert D.   "Communist Attempts to Elicit
         False Confessions From Air Force Prisoners of War."
         BUL N Y ACA MED, 1957 33 (9):616-625.

         Shows how the Communists used isolation, monopolization of
         perception, exhaustion, threats, occasional indulgences,
         futility of resistance, degradation and developing habits
         of compliance to elicit support of US Air Force POW's.

Does not deal with physical torture because it was not an effective method of inducing compliance.

1808. Biderman, Albert D. COMMUNIST TECHNIQUES OF COERCIVE INTERROGATION. Lackland Air Force Base, TX: 1956.

Describes the physical and psychological pressures brought on US POW's to force them to make statements or assertions sought by their Communist captors in Korea.

1809. Biderman, Albert D. "Effects of Communist Indoctrination Attempts: Some Comments Based on Air Force Prisoner of War Study." SOC PROB, 1959 6 (4):304-313.

Analysis of the effects of Chinese Communist indoctrination of all 235 US Air Force POW's repatriated in 1953 concludes: (1) attempts to indoctrinate prisoners were generally ineffective because they did not convert anyone, did not weaken allegiance to the US, and did not motivate prisoners to collaborate in most areas; (2) ineffectiveness was due to selective nature of indoctrination accepted and weaknesses in the enemy's presentation.

1810. Biderman, Albert D., and Herbert Zimmer, eds. THE MANIPULATION OF HUMAN BEHAVIOR. New York: Wiley, 1961.

The introduction cites a number of the studies and findings on the manipulation of American POW's during the Korean War. An author and subject index also leads the reader to key studies completed before 1960.

1811. Biderman, Albert D. MARCH TO CALUMNY: THE STORY OF AMERICAN POW'S IN THE KOREAN WAR. New York: Macmillan, 1963.

A revisionist examination of American POW's. Challenges early interpretation that US soldiers captured in Korea gave evidence of lack of character by cooperating with the enemy. Claims that American soldiers in the Eighth Army performed well and behaved much better as POW's than critics contend.

1812. Biderman, Albert D., et al. "Reading Materials in Chinese Communist Indoctrination Attempts Against American Prisoners of War." LIB Q, 1958 28 (3):187-193.

Provides a comprehensive bibliography of materials made available to US Air Force POW's in Korea and contends that the works were probably provided not so much for their propaganda value as for their availability.

1813. Brinkley, William. "Valley Forge GI's Tell of Their Brainwashing Ordeal." LIFE, 1953 34 (21):108-124.

Four prisoners of war who were taken to Valley Forge Army Hospital upon their repatriation tell of their experiences at the Pyuktong prisoner camp.

1814. Brownfield, Charles A. THE BRAIN BENDERS: A STUDY OF THE EFFECTS OF ISOLATION. New York: Exposition, 1972.

A psychological study on the impact of isolation gives considerable attention to the treatment of American prisoners of war held by the Chinese Communists during the Korean War.

1815. "Communist Indoctrination of American Prisoners." ARMY INFOR DIG, 1953 8 (7):57-64.

US Department of Defense explanation of the treatment of US, South Korean and UN soldiers being held in communist POW camps in North Korea. Tells of the intensive indoctrination, psychological pressures and physical suffering that is utilized to win over or break prisoners. Maintains the enemy is using the prisoners for propaganda purposes.

1816. Cunningham, Cyril. "Korean War Studies in Forensic Psychology." BUL BT PSY SOC, 1970 23 (81):309-311.

Points out that penology can learn a great deal about controlling prisoners from studying the techniques used on US prisoners of war by the Chinese. Areas benefiting from those studies are penology, especially the value of extensive segregation facilities and clinical psychology.

1817. Greenway, John. "The Colonel's Korean 'Turncoats.'" NATION, 1962 195 (15):302-305.

Critical account of Lt. Col. William E. Mayer's activities in setting forth his view that the conduct of American POW's in Korea was traitorous and all because of American decadence which has come with the move away from discipline. Also critical of widespread acceptance of Mayer's claim. Makes an attempt to be supportive of POW's conduct.

1818. Hunter, Edward. BRAINWASHING IN RED CHINA: THE CALCULATED DESTRUCTION OF MEN'S MINDS. New York: Vanguard, 1951.

A look at Chinese "brainwashing" techniques, written before it became a major issue related to prisoners-of-war. The author interviewed a number of people who fled the mainland and relayed to the author the methods of propaganda and indoctrination that were used to get noncommunists to support Mao's regime.

1819. Hunter, Edward. BRAINWASHING: THE STORY OF MEN WHO DEFIED IT. New York: Farrar, 1956.

Shows how the Chinese Communists used fatigue, hunger,
threats, violence and cunning to get prisoners of war to
accept what normally would have been abhorrent to them. Goes
into the background of the techniques which the author traces
to Lenin. Shows why blacks and whites were segregated and
how both groups resisted equally well. Maintains the
importance of having soldiers know what they are fighting
for.

1820. Hunter, Edward. "Our POW's Are Not Traitors." COM
      FOR J, 1953 4 (3):36-37.

Claims the Americans do not understand the nature of
brainwashing and that "progressives" should be pitied as
sick men not condemned as traitors. Notes how hunger,
fatigue, fear and violence were used to gain confessions
or convert the victims.

1821. Karsten, Peter. "The American Democratic Citizen
      Soldier: Triumph or Disaster." MIL AFF, 1966 30 (1):
      34-40.

Argues against the claims of Eugene Kinkead and William E.
Mayer that the conduct of American POW's in Korea was far
worse than in other US wars. Shows the problems existed
in previous military conflicts.

1822. Karsten, Peter. "American POW's in Korea and the
      Citizen Soldier" in Peter Karsten, ed. THE MILITARY IN
      AMERICA. New York: Free Press, 1980.

Attacks the premises, evidence and conclusions of critics
of the conduct of American POW's during the Korean War,
especially the claims of Eugene Kinkead and William E.
Mayer.

1823. Kinkead, Eugene. "Have We Let Our Sons Down?" MCCALL'S,
      1959 86 (4):23, 74-81.

Supposedly based on an official Army Report, this article
claims that one-third of the American POW's collaborated
with the enemy in some fashion, that many treated fellow
prisoners brutally and many died as a result of the
callousness of their comrades. The cause of such action
rests primarily in the breakdown of family life and lack
of discipline. Tells of Army indoctrination to avoid a
repetition of the experience.

1824. Kinkead, Eugene. IN EVERY WAR BUT ONE. New York:
      Norton, 1959.

A look at the conduct of American prisoners of war in the
Korean conflict. Maintains that one-third of the prisoners
cooperated with the enemy, one in seven committed acts

approaching treason, not one escaped from a permanent enemy
camp and nearly forty percent died because they lacked the
will to live. Kinkead claims the cause is a flaw in the
American character but does not really say what it is or what
caused it. Urges training to avoid such behavior in the
future.

1825. Martin, Harold H. "They Tried to Make Our Marines
      Love Stalin." SAT EVE POST, 1951 224 (8):25, 107-110.

      Relates the experiences of nineteen US Marines who were
      captured by the Chinese near the Changjin Reservoir in
      late November 1950 and held for six months, during which
      time they were fed Communist propaganda. They were then
      released and provided with bundles of propaganda. Based
      on interviews with the prisoners almost immediately upon
      their release.

1826. Mayer, William E. "Why Did so Many G.I. Captives Give
      In?" US NEWS W P, 1956 40 Feb. 24:56-62, 64-72.

      Interviews with William E. Mayer, US Army psychiatrist,
      a leading advocate of the view that conduct of US POW's
      in Korea was deplorable. Maintains that the sorry conduct
      was due to a serious flaw in the character of the nation's
      youth and a failure of education to teach the virtues of
      American Democracy.

1827. Peters, W.E. "When the Army Debunks the Army: A
      Legend of the Korean War." ENC, 1960 15 (1):77-79.

      Review article of the works of Eugene Kinkead the leading
      proponent of the view that American POW behavior in Korea
      was a disgrace with widespread collaboration and extremely
      unpatriotic behavior. Peters claims that Kinkead's works
      are misleading if not outrightly deceptive.

1828. "Red Torture Broke Few G.I.'s." US NEW W R, 1955 39
      (9):38-39.

      7,190 American servicemen were captured by the Communists
      in Korea of which 2,730 died in captivity. Less than 200
      succumbed to brainwashing, but most attention is focused
      on them rather than the large number who successfully
      resisted the Red indoctrination.

1829. Reinhardt, Geough C. "Frame-Up, Communist Style."
      COM FOR J, 1953 4 (3):35-36.

      Contends that collaboration of US POW's with their
      Communist captors was not widespread, but the enemy
      convinced the prisoners that all the others were cooperating.
      Warns not to jump to the conclusion that there were many
      traitors but look into the charges very thoroughly before
      making accusations.

1830.   Rogge, Oetje John. WHY MEN CONFESS. New York: Nelson,
        1959.

        An examination of how confessions have been obtained from
        unwilling subjects from the Inquisition down through the
        Korean War. Useful as an introduction to the subject but
        not much more. Does make the point that confessions by
        Korean War POW's were by no means historically unique
        events.

1831.   Schein, Edgar H. "The Chinese Indoctrination Program
        for Prisoners of War: A Study of Brainwashing." PSY,
        1956 19 (2):149-172.

        Based on extensive use of interviews with repatriated
        American POW's. Forms generalized picture of the average
        prisoner from day of capture to release. Tells of direct
        and indirect attacks on beliefs, attitudes and values. By
        disrupting social organization and use of reward and
        punishment, the Chinese were able to elicit considerable
        collaboration. Techniques used were not new.

1832.   Schein, Edgar H., et al. COERCIVE PERSUASION. New
        York: Norton, 1961.

        Many studies have been made on "brainwashing" of prisoners
        of war by Chinese Communists during the Korean War, but it
        is generally not known that a number of American civilians
        were taken prisoner and "brainwashed." This focuses on
        those civilians and the social process of coercive per-
        suasion which the Chinese used on them.

1833.   Schein, Edgar H. "Distinguishing Characteristics of
        Collaborators and Resisters Among American Prisoners of
        War." J ABN SOC PSY, 1957 55 (2):197-201.

        Study of 759 American POW's in Korea was undertaken to see
        if collaborators, resisters or neutrals were similar in
        terms of rank, civilian occupation, religion, location of
        home community or number of parents in the home. Found
        that none of the three groups differed in any of the
        variables investigated.

1834.   Schein, Edgar H. "Reaction Patterns to Severe, Chronic
        Stress in American Prisoners of War of the Chinese." J SOC
        IS, 1957 13 (3):21-30.

        Contends that the Chinese Communists were successful in
        getting US prisoners to collaborate because they aimed their
        efforts at controlling the group and not the individual.
        Maintains the Chinese were not successful at gaining converts
        but did get cooperation from individuals for reasons such as
        the receiving of special privileges and inability to identify
        with the group.

1835. Segal, Julius. "Correlates of Collaboration and Resistance
       Behavior Among US Army POW's in Korea." J SOC IS, 1957
       13 (3):31-40.

       Statistical study of 579 repatriated American POW's shows
       the Communists achieved some success in achieving collabora-
       tion and obtaining propaganda statements but not in gaining
       converts. Defends the prisoners, claiming they were put in a
       most untenable position. Claims that only 15% collaborated
       with the enemy.

1836. Tanner, Louise. HERE TODAY. New York: Crowell, 1960.

       Sketches of fifteen Americans who captured the headlines in
       the 20th century. Includes a sketch on defector, Corporal
       Claude Batchelor of Kermit, Texas, and tells of the
       Communist indoctrination of Americans captured during the
       Korean War.

1837. Ulman, William A. "The GI's Who Fell for the Reds."
       SAT EVE POST, 1954 226 (36):17-19, 64-67.

       Looks at some of the US POW's who were known collaborators
       with the Communists and tells how they were duped into
       doing what they did. Also examines their activities after
       being released, which shows that some continued to put forth
       the enemy line.

1838. US Department of Defense. POW: THE FIGHT CONTINUES
       AFTER THE BATTLE, THE REPORT OF THE SECRETARY OF DEFENSE'S
       ADVISORY COMMITTEE ON PRISONERS OF WAR. Washington:
       Government Printing Office, 1955.

       The official US government assessment of the conduct of
       American POW's in Korea is somewhat contradictory in that
       it concluded the record was very good yet also claims that
       what happened should not be permitted to happen again.
       Generally favorable to the G.I.'s captured.

1839. West, Louis J. "Psychiatry, 'Brainwashing' and the
       American Character." AM J PSY, 1964 120 (9):842-850.

       A psychiatrist refutes the "brainwashing hoax." Discusses
       the claims of William E. Mayer and counters with the work
       of Albert Biderman. Looks at the American character, that
       has historically been condemned by many, and sees it as no
       worse than in earlier times.

1840. Wilson, Richard. "How US Prisoners Broke Under Red
       'Brainwashing.'" LOOK, 1953 17 (11):80-82.

       One of the earliest accounts of American prisoners of war
       reaction to "brainwashing." Tells how the Chinese Communists

degrade the prisoners and create a deep sense of guilt which
ultimately leads to confessions of their wrongdoings.
Speculates that the consequences, about which US authorities
know little, may lead to refusal of some Americans to accept
repatriation.

B.   COMMUNIST PRISONERS

1841.   Benben, John S. "Education of Prisoners of War on Koje
        Island, Korea." ED REC, 1955 36 (2):157-173.

        Describes the handling of Communist POW's on Koje by the
        UN Command, especially the education program that was
        provided. Includes mention of the major uprising of
        March 21, 1952. Good account of the physical and
        organizational attributes of the camp. Author was chief
        of the education program for POW's.

1842.   Bradbury, William C. (Study Director), Samuel Meyers, and
        Albert D. Biderman, eds. MASS BEHAVIOR IN BATTLE AND
        CAPTIVITY: THE COMMUNIST SOLDIER IN THE KOREAN WAR.
        Chicago: University of Chicago, 1968.

        Attempts to answer the reason why two-thirds of the Chinese
        prisoners of war refused repatriation at the end of the
        Korean War. Based on interviews with forty-three prisoners.
        Contains an analysis and review of the interviews and an
        overview of the political and social behavior of communist
        prisoners and insights into Chinese and North Korean
        Communist societies.

1843.   Burchett, Wilfred, and Alan Winnington. KOJE UNSCREENED.
        Peking, 1953.

        Indictment of the US-UN operation of the POW Camp at Koje
        Island. Maintains that poor treatment of Communist prisoners
        predictably led to the uprisings in the camp. The authors are
        newspapermen, one from England and one from Australia, who
        openly collaborated with the Chinese Communists during the war.

1844.   Chinese People's Committee for World Peace. UNITED
        NATIONS POW'S IN KOREA. Peking: Foreign Languages Press,
        1953.

        Red Chinese war propaganda indicts the US and UN Command for
        mistreatment of North Korean and Chinese POW's. Claims
        Americans are forcing prisoners to say they do not wish
        to be repatriated.

1845.   Cooper, Bernan. "Radio Broadcasting to Chinese and
        Korean POW'S: A Rhetorical Analysis." Doctoral Dissertation.
        Stanford, 1956.

        Rhetorical analysis of the appeals which were made in

1952-1953 radio broadcasts to Chinese and Korean POW's
being held by the UN Command.

1846.   Hindman, Edward R. "Prisoner-of-War Hospital on Koje-
          do." MIL ENG, 1953 45 (307):360-363.

Describes the construction of a 3,000-bed hospital for
Communist prisoners of war at the UN Camp at Koje Island.
This mammoth project was accomplished by Company A, 93rd
Engineer Construction Battalion, using prisoners. The
innovativeness of the engineers is evident from their
ability to complete the building in spite of the shortage
of many construction materials.

1847.   Kalischer, Peter. "The Koje Snafu." COLLIER'S,
          1952 130 (10):15-19.

Details the May 1952 incident when Brigadier General
Francis T. Dodd, commander of the huge UN POW Camp at
Koje Island was held captive by his prisoner and released
after another Brigadier General Charles F. Colson signed
a statement admitting wrongdoing on America's part. Both
were subsequently demoted to Colonel. Good background on
Koje as well as the incident and its impact. Critical of
the US commanders of the camp and their actions.

1848.   "Koje Island in Perspective." COM FOR J, 1952 3
          (1):24-25.

Misleading title of this photo essay which concludes that
when the record is complete, it will show that the Army performed the difficult mission of putting down the rebellion "with
credit." Makes no reference to uprisings and other problems
in the first five months of the year.

1849.   National Red Cross of China. OUT OF THEIR OWN MOUTHS.
          Peking, 1952.

Communist Chinese propaganda piece that allegedly sets
forth written confessions by US soldiers admitting that
they tortured, raped, burned, looted and murdered innocent
Korean civilians and POW's during the fighting in Korea.

1850.   US House of Representatives, Committee on Appropriations.
          THE PRISONER OF WAR SITUATION IN KOREA. 82nd Cong. 2nd Sess.
          Washington: Government Printing Office, 1952.

While these June 1952 hearings examined such things as
number of enemy prisoners to be kept together, sending of
ROK guards into compounds and demands of Communist
prisoners, most attention is given to the Koje uprisings
and why they occurred.

1851.   Vetter, Hal. MUTINY ON KOJE ISLAND. Rutland, VT:
          Tuttle, 1964.

An account of the 1952 Chinese-North Korean uprisings at
the UN prison camp at Koje Island. In February and March,
prisoner riots were put down by US guards with the loss of
life of nearly one hundred prisoners. In May the US camp
Commander General Francis T. Dodd was taken hostage and
not released until his subordinate accepted humiliating
demands.

1852. Weintraub, Stanley. THE WAR IN THE WARDS: KOREA'S
       UNKNOWN BATTLE IN A PRISONER-OF-WAR HOSPITAL CAMP.
       Garden City, NY: Doubleday, 1964.

       Near the end of the war, hardcore Chinese and North Korean
       prisoners being held in a UN prison camp at Koje Island did
       everything they could to thwart American efforts to give
       prisoners a choice as to whether they should be repatriated.
       Consequently, the prisoners virtually came to control the
       camp. This is a firsthand account by an American service-
       man on duty at Koje.

1853. White, William L. THE CAPTIVES OF KOREA: AN UNOFFICIAL
       WHITE PAPER ON THE TREATMENT OF WAR PRISONERS. New York:
       Scribner's, 1957.

       Compares the prisoner of war camps of the Chinese
       Communists, who refused supervision by the International Red
       Cross, and those of the UN forces who accepted supervision.
       Concentrates on brutality of the enemy in a very descriptive
       manner. Lauds UN efforts but does not analyze what took
       place or its impact.

1854. Worden, William L. "Our Lucky Red Prisoners." SAT EVE
       POST, 1952 224 (27):32-33, 45, 47.

       Maintains that while American soldiers were brutalized and
       killed in Communist POW camps, the UN Command treated
       captured Reds better than they had ever been treated before.
       Describes the UN camp at Koje and praises its providing
       education and recreational services to the prisoners.
       (Written before the uprisings.)

                          C. REPATRIATION

1855. Alapatt, George K. "The Legal Implications of the
       Repatriation of War Prisoners in Relation to the Korean
       Armistice and in View of the Division of Korea." Doctoral
       Dissertation. St. Louis, 1958.

       Emphasis is on the creation, organization and work of
       the Neutral Nations' Repatriation Commission in implementing
       the exchange of Korean POW's.

1856. Beebe, Gilbert W. "Follow-up Studies of World War II
       and Korean War Prisoners. Part II: Morbidity, Disability
       and Maladjustments." AM J EPID, 1975 101 (5):400-422.

       A study of hospital admissions of US Army veterans who
       were prisoners of war. Examined admissions in the decade
       after confinement in terms of symptoms, disability and mal-
       adjustments. Finds the sequelae of the POW experience
       were somatic and psychiatric.

1857. Fogg, Charles. "I Saw the Struggle in the 'Explanation'
       Tents." SAT EVE POST, 1954 226 (31):28, 68-72.

       The head interpreter for the UN Command Repatriation-
       Group relates his experiences in working on the exchange
       of POW's. Extremely critical of the methods used by
       the Chinese Reds and North Koreans to convince their
       soldiers being held prisoner to return.

1858. Hansen, Kenneth K. HEROES BEHIND BARBED WIRE.
       Princeton, NJ: Van Nostrand, 1957.

       The Chief of Psychological Warfare for the UN Command
       details the story of the thousands of Chinese and North
       Koreans who chose not to return to their homes at war's
       end and the reactions of the Communist officials at
       Panmunjom as they witnessed the events. Goes overboard
       in maintaining the outcome was inevitable when people
       must choose between the good of Democracy and the evil of
       Communism.

1859. Heinecke, Roy E. "The Big Switch." LEATHERNECK, 1953
       36 (11):44-48.

       A Marine Sergeant describes what took place in the
       repatriation of UN POW's at Munsan Provisional Command
       in the summer of 1953.

1860. Keehn, Robert J. "Follow-up Studies of World War II
       and Korean Conflict Prisoners. Part III: Mortality to
       January 1, 1976." AM J EPID, 1980 111 (2):194-211.

       This mortality study of US Army veterans released from
       prisoner of war camps shows an increased risk of dying
       when compared to standard mortality rates. The major
       increase in the death rate of Korean veterans is
       attributed to trauma and cirrhosis of the liver. There
       is no evidence of differences in the death rate of former
       prisoners when it comes to chronic and degenerative
       diseases.

1861. Lavine, Harold. TWENTY-ONE G.I.'S WHO CHOSE TYRANNY:
       WHY THEY LEFT US FOR COMMUNISM. New York: Oxford
       University, 1969.

A social profile of the twenty-one American prisoners of
the Korean War who chose to remain with the Communists.
Notes that nearly all were loners who lacked direction and
security and had found a home in the Army. When faced with
returning to their earlier life, they elected not to do so.

1862. Lifton, Robert J. "Home By Ship: Reaction Patterns
       of American Prisoners of War Repatriated From North
       Korea." AM J PSY, 1954 110 (10):732-739.

       Because of the expected problems of readjustment of US
       POW's following operation "Big Switch" (August-September
       1953), the men were sent back to the US by ship rather
       than plane to provide an interlude which would help them
       bridge the gap from prisoner to free man. Tells of the
       "treatment" provided on board ship and the soldier's
       reaction to it.

1863. Moskin, J. Robert. TURNCOAT: AN AMERICAN'S TWELVE
       YEARS IN COMMUNIST CHINA. New York: Pocket, 1970.

       The story of Morris R. Wills, an American taken prisoner
       of war during the Korean conflict, who refused to be
       repatriated. He then spent twelve years in Red China
       before he became disillusioned and returned to the US.

1864. Pasley, Virginia. 21 STAYED: THE STORY OF THE AMERICAN
       G.I.'S WHO CHOSE COMMUNIST CHINA. New York: Farrar, 1955.

       Examines, with an impressive array of statistics, the
       social and economic backgrounds of the twenty-one US
       servicemen who elected to stay with their Chinese captors
       rather than be repatriated. Concludes the group was
       basically from extremely poor backgrounds, were undereducated
       and generally misfits who consequently were more apt to be
       taken in by Communist propaganda. Does not deal with why
       many others in the same situation chose to return.

1865. Potter, Pitman B. "Repatriation of Prisoners of War."
       AM J INTER LAW, 1952 46 July:508-509.

       Points out that peculiar circumstances in the Korean War
       have led to the possibility that some repatriated prisoners
       from North Korea or Red China might be mistreated by their
       governments; thus, the legal question arises if they should
       be returned. Perhaps international law will need to be
       rethought on the matter of repatriation.

1866. Schein, Edgar H., et al. A PSYCHOLOGICAL FOLLOW-UP OF
       FORMER PRISONERS OF WAR OF THE CHINESE COMMUNISTS. Cambridge:
       Massachusetts Institute of Technology, 1960.

       A follow-up study of more than 200 POW's of the Korean War.
       Undertaken five years after repatriation, this study utilized

psychological tests and interviews to examine their
experiences following release. It was revealed that the
"apathy reaction" immediately following release had not
persisted and that the repatriates made adequate adjustments
and were living lives similar to those of other average
Americans.

1867. Segal, Henry A. "Initial Psychiatric Findings of
        Recently Repatriated Prisoners of War." AM J PSY, 1954
        111 (5):358-363.

        Tells of the psychiatric planning for and conduct of
        Operation Little Switch and Big Switch, the 1953
        repatriation of 149 and 1,551 American POW's respectively.
        Identifies the anticipated problems of the prisoners and
        tells how Army psychiatrists prepared to meet those
        challenges.

1868. Strassman, Harvey D., et al. "A Prisoner of War
        Syndrome: Apathy as a Reaction to Severe Stress."
        AM J PSY, 1956 112 (12):998-1003.

        Study based on interviews of 201 recently released American
        POW's. Looked at types of stresses they faced, their initial
        reaction and reaction following repatriation. Stresses
        brought on by their captivity and uncertain future led in
        nearly all cases to apathy, but at different levels. This
        apathy continued even after they were released.

1869. "They Chose Red China and Then--Story of GI Turncoats."
        US NEWS W R, 1957 42 (26):58-64, 67-74.

        Within four years after they chose to remain in Red China,
        eight of the twenty-one Americans who refused repatriation
        had returned to the US. This article includes interviews
        with five of the turncoats--all of whom express disillusion-
        ment with life in Red China.

1870. US House of Representatives, Committee on Foreign Affairs.
        RETURN OF AMERICAN PRISONERS OF WAR WHO HAD NOT BEEN
        ACCOUNTED FOR BY THE COMMUNISTS. 85th Cong. 1st Sess.
        Washington: Government Printing Office, 1957.

        May 27, 1957 hearings were held to attempt to receive a
        satisfactory accounting of American military personnel for
        which there had been no satisfactory accounting for by
        Communist officials. Lists the names, grades and service
        numbers of 450 missing personnel.

XVII. PEACE NEGOTIATIONS AND THE ARMISTICE
A. NEGOTIATIONS - TRUMAN ADMINISTRATION

1871. Acheson, Dean G. "The Truce Talks in Korea." HARPER'S,
       1953 206 (1232):21-31.

       Excerpts from an October 24, 1952, statement on the Korean
       situation to the UN's Political Committee by US Secretary of
       State Acheson focuses on the truce talks especially the POW
       issue. Sets forth the US position from their 1951 start
       through the October 1952.

1872. Bacchus, Wilfred A. "The Relationship Between Combat and
       Peace Negotiations: Fighting While Talking In Korea."
       ORBIS, 1973 17 (2):545-574.

       Examines the prolonged peace negotiations in Korea and
       shows the relationship between military activities and
       diplomatic maneuvering. Attaining peace in a limited war is
       very difficult, but in the end military capability and the
       ability to make it clear to the enemy there is a willingness
       to use it, strongly influences negotiations.

1873. Bernstein, Barton J. "The Struggle Over the Korean
       Armistice: Prisoners or Repatriation?" in Bruce Cumings,
       ed. CHILD OF CONFLICT. Seattle: University of Washington,
       1983.

       Excellent in-depth study of the two years of peace
       negotiations that ultimately ended the fighting. Covers the
       major disputes, especially the issue of repatriation, a
       problem that stymied an agreement for fifteen months.

1874. Blumenson, Martin. "Neutrality and Armistice in Korea."
       MIL R, 1967 47 (6):3-12.

       Narrative account of the negotiating process in Korea which
       ultimately led to the 1953 agreement to be supervised by the
       Neutral Nations Supervisory Commission.

1875. Clarke, Bruce C. "Negotiations: Korean Lessons."
       MIL R, 1968 48 (6):91-93.

       Using Korean peace negotiations, the author warns against
       thinking that problems are practically over when peace
       talks begin and the US must realize that while it respects

negotiations, the Communists use it as a tool to gain
military and political advantages.

1876. Hermes, Walter G. "The Military Role in the Korean
       Truce Negotiations." MIL R, 1964 44 (1):14-23.

       Examines the role played by US military negotiators in
       the Korean peace negotiations between 1951 and 1953.

1877. Hermes, Walter G. TRUCE TENT AND FIGHTING FRONT. Vol. II
       in the series THE UNITED STATES ARMY IN THE KOREAN WAR.
       Washington: Government Printing Office, 1966.

       Official Army account of the truce negotiations held at
       Kaesong and then Panmunjom between July 1951 and July 1953.
       Details the offers and counter offers of the UN negotiators
       and Chinese Communists. Also focuses on the stalemated
       military conflict during the period. Covers the major
       communist prisoner riots at Koje Island.

1878. Joy, Charles Turner. HOW COMMUNISTS NEGOTIATE. New York:
       Macmillan, 1955.

       The author, a US Naval Admiral who served as chief of the
       United Nations Command Delegation to the Korean Armistice
       Conference, shares the frustration inherent in attempting
       to negotiate an end to the conflict.

1879. Joy, Charles Turner. "My Battle Inside the Korean
       Truce Tent." COLLIER'S, 1952 130 (7):36-43; 130 (8):
       26-31; 130 (9):70-73.

       Firsthand account of the Admiral who was senior UN delegate
       to the Korean peace talks from July 8, 1951, to May 22, 1952.
       Tells of the preparation for the talks and the frustrations
       in dealing with his Communist counterparts. Good for
       understanding the mind set of the enemy. This material
       appears in Turner's diary, NEGOTIATING WHILE FIGHTING.

1880. Joy, Charles Turner. NEGOTIATING WHILE FIGHTING: THE
       DIARY OF ADMIRAL C. TURNER JOY AT THE KOREAN ARMISTICE
       CONFERENCE. Stanford, CA: Hoover Institution, 1978.

       The Diary of Admiral Joy, the Chief of the UN Command
       Delegation to the Armistice Conference shows the difficulties
       and frustrations of trying to reach an acceptable peace
       accord in a stalemated conflict.

1881. Karolevitz, Robert F. "Peace Talks and Limited Action."
       ARMY INFO DIG, 1952 7 (4):25-36.

       Examines the military and political aspects of the Korean
       War from July through December 1951 and notes that during
       the period, words were exchanged at a comparable rate with
       bullets. Details the start of armistice talks and the

problems that surrounded them. Notes that while the
ground fighting slowed down, air interdiction and anti-
guerrilla activities were stepped up.

1882. Kim, Myong W. "Prisoners of War as a Major Problem
        of the Korean Armistice." Doctoral Dissertation. New York,
        1960.

        Focuses on the question of repatriation of POW's in the
        Korean armistice negotiations. Claims that prisoners
        should not be repatriated by force if it can be detemined
        that they truly do not want to return home.

1883. Kintner, William R. "Making an Armistice Work."
        COM FOR J, 1954 4 (6):14-17.

        While focusing on the peace negotiations that took place
        after the July 1953 armistice and the techniques used by
        both sides in the process, this article provides an
        overview of the negotiations that took place during the
        war.

1884. MacGregor, Greg. "Brother Act at the Truce Talks."
        COLLIER'S, 1952 129 (7):42, 44.

        Korean War truce talks that began in Kaesong in July 1951
        were greatly facilitated by the interpreting of two
        American brothers, Dick and Horace Underwood. One was
        an Army Reserve Officer, the other a Naval Reserve Officer.
        Born in Korea, of missionary parents, the brothers were
        not only fluent in the language but also understood the
        Korean mind.

1885. Mauldin, Bill. "Truth and Consequences." COLLIER'S,
        1952 129 (21):18-19, 61.

        Combat humorist Mauldin takes a look at the armistice
        talk at Panmunjom and concludes that the negotiators
        acted like children as their representatives tried to
        outdo each other. Demonstrates that some humor could
        be found in a serious matter.

1886. Murray, J.C. "The Korean Truce Talks: First Phase."
        US NAVAL INST PROC, 1953 79 (9):981-989.

        Traces the Korean armistice talks from their initiation by
        the communists in July 1951 through the October 8, 1952,
        recess called for by the UN negotiators. Considerable
        attention is given to communist motivation and negotiation
        techniques and the Prisoner of War issue.

1887. PANMUNJOM. Pyongyang: Foreign Languages Press, 1958.

        North Korean propaganda piece on the peace negotiations.
        Also tells how the American imperialists provoked the war
        in Korea.

1888. Scheidig, Robert E. "A Comparison of Communist
       Negotiating Methods." MIL R, 1974 54 (12):79-89.

       Compares the peace negotiations conducted during the
       Korean and Vietnam wars and concludes that the Communists
       view the negotiating process in a very different light
       and with very different values, thus making such
       activities frustrating to westerners.

1889. Sherrod, Robert. "The Inside Story of the Korean Truce."
       SAT EVE POST, 1953 226 (16):26-27, 125, 127-130.

       Discusses the difficulty historians will have in writing
       the history of the Korean War because enemy records will
       probably not be available and Communist generals do not
       write memoirs. Then traces the peace negotiations from
       their beginning in June 1951 until the cease-fire was
       signed in July 1953. Tells of the difficulties of
       negotiating a settlement with the communists on one hand
       and President Rhee on the other.

1890. United Kingdom, Secretary of State for Foreign Affairs.
       KOREA: A SUMMARY OF DEVELOPMENTS IN THE ARMISTICE
       NEGOTIATIONS AND IN THE PRISONER OF WAR CAMPS. London:
       Her Majesty's Stationery Office, 1952.

       British account of the Korean peace negotiations from
       July 1951 until the spring of 1952. Shows how the POW
       issue was crucial from the beginning.

1891. Vatcher, William H., Jr. PANMUNJOM: THE STORY OF THE
       KOREAN MILITARY ARMISTICE NEGOTIATIONS. New York:
       Praeger, 1958.

       Excellent account by a political scientist who was present
       at the negotiations as a UN advisor. Traces the problems
       of cease-fire, demarcation line and prisoner exchanges
       through the two years of negotiations. Agrees with military
       men who contend that Washington diplomats were less than
       competent and maintains that negotiators on the scene lacked
       the authority necessary to make progress.

            B. NEGOTIATIONS - EISENHOWER ADMINISTRATION

1892. Adams, Sherman. FIRSTHAND REPORT: THE STORY OF THE
       EISENHOWER ADMINISTRATION. New York: Harper, 1961.

       An inside account of the Eisenhower presidency by the
       Assistant to the President. Provides insight into the
       White House's frustrating but eventually successful
       efforts to bring the war in Korea to an end.

1893. Blechman, Barry M., and Robert Powell. "What in the
       Name of God is Strategic Superiority?" POL SCI Q,
       1982-83 97 (4):589-602.

       Looks at Eugene V. Rostow's contention that the Korean War
       was ended by President Eisenhower's hint of the use of
       nuclear weapons and contends that the enemies' willingness to
       reach agreement was due more to the threat of general
       escalation than an atomic threat.

1894. Donovan, Robert J. EISENHOWER, THE INSIDE STORY.
       New York: Harper, 1956.

       Inside look at the first Eisenhower Administration by
       a top New York Herald Tribune correspondent who was
       given access to White House files. Devotes a chapter
       to Eisenhower and the Korean truce.

1895. Eisenhower, Dwight D. MANDATE FOR CHANGE, 1953-1956.
       Garden City, NY: Doubleday, 1963.

       This first volume of Eisenhower's memoirs of the Presidency
       is reasonably well done as far as memoirs go. Covers the
       Korean issue in the 1952 election, the President's December
       1952 trip to Korea and the steps taken to achieve a truce.
       Reveals the President's policy options and his willingness
       and threats to turn to the use of nuclear weapons if the
       enemy did not begin to negotiate seriously.

1896. Ferrell, Robert H., ed. THE EISENHOWER DIARIES.
       New York: Norton, 1981.

       These excerpts from Eisenhower's diaries give some insight
       into his analysis of the Korean War from its outbreak through
       the successful armistice negotiations of July 1953. Provides
       some insights into the frustrations in dealing with President
       Rhee as well as the enemy.

1897. Millis, Walter. "Military Problems of the New
       Administration." FOR AFF, 1953 31 (2):215-224.

       Examines five major military problems that the Eisenhower
       Administration will have to deal with upon assuming office.
       One of those problems is what to do in Korea. Looks at
       the various options that might be pursued, from abandoning
       the fight to a greatly expanded effort. Also deals with
       such things as: military organization, allocation of
       resources to the various services, global strategy and
       costs.

1898. Mrozek, Donald J. "A New Look at 'Balanced Forces':
       Defense Continuities From Truman to Eisenhower." MIL
       AFF, 1974 38 (4):145-150.

Shows that there was considerable continuity in the defense
policies of Truman and Eisenhower. Eisenhower was very
supportive of the President's Korean policies until he
became a candidate. Politics forced him to be critical
of the Chief Executive's policies but in reality their
thinking remained quite similar.

1899. "New Defense Executives." ARMY INFO DIG, 1953
       8 (7):17-21.

       Pictorial section showing the individuals filling the
       civilian leadership in the US defense establishment
       under the Eisenhower Administration. Includes officials
       of the Office of Secretary of Defense as well as the
       Army, Navy and Air Force.

1900. Parmet, Herbert S. EISENHOWER AND THE AMERICAN CRUSADES.
       New York: Macmillan, 1972.

       Thoroughly researched and well-written account of
       Eisenhower's campaign for President and his two terms in
       office. Takes the reader through the frustrating and fragile
       negotiating process that finally led to an end to
       hostilities.

1901. Pruessen, Ronald W. JOHN FOSTER DULLES: THE ROAD TO POWER.
       New York: Free Press, 1982.

       Scholarly study of Dulles' career prior to becoming
       Secretary of State. Two chapters focus on his involvement in
       the Far East from just prior to the outbreak of war in Korea
       through 1952. Tells of his visits to Korea and Japan during
       that period and shows how he used the war to bring about the
       peace settlement with Japan.

1902. PUBLIC PAPERS OF THE PRESIDENTS OF THE UNITED STATES,
       DWIGHT D. EISENHOWER 1953. Washington: Government
       Printing Office, 1960.

       This compilation of President Eisenhower's public messages,
       speeches, statements and official news conferences is
       valuable in tracing the administration's efforts to secure an
       armistice in Korea during the first six months in office.

1903. Reichard, Gary W. "Eisenhower and the Bricker Amendment."
       PROL, 1974 6 (2):88-99.

       Senator John Bricker (R-Ohio) alarmed over what he
       considered President Truman's abuse of power in pursuing the
       war in Korea put forth a constitutional amendment limiting
       presidential treaty and executive agreement powers. With the
       election of Eisenhower, who opposed the measure, the chances
       for passage and ratification were weakened, and it ultimately
       was rejected in various forms.

1904. Schoenebaum, Eleanora W. POLITICAL PROFILES: THE EISENHOWER
       YEARS. New York: Facts on File, 1977.

       Brief biographies along with analysis of the contributions
       of more than 500 individuals significant in the US government
       during the Eisenhower Administration. Diplomatic, military
       and top advisors who played key roles in the Korean War
       negotiations are included.

1905. Shepley, James. "How Dulles Averted War." LIFE, 1956
       40 (3):70-72, 77-80.

       Secretary of State John Foster Dulles faced many difficult
       problems during his first eighteen months in office, but none
       more difficult than ending the Korean War. This story
       examines, among others, the Korean problems, especially those
       encountered with President Rhee.

1906. Yates, Lawrence A. "John Foster Dulles and Bipartisanship,
       1944-1952." Doctoral Dissertation. Kansas, 1981.

       Shows how the Republican lawyer had a major impact on
       Democratic foreign policy. His stands on the Korean War and
       Japanese Peace Treaty shaped the Truman policies while
       virtually assuring that if a Republican won the White House,
       he would be appointed Secretary of State.

                         C. ARMISTICE AGREEMENT

1907. Brazda, Jaroslav J. "The Korean Armistice Agreement."
       Doctoral Dissertation. Florida, 1956.

       Examines the reasons why it took so long, nearly two years,
       to negotiate the armistice. Maintains the most important
       delaying factors were: numerous political considerations;
       Cold War tensions; and complexities caused by the United
       Nations involvement.

1908. Butcher, J.O. "The Challenge." MARINE CORPS GAZ, 1966
       50 (12):20-26.

       A descriptive narrative of the July 27, 1953 signing of
       the armistice between representatives of North Korea and the
       UN Command. Also discusses the tenuous situation that
       existed in Korea in the decade following the end of
       hostilities.

1909. Carroll, E.J., Jr. "Limited War--Limited Peace?" US
       NAVAL INST PROC, 1966 92 (12):30-37.

       Maintains that limited wars tend to end in limited peace
       settlements, which are nearly always unsatisfactory. Cites
       the 1953 Korean peace settlement as an example of such an
       agreement--poorly planned and difficult to maintain.

1910. Choi, Duk-shin. PANMUNJOM AND AFTER. New York: Vantage, 1972.

The negotiations that finally led to the July 27, 1953, armistice agreements are examined as are the specific provisions of the agreement.

1911. Freymond, Jacques. "Supervising Agreements: The Korean Experience." FOR AFF, 1959 37 (3):496-503.

Claims that the armistice provision establishing a Military Armistice Commission to carry out the terms of the ceasefire agreement was doomed from the beginning because of the divergence between the understanding of both sides of the terms of the agreement. Shows how the commission was stymied and claims that in such future agreements, all details must be worked out first.

1912. Friedman, Edward. "Nuclear Blackmail and the End of the Korean War." MOD CHINA, 1975 1 (1):75-91.

Rejects US Secretary of State John Foster Dulles' claims that the war ended because of threats of nuclear escalation. Maintains China agreed to a negotiated settlement because after Stalin's death, Soviet leaders were no longer willing to issue nuclear counterthreats.

1913. Nordy, Walter H. "I Saw the Truce Arrive!" CHAP, 1953 10 (6):4.

Recounts the fighting that took place in Korea during the final hours of the war. The author was a chaplain serving with the 1st Battalion, 7th Marines. Notes that enemy shelling inflicted casualties less than three hours before the cease fire.

1914. Toner, James H. "Exceptional War, Exceptional Peace: The 1953 Cease-Fire in Korea." MIL R, 1976 56 (7):3-13.

Examines the role played by President Elect Eisenhower and the UN in trying to facilitate peace negotiations in Korea in late 1952 and early 1953.

1915. "Truce Comes In Korea." COM FOR J, 1953 4 (2):15.

One page photo-essay contains excellent maps showing the demilitarized zone and demarcation line which was based on battle positions when the truce agreement was reached.

1916. US Department of State. MILITARY ARMISTICE IN KOREA AND TEMPORARY SUPPLEMENTARY AGREEMENT. Washington: Government Printing Office, 1953.

This 130-page volume sets forth the detailed provisions of the agreement signed at Panmunjom on July 27, 1953.

1917. Winnington, Alan, and Wilfred Burchett. PLAIN PERFIDY. London: Britain-China Friendship Association, 1954.

Sets forth the Korean truce agreements from a pro-Communist, anti-American point of view. Claims the truce was so slow in coming because of US and South Korean insincerity and deceit in the negotiations.

XVIII. KOREA DURING THE WAR
A. POLITICS, ECONOMICS AND EDUCATION

1918. Bihlemeyer, Earl W. "Wartime Education in Korea."
       SCH EX, 1953 72 March:70-73.

       Shows how the task of educating South Korean children
       continued during the war in spite of the problems of
       destroyed schools, lack of supplies and shortages of
       teachers. Includes statistics of numbers of students
       being educated and salaries of teachers.

1919. Cullison, A.E. "Korean Broadcasting System ... Outpost
       of the Free World." KOREAN SUR, 1957 6 (2):6-7.

       Looks at the system in the post-war years, but half of the
       story is devoted to the problems and accomplishments seen
       during the course of the war--including the move of the
       headquarters to Taejon.

1920. Davison, W. Phillips. "The Lesser Evil." READ DIG,
       1951 58 (350):97-100.

       A member of a US Air Force Evaluation Group in the Far East
       traveled through Korea to find out if there was truth to
       stories that most Koreans wished that US-UN troops had not
       come to Korea to challenge the communist invasion and wanted
       them to leave. His study found such views to be virtually
       nonexistent, and while the civilians did not like the
       fighting, it was better than the evils of Communism.

1921. Han, Pyo W. "The Problem of Korean Unification: A Study
       of the Unification Policy of the Republic of Korea, 1948-
       1960." Doctoral Dissertation. Michigan, 1963.

       Traces the ROK policy of unification. A major portion of
       the study looks at the impact of the Korean War on South
       Korea's hopes and aspirations. The war originally led to
       hopes that the US and UN would reunite the country, but
       Chinese Communist intervention and the US decision to
       negotiate a settlement dashed those hopes. US-ROK position
       split over negotiated settlement issue.

1922. Jacobs, Harry A. "Native Labor--The Army's Ally Abroad."
       ARMY INFO DIG, 1953 8 (1):27-29.

Notes the contributions being made by native labor to the
US military effort worldwide but focuses primarily on Korea.
Tells of the contributions of the 296th Transportation Truck
Battalion and use of native porters, drivers, mechanics and
"chigebearers," men who carried supplies to nearly inaccessible
locations.

1923. Kim, Kwang Suk, and Michael Roemer. STUDIES IN THE
       MODERNIZATION OF THE REPUBLIC OF KOREA: 1945-1975: GROWTH
       AND STABILIZATION. Cambridge: Council on East Asian Studies,
       1979.

       Analyzes the growth of the South Korean economy and its
       associated changes on society and government. Good
       background on economic developments prior to and during the
       war. Statistics on economic damages, wartime agricultural
       and individual production, and imports and exports during
       the war years.

1924. Koons, William B. "Civil Assistance in Korea." ARMY INFO
       DIG, 1953 8 (2):15-23.

       Lauds the efforts of the United Nations Civil Assistance
       Command, Korea (UNCACK) in providing for the numerous
       refugees of the war. Describes the evolution of feeding and
       sheltering the victims of the conflict and tells of the
       medical and economic assistance along with the food, clothing
       and housing that were provided.

1925. KOREAN REPORT VOL. II, 1952-1953. Seoul: Korean Pacific,
       1955.

       Summary of ROK Governmental activities during the last two
       years of the war shows that advances were being made in such
       areas as agriculture, forestry, finance and banking,
       education, public health and transportation, in spite of the
       fighting.

1926. Oliver, Robert T., ed. KOREA'S FIGHT FOR FREEDOM.
       Washington: Korean Pacific, Vol. 1, 1951; Vol. 2, 1952.

       Selected addresses by South Korean statesmen on the Korean
       War. Most are messages aimed at rallying support for the
       war.

1927. Oliver, Robert T. THE TRUTH ABOUT KOREA. London:
       Putnam, 1951.

       A US scholar and friend of President Syngman Rhee examines
       the background of the war and maintains that the US has an
       obligation to the ROK and the UN to vigorously pursue the
       war.

1928. Oliver, Robert T. VERDICT IN KOREA. State College,
       PA: Bald Eagle, 1952.

Extremely pro-Korean, anti-Communist work on the will and aspirations of the Korean people. Praises the revitalized ROK Army for the job it did after the initial setbacks and gives an extremely favorable picture of Syngman Rhee and his government.

1929. Park, Chang J. "The Influence of Small States Upon the Superpowers: United States South Korean Relations As a Case Study, 1950-1953." WORLD POL, 1975 28 (1):97-117.

Studies how South Korea attempted to influence the foreign policy decisions of the US during the Korean War. Concludes that utilization of public calls for assistance and mutual cooperation and moral suasion were all very successful.

1930. Park, Chang Jin. "Seoul and Washington: A Study of Intra-Alliance Politics." Doctoral Dissertation. Washington, 1972.

Analyzes relations between the Republic of Korea and the US from 1950 to 1953. The highly temporal nature of US policies and the limited influence which the ROK had upon US policy makers is explored. The war complicated US policy with her allies throughout the world.

1931. Rhee, Syngman. KOREA FLAMING HIGH, EXCERPTS FROM STATEMENTS BY PRESIDENT SYNGMAN RHEE IN CRUCIAL 1953. Seoul: Office of Public Information, ROK, 1954.

Portions of speeches dealing with such things as the need to pursue the war, POW's, defense of his stands and actions.

1932. Smith, Paul A. "The Impact of International Events Upon Domestic Political Behavior." Doctoral Dissertation. Princeton, 1960.

This study of the relationship between four key foreign policy crises and American public opinion and voting behavior examines two events connected with the Korean War: the June 1950 North Korean invasion; and the fall 1950 Chinese intervention.

1933. Steger, Byron L. "Rehabilitation of Medical Education in South Korea." US ARM FOR MED J, 1953 4 (12):1675-1692.

Excellent study on the impact of the Korean War on medical education in South Korea. Tells of the prewar medical school system and the consequences when the war caused those facilities to be closed, and most physicans were drafted into the ROK Army. By the fall of 1952 several medical schools had reopened but were facing problems of lack of teachers and supplies.

1934. Stolzenbach, C. Darwin, and Henry A. Kissinger. CIVIL AFFAIRS IN KOREA 1950-51. Chevy Chase, MD: Operations Research Office, Johns Hopkins University, 1952.

A report based on a field study in Korea--with conditions up to September 1951. The Eighth US Army entered Korea in 1950 with no plan for Civil Affairs operations, but as in other wars, the responsibility fell to the army. The activity quickly developed into a $150 million annual operation carried out by 400 personnel. Many problems, such as lag in policy direction, confusion as to whether the ROK or US-UN Command had certain responsibilities and lack of trained and qualified civil affairs personnel, all had to be resolved.

1935. Vinocour, S.M. "Korea's Merchant Fleet." KOREAN
       SUR, 1953 2 (6):3-4.

       Problems of the ROK in meeting the Merchant Marine needs while in the midst of war. Korean ships and stevedores are assuming from the Japanese more of the responsibility of meeting the nation's shipping needs.

1936. Vinocour, S.M. "Second Front in Korea." KOREAN SUR,
       1953 2 (1):13-15.

       Examines the economic homefront in Korea during the war. Talks about the problems of rebuilding the country physically while keeping inflation under control. Good account of the physical reconstruction problems facing the ROK.

1937. Warren, Gile J. "We Worked With the Koreans." KOREAN
       SUR, 1957 6 (1):6-7, 11-12.

       Tells of the work of the First American Education Team to go to Korea in late 1952 and early 1953, when the war was still going on, as part of the UN effort to upgrade education. The team trained hundreds of key educators who in turn trained teachers at all levels of education.

                           B. SOCIAL AND CULTURAL IMPACTS

1938. Camp, Carol E. SNAPSHOTS, A SEASON IN KOREA. New York:
       Pageant, 1957.

       A young man from South Carolina presents an appreciative account of the Korea he came to know while serving there in the US Army during the war.

1939. Cutforth, Rene. KOREAN REPORTER. London: Wingate, 1952.

       A look at the impact of the war on the civilian populace of South Korea. Personal observations and interviews with the innocent people caught up in the fighting reveals the destruction, suffering and general havoc that prevailed. Questions if, when the war is over, and forces withdrawn, the Korean people will feel the war was worth it.

1940. Denson, John. "Bitter Weekend in Seoul." COLLIER'S,
          1951 127 (4):13-15, 74-76.

          Describes the chaos, confusion and terror that gripped the
          city of Seoul in December 1950 when there was fear that the
          Chinese Communists might retake the city. Although under UN
          control, Communist agents were everywhere, and they killed
          an average of eighteen anti-Communists a night. Good discus-
          sion of the refugee problem, especially as it affected the
          capitol city.

1941. Gilbert, Charles E. "Young Koreans Rebuild With Music."
          KOREAN SUR, 1953 2 (7):3-5.

          A member of the UN Civil Assistance Command shows how a
          music education program was developed and used as a major
          tool of rehabilitation of Korean war refugees.

1942. Kim, Bok Lim C. "Casework With Japanese and Korean
          Wives of Americans." SOC CAS, 1972 3 (5):273-279.

          The influx of Americans into Korea during and after the war
          led to many marriages between American men and Korean women.
          This study looks at the couples' relationships before and
          after marriage and problems of adjustment upon return to the
          US.

1943. Kim, Eul Han. I CHOSE FREEDOM. Seoul: International
          Cultural Association of Korea, n.d.

          A Korean publisher and translator recounts his experiences
          in Seoul following the June 1950 capture of the city by the
          Reds.

1944. Lee, Theresa. "Thunder in the North." KOREAN SUR,
          1957 6 (6):3-4, 10.

          A young girl living in Seoul, Korea, at the time of the
          invasion tells of the confusion that initially reigned,
          then recounts the Communist invasion and the horrors
          that followed, including the justice of the People's
          Courts. Word of the Inchon invasion and liberation are
          also described.

1945. Michener, James A. THE VOICE OF ASIA. New York:
          Random, 1951.

          Observations of the well-known American author's visit
          to a score of Asian nations, including wartime Korea.
          Tells of the destruction and suffering being inflicted
          on the civilians and claims US soldiers are unsure of why
          they are fighting and have no respect for the South
          Koreans. Defends the US involvement in the war.

1946. Republic of Korea, Statistics Bureau. STATISTICS OF
          DAMAGE SUFFERED DURING THE KOREAN WAR, JUNE 25, 1950-

JULY 27, 1953. Seoul: Office of Public Information,
ROK.

More than fifty pages of statistics on the human and
property loss sustained by the Republic of Korea during
the conflict. Claims that any errors are in the direction
of conservatism.

1947. Roh, Chang Shub. "Recent Changes in Korea Family Life
        Patterns." J COM FAM STUDIES, 1972 3 (2):217-227.

This study of changes in Korean family life during the
twenty-five years following WWII shows that the Korean War
was a major benchmark for change. Among the problems to
emerge were weakening of family ties, divorce, and
problems of the aged.

1948. Waln, Nora. "The Sunday After Korea." ATLANTIC,
        1951 187 (5):23-26.

A female American war correspondent recalls highlights
of her tour in war-torn Korea from the summer of 1950 to
December. Tells of the suffering inflicted upon the
civilians, especially children. Describes Korean treatment
of Communists after the retaking of Seoul in the fall and
notes that trials were quick and punishment cruel.

1949. "War's Tragedy in Korea." COLLIER'S, 1950 126 (9):
        24-25.

Photo essay setting forth the tremendous suffering which
the Korean War is inflicting on the innocent civilian
populace.

1950. Worden, William L. "Now They Know What Red Conquest
        Means." SAT EVE POST, 1950 223 (22):28-29, 126-128.

Description of life in Seoul from the time it fell to
advancing North Koreans in late June 1950 until it was
liberated by UN troops three months later. During that
period the one million citizens of the South Korean
capitol suffered under the oppression of their communist
captors.

                    C. REFUGEES

1951. Del Rey, Sister Maria. "Hands and Hearts Joined in
        Korea." KOREAN SUR, 1955 4 (1):10-11.

Tells how the Sisters of Maryknoll established a clinic
in Pusan during the Korean War and ministered to the
medical and material needs of Korean refugees. Describes
the work they are doing.

1952. Del Rey, Sister Maria. HER NAME IS MERCY. New York:
       Scribner's, 1957.

       Tells of the work of a Catholic missionary who as a member
       of the Maryknoll Sisters set up a clinic in Pusan, Korea, in
       April 1951. Along with eighteen other sisters, including
       several who were doctors, they ministered to the medical and
       physical needs of thousands of refugees. Tells of the
       problems and accomplishments of the group.

1953. Flavin, Martin. "Korean Diary." HARPER'S, 1951 202
       (1210):52-59.

       Observations of an American journalist who visited Seoul
       in early November 1950, six weeks after its liberation and
       before major Chinese intervention. Tells of the problems
       of refugees and the conditions in South Korean prison
       camps where thousands of political prisoners were being
       held.

1954. Goodman, Bud. "Better Than Bullets." READ DIG, 1954
       65 (392):127-128.

       How the people of Detroit, Michigan, and surrounding areas
       responded to a plea from a Marine Sergeant Parker Hallam, 7th
       Marine Transport Battalion for food, clothing and Christmas
       toys for orphans and homeless children in war-racked Korea.
       Condensed from VFW MAGAZINE, September 1954.

1955. Holt, Mrs. Harry as told to David Wisner. THE SEED FROM
       THE EAST. Los Angeles: Oxford, 1956.

       Account of the Holt family of Oregon who adopted several
       Korean war orphans and then initiated a program which
       brought hundreds of "G.I. orphans" to the US for adoption.

1956. Kennedy, Edgar S. MISSION TO KOREA. New York:
       British Book Center, 1953.

       An Englishman who spent eight months in Korea in 1952 on
       the staff of the International Refugee Organization describes
       efforts to provide food, clothing and shelter for South
       Koreans. Tells of the problem of meeting the needs of a
       people who scoff at charity. Good account of the refugee
       problem.

1957. Koh, Mrs. Taiwon. THE BITTER FRUIT OF KOM-PAWI.
       Philadelphia: Winston, 1959.

       The devastation and the suffering of war refugees
       receive considerable attention from a young woman who
       grew up in Kom-Pawi, North Korea, and went to college
       in Seoul. Tells of the invasion and occupation and
       the circumstances that enabled her family to go to the
       US to live.

1958. Koner, Marvin. "Korea's Children: The Old In Heart."
       COLLIER'S, 1953 132 (4):24, 26-27.

       Examines the problems surrounding the more than 100,000
       Korean children that ended up as orphans because of the
       war. Tells of their sufferings and the attempts of one
       US soldier, Sergeant Werner Krenzer, to help them.

1959. "Korea Today: The Plight of a Desperate People." UN BUL,
       1952 13 (1):434-436.

       Relates the devastation caused by twenty-eight months of
       fighting and tells of the tremendous impact which this has had
       on the social and economic life of South Koreans. Claims
       that refugees and those whom the conflict has rendered
       destitute number more than ten million.

1960. Mosier, Robert H. "The GI and the Kids of Korea."
       NAT GEO, 1953 103 (5):635-664.

       Account of a US Marine of the 1st Division who "adopted"
       a Korean orphan during the war. Relates the problem
       experienced by refugees and tells of many of the projects
       undertaken by US forces to help them overcome the ravages
       of war. Excellent photographs, including many in color,
       tell of Korean life in wartime.

1961. Mullen, Alyce M. "GI Ambassadors." CHAP, 1952
       9 (6):16-19.

       Describes ways in which US military personnel are
       assisting natives in the country where they are serving.
       Includes several examples of humanitarian acts in Korea
       during the war period.

1962. Riley, John W., Jr., et al. "Flight From Communism:
       A Report on Korean Refugees." PUB OP Q, 1951 15 (2):
       274-286.

       After the war started, tens of thousands of North and
       South Koreans fled from Communist-held sections to areas
       controlled by UN forces. This study, based on interviews
       of 1,319 refugees, examines the reasons they fled. Findings
       were that North Koreans generally left because of
       dissatisfaction with Communism while South Koreans tended
       to leave because they felt a family member was marked for
       liquidation or imprisonment.

1963. Scullin, George. "The Sergeant Didn't Go Home."
       READ DIG, 1953 62 (373):99-101.

       Focuses on an American Army Sergeant assigned to the
       United Nations Civil Assistance Command, a unit which
       provided aid for homeless Korean children. Relates the

suffering imposed on civilians caught up in the war and efforts of the UN and US to provide assistance.

1964. Shuler, James B. "Medical Practices With the Marines on Occupation Duty in Korea." US ARM FOR MED J, 1951 7 (7):1040-1050.

Details the medical treatment of civilians by Navy medical personnel.

1965. Sizoo, Joseph. "Korean's Story: Tragedy and Faith." KOREAN SUR, 1953 2 (4):3-5.

An American professor of religion tells of his 1953 visit to the war-ravaged country and the suffering the conflict has brought to South Korean civilians. Tells of the efforts of Christians to meet the physical needs of the people.

1966. Thompson, Reginald W. CRY KOREA. London: MacDonald, 1951.

Describes the fighting in Korea and shows the suffering that it inflicts on the civilian population. The author was a British war correspondent who witnessed the carnage.

1967. Waln, Nora. "Our Softhearted Warriors in Korea." SAT EVE POST, 1950 223 (26):28-29, 66-67.

While US soldiers were busy fighting the enemy in Korea, they also found time to take care of and provide for the numerous orphans produced by the war. Gives examples of such assistance.

1968. "The War Against Misery." KOREAN SUR, 1953 2 (7): 10-12.

The activities and accomplishments of CARE in attempting to alleviate some of the suffering among Korean War refugees are cited. Shows how many different segments of American society, including soldiers serving in Korea, joined in the effort.

1969. Worden, William L. "The Cruelest Weapon in Korea." SAT EVE POST, 1951 223 (33):26-27, 134-136.

The Communists in Korea used the refugees as a kind of military weapon as they sent their civilians fleeing South, thus harming the UN forces and hiding enemy agents who provided intelligence information and performed acts of sabotage. Tells of the danger and difficulty of not knowing hapless refugees from agents who might present a threat to the safety of US troops.

1970. Worden, William L. "What Must We Do About Korea Now?"
       SAT EVE POST, 1951 (24):32-33, 93-101.

       Examines the efforts of the UN to meet the needs of Korean
       War refugees by providing food, shelter and medical care.
       Shows the enormous task facing the UN agencies and the
       heavy cost, economically, of meeting the problem.

1971. Yong, Pak Jong, and Jock Carroll. KOREAN BOY. New York:
       Lothrop, 1955.

       Juvenile reading. A South Korean school boy recounts to a
       Canadian war correspondent the impact the war had on him,
       his family and his countrymen. Good on the consequences of
       war on civilians and their plight as they became refugees.

1972.   Air University Quarterly Staff.   "Enemy Airfields in
        North Korea."   AIR UNIV Q R, 1954 7 (2):12-28.

        In its last two years, the Korean conflict was basi-
        cally an air war, yet when the peace was negotiated,
        it was only concerned with the ceasefire line and did
        not address construction of enemy airfields in North
        Korea. Consequently, within months of the end of the
        war, the Communist forces had large operational airfields
        equipped and ready to function if combat flared again.
        Critical of the US policy which permitted this develop-
        ment.

1973.   Armstrong, O.K.   "The Communist Double-Cross in Korea."
        READ DIG, 1956 68 (405):37-41.

        Claims that in the two and a half years following the
        signing of the armistice in Korea, the Communists have
        continually violated the terms of the agreement, especially
        provisions that neither side would increase its military
        strength. Gives examples of numerous alleged violations.

1974.   Bernath, Cliff.   "No Dirtballs on the DMZ."   SOLDIERS,
        1982 37 (5):22-28.

        Describes life on the demilitarized zone in Korea nearly
        thirty years after the armistice. Describes the creation
        of the DMZ and the negotiations that led to its establish-
        ment. Tells of the frequent violations, problems of patrol-
        ing it and the overall functioning of the UN Command,
        Supply Group, Joint Security Area. Color photos.

1975.   Blumenthal, John.   "Korea's Sparetime Special."   ARMY INFO
        DIG, 1954 9 (10):39-43.

        The year following the Korean armistice saw US troops
        stationed at remote spots throughout the country. To meet
        the recreational and religious needs of those soldiers, the
        3rd Transportation Rail Command converted four railroad cars
        to a chapel, arts and craft center, library and education
        classroom and sent them to remote spots.

1976.   Burchett, Wilfred G.   AGAIN KOREA.   New York: International,
        1968.

        Australian journalist (and well-known Socialist) tells of
        his return visit to North Korea where he finds complete

reconstruction and recuperation from the Korean War. Maintains
that that devastating war was started by the South Koreans.

1977. Caldwell, John C. STILL THE RICE GROWS GREEN. New York:
Regnery, 1955.

A look at the post Korean War period in Korea and Formosa.
Finds the areas still under the threat of Communism and
Korea still showing the outward signs of war but is mildly
optimistic about the future because the people, who are a
strong and hearty lot, keep the rice fields green and
growing.

1978. Castles, Jean I. "Our Ground Defense Line in the Far
East." ARMY INFO DIG, 1955 10 (9):2-11.

Looks at US defenses in the Far East in the year following
the end of hostilities in Korea. Okinawa and Japan are
covered, as are the activities of the Eighth US Army in Korea
from July 1953 to September 1954. Brief mention of
Operations Little Switch, Big Switch, Reclaim and Glory.

1979. Chopra, Maharaj K. "Korea's Path of Unification." MIL R,
1973 53 (2):19-29.

Examines efforts to bring about unification of North and
South Korea in the aftermath of the Korean War. Covers the
1953 Truce agreement and subsequent peace negotiations and
the economic and political progress of the two Koreas in the
years that followed. Somewhat optimistic that unification
might ultimately take place.

1980. Cogswell, D.G. "Eighth Army's All-Purpose Aviation."
ARMY INFO DIG, 1963 18 (11):18-26.

Demonstrates the importance of US Army aviation in
maintaining the peace in Korea in the decade following
hostilities. Aviation was essential in deploying material,
delivering troops and maintaining equipment.

1981. "Dead End For Infiltration." ARMY DIG, 1968 23 (3):21.

1967 saw nearly 450 North Korean intrusions along the
demilitarized zone in Korea. In those attacks sixteen US
soldiers were killed and fifty-one wounded. To reduce
those intrusions, the US 2nd Infantry division constructed
an anti-infiltration system using chainlink fence, guard
towers and clearing a strip along the fence. Its
effectiveness had not yet been determined.

1982. DOCUMENTS RELATING TO THE DISCUSSION OF KOREA AND
INDO-CHINA AT THE GENEVA CONFERENCE, APRIL 27-JUNE 15,
1954. London: Her Majesty's Stationery Office, 1954.

Covers many speeches made in the fifteen plenary sessions

on Korea. The conference was convinced primarily to
provide for Korea's unification, but Communist refusal to
recognize the authority of the UN in that country led to
the failure of the conference's goal.

1983. Falk, Ray. "What the GI's in Korea Are Reading."
       NY TIMES B R, June 27, 1954, p. 19.

       Tells the leading books that are being read by US
       military leaders in the nine months after the armistice.
       Shows that accounts of WWII and the Korean War are very
       popular, but Mickey Spillane is top author. Statistics
       on books bought and borrowed and their general classifi-
       cation.

1984. Frank, Pat. THE LONG WAY AROUND. Philadelphia:
       Lippincott, 1953.

       Observations and experiences of a UN Korean Reconstruction
       Agency movie script writer who was in Seoul in the period
       immediately after the war ended. Laudatory of the humaneness
       of US policy in South Korea.

1985. Gaffe, Gordon. "The New Korea." ARMY DIG, 1967
       22 (6):16-20.

       Tells how Korea rebuilt physically and economically after
       the war. Describes conditions along the 151 mile long
       demilitarized zone.

1986. Goodsell, Vincent F. "The Panmunjom Story." ARMY
       INFO DIG, 1962 17 (8):16-22.

       Relates problems of maintaining the peace in Korea in
       the nine years after the ceasefire. Tells the role and
       functioning of the Military Armistice Commission and
       those assigned to aid it such as the Joint Observer
       Teams, Joint Duty Officer and the secretariat.
       Explains the difference between the military demarcation
       line and the demilitarized zone.

1987. Groves, Joseph R. "An Evaluation of the Neutral Nations
       Supervisory Commission in Korea." Master's Thesis.
       Georgetown, 1956.

       Describes the organization and responsibilities of the
       Commission composed of members from four nations given
       the responsibility in the 1953 truce of investigating
       complaints of truce violations outside the demilitarized
       zone.

1988. Han, Sung-Joo. US KOREA SECURITY COOPERATION: RETROSPECTS
       AND PROSPECTS. Seoul: Asiatic Research Center, 1983.

       Addresses and papers presented at a conference commemorating

the thirtieth anniversary of the 1953 signing of the Mutual
Defense Treaty between the US and the Republic of Korea.
Includes a copy of the treaty. While focus in on the
period betwen 1953 and 1983, there are numerous references
to the Korean War and its background.

1989.   Hanna, Parker D., Jr.   "KCAC in Korea." ARMY INFO DIG,
         1955 10 (9):27-32.

         Lauds the work being done by the Korea Civil Assistance
         Command (KCAC), a US command established after the war to
         assist in reestablishing agriculture, transportation,
         communications, health and welfare. The command works
         closely with the UN Korean Reconstruction Agency (UNCRA)
         which provided aid to industry, mining, education and
         housing.

1990.   Helton, Carl J. "Joint Observer Teams." ARMY INFO DIG,
         1963 18 (6):14-23.

         Explains the primary mission of the Joint Observer Team
         (JOT), an agency of the Korean Military Armistice Commission,
         which is to investigate violations of the armistice
         agreement. The five teams, made-up of three representatives
         from the UN Command and three from the Communists, also handle
         the exchange of detained personnel, recovery and exchange of
         human remains, and maintenance of safe lanes, roads and
         trails within the DMZ.

1991.   Heronemus, Michael L. "Face to Face With Communism."
         ARMY DIG, 1967 22 (10):39-42.

         Sets forth the role and responsibilities of the Military
         Armistice Commission in Korea during the post-war period.
         Explains the make-up of the Commission and gives examples
         of the types of problems they deal with and describes the
         Joint Security Area, the site of the MAC meetings.

1992.   "Korea--One Year Later." ARMY INFO DIG, 1954 9 (7):
         13-19.

         A photo essay examines the US Eighth Army in the year
         following the Korean armistice and notes its extensive
         program of field training, military reconstruction and
         rehabilitation of civilian communities.

1993.   "Korea Today: The Vigil Continues." ARMY DIG, 1969
         24 (10):41-47.

         Looks at Korea militarily, politically, socially and
         economically fifteen years after the end of the Korean
         War. Gives attention to the demilitarized zone and the
         responsibility of US and South Korean soldiers to defend
         it. The article is preceded by seven pages of color
         photos, many of the demilitarized zone.

1994. Kotch, John. "The Origins of the American Security
       Commitment to Korea" in Bruce Cumings, ed. CHILD OF
       CONFLICT. Seattle, University of Washington, 1983,
       pp. 239-259.

       Shows that the US desire to provide security for South
       Korea after hostilities had a major impact on the
       negotiations to end the war. Frustration with President
       Rhee's opposition to US proposals almost led to US
       abandonment of Rhee. What finally emerged was a ROK-US
       security agreement that was dictated by the Americans.

1995. Kriebel, Wesley P. "Korea: The Military Armistice
       Commission, 1965-1970." MIL AFF, 1972 36 (3):96-99.

       While focusing on the Commission nearly twenty years
       after its establishment and showing the continual
       tension along the ceasefire line, this article does
       describe the machinery and objectives of the ten-man
       commission.

1996. Margeson, Henry B. "Training Vigil in Korea." ARMY
       INFO DIG, 1954 9 (4):11-18.

       Examines the activities of the Eighth United States Army in
       the months immediately following the Korean armistice. Tells
       of the need to be ready militarily for anything that might
       happen, yet it was necessary to provide training, work
       projects and recreation programs that would keep soldiers
       busy and their morale high.

1997. Nesbitt, Frank M. "Pilgrimage to Panmunjom." ARMY
       INFO DIG, 1965 20 (7):52-53.

       Observations of a young US Army private who visited
       Panmunjom, on the twelfth anniversary of the ceasefire, to
       witness the continuing truce talks.

1998. Norton, Robert F. "Armor Helps Defend the ROK."
       ARMOR, 1968 77 Sept/Oct:18-20.

       Examines the US commitment to the defense of South Korea
       fifteen years after the ceasefire was signed. Tells of
       the missions of US Army units and recounts the role
       those units played in the Korean War. Claims a strong
       US-ROK defense will likely forestall an attack like that
       of June 1950.

1999. O'Neill, Arthur C. "Flight to Freedom." AERO HIST,
       1969 16 (2):19-20.

       Tells the story of North Korean pilot, Lieutenant Kum Sok
       No, who on September 21, 1953, defected by flying a
       Russian-built MIG-15 aircraft from Pyongyang to the US
       base at Kimpo, South Korea. No received a $100,000 reward

which General Mark Clark had offered to anyone who would
deliver the aircraft intact to US custody. Tells of No and
his defection.

2000. Richard, Duke. "Action Zone--Korea." ARMY DIG, 1968
      23 (3):20.

Shows the tense situation along the demilitarized zone some
fourteen years after the armistice by relating details of a
1967 North Korean attack on a unit of the 2nd US Infantry
Division which resulted in three Americans dead and twenty-
six wounded.

2001. Schwartz, Michael G. "Advance Camp--Korea." ARMY DIG,
      1970 25 (1):12-13.

Traces the history and explains the mission of the US
Army Support Group (USASG) for the Joint Security Area
at Panmunjom, North Korea. The 300-man force provides
security and logistical support to the Military Armistice
Commission.

2002. Sharp, John D., Jr. "A Truce With Teeth." ARMY INFO
      DIG, 1965 20 (6):22-24.

Describes the activities of the men of the 1st Cavalry
Division as they keep watch over the North Koreans in the
Demilitarized Zone--an activity that had already been going
on twelve years when this article was written.

2003. Staley, J.W. "Eyes Across the DMZ." ARMY DIG, 1969
      24 (10):29-32.

An examination of the typical North Korean soldier that is
protecting his country from intrusions by US or ROK soldiers
along the demilitarized zone. The soldiers are urban youth,
well-indoctrinated in Communist philosophy who are well
trained and equipped (with Soviet weapons). North Korea
puts its best soldiers on duty along the demarcation line.

2004. Stanley, David L. "Unrest in Indian Country." ARMY
      DIG, 1967 22 (11):52-53.

Experiences of men of the 1st Battalion, 23rd Infantry,
positioned north of the Imjin River, who are protecting the
DMZ. Tells of North Korean penetrations and American
attempts to halt them. All this fourteen years after the
ceasefire.

2005. Strauss, William L. "A Continuing Threat to Peace--
      Korean War 24 Years Later." J KOREAN AFF, 1974 4 (2):
      41-50.

Discusses the political and military impacts that the
Korean War had on both the North and South in the two

decades following the armistice.

2006. Strauss, William L. "The Military Armistice Commission:
       Deterrent of Conflict." J KOREAN AFF, 1975 5 (1):24-46.

       Explains the problems and effectiveness of the Military
       Armistice Commission established at the end of the conflict
       to enforce the boundary lines agreed to in the armistice.

2007. Thomas, S.B. "The Chinese Communists' Economic and
       Cultural Agreement with North Korea." PAC AFF, 1954
       27 (1):61-65.

       In the aftermath of the Korean War armistice, North Korea
       and Communist China moved to solidify their wartime
       cooperation by signing a ten-year agreement to share economic
       and technical aid and promote cultural exchanges; Kim Il Sung
       went to Peking to negotiate the agreement. The two sides
       made it clear that they would cooperate in Korea as long as
       the UN-US threat remained in the south.

2008. US Department of State. FOREIGN RELATIONS OF THE UNITED
       STATES, 1952-1954. Vol. XVI: THE GENEVA CONFERENCE.
       Washington: Government Printing Office, 1981.

       Official US government documents relating to the April 26-
       June 15, 1954 Geneva Conference On Korea. Includes pre-
       conference memorandums of State Department officials as
       well as exchanges during the conference. List of sources
       and participants.

2009. US Department of State. THE KOREAN PROBLEM AT THE
       GENEVA CONFERENCE, APRIL 26-JUNE 15, 1954. Washington:
       Government Printing Office, 1954.

       Collection of documents emanating from the 1954 Geneva
       Conference shows that considerable attention was given to
       the question of Korean unification but no agreements could
       be reached.

2010. US Department of State. MUTUAL DEFENSE TREATY BETWEEN
       THE UNITED STATES AND THE REPUBLIC OF KOREA. Washington:
       Government Printing Office, 1955.

       Official version of the agreement signed in Washington on
       October 1, 1953, provided for consultation between the two
       when either was threatened by attack, action by each to
       meet a common danger, and ROK permission to US to maintain
       land, air and sea forces in South Korea.

XX.   US HOMEFRONT
A.   CONGRESS AND THE POLITICS OF WAR

2011.   Armstrong, John P.   "The Enigma of Senator Taft and
        American Foreign Policy."   R POL, 1955 17 (2):206-231.

        Examines some of Taft's foreign policy views as expressed
        in his public statements and concludes that most of what he
        said was "political nonsense."   Considerable attention is
        given to Taft and the Korean War, and the author concludes
        there was little, if any, consistency in his position.   A
        significant study since Taft was the leading Republican
        spokesman.

2012.   Caridi, Ronald J.   "The G.O.P. and the Korean War."
        PAC HIST R, 1968 37 (4):423-443.

        When the war broke out, congressional Republicans openly
        supported the President's policy.   However, when the US
        military began suffering setbacks, the GOP members began
        criticizing the President's conduct of the war and
        continued to do so as long as he remained in office.   Some
        attacks were the result of genuine concern while others
        were clearly for partisan reasons.

2013.   Caridi, Ronald J.   THE KOREAN WAR AND AMERICAN POLITICS:
        THE REPUBLICAN PARTY AS A CASE STUDY.   Philadelphia:
        University of Pennsylvania, 1969.

        Indicts the Republican Party's actions during the Korean
        War by claiming its members in Congress were driven by
        partisan motives and political expediency to criticize the
        Democratic Administration's handling of the conflict without
        giving viable alternatives.   A scholarly study which relies
        heavily on the public record.

2014.   Caridi, Ronald J.   "The Republican Party and the Korean War."
        Doctoral Dissertation.   New York, 1967.

        Examines the GOP's response to the Korean War from its
        outbreak through the inauguration of Eisenhower.   Maintains
        that the Republicans capitalized on and helped promote
        discontent over the Truman policies and ultimately turned
        that dissatisfaction into a victory in the 1952 presidential
        race.   Published in 1969 under title, THE KOREAN WAR AND
        AMERICAN POLITICS.

2015. Connally, Tom. MY NAME IS TOM CONNALLY. New York:
       Crowell, 1954.

       This autobiography of the Democratic Senator from Texas,
       who was chairman of the Senate Committee on Foreign Relations,
       includes a chapter on the background to the Korean War and US
       response and another chapter on the impact of the war on
       bipartisan foreign policy. Inside information on Connally's
       talks with Truman during the period of the decision to
       intervene.

2016. Dewey, Thomas E. JOURNEY TO THE FAR PACIFIC. Garden
       City, NY: Doubleday, 1952.

       In 1951 the former Republican presidential candidate and
       party leader toured the Far East, including Korea. Praises
       the performance of the Americans fighting there and, as
       would be expected, is critical of the Truman Administration's
       conduct of the war.

2017. Glassen, Chester E. "Development of the Performance of
       Budget Structure in the Department of the Army, September
       1947 to June 1951." Master's Thesis. Syracuse, 1953.

       Shows the impact that the Korean War had on the budgets and
       budgeting of the US Army.

2018. Graham, Charles John. REPUBLICAN FOREIGN POLICY, 1939-
       1952. Doctoral Dissertation. Illinois, 1955.

       Contains a discussion of the Republican Party's position
       on President Truman's handling of the Korean War. The GOP
       was caught in the dilemma of being supportive of US military
       forces while trying to make political gain at the expense
       of the Democrats.

2019. Huzar, Elias. THE PURSE AND THE SWORD: CONTROL OF THE
       ARMY BY CONGRESS THROUGH MILITARY APPROPRIATIONS, 1933-1950.
       Ithaca, NY: Cornell University, 1950.

       Shows that the US Army is at the mercy of Congress which
       influences the military by the dollars it permits it to have.
       This was especially true in the post-WWII period when Congress,
       for various reasons, chose to severely limit funds with the
       consequence that the Army was unprepared to fight in Korea
       in 1950. When war came Congress quickly provided funds, but
       it could not be turned into equipment and well-trained
       soldiers overnight.

2020. Kinnard, Douglas. "President Eisenhower and the Defense
       Budget." J POL, 1977 39 (3):596-623.

       President Eisenhower's defense budgets throughout his years
       in office were heavily influenced by his 1952 campaign
       promises to end the war in Korea and cut taxes, both of which
       led to a position to reduce defense spending. To save

dollars he thus turned from Truman's position of balanced
forces to advocacy of strategic deterrence.

2021. Lo, Clarence Y.H. "Military Spending as Crisis Management:
       The US Response to the Berlin Blockade and the Korean War."
       BERK J SOC, 1976 20:147-181.

       The positive and negative impacts of the big increase in
       military spending that came with the Korean War. Rearmament
       improved the deficit because of increased purchases of raw
       materials from Europe's colonies but eventually increased raw
       material prices, intensified inflation and increased Europe's
       balance of payments deficit.

2022. Lo, Clarence Y.H. "The Truman Administration's Military
       Budgets During the Korean War." Doctoral Dissertation.
       California, Berkeley, 1978.

       An examination of the impact that the Korean War had on
       US military spending. During the war the budget quadrupled,
       but more money was spent to arm US allies and to expand
       military capabilities at home than was spent on the war.

2023. Lofgren, Charles A. "Congress and the Korean Conflict."
       Doctoral Dissertation. Stanford, 1966.

       Congressional attitudes toward the war and its conduct
       are examined. While extreme hawkish or dovish views were
       expressed by a few politicians from both parties, generally
       Democrats remained supportive and Republicans walked a middle
       line by trying to be supportive of the fighting men, yet
       criticizing the President's conduct of the war.

2024. Martin, Harold H. "The Man Behind the Brass." SAT
       EVE POST, 1951 223 (49):22-23, 42, 45-48.

       Examines the activities of the chairman of the US Senate
       Armed Services Committee, Richard Russell (D-Georgia) as
       he attempted to see that the nation could meet its
       worldwide military commitments while fighting in Korea.
       A look at the Senate during the war.

2025. Martin, Joe. MY FIRST FIFTY YEARS IN POLITICS.
       New York: McGraw, 1960.

       The Republican Minority Leader in the House of
       Representatives at the time of the MacArthur dismissal
       includes in this autobiography his role in the
       Truman-MacArthur controversy. Martin, a staunch supporter of
       the General, was the recipient of MacArthur's letter
       criticizing the President's Korean policy, and when he
       made it public, Truman decided to act.

2026. Marwell, Gerald. "Party, Region and the Dimensions
       of Conflict in the House of Representatives." AM POL
       SCI R, 1967 61 (2):380-399.

This study looks at the 81st, 82nd and 83rd Congresses
and shows the consistency of congressmen in their legislative
voting over a broad range of issues. While there were
several factors which led to changes in voting behavior,
it was the Korean War which had the most far-reaching
impact.

2027. Michalak, Stanley J. "The Senate and the United Nations."
       Doctoral Dissertation. Princeton, 1967.

       Examines the US Senate's perceptions about the value of the
       UN as an instrument of international peace and shows how the
       Korean War impacted those views.

2028. Morgan, Anne Hodges. ROBERT S. KERR: THE SENATE YEARS.
       Norman: University of Oklahoma, 1977.

       This biography of the influential Democratic Senator from
       Oklahoma covers the Washington scene during the Korean War
       and shows many of the impacts the conflict had on politics.
       Interesting because Kerr was a major critic of MacArthur
       even before the dismissal. Afterward, he stood firmly
       behind Truman.

2029. Patterson, James T. MR. REPUBLICAN: A BIOGRAPHY OF
       ROBERT A. TAFT. Boston: Houghton, 1972.

       This first-rate study of the key Republican spokesman at
       the time of the Korean conflict shows the legislative
       problems that developed for members of both parties when
       war broke out and as it developed into a stalemate. Taft
       was supportive of the war but critical of Truman's handling
       of it.

2030. Republican National Committee. BACKGROUND TO KOREA.
       Washington: Republican National Committee, 1952.

       A sixty-four page campaign document traces the Truman
       Administration's mishandling of the Korean situation
       from the establishment of the ROK through the summer of
       1952. Not so critical of the decision to intervene
       but sees the war resulting in part from Democratic
       failures and sees the conduct of the war as anything but
       well handled.

2031. Riggs, James R. "Congress and the Conduct of the
       Korean War." Doctoral Dissertation. Purdue, 1972.

       While Congress was extremely interested in the Korean War
       and debated various issues related to it from 1950 through
       1953, it took little action. Examines congressional
       responses to US intervention, objectives and strategy,
       Chinese intervention, MacArthur's dismissal, and domestic
       consequences of the war.

2032.   Rovere, Richard H. "Letter From Washington." NEW
        YORKER, 1950 26 (July 8, 1950):69-73.

        Inciteful assessment of the mood in Washington, D.C., in
        the days following Truman's decision to intervene in Korea.
        Claims there was a certain calmness brought on by the
        feeling that earlier (Cold War) tensions were being replaced
        by something more certain, more concrete. Notes that while
        it was uncertain who pushed for what in the inner circle,
        it was evident Congress played a minor role.

2033.   Schilling, Warner R., et al. STRATEGY, POLITICS, AND
        DEFENSE BUDGETS. New York: Columbia University, 1962.

        Three in-depth studies which look at the evolution of US
        defense strategies from ideas to appropriations to purchase
        of weapons. Examination of the 1950 defense budget goes
        a long way toward explaining the military's lack of prepara-
        tion on the eve of the Korean War and a look at NSC-68
        (National Security Council Policy Paper No. 68) shows how
        that plan for rearmament became a reality because of the
        Korean War.

2034.   Smith, Beverly. "He Makes the Generals Listen."
        SAT EVE POST, 1951 223 (37):20-21, 134-138.

        Inside look at the powerful chairman of the US House of
        Representatives Armed Services Committee, Carl Vinson
        (D-Georgia) in the early months of the Korean War. Tells
        of his battle with fellow congressmen and civilian and
        military leaders at the Pentagon to provide the material
        and manpower to meet the military needs of the conflict.

2035.   Thompson, Jo. "He Makes the Brass See Red." SAT EVE
        POST, 1952 (45):36-37, 105.

        Looks at the Washington activities of Congressman F. Edward
        Herbert (D-Louisiana), member of the House Armed Services
        Committee, who was a major critic of military spending during
        the Korean War. Herbert was a thorn in the side of military
        leaders who were concerned about military performance and
        not cost. He was a critic yet was supportive of the military
        effort.

2036.   US Air Force Academy Library. THE HOME FRONT AND WAR IN
        THE TWENTIETH CENTURY. Special Bibliography Series No. 65,
        USAF Academy, 1982.

        Lists forty-five books, articles and reports which focus on
        domestic developments in the US during the Korean War.

2037.   Vandenberg, Arthur H., Jr., ed. THE PRIVATE PAPERS OF
        SENATOR VANDENBERG. Boston: Houghton, 1952.

        The Republican Senator from Michigan who turned from post-

WWII isolationism and helped bring about a bipartisan foreign
policy in the Cold War era was not pleased with the US's
Korean foreign policy and our involvement in the war. Covers
only the initial months of the war before his death from
cancer in April, 1951.

2038. White, William S. CITADEL: THE STORY OF THE US SENATE.
       New York: Harper, 1957.

       This study contains an examination of the conduct,
       importance and significance of the MacArthur Hearings. Sees
       the importance of open inquiry and the contribution of the
       preservation of civilian supremacy over the military as being
       very beneficial to the US.

                    B. INDUSTRIAL MOBILIZATION

2039. Aber, John W. "The Navy and the Merchant Marine." US
       NAVAL INST PROC, 1970 96 (3):40-44.

       When the US became involved in Korea, there was a surge of
       interest in providing naval protection to the Merchant Marine
       to assure that needed supplies could reach the war front.
       As a result the Naval Control of Shipping Organization was
       developed near the end of the war but was never really tested.

2040. Bernard, Tom. "We Are Counting on Women." AMERICAN,
       1951 152 (2):36-37, 110-112.

       As in WWII women played a major role in the industrial
       mobilization effort during the Korean War. Tells of the
       labor shortage that resulted when nearly 4,000,000 new
       workers were hired for defense industries in the first
       eighteen months of the conflict, and women provided nearly
       one-third of that number. Women played an important part
       in the aircraft, ship, tank and munitions industries.

2041. Conner, John. "Do We Have Enough Strategic Materials
          For War?" COLLIER'S 1950 126 (11):34, 72-73.

       Describes the machinery in the US government to see that
       the raw materials and finished products necessary to pursue
       the Korean War are provided. Procurement of such materials
       as rubber, aluminum and tungsten is described. Tells of
       the functioning of the National Security Resources Board
       and National Munitions Board.

2042. Crawford, D.J. "A Tank Isn't Born Overnight." ARMOR,
       1951 60 (4):6-11.

       Relates the problems and time required to get a tank from
       the drawing board to production.

2043.   David, Charles. "Price Wage Boss." QM R, 1951
        30 (6):12-13, 137-138.

        Delves into the problems facing Eric A. Johnson as head of
        the government's Economic Stabilization Agency, a body
        established to head off inflation caused by the war. As
        such, he headed the two-pronged drive to hold the line on
        prices and wages by being the boss of both the Office of
        Price Stabilization and Wage Stabilization Board. His holding
        the line on wage and price increases won him few friends in
        Washington.

2044.   DiSalle, Michael V. "What About Prices." AMERICAN,
        1951 151 (4):24-25, 118-121.

        The head of the US Office of Price Stabilization, whose
        responsibility was to assure there was a lid on prices of
        consumer items to assure that inflation did not get out of
        hand, tells of the problems facing him and his approach to
        those difficulties. Answers questions frequently asked by
        consumers.

2045.   Douglas, Paul H. "The Problem of Tax Loopholes." AM SCH,
        1968 37 (1):21-43.

        During the Korean War, Senator Paul Douglas (D-Illinois)
        joined with Senator Hubert Humphrey (D-Minnesota) and used
        the wartime atmosphere to push for tax reform which would
        place a heavier burden on industry and the wealthy. In the
        years after the conflict, they continued to play a major
        role in tax reform. Shows how war can affect tax policies.

2046.   Drucker, Peter. "This War is Different." HARPER'S,
        1950 201 (1206):21-27.

        Assesses the economic problems facing the US at the beginning
        of the war in Korea. Maintains the US does not know how to
        gear up for "near war," only total war. Claims that initially
        close control of the industrial machine by government will be
        essential but later it could be relaxed.

2047.   Eaton, Edgar I. "Comparison of Price Movements, World War
        II-1950." MONT LAB R, 1950 71 (3):318-322.

        This five-year study of US consumer prices shows the impact
        that the outbreak of war in Korea had on them. The rapid
        increases that took place in the first few months resulted
        as consumers, who recalled the effects of WWII on the supply
        of goods, wished to stock up on consumer goods.

2048.   Heller, Francis H. ECONOMICS AND THE TRUMAN ADMINISTRATION.
        Lawrence: Regents Press of Kansas, 1981.

        President Truman made a determined effort to balance the

annual budget and was quite successful. It was that
determination that led him in the post- WWII period to cut
defense spending, which had a major impact on the armed
forces on the eve of the Korean War. This work relates the
views of participants and scholars in economic matters.
Considerable discussion of the impact of the war on those
policies.

2049.   Hewlett, Richard G., and Francis Duncan. ATOMIC SHIELD,
        1947-1952. University Park, PA: Pennsylvania State
        University, 1969.

        Volume 2 of the History of the United States Atomic Energy
        Commission is a well-written, scholarly study which shows
        the development of atomic weapons just prior to and during
        the Korean War. Shows how the 1949 Soviet detonation of
        an atomic weapon and the war in Korea stimulated US
        production of atomic bombs and development of a hydrogen
        bomb.

2050.   Hickman, Bert G. THE KOREAN WAR AND US ECONOMIC ACTIVITY,
        1950-1952. New York: National Bureau of Economic Research,
        1954.

        The impact of the war on American business through 1952.
        Shows the stimulus which the war gave to the industrial
        economy and the problems which the war brought to the fore.

2051.   Janeway, Eliot. "The International Imperative of
        Mobilization." YALE R, 1951 40 (3):452-468.

        Examines US's partial mobilization for the Korean War
        and is critical of the Truman Administration's inappropriate
        measures to control inflation. Looks at some of the domestic
        mobilization efforts but also shows how the war is impacting
        US foreign trade. Calls for international mobilization and
        more US initiative in world affairs.

2052.   Janeway, Eliot. "Mobilizing the Economy: Old Errors in
        a New Crisis." YALE R, 1950 40 (2):201-219.

        One of the foremost mobilization experts warns that the
        mistakes of WWI and II not be repeated as the nation goes
        to war in Korea. Says the US must control inflation and
        coordinate mobilization of materials, manpower and foreign
        aid.

2053.   Keller, K.T. "The Truckmakers and the Soldier."
        COM FOR J, 1953 3 (8):32-34.

        The Chairman of the Board of Chrysler Corporation talks
        of how the automobile industry is meeting the vehicular
        needs of the US armed forces. Uses the military truck
        to show how the manufacturer and the government cooperate
        in the production effort.

2054. Kupinsky, Mannie. "Expansion of Employment in the
       Aircraft Industry." MONT LAB R, 1951 73 (1):15-19.

       Rapid expansion of the US Air Force and naval and marine
       aviation during the conflict in Korea led to tremendous
       expansion of the workforce in the aircraft industry.
       This article looks at the expansion during the first ten
       months of the war, the employment outlook, occupational
       requirements and the employment of women in the industry.

2055. LeRoy, Dave. "OPS vs. Inflation." QM R, 1951 30
       (6):14-15, 138, 141-148.

       Looks at the problems encountered by Michael V. DiSalle,
       head of the Office of Price Stabilization. Brought to the
       position months after the war began, DiSalle by pushing for
       a virtual freeze on prices immediately split with his boss,
       Alan H. Valentine, and precipitated the latter's resignation.
       DiSalle's hard line approach was assaulted by businessmen
       but was successful in halting runaway inflation.

2056. McConnell, Grant. THE STEEL SEIZURE OF 1952.
       Indianapolis, Bobbs-Merrill, 1960.

       Case study of the April 8, 1952 seizure of the nation's
       steel mills by President Truman. Looks at the events
       leading up to the seizure, the legal happenings and its
       consequences from the perspective of the White House.
       Part of The Inter-University Case Program.

2057. Mack, Louise J. "Price Movements During a Year of
       Korean Hostilities." MONT LAB R, 1951 73 (2):141-143.

       The outbreak of war marked the beginning of six months of
       rapid inflation in the US. In December 1950, under the
       provisions of the Defense Production Act, an attempt at
       voluntary price controls was attempted, but five weeks
       later, when it was apparent such an approach would not
       work, the Price Administration imposed the General Ceiling
       Price Regulation which ushered in a year of stability.

2058. Marcus, Maeva. TRUMAN AND THE STEEL SEIZURE CASE:
       THE LIMITS OF PRESIDENTIAL POWER. New York: Columbia
       University, 1977.

       In 1951, President Truman, claiming a steel strike would
       hurt the production of war goods needed by troops in
       Korea, seized the mills to prevent the strike. The US
       Supreme Court ruled he did not have that right. The
       dispute between labor and the companies was settled, and
       there was no real impact on the fighting. This scholarly
       account talks of the dispute and its significance, which
       was more constitutionally than militarily important. Good

look at Congress and the public during the Korean War period.

2059. Maynard, Lemuel. "Mobilizing Munitions." QM R, 1951 30 (6):22-23, 115-117.

Looks at the responsibilities and operations of the US Munitions Board whose defense mobilization tasks included: coordination of all industrial matters, including production, procurement and distribution; planning military aspects of industrial mobilization; supervising the national stockpile of strategic materials and the maintenance of reserves of industrial plants and equipment. Tells how it is moving to meet those responsibilities.

2060. Mitchell, Donald W. "Mobilization Progress." CUR HIST, 1952 23 (133):139-143.

US Government supervision of production and allocation of many valuable resources such as steel, copper and aluminum made it possible to adequately meet military and civilian demands for those items. Puts forth the US economic mobilization policy and tells how the National Production Authority was set up to implement it.

2061. "Mobilization Plans for Industry." ARMY INFO DIG, 1951 6 (2):11-21.

Explains the program for US industrial mobilization on which the expanded defense production of late 1950 was based. Details the planning that took place in the four years prior to the Korean War and tells what programs were in place when, on December 16, 1950, President Truman proclaimed a national emergency.

2062. Morgan, John D. "The National Security Resources Board in Mobilization Planning." MIL ENG, 1950 42 (289):379-381.

Describes the organization and functions of the National Security Resources Board, set up in 1947 to advise the President on the coordination of military, industrial and civilian mobilization. The secretaries of seven departments - State, Defense, Treasury, Interior, Agriculture, Commerce and Labor - are members of the board, and they use the resources of their departments to assure the effective use of all the nation's vital resources in time of war.

2063. Nelson, Harold B. "Emphasis on Production." QM R, 1951 30 (6):8-9.

Sketches the career of William H. Harrison, head of the US Defense Production Administration, during the early period of the Korean War and tells what his job entailed. Having some form of direction over fifteen government agencies, his responsibility was to see that the nation's factories

produced adequately and promptly to meet the demands of the
Korean conflict.

2064. Newhall, Shirley. "Brake on Wages." QM R, 1951 30
       (6):16, 134, 137.

       Explains the organization, problems and responsibilities
       of the revamped eighteen member Wage Stabilization Board.
       The group passed on requests for wage increases that
       exceeded their guidelines and had authority in noneconomic
       matters, such as senority rules, as well.

2065. Newlon, Clarke. "How to Make Tanks in a Hurry."
       COLLIER'S, 1951 128 (22):24-25, 60-62.

       Good example of how US industry was able to gear up for
       war during the Korean conflict. On August 15, 1950,
       representatives from Cadillac inspected a rundown WWII
       bomber plant in Cleveland, Ohio, and seven months later,
       T-41 Walker Bulldog Tanks, a weapon of new design, were
       rolling off the assembly line at a rapid rate.

2066. "NSRB Rushes 1950 Mobilization Plan." BUS WK, 1950
       August 5, No. 1092:22-24.

       Sets forth the planning taking place in the National
       Security Resources Board, chaired by W. Stuart Symington.
       The group is examining and relying on the plans instituted
       in 1940 and 1941. Truman and Symington favor limited
       mobilization, basically intending to examine military
       requests and determine if they should be granted.

2067. Pace, Frank, Jr. "Training and Industrial Mobilization."
       QM R, 1951 30 (6):36-37, 100, 103-104.

       Tells the major role played by American small businesses in
       meeting the procurement needs of the Army in the period of
       rapid industrial mobilization that occurred in the year
       following the outbreak of the war.

2068. Pachley, Walter A. "Controlling the Purse Strings."
       QM R, 1951 30 (6):18, 123-127.

       Relates the activities of the Federal Reserve Board and
       the Reconstruction Finance Corporation as they took steps
       to control inflation while assuring that the defense
       mobilization program could be funded. Explains the
       various pressures for inflation and describes actions
       utilized to quell them.

2069. Pastalove, Ester. "Antiaircraft Weapons Protect Industry."
       ARMY INFO DIG, 1953 8 (5):43-45.

       Examines one aspect of US civil defense during the Korean
       War by focusing on the 69th AAA Gun Battalion at Fort Tilden,

New York, and showing how it worked with the Civilian Ground
Observer Corps to "protect" American cities from enemy air
attack.

2070. Pasternak, Robert. "A Review of Prices in a Year of Price
Stabilization." MONT LAB R, 1952 74 (4):386-389.

To halt the rapid rise in inflation that marked the first
six months of the Korean War, the US government issued the
General Ceiling Price Regulation in January 1951. The action
worked and 1951 witnessed a modest 3% increase in the
Consumer Price Index and a slight reduction in wholesale
prices. Shows the impact the war had on food, rent, apparel
and other prices.

2071. Patrick, Ed. "Old Line Bureaus Re-Geared for Defense."
QM R, 1951 30 (6):24, 119-123.

While many aspects of the Defense Mobilization Program of
the US was carried on by newly created agencies, a large
part of the burden fell to old-line offices converted from
peacetime to emergency operations. Sub groups in departments
such as Agriculture, Interior and Commerce contributed in
some fashion to the overall mobilization effort.

2072. Pearse, Ben. "Can We Outproduce the Russians?" SAT
EVE POST, 1951 224 (3):22-23, 98-101.

Describes how the US was able to supply its front line
troops with the 3.5 inch rocket launcher in great quantities
early in the Korean War. Tells how the American Ordnance
Association facilitated the development, production and
transportation of the weapon which was essential in
stopping the Russian built T-34 tank.

2073. "Plane Makers Turn It On." LIFE, 1950 29 (9):45-48.

Tells of the actions by US aircraft industry to expand
military aircraft production from its June 1950 level of
2,500 per year to 8,000 a year by July of 1951.

2074. Ragan, Bill. "Mr. Mobilization." QM R, 1951 30
(6):5-7, 152-155.

A look at the US Director of Defense Mobilization during
the Korean War, Charles E. Wilson. Traces his career
and looks at the burdens of direction, control and
coordination of all mobilization activities of the
government.

2075. Ramsett, David E., and Tom R. Heck. "Wage and Price
Controls: A Historical Survey." NO DAK Q, 1977 45
(4):5-22.

Examines US wage and price control policies in WWI and II
and Korea. The Truman Administration turned to price-wage

policies to assure that consumer and government interests
were protected, but it soon became apparent that such
actions were unnecessary.

2076. Reday, Joseph Z. "Industrial Mobilization in the US."
       US NAVAL INST PROC, 1953 79 (10):1065-1075.

       US industrial mobilization during the Korean War is
       examined. The fact that the nation followed only limited
       mobilization presented more difficulties than if an
       all-out effort was needed. Discusses production levels,
       plant expansion, mobilization machinery and the impact on
       the civilian economy.

2077. Rings, E. Eleanor. "The Effects of Mobilization on
       Automobile Employment." MONT LAB R, 1952 74 (1):1-6.

       The impact of war was definitely felt by the American
       automobile industry as it was forced to divert its efforts
       from passenger vehicles to war production. Although focus-
       ing upon the impact of the change on the labor force, it
       includes statistics on production levels and discusses the
       defense activities of the automotive companies.

2078. Rosenberg, Herbert. "ODM: Civil-Military Relations
       During the Korean Mobilization." Doctoral Dissertation.
       Chicago, 1957.

       Study of the Office of Defense Mobilization, the federal
       agency designed to assure that US industry and the civilian
       economy provided the goods necessary for the military to
       conduct the war in Korea.

2079. Schwarz, Jordan A. THE SPECULATOR: BERNARD M. BARUCH
       IN WASHINGTON, 1917-1965. Chapel Hill: University of
       North Carolina, 1981.

       Although Baruch, who was the man behind WWI and WWII
       industrial mobilization, was basically on the sidelines
       during the Korean conflict, he made his opinions on the
       subject known, and the section on the period 1950-51 explains
       the government's efforts to meet the war's needs and control
       inflation.

2080. Spector, Eugene P. "Manpower Problems in the American
       Merchant Marine." MONT LAB R, 1951 73 (5):564-567.

       An increase of 1,910 merchant marine vessels created a
       great need for American seamen to operate them.
       Unfortunately, not enough men could be attracted into that
       labor force, and thus, sailings were delayed because of crew
       shortages. Concludes that while more ships could be
       outfitted, it would be difficult to get the personnel to
       operate them.

2081. Staring, Graydon S. "The Mobilization of Shipping For
       War." US NAVAL INST PROC, 1953 79 (5):495-503.

382

US HOMEFRONT

A brief look at US shipping mobilization in WWII is followed
by a more detailed look at developments just prior to and
during the war in Korea. The establishment and operation
of the Military Sea Transportation Service (MSTS) is covered.

2082. Stein, Bruno. "Wage Stabilization in the Korean War
Period: The Role of the Subsidiary Wage Boards." LAB
HIST, 1963 4 (2):161-177.

To help control inflation in the US during the Korean War,
the Wage Stabilization Board moved to control wages. Wage
problems and requests for wage increases were heard by
fourteen regional boards, and parties dissatisfied with
decisions could carry their case to an appeals committee.

2083. Stein, Harold. "Notes on Economic Mobilization."
PUB ADM R, 1950 10 (4):236-244.

Points out criteria by which the soundness of the US
economic mobilization for Korea can be judged. Warns of
problems such as the inflationary gap and indicates it
will be more difficult to get the citizens of the US to
mobilize for a limited engagement in the Cold War
than it was for total war in WWII.

2084. Stieber, Jack. "Labor's Walkout From the Korean War
Wage Stabilization Board." LAB HIST, 1980 21 (2):
239-260.

Recounts the United Labor Policy Committee's walking out
of participation in the Wage Stabilization Board in
February 1951. This action, by a body representing
organized labor, resulted in the Stabilization Board
taking a greater interest in labor issues than it otherwise
would have.

2085. "Tank Production." ARMOR, 1950 59 (5):32-33.

Photo essay on the US M46 Patton Tank from the production
line in Detroit to the battle line in Korea.

2086. Tobin, Maurice J. "Labor-Supply Aspects of Mobilization."
MONT LAB R, 1950 71 (5):564-567.

Expansion of the armed forces and armament production during
the early months of the Korean conflict put new demands on
the labor force. This analysis and projection of manpower
needs concludes that if the current level of partial mobilization was maintained, there would be no overall manpower
shortage. If however, all-out mobilization occurred, there
would be a major problem. Suggests ways shortages could be
met.

2087. Ullman, Victor. "Oh, How You'll Hate Him." SAT EVE

POST, 1951 223 (38):30-31, 139-141.

Michael DiSalle, Mayor of Toledo, Ohio, was appointed US
Price Stabilizer in late 1950. His responsibility was to set
and enforce price controls so as to halt inflation. This was
not a popular position, that of telling Americans how much
they could spend for items, but he held his ground and
achieved the administration's goal of controlling inflation.

2088. "The US Tries to Catch Up On Tanks." LIFE, 1950
       29 (5):13-19.

       Admits that US tanks are inferior to the T-34 being used
       by the North Koreans and tells how US Army and industry are
       trying to overcome that shortcoming.

2089. Wood, Helen. "Effect of Mobilization Programs on
       Employment Opportunities." MONT LAB R, 1950 71
       (6):680-681.

       Looks at occupations where job opportunities abounded as a
       consequence of the war. Shortages in fields such as the
       health profession, teaching, electronics, metal working
       and the railroad industry made it very easy for individuals
       in those fields to secure jobs and command good pay.

                C. SOCIAL, INTELLECTUAL AND CULTURAL IMPACTS

2090. Breyer, William R. "Coffee and Doughnuts." ARMY INFO
       DIG, 1952 7 (2):15-19.

       Describes the role of the American Red Cross in providing
       an attractive young lady serving a cup of coffee and a fresh
       doughnut to US servicemen in Korea. By the fall of 1951, the
       Red Cross had established one club and four canteens and used
       mobile "clubmobiles" to serve more than 800,000 visitors a
       month in Korea.

2091. Clark, Maurine. CAPTAIN'S BRIDE, GENERAL'S LADY.
       New York: McGraw, 1956.

       The memoirs of the wife of US General Mark Clark show the
       impact that war, especially the Korean War, had on her life.
       Tells of life in Tokyo during the last fifteen months of the
       fighting. Shares the disillusionment her husband experienced
       in having to settle as Commander of the UN Command for a
       stalemate which he felt the US could have won.

2092. Goldman, Eric F. THE CRUCIAL DECADE: AMERICA 1945-55.
       New York: Knopf, 1956.

       Popular diplomatic and social history of the US in the
       decade after WWII. Especially good on American decision to
       enter the conflict and an excellent job of life on the

homefront during that period.

2093. Griffith, Robert. "The Chilling Effect." WILSON Q,
       1978 2 (3):135-136.

       Influences of the Korean War on the loyalty-security
       issue and the negative impact on the liberal Democratic
       domestic reforms are examined.

2094. Hardaway, Eleanor S. "We are the Widows of West Point
       '49." SAT EVE POST, 1951 223 (50):30-32, 143-146.

       In June of 1949, West Point graduated 576 cadets. Two
       years later, fourteen of those men, nearly all of whom
       were married, died in combat in Korea. This is the story
       of their widows and the events of that two year period.
       Told by one of the widows.

2095. Harper, Alan D. THE POLITICS OF LOYALTY: THE WHITE
       HOUSE AND THE COMMUNIST ISSUE, 1946-1952. Westport, CN:
       Greenwood, 1969.

       Excellent study of the loyalty issue in the Truman
       Administration shows the impact of the Korean War on that
       issue. Very good chapter on how Truman's dismissal of
       MacArthur fit into the larger issue of loyalty and how
       Joseph McCarthy attempted to capitalize on the relief
       of the general.

2096. Harriman, E. Roland. "The Red Cross in the Nation's
       Service." ARMY INFO DIG, 1951 6 (3):17-24.

       Describes the services offered by the Red Cross to US
       military personnel and their families during the Korean
       War. Many statistics on the personnel and the services
       provided.

2097. Herz, Martin. "How the Cold War is Taught." SOC ED,
       1979 43 (2):118-122.

       Maintains that textbooks used in US secondary schools are
       extremely biased and therefore inaccurate in reporting the
       Cold War and such key events as the Korean War. Those books
       make it appear that the conflict was between the evil system
       of communism, which was responsible for the war, and the good
       system of Democracy, which upheld the rights of a free
       country.

2098. Keighley, Larry. "The Wives Wait Out the War." SAT
       EVE POST, 1950 223 (14):29, 116.

       Tells of the families of US pilots who flew combat
       missions over Korea from Japanese airbases early in the war.
       These wives and children were living in Japan with their
       husbands when war came; thus, they saw their husbands going

off to war in the morning and returning that evening having
spent the day in combat.

2099. Schaich, Warren. "A Relationship Between Collective
       Racial Violence and War." J BLACK STUDIES, 1975 5 (4):
       374-394.

       Studies racial violence in the US between 1910 and 1967
       and shows a correlation between war and racial violence.
       Yet the Korean War does not fit into that pattern as
       racial difficulties were avoided.

2100. Time Magazine. TIME CAPSULE: 1950. New York: Time-
       Life, 1967.

       The year 1950 is examined by excerpts from hundreds of
       stories that appeared in TIME magazine during that crucial
       year. In addition to the start of the war, there is a
       summary of key economic developments as well as a look at
       American society and culture during the early months of
       the fighting in Korea. News account format rather than
       in-depth analysis.

2101. Toner, James H. "American Society and the American Way
       of War: Korea and Beyond." PARAMETERS, 1981 11 (1):79-90.

       An excellent study of the impact of US societal views on
       the conduct of the Korean War. For example, aversion to
       the loss of lives led to such things as: less than stringent
       training so as to not lose lives in such activity even
       though the policy led to increased battlefield casualties;
       rotation of combat troops, which frequently led to a shortage
       of combat-experienced personnel; and wholesale destruction of
       villages with the hope it would save American combat soldiers.

2102. Wallrich, William. AIR FORCE AIRS: SONGS AND BALLADS
       OF THE UNITED STATES AIR FORCE, WORLD WAR ONE THROUGH KOREA.
       New York: Duell, 1957.

       A collection of the lyrics of songs sung by USAF personnel
       during the nation's 20th century wars, including Korea.
       Songs are a unique way for combatants to express their
       feelings about the enemy and themselves.

2103. Wiltz, John E. "The Korean War and American Society" in
       Francis H. Heller, ed. THE KOREAN WAR: A 25-YEAR PERSPECTIVE.
       Lawrence, KS: The Regents Press of Kansas, 1977, pp. 112-158.

       Contends that the war was frustrating but not traumatic
       for the American people. Sees good things, such as stimula-
       tion of the economy and confirmation of civilian control of
       the military, as well as negative, such as intensification
       of Cold War attitudes.

D. PUBLIC OPINION

2104.   Adler, Selig. THE ISOLATIONIST IMPULSE: ITS TWENTIETH
        CENTURY REACTION. New York: Abelard, 1957.

        This classic study of American isolationism in the 20th
        Century has a chapter focusing on the Korean War. Shows
        how the isolationists used the MacArthur dismissal and
        stalemate to assail Truman's policy of containment in
        the Far East. Examines Senator Taft's moderate
        isolationist policy.

2105.   Caine, Philip D. "The United States in Korea and
        Vietnam: A Study in Public Opinion." AIR UNIV Q R,
        1968 20 (1):49-58.

        Points out the importance of favorable public opinion
        when a Democracy is involved in a war. Examines this
        concept in Korea and Vietnam. In Korea he concludes
        that when war was going well, people were supportive
        of the President and his war policy, but when things
        were not going well, support for the war and the President
        faded very quickly.

2106.   Caspary, William R. "Public Reactions to International
        Events." Doctoral Dissertation. Northwestern, 1968.

        Examines how people react to certain events and how their
        attitudes change over a period of time as a series of
        events unfold. One chapter looks at American reactions
        to the Korean War and concludes that there was constant
        support for offensive action against Red China.

2107.   Dowell, Arthur E. "Appeasement or Conciliation in
        Global Crises, 1938 to 1951." Doctoral Dissertation.
        Chicago, 1967.

        One of the crises examined in this study is the Korean War
        with specific focus on the impact of McCarthyism on the
        government process and the forestalling of a negotiated
        settlement by General MacArthur prior to his dismissal.

2108.   Elowitz, Larry, and John W. Spanier. "Korea and
        Vietnam: Limited War and the American Political System."
        ORBIS, 1974 18 (2):510-534.

        An examination of public support of the President in the
        limited wars in Korea and Vietnam. In Korea, Truman
        initially had considerable public and congressional support,
        but as the war dragged on, he lost both. Follows the
        changing course of public support.

2109.   Epstein, Laurence B. "The American Philosophy of War,
        1945-1967." Doctoral Dissertation. Southern California,
        1967.

This study of American attitudes toward war, which contends
that the philosophy of war is changing, looks at views of
the conflict in Korea.

2110.   Erskine, Hazel. "The Polls: Is War a Mistake." PUB
        OP Q, 1970 34 (1):134-150.

        Analysis of seven major polling organizations findings on
        public support of 20th Century US Wars. At the peak of
        discontent, 64% considered WWI a mistake compared to 31%
        in WWII, 62% in Korea and 58% in Vietnam (through 1969).
        Discusses breakdown of various groups in each war.

2111.   Gallup, George. THE GALLUP POLL: PUBLIC OPINION,
        1935-1971 Vol. 2, 1949-1958. New York: Random, 1972.

        Essential reference for anyone examining American public
        opinion concerning the Korean War and its conduct. Per-
        centage breakdown on dozens of questions, such as
        support for the war, crossing the 38th Parallel, role
        of the UN, use of atomic weapons, size of military forces,
        Truman and the war, Eisenhower and the war and the peace
        negotiations. Also looks at public support for the war
        in other UN nations such as Canada, Australia, Holland
        and England.

2112.   Gietschier, Steven P. "Limited War and the Home Front:
        Ohio During the Korean War." Doctoral Dissertation.   Ohio
        State, 1977.

        An investigation of the impact which the Korean War had
        on people and institutions in the state of Ohio. Looks
        at such things as public opinion, economic impact, labor
        reaction and freedom of speech. Maintains that the
        impact on attitudes was major as people came to accept
        that international problems were of more importance than
        domestic issues.

2113.   Hamby, Alonzo L. "Public Opinion: Korean and Vietnam."
        WILSON Q, 1978 2 (3):137-141.

        Comparison of popular attitudes of Americans toward the
        Korean and Vietnam Wars. The groups voicing disapproval
        of the two wars and their attitudes were very different.
        For example, protests against Korea came from the Right,
        while protests against Vietnam came from the Left, and
        Korean War protestors honored the flag, while Vietnam
        protestors burned it. Charts measure popular support for
        both wars.

2114.   Hamilton, Richard F. "A Research Note On the Mass Support
        for 'Tough' Military Initiatives." AM SOC R, 1968 33 (3):
        439-445.

An analysis of a 1952 public opinion survey on whether the US should have become involved in Korea and whether it should continue the fight. It shows that support for a "tough" policy was strongest among the highly educated, those in high status jobs, those with high incomes, younger people and those regularly reading newspapers and magazines.

2115. Herzon, Frederick D., et al. "Personality and Public Opinion: The Case of Authoritarianism, Prejudice and Support For the Korean and Vietnam Wars." POLITY, 1978 11 (1):92-113.

Argues that personality traits and public opinion are interrelated. The study claims there is a substantial correlation between those individuals steeped in authoritarianism and racial prejudice and aggressive views on the wars in Korea and Vietnam.

2116. Hoover, Herbert. ADDRESSES UPON THE AMERICAN ROAD, 1950-1955. Stanford, CA: Stanford University, 1955.

Excerpts of the former President's public speeches from December 1950 to late 1954, including a number of references to the Korean War. He was generally supportive of the US-UN decision to intervene but critical of the Truman Administration's conduct of war.

2117. Hunter, Edward. "Defeat by Default." AM MERCURY, 1952 75 (345):40-51.

Claims that the US is discouraging Asians from siding with Democratic nations by being taken in by Communist propaganda and not condemning their actions. The Asians, he believes, see the US being taken in and are reluctant to take a stand against the communists. Cites many examples of how the Communists exploited the POW issue to their advantage.

2118. Johnson, Ronald W. "The Korean Red Scare In Missouri." RED RIV VAL HIST R, 1979 4 (2):72-86.

A look at how communities in one state reacted to the war against communism in Korea. In Missouri many anti-Communist ordinances were enacted and many anti-Communist, pro-American organizations sprung up.

2119. Lipset, Seymour M. "The Wavering Polls." PUB INT, 1976 (43):70-89.

During the Korean War, there was extensive polling of American public opinion on the war, frequently with conflicting results. This article discusses how sample design, wording of questions, and complexity of issues can lead to disparate results. Necessary for those looking at public opinion during the war.

2120. Lubell, Samuel. "Is America Going Isolationist
       Again?" SAT EVE POST, 1952 224 (49):19-21, 48, 51-54.

       By 1952 the war in Korea was becoming increasingly
       frustrating for many US citizens. This story examines
       the growing unpopularity of the conflict and reveals
       that many Americans favored either an all out commitment
       or disengagement rather than the half-hearted effort
       being put forth.

2121. Mantell, Matthew E. "Opposition to the Korean War:
       A Study in American Dissent." Doctoral Dissertation.
       New York, 1973.

       Identifies three groups opposed to the war: (1) pacifists
       who opposed all wars; (2) political parties on the left who
       considered the war imperialistic in design; and (3)
       pragmatists who initially supported the effort then became
       critical because the limited war seemed to be getting
       nowhere. Generally, however, criticism was restrained
       because of fear it would be interpreted as being
       anti-American.

2122. Modigliani, Andre. "Hawks and Doves, Isolationism and
       Political Distrust: An Analysis of Public Opinions on
       Military Policy." AM POL SCI R, 1972 66 (3):960-978.

       A study of public opinion in the US to determine if there
       was a relationship between socioeconomic status and support
       for the war in Korea. Concludes there was no clear "Hawk
       to Dove" continuum. Those favoring disengagement and those
       supporting escalation did not reject the opposite alternative;
       thus, both groups were similar in that they were opposed to
       the policy being pursued.

2123. Mueller, John E. "Presidential Popularity From Truman
       to Johnson." AM POL SCI R, 1970 64 (1):18-34.

       The Gallup Poll's presidential popularity questions were
       examined to see factors impacting support. International
       crises usually raise popularity as the public rallies
       around the President. This was initially the case with
       Truman in Korea, but as the war dragged on, his popularity
       suffered considerably.

2124. Mueller, John E. "Trends In Popular Support For The
       Wars In Korea And Vietnam." AM POL SCI R, 1971 65 (2):
       358-375.

       Compares public opinion of the two wars and finds the
       pattern to be very similar; i.e., considerable initial
       support which eroded with time. The Korean War was different
       from other US wars in that its popularity rose after the war
       ended.

2125. Mueller, John E. WAR, PRESIDENTS AND PUBLIC OPINION.
       New York: Wiley, 1973.

       Excellent study on American public opinion as it related
       to the wars in Korea and Vietnam. Maintains that both wars
       generated about the same amount of support and from the
       same groups but that there was not much vocal opposition
       to the war in Korea. Popular support for the wars is
       compared by looking at responses to questions such as
       escalation and withdrawal. Good bibliography.

2126. Perkins, Dexter. "Dissent in Time of War." VIR Q R,
       1971 47 (2):161-174.

       An examination of public dissent in ten American wars,
       noting that there was considerable discontent expressed
       in all wars except WWII and Korea. Concludes that dissent
       did not harm the war effort even when it was of consider-
       able proportions.

2127. Roper, Elmo. YOU AND YOUR LEADERS: THEIR ACTIONS AND
       YOUR REACTIONS, 1936-1956. New York: Morrow, 1957.

       One of the leaders in determining American public
       opinion analyzes his organization's findings about the
       public's attitudes towards nine leaders at the center
       of public attention, including President Truman and
       General MacArthur. Included in Truman's study is a
       look at public support for his Korean decisions and
       for MacArthur, both the Korean War and the dismissal.

2128. Suchman, Edward A., et al. "Attitudes Toward the
       Korean War." PUB OP Q, 1953 17 (2):171-184.

       This study attempts to explain why the Korean War
       lacked the united and wholehearted support that
       Americans gave to WWII. Concludes that partisanship,
       divided opinion and doubt were present. Three sets of
       criteria--public opinion, ideological conviction, and
       partisan allegiance--were often in conflict with one
       another, thus causing many people to question the
       nation's involvement.

2129. Thomas, James A. "Collapse of the Defensive War
       Argument." MIL R, 1973 53 (5):35-38.

       The Korean War forced the citizens of the US to
       justify the war in a very different fashion than they
       did WWII, which had been characterized as a defensive
       war. These new attempts at justification were not
       successful and that fact was instrumental in the
       failure to maintain public support for the war in
       Korea.

2130.   Wood, Hugh G. "American Reaction to Limited War in
        Asia: Korea and Vietnam, 1950-1968." Doctoral
        Dissertation. Colorado, 1974.

        An impressionistic study of American thought and
        opinion on the US policies of limited war and
        containment in Asia. Reconstructs American opinion
        as reflected in newspapers, magazines, opinion polls
        and public statements. Claims that US political
        objectives in Asia in the period studied were
        unrealistic, but Americans did not realize that during
        the Korean War. Only when the war in Vietnam turned
        into a stalemate did Americans begin to realize that
        they could not save the world.

                    E. IMPACT ON FOREIGN POLICY

2131.   Aduard, E.J. Lewe. JAPAN: FROM SURRENDER TO PEACE.
        New York: Praeger, 1954.

        A Dutch author gives a balanced account of what was
        going on in Japan from 1945 to 1951. Very laudatory
        of Ambassador Joseph Grew and General MacArthur and
        the benevolent US occupation policy. Sees the 1951
        treaty with Japan as a major political victory for the
        US.

2132.   Allen, Harry C. GREAT BRITAIN AND THE UNITED STATES.
        New York: St. Martin's, 1955.

        A history of Anglo-American relations from 1783-1952.
        Good coverage of the impact of the Korean War on the
        relations between the two nations. While Britain joined
        actively in the UN commitment, she was continually at
        odds with the US over the recognition of Red China at
        the UN. Tells of British dislike of MacArthur and his
        policies and their pleasure with his dismissal. Ends
        with the 1952 election of Eisenhower.

2133.   Allison, John M. AMBASSADOR FROM THE PRAIRIE: OR
        ALLISON WONDERLAND. New York: Houghton, 1973.

        Memoirs of a US diplomat who had many top posts in the
        Far East in the 1940's and 50's, including special
        assistant to John Foster Dulles in 1951, when he played
        a major role in negotiating the Japanese Peace Treaty,
        Assistant Secretary of Far Eastern Affairs and in 1953
        Ambassador to Japan. Good character studies of people
        such as MacArthur, Dulles, Sebald and Acheson.

2134.   AMERICAN ARMED INTERVENTION IN KOREA. London: Soviet
        News, 1950.

A sixty-page Soviet propaganda piece which blasts the
US for unwarranted and aggressive action against North
Korea in the summer of 1950.

2135.   "American Strategy in the Western Pacific:
        The Ryukyu Islands." BT SUR, 1963 25 (175):1-19.

        The start of war in Korea stimulated the US to
        strengthen its military position throughout the Far East.
        A vital component of the new strategy was to build
        installations in the Ryukyu Islands (including Okinawa)
        which stretch from Japan to Formosa.

2136.   Andrusiak, Nicholas. "Soviet Anti-Americanism."
        UKR Q, 1970 26 (3/4):270-276.

        Discusses Soviet anti-American propaganda which flourished
        in the post-WWII era and reached its peak during the Korean
        War. The US as the champion of financial imperialism was
        always the major theme.

2137.   Attlee, Clement R. AS IT HAPPENED. New York: Viking,
        1954.

        These memoirs of the British labor leader and Prime
        Minister from 1945 through 1951, contain his views on the
        Korean War including his belief that support of the UN was
        essential, that the war should be confined to Korea and that
        General MacArthur presented a threat to maintenance of the
        latter.

2138.   Bess, Demaree. "How Long Will This War Last?"
        SAT EVE POST, 1950 (11):22-23, 95, 98, 100, 102.

        Sees good news in the Communist aggression in Korea
        because he claims such action shows that Russia is not
        willing or able to fight an all-out war and thus has
        resorted to expanding piecemeal. Furthermore, it concludes
        the Soviet Union would not be able to wage all-out war
        for at least ten years because it lacks the necessary
        strategic materials.

2139.   Bohlen, Charles E. WITNESS TO HISTORY 1929-1969.
        New York: Norton, 1973.

        Reminiscences of a leading US foreign service officer and
        confidant of top foreign policy makers from the 1930's
        through 1960's held some views on Korea that were not held by
        his colleagues. His chapter on the Korean war puts forth his
        belief that it was not part of a larger Soviet move, and
        there was a danger of Chinese intervention. Tells of trips
        to Korea and the problems caused by the prisoner of war
        issue.

2140.   Borneman, Ernest. "The British Disagree With Us."
        HARPER'S, 1951 202 (1212):35-42.

Maintains that the British are not in agreement with nor
sympathetic toward American policy in Korea. Claims they feel
UN involvement was actually a violation of its charter
because Communist China is not represented,and the absence of
the Soviet delegate, regardless of the reason, in the
Security Council vote invalidated the decision to intervene.

2141. Bowles, Chester. AMBASSADOR'S REPORT. New York: Harper,
        1954.

        Firsthand account by the US Ambassador to India from 1951
        through 1953 gives a good perspective of the impact of the
        Korean War on US-Indian relations. Examines the Indian
        policy on the war, role in seeking peace and the repatriation
        of POW's.

2142. Brown, Seyom. THE FACES OF POWER: CONSTANCY AND CHANGE
        IN UNITED STATES FOREIGN POLICY FROM TRUMAN TO REAGAN.
        New York: Columbia University, 1983.

        The chapter on the Korean War maintains that on the matter
        of military planning the conflict produced greater differences
        rather than consensus. There developed a general feeling that
        local imbalances of power would lead to more "Koreas" and thus
        the US needed to strengthen NATO to prevent such imbalances
        in Europe. Shows impact of the Korean War on US foreign and
        military policies toward Europe.

2143. Chang, Yu Nan. "American Security Problems in the Far
        East, 1950-1952." Doctoral Dissertation. Washington, 1954.

        While Japan, Indo-China and Indonesia were all of concern
        to US national security advisers during the period under
        consideration, it was the war in Korea that overshadowed
        and thus shaped US defense and foreign policies. Several
        chapters focus on the impact of the war.

2144. Cohen, Warren I. "Ambassador Philip D. Sprouse on the
        Question of Recognition of the People's Republic of China
        In 1949 and 1950." DIP HIST, 1978 2 (2):213-217.

        Years after the war Ambassador Sprouse revealed that in
        1949 and 1950 the Truman Administration gave serious
        consideration to granting recognition to Red China, but
        when that nation entered the Korean War any possibility
        that recognition would be granted came to an end.

2145. Cohen, Warren I. AMERICA'S RESPONSE TO CHINA.
        New York: Wiley, 1971, 1980

        Survey of US-Chinese relations from the 1840's to the
        present. Examines the Truman Chinese and Korean policies
        and is critical of the failure to understand the conflicts
        in those countries as civil wars.

2146. Crozier, Brian. THE MAN WHO LOST CHINA: THE FIRST
       FULL BIOGRAPHY OF CHIANG KAI-SHEK. Scribner's, 1976.

       Well-researched, well-written account that not only looks
       at Chiang but China as well from 1920-1950. A balanced
       account of Chiang which exposes readers to both extremes
       of his nature. Does not go into Chiang and the
       Korean War but helps the reader understand the man.
       Some errors of fact.

2147. Dawson, Raymond, and Richard Rosecrance. "Theory and
       Reality in the Anglo-American Alliance." WORLD POL, 1966
       19 (1):21-51.

       The Anglo-American alliance has survived many challenges
       in the post-war period in many situations where theory
       would say it would breakdown. This was true during the
       Korean War where relations between US and Britian remained
       good in spite of some conflicting policies.

2148. Dulles, Foster R. AMERICAN POLICY TOWARD COMMUNIST
       CHINA 1949-1969. New York: Crowell, 1972.

       Survey of Chinese-American relations by a top scholar
       with a readable style. Fits Chinese policy into the
       Korean question, and a chapter on the impact of the
       Korean War maintains it marked a major turning point
       not only in Far Eastern policy but commitment to building
       up the military power of Western Europe. Good account of
       Chinese intervention and the Truman-MacArthur split.

2149. Dunn, Frederick S. PEACE MAKING AND THE SETTLEMENT WITH
       JAPAN. Princeton, NJ: Princeton University, 1963.

       Case study of American decision making in regard to post-
       WWII Japan and the 1951 Peace Treaty. Straightforward
       narrative focuses on the 1950-1951 negotiations by John
       Foster Dulles and shows how the war in Korea impacted US
       policy toward Japan.

2150. Eden, Anthony. FULL CIRCLE: THE MEMOIRS OF ANTHONY
       EDEN. Cambridge, MA: Riverside, 1960.

       British Conservative leader who served as both Foreign
       Secretary and Prime Minister during the 1950's covers
       the period from October 1951-July 1953 as he tells of
       the efforts to achieve a ceasefire in Korea. Covers
       the armistice talks, prisoners of war issue and problems
       with President Rhee. Tells nothing of friction between
       US and Britain over Red China policy.

2151. Fitch, Geraldine. FORMOSA BEACHHEAD. Chicago:
       Regnery, 1953.

An intimate friend of General Chiang Kai-shek writes of
his plans and desires to regain control of the mainland
from the Communists. Tells of the General's desire for
material assistance from the US while he would supply the
manpower for engaging the Communists, either in Korea or
in invasion of the mainland.

2152. Gosnell, Harold. TRUMAN'S CRISES: A POLITICAL BIOGRAPHY
        OF HARRY S. TRUMAN. Westpoint, CT: Greenwood, 1980.

        Part three of this study does a good job of putting the
        Korean War in the context of US domestic and foreign
        policy developments immediately prior to and during the
        conflict. Includes coverage of labor, agriculture and
        civil rights developments during the war.

2153. Japan, Ministry of Foreign Affairs. OUR POSITION IN THE
        KOREAN CONFLICT. Tokyo: Public Information Division, 1950.

        Pamphlet setting forth Japanese support for the US-UN
        stand against Communist aggression in Korea.

2154. Kalischer, Peter. "I Raided Red China With the Guerrillas."
        COLLIER'S, 1953 131 (13):20-23.

        During the Korean War, Red China could not concentrate all
        its military might on that conflict because guerrillas from
        Chiang Kai Shek's Nationalist Army made raids on the mainland
        coast. This article tells of those attacks and focuses on
        one particular such Nationalist operation.

2155. Kaplan, Lawrence S. "The Korean War and US Foreign
        Relations: The Case of NATO" in Francis H. Heller, ed.
        THE KOREAN WAR: A 25-YEAR PERSPECTIVE. Lawrence, KS:
        Regents Press of Kansas, 1977, pp. 36-75.

        Proposes that the changes brought by the war were more
        significant to US policy in Europe than Asia. Shows that
        the war led to a major strengthening of NATO; thus,
        transforming it into a meaningful alliance, politically
        and militarily.

2156. Kennan, George F. "Japanese Security and American
        Policy." FOR AFF, 1964 43 (1):14-28.

        This examination of Japanese security in the post-WWII
        period shows the impact that the Korean War had on US-
        Japanese relations and the subsequent peace treaty.
        Looks at the Japanese-Korean relationship from 1945 through
        the early 1960's and decries their failure to bring about
        a working relationship.

2157. Macmillan, Harold. TIDES OF FORTUNE 1945-1955.
        New York: Harper, 1969.

This volume of the memoirs of the British Conservative
leader, who was Prime Minister from 1957 to 1963, covers
the post-WWII decade and looks at British policy during
the Korean War. Although he served as Minister of
Housing from 1951-1954, he gives good insight into the
party's foreign and domestic policy during the war
period.

2158. Morley, James W. JAPAN AND KOREA: AMERICA'S ALLIES
IN THE PACIFIC. New York: Walker, 1965.

Survey of political developments in Japan and Korea
from 1945-1965. Discusses US relations with the two
countries and the development of both North and South
Korea. Chronology of key developments.

2159. Murphy, Robert. DIPLOMAT AMONG WARRIORS. Garden
City, NY: Doubleday, 1964.

Memoirs of one of the US's most experienced diplomats
who served as the first postwar Ambassador in Japan,
1952-1953. In that position he was deeply involved in
the armistice negotiations. Gives inside information on
reaching an agreement and the problems that had to be
overcome.

2160. O'Neill, Robert. "Constraint With Honor." INTER J,
(Canada) 1974 29 (3):350-355.

US-Canadian diplomatic relations during the Korean War
are examined in this review article of Denis Stairs' book
THE DIPLOMACY OF CONSTRAINT: CANADA, THE KOREAN WAR AND
THE UNITED STATES.

2161. PARK, CHANG J. "American Foreign Policy in Korea and
Vietnam: Comparative Case Studies." R POL, 1975 37 (1):
20-47.

A study of the reasons behind US military involvement in
Korea and Vietnam which concludes that the concepts of
international prestige and a sense of morality were
primary factors.

2162. Rankin, Karl L. CHINA ASSIGNMENT. Seattle: University
of Washington, 1964.

Ambassador Rankin, the ranking US diplomat to the Nationalist
Chinese Government from 1949 to 1958 tells the problem of
keeping Chiang satisfied and keeping the morale of his
followers up during the Korean War.

2163. Scalapino, Robert A. "The American Occupation of
Japan--Perspective After Three Decades." AN AM AC POL
SOC SCI, 1976 428:104-113.

Examines Japan from 1945-1951, especially the occupation policies of General MacArthur. Shows how the war in Korea pushed the US into a growing acceptance of Japan as a defensive partner in the Far East and helped lead to the end of US occupation.

2164. Sodhy, Pamela. "Passage of Empire: United States-Malayan Relations to 1966." Doctoral Dissertation. Cornell, 1982.

Includes one chapter which shows how the Korean War increased Malaya's importance to the US as it became a producer of strategic materials needed for the American war effort.

2165. Soustelle, Jacques. "Indo-China and Korea: One Front." FOR AFF, 1950 29 (1):56-66.

Claims that the wars in Indo-China and Korea both resulted from Soviet expansion and that the governments of both President Syngman Rhee and Emperor Bao Dai cannot survive without external aid. Virtually all attention is focused on the situation in Indo-China.

2166. Spanier, John W. AMERICAN FOREIGN POLICY SINCE WORLD WAR II. New York: Praeger, 1960.

One of the best single volumes on US foreign policy in the decade and a half after WWII. Puts the Korean War in the perspective of US's Far East policy and gives considerable attention to the conduct of the war in light of the Truman-MacArthur controversy.

2167. Stemons, James S. THE KOREAN MESS AND SOME CORRECTIVES. Boston: Chapman, 1952.

Brief critical account of US involvement in the Korean conflict urges the US and Soviet Union to permit the Koreans to determine their own destiny.

2168. Stevenson, Adlai E. MAJOR CAMPAIGN SPEECHES OF ADLAI E. STEVENSON, 1952. New York: Random, 1953.

Included in this collection are four of the Democratic Presidential candidate's speeches on Korea. An August address broadcast to US Armed Forces overseas, an attack on General Eisenhower's criticism of the Truman conduct of the war, a call for bipartisan support of the war effort and a final attack on Eisenhower's claim to let "Asians fight Asians" are set forth.

2169. Thayer, James R. "Japanese Opinion on the Far Eastern Conflict." PUB OP Q, 1951 15 (1):76-88.

Japanese public opinion poll revealed that a majority of
those surveyed believed that their country should not
actively participate in the Korean War. Also discusses
the impact of the war on the Japanese, especially
increased attention to war news.

2170. US Department of State. FOREIGN RELATIONS OF THE UNITED
       STATES 1951. Vol. VII, 2 Pts. KOREA AND CHINA. Washington:
       Government Printing Office, 1983.

       Diplomatic correspondence and memoranda of the State
       Department in regard to Korea and China for 1950 covers
       activities in the UN, the decision to dismiss MacArthur,
       initiation of ceasefire talks, negotiations, policy toward
       Red China and trade restriction policy with North Korea.

2171. US Department of State. FOREIGN RELATIONS OF THE UNITED
       STATES, 1952-1954. Vol. XV, 2 Pts. KOREA. Washington:
       Government Printing Office, 1984.

       Official department documents relating to the continuing
       peace negotiations, UN debates and discussions, transition
       from the Truman to Eisenhower administrations, the armistice
       and post-armistice issues.

2172. Williams, J.A. "Korea and the Malayan Emergency: The
       Strategic Priorities." ROY UNI SER INST J, (Great
       Britain) 1973 118 (2):56-62.

       Friction developed between Britain and the US during the
       Korean War because Britain was having problems in Malaya
       and chose to give that and the defense of Hong Kong priority
       over support of the UN effort in Korea. The US was critical
       of Britain's foot dragging.

2173. Yoshida, Shigeru. "Japan and the Crisis in Asia."
       FOR AFF, 1951 29 (2):171-181.

       The author, who was the Prime Minister of Japan when war
       came to Korea, pledges his nation's support for the meeting
       of aggression while arguing they could be of more assistance
       if they could conclude a WWII peace treaty.

XXI. THE MEDIA AND THE WAR
A. THE PRESS

2174. Andrews, Marshall. "Top Reporting From the Horizon of
Battle." ARMOR, 1951 60 (5):51-53.

Critical review article of David D. Duncan's pictorial book
THIS IS WAR! Praises the first-rate photos of the Korean War,
including those of non-combatants as well as combatants, but
says it does not add much to the study of warfare.

2175. Andrews, Marshall. "What Can You Believe?" COM FOR J,
1950 1 (3):20-21.

Criticizes the accuracy of war correspondents' news
accounts of the war. Places blame on reporters for
frequently writing about things which they obviously know
nothing about and the US Army's failure to provide adequate
information. Claims there is a need for Army censorship and
maintains women correspondents should not be permitted at the
front. The author is a staff member of the WASHINGTON POST.

2176. Beech, Keyes. TOKYO AND POINTS EAST. Garden City, NY:
Doubleday, 1954.

A firsthand account of the war by the highly respected war
correspondent of the CHICAGO NEWS. The author includes
reminiscences of the early days of the fighting and the
perils that face frontline war correspondents. Good
firsthand observations of General MacArthur.

2177. Burchett, Wilfred. AT THE BARRICADES: FORTY YEARS ON
THE CUTTING EDGE OF HISTORY. New York: Times Books, 1981.

Autobiography of a well-known leftist Australian news
correspondent who made headlines during the Korean War
when he turned up on the North Korean-Communist side at
the truce negotiations. In spite of his pro-Communist
views, he provided valuable information to western
correspondents from his contacts with communist negotiators.
As would be expected, he is extremely critical of US
policy in Korea.

2178. Cleary, Thomas J., Jr. "Aid and Comfort to the Enemy."
MIL R, 1968 48 (8):51-55.

An examination of the question of how much freedom the press
has to report war happenings that can hurt the war effort and
morale at home. Cites examples during the Korean War where
conflict developed between the military and reporters over
the nature of reports. Maintains the press should report the
truth but do so without damaging the armed forces.

2179. "Combat Photographer." COM FOR J, 1951 2 (1):10, 20-21.

Tribute to the members of the US Signal Corps serving as
combat photographers in Korea. Notes that they not only
contribute to knowledge of the war but do a great job that
is of military value as a way to improve morale and to
provide intelligence.

2180. DiCola, Louis F. "The Korean War as Seen by the Chicago
Tribune, The New York Times and The Times of London."
Master's Thesis. Kent State, 1981.

Comparison of the coverage and editorial position of the
conflict by three major US newspapers.

2181. Dorn, Frank. "Briefing the Press." ARMY INFO DIG, 1951
6 (5):36-41.

Describes the Department of Defenses' means of
disseminating news of the fighting to the press during the
first six months of the war. Describes the difficulty of
trying to provide accurate information and not sounding negative when things were not going well for the US.

2182. Douglas, James S. "The Army's Newspaper Chain." ARMY
INFO DIG, 1951 6 (6):33-37.

The US military, because of its defense of a free society,
has always gone to great efforts to keep its personnel
informed of local, national and international events. This
was especially true in Korea where the Korean edition of the
PACIFIC STARS AND STRIPES and local unit newspapers spread
the news. Tells of the problems of producing newspapers in
the combat zone.

2183. Echols, M.P. "Information in the Combat Zone." ARMY INFO
DIG, 1951 6 (4):60-64.

Describes the efforts of the Public Information Office, Far
East Command to provide information on the Korean War. The
primary means of meeting its objectives was to issue official
releases by military authorities and extending assistance to
accredited civilian news representatives. The latter was
especially difficult since by September 1950 there were more
than 300 war correspondents in Korea.

2184. Emery, Michael C. "The American Mass Media and Coverage
of Five Major Foreign Events, 1900-1950." Doctoral
Dissertation. Minnesota, 1968.

One of the major events covered is the North Korean
invasion with coverage of the South's retreat from Seoul and
the defense of Taejon being examined in depth.

2185. Erwin, Ray. "Censorship, Communications Worry 200
        K-War Correspondents." ED PUB, 1950 83 (30):7, 44.

        Details the problems of US war correspondents during the
        early weeks of the war. Confusion reigned as American
        military authorities imposed, then rescinded, then revised
        the rules governing the battlefield reporters. Includes
        names of many correspondents covering the fighting.

2186. Higgins, Marguerite. WAR IN KOREA: THE REPORT OF A WAR
        COMBAT CORRESPONDENT. New York: Doubleday, 1951.

        Pulitzer Prize winner "Maggie" Higgins was in Tokyo when
        the war broke out, flew on MacArthur's plane to Seoul on
        his initial visit and then spent the next six months covering
        the war for the New York HERALD TRIBUNE. Her propensity for
        being where major stories were breaking, such as Inchon on
        invasion day, and ability to describe the American G.I. and
        his problems during the early months of the war make this a
        very useful book, even though the author tends to overplay
        her experiences.

2187. Johnson, Lisa D. "No Place for a Woman: A Biographical
        Study of War Correspondent Marguerite Higgins." Master's
        Thesis. East Texas State, 1983.

        Prize-winning war correspondent Marguerite Higgins
        covered WWII, Korea and Vietnam, but it was in Korea that
        the controversial reporter did her best work. In addition
        to such well-known stories as those of MacArthur's initial
        visit to Korea and the Inchon invasion, she issued daily
        stories from the front lines. Her aggressiveness won her
        the adulation of the public but the contempt of her male
        colleagues.

2188. Jones, Ken. I WAS THERE. New York: Lion, 1953.

        An American war correspondent recounts many of the human
        interest stories he witnessed in covering the conflict.

2189. Knightley, Phillip. THE FIRST CASUALTY: FROM THE CRIMEA
        TO VIETNAM: THE WAR CORRESPONDENT AS HERO, PROPAGANDIST
        AND MYTH MAKER. New York: Harcourt, 1975.

        This work contains a very good chapter on war correspondents
        covering the Korean War. Reporting the war was difficult
        because reporters were dependent upon the military for
        transportation and communication, and after describing the
        setbacks early in the war, the military was suspicious of
        newsmen. Mentions many of the top correspondents and the
        problems they encountered.

2190.   "The Korean Air War in Color." LIFE, 1950 29 (12):79-
         82.

         The first aerial color photographs taken in the Korean
         War and the first ever taken from a jet fighter show the
         beauty and destruction that characterize the air war.

2191.   Lee, Raymond S.H. "Early Korean War Coverage." JOU Q,
         1978 55 (4):789-792.

         A comparison of news coverage just before the outbreak
         of war and immediately after in the NEW YORK TIMES,
         WASHINGTON POST and four South Korean newspapers. Notes
         that the uncensored US papers gave more indications
         that an attack was imminent than did their censored South
         Korean counterparts. As would be expected after war came,
         the US papers more accurately reported the military picture.

2192.   Lucas, Jim G. REPORT FROM KOREA. New York: World-
         Telegram, 1953.

         A pamphlet containing a number of the well-known Scripps-
         Howard war correspondent's dispatches from the Korean war
         front.

2193.   Marshall, Cate, ed. BRINGING UP THE REAR: A MEMOIR
         S.L.A. MARSHALL. Novato, CA: Presidio, 1979.

         Recollections, observations and evaluations by one of the
         most prolific and respected writers of modern warfare and
         author of more than a dozen of the most significant
         articles and books on the Korean War. Includes some
         information not previously included on his experiences
         in Korea.

2194.   May, Antoinette. WITNESS TO WAR: A BIOGRAPHY OF
         MARGUERITE HIGGINS. New York: Beaufort, 1983.

         Favorable account of the life and career of perhaps the
         most famous American war correspondent to cover the Korean
         War. While covering her reporting in WWII and Vietnam,
         the Korean story dominates. Good coverage of the early
         weeks of the fighting. Tells the problems and challenges
         of covering the fighting.

2195.   Mee, Charles L., Jr. "Are You Telling Them That it is an
         Utterly Useless War?" HORIZON, 1976 18 (1):110-111.

         An essay critical of US press coverage of the Korean War.
         Claims reporters such as Wilfred Burchett and Alan Winnington
         gave a truer picture of what was happening. The American
         press, it claims, would not report stories critical of the
         American military.

2196.   Miller, Robert C. "We Haven't Been Getting the Facts

About Korea." READ DIG, 1952 61 (368):29-31.

An experienced American war correspondent maintains that
the public has not been getting the true story about Korea
because of overzealous military censors. Critical of the
Far East Command's censorship code of 1951 which he claims
is destroying the best weapon against Communism--the truth.
Lacks objectivity, sees no merit in the military's position.
Condensed from NIEMAN REPORTS, July 1952.

2197. Mydans, Carl. "Girl War Correspondent." LIFE, 1950
       29 (14):51-60.

The problems and successes encountered by female war
correspondent, Marguerite Higgins, in the early months
of the Korean War.

2198. Mydans, Carl. MORE THAN MEETS THE EYE. New York: Harper,
       1959.

One of LIFE magazine's most distinguished photographers, who
covered both WWII and Korea, tells of his experiences in
those sojourns. Surprisingly, this book has no photos.

2199. Namenwirth, J. Zvi, and Richard Bibbee. "Speech Codes
       in the Press." J COMM, 1975 25 (2):50-63.

An analysis of 288 editorials dealing with the Korean War
from mass and prestige American and British newspapers.
Found that mass newspapers tend to be parochial, militarily-
oriented, and focused on material concerns while prestige
papers are more apt to be cosmopolitan, economically-oriented
and focus more on symbolic issues.

2200. Oldfield, Barney. "USAF Press Relations in the Far East."
       ARMY INFO DIG, 1950 5 (11):40-45.

A staff member of the Air Force's Office of Public
Relations tells the importance of getting as much news
coverage as possible from the war front and putting it forth
in a way that helps the war effort. In urging support of
and cooperation with war correspondents, it shows the
importance of a free press to an open society.

2201. Osmer, Harold H. US RELIGIOUS JOURNALISM AND THE KOREAN
       WAR. Lanham, MD: University Press of America, 1980.

An analysis of how various religious groups in the US
reacted to the nation's involvement in the war and then
displayed those attitudes through their journals. Shows
that the religious media's response was as varied as
that of American society in general.

2202. Richards, Edward B. "The Soviet Press, the UN and
       Korea." JOU Q, 1958 35 (Fall):455-463.

An analysis of Soviet press coverage of the Korean question from 1945 to the 1950 outbreak of war shows that Soviet readers received only one side of the story. Accounts were extremely anti-US and UN.

2203. "SLAM." COM FOR J, 1951 1 (11):10-12.

Brief biography of Samuel Lyman Atwood Marshall, perhaps the most prolific and authoritative writer on military topics in the Korean War. Marshall had established himself prior to WWII and by 1950 was the most influential military analyst in the US. His half-dozen books and dozen articles on Korea further solidified his reputation.

2204. Sondern, Frederic. "Dave Duncan and His Fighting Camera." READ DIG, 1951 58 (349):43-46.

Human interest story on perhaps the best known combat photographer of the Korean War. As a photographer for LIFE magazine, he captured the American fighting man and the suffering inflicted upon the civilians caught up in war. Tells of his early career and his assignment to and experiences in Korea.

2205. Spahr, W.J. "The Korean Question as Presented in the Soviet Press, January 1 to June 25, 1950." Master's Thesis. Columbia, 1953.

Sets forth the Soviet view of Korea in the six months preceding the outbreak of war. In predictable Cold War rhetoric, Tass set forth the position that US imperialism was trying to dominate Korea while the Soviets were attempting to save it.

2206. Tallent, Robert W. "An Early Afternoon." LEATHERNECK, 1951 34 (6):14-18.

Experiences of a Marine Corps combat photographer during the Battle of Hoengsong, on the eastern front, in February 1951.

2207. Von Voigtlander, Karl A. "The War for Words." ARMY INFO DIG, 1953 8 (1):54-59.

Examines the unusual censorship problems created by the Korean War for the US press and the military. Describes the voluntary code of censorship presented by General MacArthur early in the war and tells why it did not work. No code was needed in the early fall of 1950 when the war was going well, but the entrance of Chinese Communists presented many new problems. Covers the first year of the conflict.

B. MOTION PICTURES

2208.   Altieri, James J. "The Story Behind Army Feature Films."
        ARMY INFO DIG, 1952 7 (9):37-42.

        The Korean War did a great deal to stimulate the US motion
        picture industry's production of war movies, with thirty-
        five features and short subjects under production in 1952.
        The Army cooperated with the film industry on many of these
        projects because it helped the public's understanding of the
        military. Details the making of "The Big Push," a film on
        combat in Kora, and shows how the US Army contributed to its
        production.

2209.   Avery, Robert K., and Timothy L. Larson. "US Military
        Documentary Films: A Chronological Analysis." Paper
        Presented at the 65th Annual Meeting of the Speech
        Communication Association (San Antonio, Texas, November
        1979).

        Reviews the history of US military documentary films from
        WWI through Vietnam, including Korea. Compares the themes
        and effectiveness of the film, including the propaganda film
        "Why Korea" which attempted to explain to US servicemen why
        they were fighting in Korea.

2210.   Butler, Lucius A., and Chaesoon T. Youngs. FILMS FOR
        KOREAN STUDIES. Honolulu: Center for Korean Studies, 1978.

        This useful work identifies more than one hundred twenty
        readily available 16mm films on different facets of the
        Korean War, including land, air, and sea engagements; POW's;
        UN Activities; Relief Programs; Medical Services and
        activities of various nations. Tells where and how to secure
        the films. Excellent index.

2211.   Farmer, James H. "The Making of the Battle Hymn." AVI
        HIST SOC J, 1978 23 (1):37-48.

        An account of the filming of "Battle Hymn," a story about
        US Air Force Captain, Dean E. Hess, a fighter pilot, and his
        work with hundreds of Korean war orphans.

2212.   Jones, Charles, and Eugene Jones. THE FACE OF WAR.
        New York: Prentice, 1951.

        The authors are brothers who covered the war with their
        movie cameras for NBC Television. Nearly 150 photographs
        are produced from movie film and thus are not of high
        technical quality. Includes an excellent narrative which
        relates some of the authors' combat experiences, including
        combat landings and parachuting behind enemy lines.

2213.   Myrick, Howard A. "A Critical Analysis of Thematic
        Content of United States Army Orientation Films of the

Korean War." Doctoral Dissertation. Southern California, 1968.

Empirical and critical methods were used to evaluate five government films designed to sell the war to US soldiers. Found that except for the limited war concept these Korean War films were similar to those of WWII.

2214. "Retreat Hell." LEATHERNECK, 1952 35 (4):54-55.

Photographs and brief narrative on the filming of "Retreat Hell," a Hollywood production dealing with the Chosin Reservoir Campaign. Many veterans of the operation were utilized in recreating the action.

C. ARTISTS AND CARTOONISTS

2215. Brodie, Howard. "Hill 233." COLLIER'S, 1951 27 (11): 28-29.

A combat artist's sketches of an attack by an unidentified infantry company as it stormed an enemy-held hill (233) to secure the body of a platoon leader who had fallen two days earlier. The mission was successful.

2216. Brodie, Howard. "Under Fire." COLLIER'S, 1951 127 (17):36-37, 49.

Drawings and a short account by COLLIER'S Korean War combat artist of a brief but deadly engagement between men of G Company, 2nd Battalion 7th Regiment, 3rd Division, US Army in early 1951.

2217. Brodie, Howard. WAR DRAWINGS: WORLD WAR II, KOREA. Palo Alto, CA: National, 1963.

Sketches from two wars by one of the most famous American combat artists include scenes of US Marine units in Korea.

2218. Dickinson, Theodore, and Dave McNichol. KOREA ILLUSTRATED. Rutland, VT: Tuttle, 1952.

Illustrations of combat scenes by two US Marine artists.

2219. "Korea Five Years Ago." LIFE, 1950 29 (15):70-72.

When the US Army liberated Korea in 1945, combat artists Sgt. Steven Kidd and civilian John Pike came along. This tells of fifty pictures they painted of the liberation, five of which are reproduced in the article.

2220. Mauldin, Bill. "Chogies and Chow." COLLIER'S, 1952 129 (16):22-23, 32.

In another "letter" to Willie, Joe recounts his visit
to Company I, 31st Regiment, which is dug in on what a
year before had been called Heartbreak Ridge. Tells of the
hardships and frustrations of conducting static warfare in
the cold, mountainous terrain of Korea.

2221. Mauldin, Bill. "Hostilities Ahead." COLLIER'S, 1952
      129 (17):47, 50-51.

      Another tongue-in-cheek look at US infantrymen on the
      front lines of Korea in the winter of 1951-52. America's
      well-known combat cartoonist writes and sketches about
      what he witnessed.

2222. Mauldin, Bill. "Meeting the Marines." COLLIER'S,
      1952 129 (22):52, 54.

      A look at the US Marines (5th Regiment) in front line
      positions in early 1952. Humorist Mauldin praises the
      Marines and the job they are doing by using outlandish
      stories to demonstrate their sense of pride and commitment.

2223. Mauldin, Bill. "This is the Navy and this is War."
      COLLIER'S, 1952 129 (23):22-23, 51.

      Mauldin concludes his series on the Korean War with a
      look at the role of the US Navy airpower, as it operated
      from aircraft carriers. As in the other articles, he
      shows his respect for the Navy by poking fun at it.

2224. Mauldin, Bill. "Up Front in Korea." COLLIER'S, 1952
      129 (15):20-21, 72-73.

      The author and cartoonist of "Willie and Joe" of WWII fame
      paid a visit to Korea and used his wry sense of humor to
      describe conditions in places like Seoul as well as the
      front lines. In his letter to Joe, Willie tells of a visit
      to units of the 7th Division and compares what he sees with
      some WWII experiences.

2225. Mauldin, William H. (Bill). BILL MAULDIN IN KOREA. New York:
      Norton, 1952.

      The well-known WWII cartoonist went to Korea from January
      to April 1952, and this is his account of what he saw and
      experienced. A well-written narrative and good drawings but
      no cartoons. Rather serious account; not much humor as was
      found in WWII.

2226. Pacific Stars and Stripes, eds. OUT OF LINE: CARTOONS
      BY ARMED FORCES ARTISTS. Tokyo: Toppan, 1953.

      Contains nearly 200 cartoons, from G.I. artists, that
      appeared in the PACIFIC STARS AND STRIPES during the first
      two years of the war.

2227. Packwood, Norval E., Jr. "Korean Sketches." MARINE
      CORPS GAZ, 1952 36 (2):50-53.

      Pen sketches of Marines in combat in Korea.

2228. Packwood, Norval E., Jr. LEATHERHEAD IN KOREA.
      Quantico: Marine Corps Gazette, 1952.

      Collection of cartoons by a Marine combat artist on
      Marine Corps life in Korea.

2229. Shaw, Charles S. LOOKING BACK WITH LAUGHTER.
      Pietermaritzburg, South Africa: Shuter, 1973.

      A South African pilot who flew in Korea during the war tells
      of his humorous and harrowing experiences and the conduct of
      aerial operations.

2230.   Aichinger, Peter.   THE AMERICAN SOLDIER IN FICTION, 1880-
        1963. Ames: Iowa State University, 1975.

        Contends that the demoralizing aspects of the Korean War,
        namely limited war and conscription, were evident in some
        of the most important novels to come out of the war.
        Examines the works of William Styron (The Long March),
        James Michener (Bridges at Toko-ri) and Pat Frank (Hold
        Back the Night).

2231.   Bright, Charles D. "Aviation Literature--A Changing
        Art." AERO HIST, 1984 31 (1):68-73.

        Since 1907 aviation fiction has been quite important to
        the American literary field. This article explores the
        leading works on aviation themes from the 1930's through
        1970's, including the Korean war era. The latter saw
        many books focusing on the jet pilot as hero. Mentions
        such works as: James Salter's THE HUNTERS; Robert Eunson's
        MIG ALLEY; and James Michener's BRIDGE OF TOKO-RI. Some
        leading Hollywood aviation films are also discussed.

2232.   Fowler, Miok Lee. "Korean War and Korean Consciousness."
        Doctoral Dissertation. Northern Colorado, 1974.

        Anthology of Korean War literature that deals with the
        changes in the Korean consciousness which resulted from
        the war. Includes the works of ten Korean writers,
        nearly all of whose works were in Korean only, and critiques
        each work.

2233.   Mason, F. Van Wyck. AMERICAN MEN AT ARMS. Boston:
        Little, 1964.

        Anthology of fictional accounts of WWI, WWII and the Korean
        War. Section on Korea contains excerpts from ten works on
        combat and non-battlefield situations to give insight into
        the American fighting man. Authors whose works are utilized
        include: Glen Ross, Quentin Reynolds, Ernest Frankel, John
        Sack, James A. Michener, Curt Anders, and Thomas Anderson.

409

B. KOREAN WAR NOVELS

2234. Anders, Curtis. THE PRICE OF COURAGE. New York: Sagamore,
       1957.

       The war as experienced by a US infantry company, commanded
       by Lt. Eric Holloway, a young officer whose performance
       ultimately wins the respect of his men. Good description of
       life on the front lines.

2235. Anderson, Thomas. YOUR OWN BELOVED SONS. New York:
       Random, 1956.

       Sergeant Stanley, a paternalistic, wise Army veteran leads
       five inexperienced volunteers on a reconnaissance mission.
       Through his leadership, the group becomes an effective team.
       The author, a Korean veteran, explores the conflicts and
       mental anguish the soldier experiences.

2236. Buck, Pearl S. THE LIVING REED. New York: Day, 1963.

       This novel gives a panorama of Korean history from 1881 to
       1950 by tracing the noble and patriotic Kim family through
       that period. While the story does not go into the war
       period, it gives good insight into the period from 1945
       to 1950.

2237. Clark, Roger W. RIDE THE WHITE TIGER. Boston: Little,
       1959.

       Fictionalized account of a Korean boy adopted by an
       American soldier. Written for young people, this work
       does a good job of revealing the grim impact of war on
       the civilian populace of Korea.

2238. Cole, Connor. THE CROSS AND THE STAR. New York:
       Vantage, 1960.

       Tells of three chaplains in the US Army--Robbie Metzer,
       Chaplain Kimberly and Father Ferrera--who were sent to
       Korea, where they were taken prisoner, suffered the
       horrors of captivity and ultimately died. Comradeship
       and respect emerged in spite of their religious
       differences.

2239. Coon, Gene L. MEANWHILE BACK AT THE FRONT. New York:
       Crown, 1961.

       The story of a Public Information Section of the 1st
       Marine Division during the war in Korea.

2240. Crawford, William. GIVE ME TOMORROW. New York:
       Putnam's, 1962.

The personal impact of the Korean War on a young Marine, David Martin. Deals with physical and psychological stress that combat puts on the individual.

2241. Frank, Pat. HOLD BACK THE NIGHT. Philadelphia: Lippincott, 1952.

While not a great literary work, this book is significant as the first important novel about the Korean War. Tells of a Marine Company being driven back by Chinese forces in the November-December 1950 Chosin Reservoir operation. Describes the hardships imposed by the enemy and the elements.

2242. Frankel, Ernest. BAND OF BROTHERS. New York: Macmillan, 1958.

A story of a Marine Company involved in the Chosin Reservoir operation. The central figure is Bill Patrick, a company commander who experiences the frustrations of battlefield command.

2243. Harris, A.M. THE TALL MAN. New York: Farrar, 1958.

The hero, who is referred to only as the tall man, is an Australian who takes two South Korean civilians on a dangerous mission late in the war. Although they lose their lives, they perform their mission successfully.

2244. Hollands, Douglas J. ABLE COMPANY. Houghton, 1956.

This novel, by a young Briton who served in Korea, gives a vivid portrait of a platoon commander's day-to-day activities on the twenty mile front of the British Commonwealth Division.

2245. Hollands, Douglas J. THE DEAD, THE DYING AND THE DAMNED. London: Cassell, 1956.

This literary work about men fighting with a company of Britain's Rockinghamshire Regiment in Korea asks if there is any purpose to their fighting, except to further their military careers.

2246. Hooker, Richard (pseudonym). MASH. New York: Morrow, 1968.

One of the most famous novels that served as the basis for a long-running television series. Tells of three American M.D.'s stationed in Korea with the 4077th MASH (Mobile Army Surgical Hospital). While their medical activities are covered, primary focus is on their zany off-duty activities. Humorous but warm.

2247. Kantor, MacKinley. DON'T TOUCH ME. New York: Random, 1951.

While there are a few good descriptions of air warfare in
Korea, most of this book looks at the sexual exploits of
B-29 pilot Major Gregory Wolford. Not one of Kantor's
better works.

2248.   Kent, Simon. A HILL IN KOREA. London: Hutchinson,
        1953.

        Tells of the various acts of heroics performed by members
        of a British platoon cut off on a Korean hill.

2249.   Kim, Richard E. THE MARTYRED. New York: Braziller,
        1964.

        The author of this Korean War novel was himself an ROK
        officer, but the story is far from a story of war. Instead,
        it is a mystery which revolves around a Captain Lee who is to
        investigate why, of fourteen Christian ministers captured in
        North Korea early in the war, twelve died. The story looks
        at the suffering and pangs of conscience that war can bring to
        those caught up in it.

2250.   Lasly, Walt. TURN THE TIGERS LOOSE. New York:
        Ballantine, 1956.

        The life of Colonel Tom Loving, while serving as a US
        Air Force squadron commander and wing operations officer
        in Korea, is a difficult one. Very frustrating is the fact
        that his B-26 night bomber squadron gets virtually no
        public adoration whereas the fighter pilots get it all.

2251.   McAleer, John, and Billy Dickson. UNIT PRIDE.
        Garden City, NY: Doubleday, 1961.

        Poorly written story of two young American soldiers,
        a naive New Englander and a tough Southerner, serving in
        the US Army in Korea. Tells of suffering, combat and
        personal lives of sex and booze.

2252.   McDowell, Edwin. TO KEEP OUR HONOR CLEAN. New York:
        Vanguard, 1980.

        A story about a recruit class going through basic training
        at Parris Island, South Carolina, in the summer of 1952.
        Describes the ordeal as rather brutal. The author, a Marine
        Sergeant who trained at Parris Island, writes a critical yet
        loving story of the Corps.

2253.   Michener, James A. THE BRIDGES OF TOKO-RI.
        New York: Random, 1953.

        One of the best known novels of the war by one of
        America's best known authors. The story of a carrier
        task force operating off the Korean coast. The title
        is the name of the target that the US pilots are
        committed to destroy in spite of formidable odds
        against them.

2254.   Oden, Kenneth L.   YEAH, BRAVE COWARD.   Rutland, VT:
        Tuttle, 1960.

        A Korean war veteran has written this novel which deals
        with the conflict in a highly humorous and entertaining
        way. Shows how American soldiers were able to see the
        "lighter side" in a time of peril and frustration.

2255.   Peacock, Jere.   VALHALLA.   New York: Putnam's, 1961.

        This story takes place in Japan where a group of US
        Marines are stationed after the war in Korea. Utilizes
        flashbacks to recount the suffering, danger and heroism
        that unfolded during the conflict.

2256.   Philpot, Van B.   BATTALION MEDICS.   New York: Exposition,
        1955.

        Experiences of a US Army medic serving in Korea.

2257.   Pollini, Francis.   NIGHT.   Boston: Houghton, 1961.

        US Army Sergeant Marty Landi, a POW in a Communist Camp
        on the Yalu River, is pitted against a Chinese "Education
        Officer" named Ching who attempts to brainwash him. The
        camp is full of Progressives who cooperate with the enemy,
        thus making the task of Landi and other Reactionaries very
        difficult.

2258.   Ross, Glenn.   THE LAST CAMPAIGN.   New York: Harper,
        1962.

        This story of a US Army Corporal, named Hunter, who was
        stationed in Japan in 1950 as part of a division band.
        When war came he and his buddies are sent to Korea to help
        halt the North Korean onslaught. What they experience
        are the horrors and sufferings of war.

2259.   Salter, James.   THE HUNTERS.   New York: Harper, 1956.

        An experienced flight commander is the central figure
        in this work on a US Air Force group whose mission is to
        guard Korean skies near the Yalu River. An excellent,
        authentic novel by a West Pointer who served as a jet
        fighter pilot in Korea.

2260.   Sheldon, Walt.   TROUBLING OF A STAR.   Philadelphia:
        Lippincott, 1952.

        Activities of the men of the 66th Fighter-bomber wing
        in Korea gives a good picture of military life and aerial
        combat.

2261. Skomra, Fred. BEHIND THE BAMBOO CURTAIN. New York:
       Greenwich, 1957.

       Story of US airmen and the airwar over Korea.

2262. Slaughter, Frank. SWORD AND SCALPEL. Garden City, NY:
       Doubleday, 1957.

       Captain Paul Scott, a US Army doctor, is taken prisoner by
       the Chinese, held prisoner and released. He is then accused
       of collaborating with the enemy and is court-martialed.
       Ultimately, evidence is brought forth to clear him.

2263. Styron, William. THE LONG MARCH. New York: Random,
       1968.

       Short novel about US Marine training during the Korean
       War. Originally published in 1952, this work shows the
       difficulties encountered by men thrown from placid
       civilian life into the rigorous training provided for
       Marines headed into combat. Lieutenant Tom Culver
       observes the conflict between a traditional colonel
       and a rebel captain.

2264. Thorin, Duane. A RIDE TO PANMUNJOM. Chicago: Regnery,
       1956.

       This novel by a Swedish-American helicopter pilot in Korea,
       who was taken prisoner, tells of the war and life in a
       Communist prison camp.

2265. Voorhees, Melvin B. SHOW ME A HERO. New York: Simon,
       1954.

       The story of three American military men and their
       experiences during the period of the peace negotiations.
       A US General, Lark Logan, a journalist, Tosser, and a
       chaplain, Dakin, suffered in various ways from the ironies
       of war.

XXIII. CRITIQUES, ANALYSES AND CONSEQUENCES

2266. Acheson, Dean. POWER AND DIPLOMACY. Cambridge: Harvard
       University, 1958.

       A series of lectures presented by the former Korean era
       Secretary of State notes that power no longer can play the
       role it once did because of the danger of destruction of the
       human race. In that way he seems to defend the
       administration's Korean policy, but his warning that
       political and military policy rather than reliance on the UN
       for peace seems to refute the policy he had championed.

2267. Air University Quarterly Staff. "Korea--An Opportunity
       Lost." AIR UNIV Q R, 1957 9 (2):20-27.

       An account critical of US policy makers for making the
       decision not to unleash airpower during the war. Contends
       that if leaders had understood the value of airpower it
       could have eliminated thousands of UN casualties and
       enhanced the prestige of the US.

2268. Air University Quarterly Staff. "The Korean War Speaks
       to the Indo-Chinese War." AIR UNIV Q R, 1954 7 (1):44-62.

       One of the first attempts to apply the military lessons
       learned by the US in the Korean War to the war in Indo-China.
       Compares and contrasts the political situation, military
       context, terrain and weather and concludes that getting
       involved in Indo-China would be very risky. Says best
       hope is to achieve a political settlement.

2269. Alsop, Joseph and Stewart. "The Lesson of Korea."
       SAT EVE POST, 1950 223 (10):17-19, 96, 98, 100.

       Claims the attack by North Korea was really a Soviet move
       and is the first step in a world-wide move to extend Russia's
       influence. The aggression occurred because the US was
       militarily weak, and the Truman Administration had not
       indicated its willingness to stand up to Soviet expansion.
       Critical of Truman, his limited defense budgets and the
       economy moves of Secretary of Defense Johnson.

2270. Barclay, C.M. "Lessons of the Korean Campaign."
       BRAS AN, 1954: 122-133.

       A British officer looks at the fighting in Korea and sees
       positive contributions in combined UN operations and taking

to the hills to halt the enemy but questions the use of the
tank in mobile operations. Claims that the importance of air
superiority is overemphasized and says the British must
cut down on the field administrative structure, fight more
at night, learn to "dig-in", provide suitable equipment,
and learn to conserve ammunition.

2271. Barham, Pat, and Frank Cunningham. OPERATION NIGHTMARE.
      Los Angeles: Sequoia University, 1953.

      Condemnation of US policy which did not permit the US and
      UN to achieve military victory in Korea. Calls for all-out
      support for President Rhee and his efforts to defeat Communism
      in Asia. Extremely anti-Communist work by two newspaper
      correspondents.

2272. Bartel, Ronald F. "Attitudes Toward Limited War: An
      Analysis of Elite and Public Opinion During the Korean
      Conflict." Doctoral Dissertation. Illinois, 1970.

      Maintains that while the Truman Administration was not
      very successful in defining the goals or enemy in Korea
      it did succeed in convincing congressional and military
      elites that the fate of the free world depended on stopping
      aggression in Korea. The elites were, like the American
      public, divided over the conduct of the conflict--some
      favoring traditional victory while others felt such a concept
      was obsolete. Consequently, there was considerable
      frustration and vacillation regarding the war.

2273. Bhagat, B.S. "Military Lessons of the Korean Conflict."
      MIL R, 1952 32 (9):73-79.

      After summarizing operations in the first year of the war
      and examining the impact of terrain, the author tells of a
      number of military lessons that have become evident. Lessons
      examined include the overriding consideration of political
      expediency over military strategy, limitation of air power,
      need for a supreme commander, value of concentrated fire
      power, importance of patrolling, and the need for cooperation
      among the services. From the January-April 1952 issue of THE
      JOURNAL OF THE UNITED SERVICE INSTITUTION OF INDIA.

2274. Braestrup, Peter. "Back to the Trenches." MARINE CORPS GAZ,
      1955 39 (3):32-36.

      Following WWII the use of trench warfare seemed a thing of
      the past, but when the Korean War turned into a stalemate
      in late 1950 and early 1951 that form of fighting came into
      vogue. Many lessons had to be learned and some relearned
      about trench warfare.

2275. Bridges, Styles. "Korea: A Positive Proposal." AM
      MERCURY, 1952 75 (347):11-19.

A leading Republican Senator deplores the fact that the matter of what to do in Korea was not really debated in the 1952 Presidential campaign, then proceeds to suggest what can be done. Claims the US can't win militarily in Korea and to withdraw would be devastating to the welfare of the region; thus, he proposes that the US arm and train South Koreans and Japanese to carry on the fight. Furthermore, worldwide pressure should be brought against Communism by sending aid and encouragement to those fighting tyranny.

2276. Brier, John K. "What Can an Armor Officer Learn in Korea?" ARMOR, 1953 62 (1):47-49.

Maintains that while the war in Korea was not a mobile conflict there is considerable opportunity for an Armor officer to gain valuable experience about the capabilities of his men, organizational structure and equipment.

2277. Bullitt, William C. "We Can Win the War in Korea." READ DIG, 1953 62 (371):29-34.

Assessment of the US position in Korea by a well-respected American diplomat concludes that the war should and could be won if the restraints on the military were to be removed. Acknowledges this would mean hitting targets in China but maintains Russia would not go to war over that.

2278. Campbell, James W. "What the Russians Have Learned in Korea." YALE R, 1952 42 (2):226-235.

Focuses on the weaknesses, material and human, of the Soviet-trained and equipped Chinese and North Korean Armies in Korea. Shortages of trucks and drivers force men to march and supplies to be moved by night. Weapons were obsolete and communications equipment was virtually nonexistent. Although the amount of firepower increased with the passage of time, its accuracy did not. Morale of troops was low.

2279. Cheek, Leon B., Jr. "Korea: Decisive Battle of the World." MIL R, 1953 32 (12):20-26.

Attempts to analyze the true significance of the Korean War. Claims that the conflict may be a decisive event in the history of the world--the bulwark needed by the non-Communist peoples to reach a decision and enable them to stem the tide of Communism. Rather than destroy the UN and weaken the US, as the enemy expected, the war actually strengthened both.

2280. Collins, George W. "Korea in Retrospect." AIR UNIV Q R, 1968 20 (1):113-117.

A review essay of General Matthew Ridgway's THE KOREAN

WAR (1967) is favorable to the General and his book.

2281.   Cottrell, Alvin J., and James E. Dougherty. "The
         Lessons of Korea: War and the Power of Man" in Allen
         Guttmann, KOREA AND THE THEORY OF LIMITED WAR.
         Lexington, MA: Heath, 1967, pp. 79-92.

         Critical of the self-imposed limitations that the US
         put on itself in Korea. Faults the Truman Administration's
         failure to respond decisively to Chinese intervention,
         failure to accept Chiang's offer of help, refusal to
         invoke economic warfare, and refusal to carry the war
         across the Yalu. Claims the US was not ready for the
         limited war it encountered.

2282.   Cumings, Bruce. "The Course of Korean-American Relations,
         1943-1953" in Bruce Cumings, ed. CHILD OF CONFLICT.
         Seattle University of Washington, 1983, pp. 3-55.

         Scholarly and thought-provoking essay which maintains that
         between 1943 and 1953, but essentially between 1945 and 1950,
         US foreign policy progressed from the globalism of Roosevelt
         (1943-1945) to containment (1946-1949) to a rollback policy
         (1949-1950). Claims only in Korea was rollback actually
         pursued. Defends Acheson's handling of Korea from his
         January 1950 speech on.

2283.   Davidson, Bill. "Why Half Our Combat Soldier's Fail to
         Shoot." COLLIER'S, 1952 130 (19):16-18.

         Probes the question of why in any given action in Korea
         only a maximum of twenty-five percent of the combat soldiers
         who were armed and in a position to fire their weapons did
         so. Maintains that inhibitions that go back to childhood
         are responsible. Suggests solutions, such as development of
         mob psychology and securing "natural" military leaders.

2284.   Deshingkar, G.D. "US-China Relations: Retrospect and
         Prospect." CHINA REPORT (India) 1970 6 (1):23-29.

         Relations between the Chinese Communist regime and the
         US have remained very cool in large part because of long-
         standing Chinese anger at American support of the
         Nationalists and American involvement in the Korean War.
         Contends that the US has been more anxious to normalize
         relations than has China.

2285.   DeWeerd, Harvey A. "Lessons of the Korean War."
         YALE R, 1951 40 (4):592-603.

         A former Army historian looks at war in Korea with its
         "befuddling objectives" and "baffling situations" which
         produced a bizarre conflict. Nevertheless, he concludes
         that some lessons are evident. They include the need

for more equipment and firepower, the need for improved concepts of motivation, the need for a mobile
striking force to meet similar future challenges, and
a need to properly assess the theater of operations
to arrive at strategic objectives.

2286. Drummond, S. "Korea and Vietnam: Some Speculations
About the Possible Influences of the Korean War on
American Policy in Vietnam." ARMY Q DEF J, 1968
97 (1):65-71.

A comparison of US policies in Korea and Vietnam concludes
that a misreading of some of the experiences in Korea led
to some mistaken decisions in the later conflict. Particularly important was the decision to rely on air bombardment to force the enemy to negotiate. Convinced that
such activity had worked in Korea, policy makers mistakenly
jumped to the conclusion that it would work in Vietnam.

2287. Germains, Victor W. "Military Lessons From Korea."
CONT R, 1953 184 (1055):264-269.

After maintaining that none of the nations that got
involved in the Korean War really knew what they were getting
into, this author claims that the outstanding lesson learned
is the extent to which the Russians could instill military
fanaticism into their Chinese and North Korean allies. Also
claims that the Chinese did so well because they fought across
country and avoided the mechanized UN units that operated on
or near roads.

2288. Greenough, Robert B. "Communist Lessons From the
Korean Air War." AIR UNIV Q R, 1952-53 5 (4):22-29.

Notes that while the US has downed many more aircraft
than the enemy, this situation could change because the
Communists were learning lessons from the air war. The
biggest gain for them was the technological information
they were able to gather from downed US aircraft; which
enabled them to determine its structural vulnerability.
They also utilized their observation of US tactics to
adjust their tactical and logistical thinking.

2289. Hayes, Thomas H. "Corridors." COM FOR J, 1953
3 (7):23-24.

Takes to task Marine Major Gerald Averill who wrote in
the October 1952 issue of COMBAT FORCES JOURNAL that the
US Army tended to stress the corridors as the way to
enter the battle position rather than utilizing the
ridges. Claims the Army maintained that a corridor is not
a valley, but the crests of two ridges and the ground
between. Consequently, what the Army meant was to
"Run two Ridges and Win."

2290.   Heren, Louis. "The Korean Scene." BRAS AN, 1951:
        97-111.

        A British war correspondent's account of the fighting
        in Korea from the August 1950 retreat to Pusan to the
        September-October drive to the Yalu. Excellent analysis
        of the initial North Korean successes and the later
        successes of the UN Command. A well-balanced article.

2291.   Hittle, J.D. "Korea--Back to the Facts of Life."
        US NAVAL INST PROC, 1950 76 (12):1289-1297.

        Maintains that US involvement in Korea served to bring
        the nation's military thinking back to reality. The
        nation came to believe its security could be provided
        relatively inexpensively by airplanes and atomic bombs.
        Claims the war shows that: no one weapon wins war; the
        capabilities of A-bombs and air power should not be
        overestimated; sea power still provides a mobile
        strategic fighting force; and the US may be starting an
        era of limited objective wars.

2292.   Jessup, Alpheous W. "Korea's Air Power Lessons. They
        Will Influence Plans for the Future Planes, Equipment."
        AVI WK, 1950 53 (14):16-18.

        A look at US air activities such as use of tactical air
        power, airlift operations, the role of the F-80 and
        runway construction during the Korean War. Tells lessons
        that can be learned from those experiences.

2293.   Kim, Sang Mo. "The Implications of the Sea War in
        Korea." NAV W C R, 1967 20 Summer:105-139.

        A Captain in the ROK Navy discusses the lessons to be
        learned from the war from the standpoint of the South
        Korean Navy. Sees the significant lessons as centering
        on: (1) the Communists' effective use of sea mines;
        (2) the value of amphibious operations; (3) the importance
        of blockading operations; and (4) the overconfidence of
        the impact of air power.

2294.   "The Korean War: A 25 Year Perspective." WHISTLE
        STOP, 1975 3 (3):1-4.

        Brief description of the May 1975 conference on the
        Korean War held at the Truman Library. Includes brief
        comments on aspects of the war by participants such as
        Generals J. Lawton Collins and Matthew B. Ridgway,
        Special Assistant to the President, W. Averell Harriman
        and Ambassador to the Republic of Korea, John J. Muccio.
        Full account of the conference is found in Francis H. Heller,
        THE KOREAN WAR: A 25 YEAR PERSPECTIVE (Lawrence: University
        Press of Kansas, 1976).

2295. Lee, Asher. "Air Lessons in Korea." TWEN CENT, 1951
       149 (889):193-198.

       An expert on the Soviet Air Force notes that the US has
       learned a number of tactical lessons as well as the value
       of transport aircraft and helicopters but warns against
       putting too much reliance on claims of casualties and
       damages inflicted on the enemy.

2296. Marshall, S.L.A. "A New Strategy for Korea." REPORTER,
       1953 8 (5):17-21.

       Criticizes the Truman Administration for not making a
       major commitment to win the war in Korea. Claims the US
       has not made a "first-class" effort in the war and should
       add four or five more divisions and go on the offensive.
       Examines Mao's strategy and concludes the protracted war is
       what he wants.

2297. Marshall, S.L.A. "Our Mistakes in Korea." ATLANTIC,
       1953 192 (3):46-49.

       A critical account of the US conduct of the war. Claims
       the Truman Administration was unduly optimistic about the
       outcome when it decided to intervene and was then unwilling
       to make the kinds of military commitments, especially in
       manpower, that were needed to achieve victory.

2298. Martin, H.G. "Korea--Some Tactical Lessons." BRAS
       AN, 1951:233-249.

       Good analysis of the combatants in Korea. Looks at the
       Communist and UN soldiers. Critical of US forces for
       sticking to the roads and inability to fight at night.
       Rejects as myth the idea that the enemy frequently used
       "human sea" tactics. Claims tactical air support still
       leaves much to be desired. Critical of much of the
       equipment being used by the British.

2299. Michaelis, John H. "Mike", and Bill Davidson. "This
       We Learned in Korea." COLLIER'S, 1951 128 (7):13-15,
       38-43.

       Michaelis, a thirty-eight year old Brigadier General,
       who won the Distinguished Service Cross while serving with
       the 27th "Wolfhound" Regiment, maintains the major benefits
       to come out of the fighting are that the US learned to beat
       the Communist infantry at their own game--guerila warfare
       and that it developed a battle-wise Army. Includes many of his
       experiences in combat situations.

2300. Mildren, Frank T. "What Has Korea Taught Us?" INF
       SCH Q, 1953 43 (2):6-13.

       Says that new things were not learned in Korea, but many

things were relearned. Urges that the US examine its errors
in Korea and not make them again. Some of the mistakes the
military made were: infantry did not make good use of
support weapons; planning was made too hastily; failure to
study and use terrain; failure to fight at night; attacking
fortified positions that should have been avoided; and
failure to withdraw in an orderly fashion.

2301. Rougeron, Camille. "Some Lessons of the War in Korea."
       US NAVAL INST PROC, 1953 79 (6):635-643.

       Discusses the problems encountered by the Russian and
       Chinese land powers in successfully pursuing the war in
       Korea as well as the difficulties facing the US-UN
       Command.

2302. Rush, Eugene J. MILITARY STRATEGIC LESSONS LEARNED
       FROM THE KOREAN CONFLICT AS THEY RELATED TO LIMITED
       WARFARE. Carlisle Barracks, PA: US Army War College,
       1974.

       Shows the impact of the war on US strategic thinking of
       US military planners and leaders.

2303. Seversky, Alexander P. de. "Korea Proves Our Need
       for a Dominant Air Force." READ DIG, 1950 57 (342):
       6-10.

       One of the foremost aeronautical authorities and advocates
       of greatly expanded air power argues that the war in Korea,
       rather than refuting his air advocacy, actually demonstrates
       its validity. Unless a global air force becomes a reality,
       the US will be challenged by a series of small wars, such
       as Korea, that will sap the nation's resources until it
       collapses.

2304. Smith, Gaddis. "After 25 Years--The Parallel." NY TIMES
       MAG, June 22, 1975:15-25.

       A top diplomatic historian examines the origins of the
       Korean War along with the US decision to intervene and the
       consequences of the conflict on US-Korean relations.

2305. Smith, Gaddis. "A History Teacher's Reflections on the
       Korean War." VEN, 1968 8 (1):57-65.

       The limited war in Korea saw President Truman move to meet
       the Communist expansion, confine the war geographically,
       refrain from using atomic weapons and strengthen NATO. The
       success of the war led the US to conclude that quick and
       confident responses to international challenges could shape
       world affairs as desired.

2306. Spaight, J.M. "Crimea and Korea." US NAVAL INST PROC,
       1953 79 (7):753-757.

       Perceptive comparison of the war in the Crimea, 1854-1856,
       and Korea, 1950-1953. Finds many similarities such as: both
       began with acts of aggression by Russia; both saw major
       powers go to the aid of a victim of aggression; both were
       limited wars. Draws conclusions of lessons to be learned
       and especially warns of problems inherent in a stalemate.

2307. Tarpley, John F. "Korea: 25 Years Later." US NAVAL
       INST PROC, 1978 104 (8):50-57.

       In spite of the fact that all sides may have considered the
       Korean armistice settlement as less than satisfactory,
       it did have the salutary effect of providing twenty-five
       years of stability to northeast Asia.

2308. Van Fleet, James A. "The Truth About Korea." LIFE,
       1953 34 (19):127-128, 131-142; 34 (20):156-158, 160-172.

       The commander of the US Eighth Army for twenty-two
       months of the Korean War speaks out after his retirement
       in March 1953 and is critical of the way the US conducted
       the war. Claims policy makers underestimated the strengths
       of the South Koreans and overestimated the Chinese Reds.
       Claims an all-out military effort by the UN forces could
       bring the war to a successful conclusion. Examines the
       strengths and weaknesses of both sides.

2309. Wells, Samuel F., Jr. "The Lessons of the War."
       WILSON Q, 1978 2 (3):119-126.

       Examines US policy toward South Korea before the war
       began and toward North Korea after it started. The
       Truman Administration's security policy and the Cold
       War mentality were instrumental in a major defense
       policy change. Consequently, the era saw increased
       commitments to Europe and Asia, stepped up CIA
       covert operations and an increased willingness to
       resist Communist aggression.

2310. Wint, Guy. WHAT HAPPENED IN KOREA: A STUDY IN
       COLLECTIVE SECURITY. London: Batchworth, 1954.

       Analysis of the war, its conduct and its consequences
       by a British Far Eastern expert. Very little is done
       on military matters and not much more on politics but
       looks at such factors as the motives of the participants
       in fighting and negotiating.

2311. Yool, W.M. "Air Lessons From Korea." BRAS AN,
       1951:397-404.

       A British air commander notes the limitation of

strategic air power by noting that in the first eleven
months of fighting it was not able to have a decisive
influence on the campaign. He praises tactical air
support, however, and sees it as the decisive factor
in keeping the Allies from being thrown into the
sea.

SUBJECT INDEX

Aces, US Air, 854, 908-913, 1300
Acheson, Dean, 89, 128, 129, 143, 144, 267, 305, 391, 404, 429,
    430, 432, 472, 483, 489, 490, 501, 505, 531, 1637, 1871,
    2133, 2266, 2282
Adventist Medical Cadet Corps, 1721
Afghanistan, 400
air drops, 1127, 1131, 1143, 1150
Air Force, US, 18, 23, 52, 69-71, 287, 595; sec Chapter VIII;
    training, 620, 626
Air Group Five (Carrier), 937
Air Logistic Force (USAF), 859
air power, 577, 837-867, 2267, 2288, 2293, 2303, 2311
air rescue, 1118, 1126, 1641, 1644
Air Rescue Service, 1641, 1644, 1650
airborne operations, 666, 675, 704, 830, 941, 1116, 1120, 1124
aircraft (US), 852, 853, 858, 871, 921-948, 991, 2073
aircraft carriers, 965, 981-1011, 2223
airfields, 861, 949, 1190, 1193, 1203, 1221, 1223, 1225, 1229, 1538,
    1972, 2098, 2292
airlifts, 840, 2292
American Ambassador to Korea, 407, 408, 445
American Ambassador to the UN, 1323
American Embassy (Seoul), 399
American Military Government, 223, 226, 230-232, 245, 257, 268, 270,
    277, 283, 291, 292, 299, 319, 324, 369
ammunition, 1166, 1339
Amphibious Construction Battalion One, 949
amphibious landings, 702, 1054-1057, 1059, 1069, 2293
amphibious tractors, 1029
Anders, Curt, 2233
Anderson, Thomas, 2233
Anglican Bishop of Korea, 394
animals, use of, 1234-1240
Anju, North Korea, 712
ANTIETAN USS, 983, 995
Archives, 2, 28, 58, 67, 136
Argyll and Sutherland Highlanders, 1408
Arlington National Cemetery, 1299
Armed Forces Reserve Act, 596, 606, 608
Armistice Agreement, 176, 383, 1314, 1855, 1907-1917, 1979, 2307
Armistice Agreement, violations of, 1972, 1973, 1981, 1986, 1987
Armistice Negotiations, 176, 366, 538, 724, 1422, 1562, 1754, 1786;
    See Chapter XVII, especially 1871-1906; 2170, 2171, 2177, 2265
artillery, 62, 553, 762, 764-766, 787, 792, 798, 801, 1089, 1512

artists, 2215-2219, 2226, 2227
Associated Services, 1279
ATHABASKON (Canada), 1376
Atomic bomb(s), 287, 306, 522, 530, 545, 554, 558, 561, 2049, 2291
Atomic Energy Commission, 440, 2049
atomic weapons, 244, 315, 503, 530, 532, 533, 542, 1893, 1912,
    2049, 2111, 2305
atrocities and crimes, 397, 1412, 1556, 1558, 1570, 1571, 1849
Attack Squadron 702 (US Navy), 1007
Attlee, Clement R., 2137
Austin, Warren R., 1323
Australia, 793, 1341, 1362-1368, 1395, 1432, 1763, 1801, 1843,
    2111
Australia New Zealand United States Pact (ANZUS), 1366
Australian Fighter Air Squadron, 1367
awards and honors, 1284-1301

B-26, 900, 942, 944, 948, 1701, 2250
B-29, 563, 902, 931, 934, 935, 938, 942, 989, 2247
Background to the War, See Chapter III
BODOENG STRAIT USS, 1011
bands, 1036
Bao Dai, 2165
Barth, George B. Gen., 682
Baruch, Bernard M., 2079
Batchelor, Claude Corporal, 1836
"Battle Hymn," 2211
bazooka (3.5 inch rocket launcher), 789, 797, 1167, 2072
Belgian Battalion, 741
Bibliographies, See Chapter I; 197, 581, 656, 1812, 2036
Biderman, Albert, 1803, 1839
Big Switch, 1859, 1862, 1867, 1978
Biological (Bacteriological) Warfare, 25, 1483, 1555, 1557-1569,
    1782
Black Sheep Squadron, 1114
blacks, 628-631, 633-635, 638-651, 836, 1286, 2099
blockades, 957, 1599, 1600, 1616, 1617, 2293
blood, 1692, 1696, 1738, 1748, 1751
body armor, 759, 772, 1044
Bohlen, Charles E., 2139
Bold, John F. Maj., 909
Bombardier's Palsy, 1701
bombs (conventional), 788
BON HOMME RICHARD USS, 1004
Bong, Dick, 919
Boulder City, 1101
Bowles, Chester, 2141
BOXER USS, 1007
Bradley, Omar General, 467, 469-471, 654
Brainwashing, 60, 1798, 1803-1840
Bricker, John Senator, 1903
bridges, 1194-1201, 1203, 1210, 1222, 1224, 1226, 1228, 1232,
    1233, 1443
British Ambassador to the UN, 1405

432, 441, 442, 444, 450, 451, 464, 531, 532, 566, 1547, 1572-
1586, 1592, 1617, 2056, 2058, 2095, 2108, 2111, 2123, 2127,
2148, 2152, 2269; MacArthur controversy and dismissal, 1576,
1579, 1612-1640, 1898, 2025, 2031, 2066, 2104, 2166
Truman Institute, 148, 149
Tunisia, 883
Turkey, 1356, 1431, 1436, 1441
Turncoats, See defectors
27th British Brigade, 1413
Twining, Nathan F. General, 558

Uijongbu, 1064
Uiju POW Camp, 1757
underwater demolition, 953, 955
Underwood, Dick, 1884
Underwood, Horace, 1884
unification, 1921, 1979, 1982
United Nations, 32, 68, 181, 219, 243, 255, 256, 271, 280, 294,
297, 300, 305, 322, 328, 333, 336, 383, 390, 425, 435, 439,
441, 447, 451, 461, 540, 548, 568, 580, 652; See Chapter XII,
1496, 1563, 1565, 1907, 1914, 2140, 2270, 2271, 2279;
Blockading Force, 1341; Civil Assistance Command, 1924, 1963;
Command, 141, 156, 271, 467, 468, 473, 474, 481, 496, 498,
520, 793, 867, 875, 998, 1046, 1173, 1336-1349, 2091, 2301;
Command Delegation, 1878-1880; Command, Supply Group, Joint
Security Area, 1974; Commissions, 254, 323, 333, 369, 1384;
Forces, 141, 156, 176, 550, 568, 736, 751, 979, 1006, 1342,
1347, 1350-1441, 1472, 1527, 1684; General Assembly, 1327,
1348, 1565, 1566; Korean Reconstruction Agency, 1322, 1984
United Press, 424
unpreparedness, 421, 522, 577, 696, 697, 952
US Air Force, See Chapter VIII; US Air Force, 3rd Air Rescue
Group, 1642, 1647; 3rd Bomber Wing, 860, 948; 4th Aerial
Photo Interpretation Company, 515; 4th Fighter Interceptor
Wing, 878, 891, 906, 913, 916, 918; Fifth Air Force, 841,
866, 871, 917, 946, 1263, 1649; 5th Fighter Interceptor
Wing, 891; 18th Fighter Bomber Wing, 901; 51st Fighter
Interceptor Wing, 919; 68th Fighter Squadron, 852, 914;
315th Air Division, Combat Cargo Command, 1189; 319th
Fighter Interceptor Squadron, 922
US Air Force Chief of Staff, 477, 864
US Army, 20, 21, 102, 108; See Chapter VII, 133, 134, 145, 146,
165, 166, 172, 189, 286, 287, 2017, 2019; Eighth Army, 188,
484, 493-495, 498, 503, 504, 564, 660, 668, 669, 716, 718,
720, 728, 941, 1811, 1978, 1980, 1992, 1996, 2308; 1st
Armored Division, 609; 1st Cavalry Division, 661, 665, 680,
701, 738, 777, 817, 1137, 1164, 1271, 2002; 2nd Infantry
Division, 665, 672, 686, 687, 708, 717, 731, 745, 751, 755,
835, 1981, 2000; 3rd Infantry Division, 659, 731, 744, 815,
2216; 5th Cavalry Regiment, 752; 6th Transportation
Helicopter Company, 1121; 7th Infantry Division, 251, 657,
665, 677, 701, 709, 711, 723, 725, 743, 752, 808, 833, 1442,